Charles Harding Firth

Scotland and the Commonwealth

Letters and papers relating to the military government of Scotland

Charles Harding Firth

Scotland and the Commonwealth
Letters and papers relating to the military government of Scotland

ISBN/EAN: 9783743347496

Manufactured in Europe, USA, Canada, Australia, Japa

Cover: Foto ©ninafisch / pixelio.de

Manufactured and distributed by brebook publishing software (www.brebook.com)

Charles Harding Firth

Scotland and the Commonwealth

PUBLICATIONS

OF THE

SCOTTISH HISTORY SOCIETY

VOLUME XVIII

SCOTLAND AND THE COMMONWEALTH

October 1895

SCOTLAND AND THE COMMONWEALTH

LETTERS AND PAPERS RELATING TO THE MILITARY GOVERNMENT OF SCOTLAND, FROM AUGUST 1651 TO DECEMBER 1653

Edited, with Introduction and Notes, by
C. H. FIRTH, M.A.

EDINBURGH

Printed at the University Press by T. and A. Constable
for the Scottish History Society

1895

CONTENTS

	PAGE
INTRODUCTION, ...	xvii-lv
I. Narrative or Diary of the Proceedings of the Forces under Lieutenant-General Monke, after their parting from the Army. August 4, 1651, .	1-18
II. Mr. William Clarke to Speaker Lenthall, . .	18-20
III. Mr. William Clarke to Speaker Lenthall, . .	20-21
IV. A Brief Relation of the Proceedings of the Committee of Estates and Affairs of Scotland, since the King's Majestie went from thence to England, ...	21-28
V. A News-Letter from Dundee, . .	28-30
VI. A News-Letter from Dundee, . . .	30-31
VII. A Letter from the Commissioners of the Parliament in Scotland to the Speaker, . . .	31-32
VIII. A News-Letter from Scotland, . . .	32-33
IX. Mr. William Clarke to Speaker Lenthall, . .	33
X. A News-Letter from Leith, ...	34-35
XI. Henry Whalley to Scoutmaster General Downing,	35-36
XII. Colonel Overton to General Cromwell, . .	36-37
XIII. The Marquess of Argyll to the Commissioners of the Parliament, ...	37-38
XIV. A News-Letter from Scotland, . . .	38-39
XV. An Order by the Commissioners of the Parliament of England, ...	39-40
XVI. A Letter from the Commissioners of the Parliament of England to the Marquess of Argyll, .	40

		PAGE
XVII.	The Marquess of Argyll to the Commissioners of the Parliament of England,	40-41
XVIII.	A News-Letter from Leith,	41-42
XIX.	A Letter from the Commissioners of the Parliament of England to the Marquess of Argyll,	43
XX.	A News-Letter from Leith,	42
XXI.	A Declaration of the Commissioners for regulating the Universities,	44-45
XXII.	A Declaration by Major-General Deane,	45-46
XXIII.	A Circular Letter from Charles II. to the Nobles and Gentlemen of Scotland,	46-47
XXIV.	A Letter from Charles II. to the Moderator of the General Assembly,	47-48
XXV.	Articles of Agreement between Archibald, Lord Marquess of Argisle, on the behalf of himself and freinds on the one parte, And Major-Generall Richard Deane on the behalf of the Parliament of the Commonwealth of England on the other side,	48-50
XXVI.	Charles the Second's Instructions to General Middleton,	50-53
XXVII.	A News-Letter from Leith,	53-54
XXVIII.	Lieutenant-General Middleton to the Count of Oldenburg,	54-55
XXIX.	An Agreement made between Major-General Richard Deane, in the name of the Parliament of the Commonwealth of England on the one part, And Archibald, Lord Marquesse of Argile, in the behalf of the Gentlemen and Inhabitants of the Shire of Argile on the other parte. This 27th Day of October 1652,	55-57
XXX.	Agreement between Major-General Deane and the Marquess of Argyll concerning his Guns,	57-58

CONTENTS

		PAGE
XXXI.	Major-General Deane to Captain Mutlow, .	58-59
XXXII.	Major-General Deane to the Marquess of Argyll,	59
XXXIII.	Major-General Deane to the Marquess of Argyll,	59-60
XXXIV.	Charles II. to Lieutenant-General Middleton, .	60-61
XXXV.	Charles II. to Lieutenant-General Douglas, .	61
XXXVI.	Circular Letter from Major-General Deane to the Commanders of the English Forces in Scotland, ...	62
XXXVII.	Commission from Major-General Deane to Colonel Overton, ...	62-63
XXXVIII.	Instructions for Colonel Overton, . . .	63-64
XXXIX.	Instructions for Colonel Morgan, . . .	64-65
XL.	A Commission from Charles II., . . .	65-67
XLI.	Instructions to the Commissioners, .	67-70
XLII.	A Letter from Colonel Lilburne, . . .	71-72
XLIII.	Colonel Lilburne to the Lord General Cromwell,	72-73
XLIV.	Colonel Lilburne to the Council of State, .	73-74
XLV.	The Commissioners at Leith to the Speaker, .	74
XLVI.	Circular Letter from Colonel Lilburne to the Commanders of the Army in Scotland, .	74-75
XLVII.	Petition of Major Fisher to Maj.-Gen. Deane,	75-77
XLVIII.	Col. Lilburne to the English Judges in Scotland,	77
XLIX.	Charles II. to the Duke of Courland, . .	78
L.	Colonel Lilburne to Lord General Cromwell, .	79
LI.	Col. Lilburne to the Lord General Cromwell,	80
LII.	Colonel Lilburne to Colonel Okey, . .	81
LIII.	Colonel Lilburne to Mr. Rowe, . . .	81-82
LIV.	Sir James M'Donell to Colonel Fitch, . .	82-83
LV.	Colonel Lilburne to Colonel Cooper, . .	83
LVI.	Col. Lilburne to the Lord General Cromwell,	84
LVII.	Colonel Lilburne to the Marquess of Argyll, .	85
LVIII.	Colonel Lilburne to Colonel Alured, . .	86
LIX.	Col. Lilburne to the Lord General Cromwell,	86-87
LX.	Colonel Lilburne to Lord General Cromwell, .	87-88
LXI.	Letter to Sir James M'Donell, . . .	88-89
LXII.	Sir Edward Hyde to Lieut.-Gen. Middleton, .	89-93

		PAGE
LXIII.	Charles II. to Captain Smith,	94
LXIV.	Warrant for Apprehending Colonel Bampfield,	94-95
LXV.	Colonel Lilburne to Lord General Cromwell,	95-96
LXVI.	Colonel Lilburne to Mr. William Rowe,	96-97
LXVII.	Charles II. to Lord Balcarres,	97-98
LXVIII.	Sir Edward Hyde to Lieut.-Gen. Middleton,	98-99
LXIX.	Instructions to Lord Glencairne,	99-101
LXX.	Charles II. to the Highland Chieftains,	101-102
LXXI.	Charles II. to the Earl of Glencairne,	102-103
LXXII.	Sir Edward Hyde to Lieut.-Gen. Middleton,	103-105
LXXIII.	Sir Edward Hyde to Lieut.-Gen. Middleton,	106-107
LXXIV.	Charles II. to Lord Balcarres,	107
LXXV.	Address to Colonel Lilburne,	108-109
LXXVI.	Charles II. to Lieutenant-General Middleton,	109-110
LXXVII.	The Earl of Loudoun to Charles II.,	110-111
LXXVIII.	Expenses of the English Army in Scotland,	111-114
LXXIX.	Expenses of the English Army in Scotland,	114-119
LXXX.	Colonel Lilburne to the Speaker,	120
LXXXI.	Lord Lorne to Lord Wilmot,	120
LXXXII.	Lord Lorne to Charles II.,	120-121
LXXXIII.	The Earl of Loudoun to the Earl of Rochester,	121-122
LXXXIV.	Colonel Lilburne to ——,	122-123
LXXXV.	The Count of Waldeck to Lieut.-Gen. Midleton,	123-124
LXXXVI.	Memorial from the Count of Waldeck,	124-126
LXXXVII.	A Letter from Colonel Lilburne,	126-127
LXXXVIII.	The Earl of Seaforth and the Heads of the Clans to Charles II.,	127-128
LXXXIX.	A Letter to the Council of the Army at Whitehall,	129-130
XC.	Sir Robert Moray to Charles II.,	130-134
XCI.	Colonel Lilburne to Major-General Lambert,	134-135
XCII.	Colonel Lilburne to General Cromwell,	135-136
XCIII.	Colonel Lilburne to the Officer in Command at Dunotter?,	136-137
XCIV.	Memorandum on the Rising in Scotland,	137-139
XCV.	Proclamation by Colonel Lilburne,	139

CONTENTS

		PAGE
XCVI.	Summons to the Captain of the 'Fortune,' and Answer,	140
XCVII.	Glengarry to the Earl of Athol,	141
XCVIII.	Proclamation by Colonel Lilburne,	141-142
XCIX.	Col. Lilburne to the Lord-General Cromwell,	142-143
C.	A Letter to the Earl of Glencairne,	143-144
CI.	To Sir Arthur Forbes,	144-145
CII.	An Engagement of the Gentlemen of Blair, etc.,	145
CIII.	Lord Balcarres to Colonel Lilburne,	146
CIV.	Sir Arthur Forbes to Colonel Lilburne,	147
CV.	Col. Lilburne to the Lord-General Cromwell,	147-148
CVI.	Col. Lilburne to the Lord-General Cromwell,	148-150
CVII.	A Letter of Intelligence,	150-151
CVIII.	Colonel Lilburne to Mr. John Rushworth,	151
CIX.	The Earl of Seaforth to Lieut.-Col. Blount,	151-152
CX.	Colonel Lilburne to Mr. Thurloe,	152
CXI.	Colonel Lilburne to the Laird of Pluscarty,	153
CXII.	Col. Lilburne to the Lord-General Cromwell,	153-154
CXIII.	A Proclamation by Colonel Lilburne,	154-155
CXIV.	A Proclamation against Beggars,	155-156
CXV.	Col. Lilburne to the Lord-General Cromwell,	156-157
CXVI.	The Earl of Glencairn to Lieutenant-General Middleton,	157-159
CXVII.	Warrant from Colonel Lilburne,	159-160
CXVIII.	Col. Lilburne to the Lord-General Cromwell,	160-161
CXIX.	Col. Lilburne to the Marquess of Argyll,	161-162
CXX.	Order by Colonel Lilburne,	162
CXXI.	Col. Lilburne to the Lord-General Cromwell,	162-164
CXXII.	Proclamation by Colonel Lilburne,	164-165
CXXIII.	The Marquess of Argyll to Colonel Lilburne,	165-166
CXXIV.	The Marquess of Argyll to Lord Lorne,	166-167
CXXV.	Letter to Lord Lorne,	167-168
CXXVI.	The Marquess of Argyll to Colonel Lilburne,	168-169
CXXVII.	The Valuation of Scotland,	170-171
CXXVIII.	Order Concerning the Valuation of Scotland,	172-173
CXXIX.		173

CXXX.	The Assesse laid uppon Scotland for the 4 monthes of July, August, September, October, 1653, . . .	174–179
CXXXI.	Warrant for Levying the Assessment, .	180
CXXXII.	Warrant for Levying the Assessment, . .	180–181
CXXXIII.	Warrant for Levying Confiscated Revenues, .	181
CXXXIV.	Sir Edward Hyde to Lieut.-Gen. Middleton, .	182–183
CXXXV.	The Earl of Athole to Charles II., . . .	183–184
CXXXVI.	A Letter of Intelligence, ...	184–186
CXXXVII.	Colonel Lilburne to Colonel Cobbett, . .	186–188
CXXXVIII.	Colonel Lilburne to Captain Drew, . .	188–189
CXXXIX.	The Earl of Roxburgh to Charles II., . .	189–190
CXL.	Col. Lilburne to the Lord-General Cromwell,	190–192
CXLI.	Col. Lilburne to the Lord-General Cromwell,	192–193
CXLII.	Colonel Lilburne to Colonel Reade, . .	194
CXLIII.	Col. Lilburne to the Lord-General Cromwell,	195
CXLIV.	Col. Lilburne to the Lord-General Cromwell,	195–196
CXLV.	Engagement of the Gentlemen of Renfrew, .	196–197
CXLVI.	Colonel Lilburne to Campbell of Glenorchy, .	197–198
CXLVII.	Col. Lilburne to the Lord-General Cromwell,	198–199
CXLVIII.	Colonel Lilburne to Sir James MacDonald, .	199–200
CXLIX.	Lord Newburgh to Charles II., . . .	200–201
CL.	Charles II. to the Earl of Seaforth, . .	201–202
CLI.	Col. Lilburne to the Lord-General Cromwell,	202–203
CLII.	Colonel Lilburne to the Marquess of Argyll, .	204
CLIII.	Col. Lilburne to the Lord-Generall Cromwell,	204–205
CLIV.	Charles II. to C. M., ...	205
CLV.	Charles II. to the Earl of Southesk, .	206
CLVI.	The Earl of Loudoun to Charles II., . .	206–208
CLVII.	The Earl of Loudoun's Narrative of the Union of England and Scotland, ...	208–213
CLVIII.	A Proposed Declaration of Charles II. drawn up by the Earl of Loudon, . . .	213–216
CLIX.	Colonel Bampfield's Advice, . . .	217–218
CLX.	Colonel Bampfield's Advice, . . .	218–219
CLXI.	Order concerning the Shire of Dunbarton, .	219–220

		PAGE
CLXII.	A Letter of Intelligence, ...	220
CLXIII.	Col. Lilburne to the Lord-General Cromwell,	221-222
CLXIV.	Warrant from Colonel Lilburne, . . .	222-223
CLXV.	General Douglas to Charles II., . . .	223-224
CLXVI.	Col. Lilburne to the Lord-General Cromwell,	224-225
CLXVII.	Colonel Lilburne to the Council of State, .	225-226
CLXVIII.	Col. Lilburne to the Lord-General Cromwell,	226-227
CLXIX.	A Warrant from Lord Kenmore, . . .	228
CLXX.	Proclamation by Colonel Lilburne, . .	229-230
CLXXI.	Col. Lilburne to the Lord-General Cromwell,	230-232
CLXXII.	Col. Lilburne to the Lord-Generall Cromwell,	232
CLXXIII.	Memorial from Lieutenant-General Middleton to the States-General, . . .	233-235
CLXXIV.	A Second Memorial from Lieutenant-General Middleton, ...	235-237
CLXXV.	Colonel Lilburne to Lord-General Cromwell, .	238-239
CLXXVI.	Colonel Lilburne to the Scottish Judges, .	239
CLXXVII.	Pass for the Marquess of Argyll, . .	239-240
CLXXVIII.	Col. Lilburne to the Lord-General Cromwell,	240-241
CLXXIX.	Col. Lilburne to the Lord-General Cromwell,	241-242
CLXXX.	Col. Lilburne to the Lord-General Cromwell,	242-243
CLXXXI.	Colonel Lilburne to the Marquess of Argyll, .	244
CLXXXII.	Sir Edward Hyde to Lieut.-Gen. Middleton, .	244-246
CLXXXIII.	Instructions for our Trusty and Wellbeloved Collonell William Drummond: imployed by us upon our especiall service into our Kingdome of Scotlande, ...	246-249
CLXXXIV.	Instructions to our Trusty and Wellbeloved Coll. Norman Mackcloude: imployed by us to our good subjects now in armes in Scotland, ...	250-253
CLXXXV.	Instructions for Captain Shaw, . . .	253-254
CLXXXVI.	The King to the Laird of Macnaughton, .	254-255
CLXXXVII.	The King to the Tutor of Macleod, . .	255
CLXXXVIII.	Charles II. to the Tutor of Struan, . . .	256
CLXXXIX.	Col. Lilburne to the Lord-Generall Cromwell,	256-258

		PAGE
cxc.	Order concerning the Shire of Argyll,	258
cxci.	Proclamation by Colonel Lilburne,	259
cxcii.	Sir Edward Hyde to Lieutenant-General Middleton,	259-261
cxciii.	A Letter to Colonel Lilburne,	261-262
cxciv.	Col. Lilburne to the Lord General Cromwell,	262
cxcv.	Colonel Lilburne to the Judges,	262-263
cxcvi.	A Warrant by John Graham,	263
cxcvii.	Letter from John Graham,	263-264
cxcviii.	Warrant from Sir Mungo Murray,	264
cxcix.	Col. Lilburne to the Lord General Cromwell,	264-266
cc.	Colonel Lilburne to the Council of State,	266-267
cci.	A Letter from Lord Lorne to the Gentlemen of Badenoch,	267-268
ccii.	The Governor of Ruthven Castle to the Gentlemen of Badenoch,	268-270
cciii.	Col. Lilburne to the Lord General Cromwell,	270-272
cciv.	Col. Lilburne to the Committee of the Army,	272
ccv.	Col. Lilburne to the Lord General Cromwell,	272-274
ccvi.	Col. Lilburne to the Lord General Cromwell,	274-275
ccvii.	Colonel Lilburne to Major-General Lambert,	275-276
ccviii.	Orders issued by the Judges,	276-281
ccix.	Colonel Lilburne to Andrew Hay,	281
ccx.	A Letter of Intelligence,	281-282
ccxi.	Col. Lilburne to the Lord General Cromwell,	282-283
ccxii.	Order of the Judges on the Custody of Deeds,	283-285
ccxiii.	Colonel Lilburne to Lord General Cromwell,	285-287
ccxiv.	Col. Lilburne to the Committee for the Army,	287-288
ccxv.	Col. Lilburne to the Lord General Cromwell,	288-289
ccxvi.	Col. Lilburne to the Admiralty Commissioners,	289-290
ccxvii.	A Letter of Intelligence,	290-291
ccxviii.	Charles ii. to the Earl of Murray,	291-292
ccxix.	A Commission from the Earl of Glencairne,	292
ccxx.	An Intercepted Letter,	292-293
ccxxi.	Sir Edward Hyde to Lieut.-Gen. Middleton,	293-294
ccxxii.	Col. Lilburne to the Commissioners at Leith,	294-295

ccxxiii.	Proposals from Colonel Lilburne,	295-296
ccxxiv.	Letter to Colonel Lilburne,	296-297
ccxxv.	Colonel Lilburne to the Council of State,	298
ccxxvi.	Proclamation by Colonel Lilburne,	298-299
ccxxvii.	Instructions to Officers for the Seizure of Horses,	299-300
ccxxviii.	Charles II. to the Marquess of Huntly,	301
ccxxix.	Col. Lilburne to the Lord General Cromwell,	301-303
ccxxx.	Colonel Lilburne to the Lord Protector,	303-304
ccxxxi.	Colonel Lilburne to the Lord Protector,	304-305
ccxxxii.	Proclamation against Sir Arthur Forbes,	305-306
ccxxxiii.	Form of Engagement for Prisoners,	306
ccxxxiv.	Colonel Lilburne to ———,	306-308
ccxxxv.	Colonel Lilburne to ———,	308
ccxxxvi.	The Earl of Glencairne's Instructions to Major Strachan,	308-310
ccxxxvii.	Charles II. to Lord Balcarres,	310-311
ccxxxviii.	Charles II. to Glengarry,	312-313

APPENDIX

EXTRACTS AND LETTERS SELECTED FROM NEWSPAPERS PUBLISHED DURING 1651 AND 1652.

i.	*Mercurius Scoticus*: Or the True Character of Affairs in England, Scotland, Ireland, and other Forraign Parts,	315-316
ii.	A Letter from Colonel Okey to the Lord President of the Council of State,	316-317
iii.	Extract from *Mercurius Scoticus*,	317-318
iv.	A Proclamation against Moss-troopers,	318-319
v.	A Letter from Colonel Alured,	320
vi.	Letters from Major Scot and his Party at Drumlanerick,	320-322
vii.	Proclamation against Intercourse with the Garrison of the Bass,	322-323

		PAGE
VIII.	Mr. William Clarke to the Speaker of the Parliament, ...	323-324
IX.	A Proclamation by Major-General Monk, . .	324
X.	A Proclamation against Plundering by Major-General Monk, ...	325
XI.	Mr. William Clarke to the Speaker, . . .	325-327
XII.	Extract from *Mercurius Scoticus*, Tuesday (Sept. 30), ...	327-328
XIII.	A Proclamation against Enforced Oaths by Major-General Monk, ...	328
XIV.	The Submission of the Gentlemen of Fife, . .	328-330
XV.	A News-Letter from Leith, ...	330-333
XVI.	The Marquess of Argyle to Major-General Monk,	333
XVII.	Extracts from *Mercurius Scoticus*, ...	333-335
XVIII.	Mr. William Clarke to the Speaker, . . .	335-336
XIX.	A Proclamation by Lieutenant-General Monk, .	336
XX.	A Letter from Lieutenant-General Monk, . .	337
XXI.	Extract from *Mercurius Scoticus*, ...	337-338
XXII.	Some heads of what hath been concluded touching an Agreement of a Treaty to be between the Marquesse of Arguile and the Commissioners from Lieutenant-General Monke, .	338-339
XXIII.	Extract from *Mercurius Scoticus*, ...	339-340
XXIV.	Articles agreed on with the Marquess of Huntley,	340-341
XXV.	Extracts from *Mercurius Scoticus*, ...	341-344
XXVI.	A Proclamation concerning the Price of Hay, .	344
XXVII.	Extract from Newsletter of Dec. 2, 1651, from Edinburgh, ...	344-345
XXVIII.	Extract from *Mercurius Scoticus*, .	345-346
XXIX.	A Proclamation concerning Bread, . . .	346-347
XXX.	A Proclamation concerning Lighting and Cleaning the Streets [of Edinburgh], ...	347-348
XXXI.	A Summons given by the Presbytery of Aberdeen to Sir Alexander Irving of Drum, . .	348-349
XXXII.	The Appeal of Sir Alexander Irvine of Drum from the Presbytery of Aberdeen, . .	349-350

CONTENTS

		PAGE
XXXIII.	The Summons of Mr. Row, Moderator of Aberdeen, to Sir Alexander Irvine,	351-352
XXXIV.	A Letter of Sir Alexander Irving to Lieutenant-General Monke,	352-353
XXXV.	A Letter from Sir Alexander Irvine to Mr. Row, Moderator of the Assembly at Aberdeen,	353-354
XXXVI.		355-357
XXXVII.	A Proclamation by the Deputy-Governor of Leith,	358
XXXVIII.	A Letter from Inverness,	358-359
XXXIX.	A Letter from Glasgow,	359-360
XL.	A Letter from Major-General Deane,	360-361
XLI.	A Letter from the Highlands,	361-362
XLII.	Mr. William Clarke to the Speaker,	362-363
XLIII.	A Letter from the Highlands,	363-364
XLIV.	A Letter from the Highlands,	364-365
XLV.	A Letter from Inverary,	365
XLVI.	A Letter from Paisley,	366
XLVII.	Mr. William Clarke to the Speaker,	367-369
XLVIII.	A Letter from Edinburgh,	369-370
	INDEX,	371-383

ERRATUM

P. xviii. line 19, *for* August *read* September.

INTRODUCTION

On August 3, 1651, Perth surrendered to Cromwell, and on the following day he began his pursuit of Charles II. Monk, who then held the rank of Lieutenant-General of the Ordnance, was left behind to complete the conquest of Scotland. The forces at his disposal for this task were not more than ten thousand men, if indeed so many, but as there was no organised army to meet him in the field his numbers were for the moment sufficient. Garrisons had been left in Leith, Edinburgh, and Perth, and probably also in Burntisland and some smaller places. Monk's field force consisted of four regiments of horse and three of foot with some troops of dragoons and the greater part of the train of artillery. Cromwell estimated the numbers of Monk's force at 4000 or 5000 men, but Downing the Scout-master-General mentions 7000 or 8000. The discrepancy can be explained by supposing that Downing included in his total some of the recently established garrisons.

Monk's first object was to capture Stirling. The town surrendered on August 6, at the first summons, and the castle, unable to resist Monk's well served artillery, yielded on August 14 (pp. 1-4). During the siege Colonel Okey and his regiment of horse were despatched into Lanarkshire, and having dispersed some new levies and captured the King's Commissioners at Paisley, rejoined Monk at Stirling (pp. 5, 316). From Stirling Monk set out for Dundee, which he summoned on August 26, and stormed on September 1. Between four hundred and five hundred soldiers and townsmen were killed, or according to a later account nearly eight hundred. The town was plundered for a day and a night, but except during the first heat of the storm no bloodshed seems to have taken place (pp. 7-12).¹ A few days before its fall, on the night of August 27, Colonel Matthew Alured and eight hundred of Monk's cavalry surprised and captured, at Alyth in Perthshire, the Scottish Committee of Estates. Eight noblemen, including the Earl of Leven and the Earl Marischal, and a number of gentlemen of rank, fell into Alured's hands. This was, in Chancellor Loudoun's words, a sad disaster and blow, for it deprived Scotland of the central authority necessary to unite the national efforts against the English invaders (pp. 9, 23, 320). At Alyth and Worcester so many prisoners of rank were taken, that an English newspaper scoffingly observed : 'all the nobility of Scotland that are at liberty may all sit about a joint-stool' (*Mercurius Politicus*, Sept. 11-18, 1651). St. Andrews, which had at first refused Monk's summons, yielded on August 30 (pp. 7, 8, 10). Aberdeen was occupied about the 10th of September and Montrose about the same time (pp. 14, 15). The news of the rout of the Scottish army at Worcester reached Monk's camp on August 9, but even before it could produce its results in putting an end to further resistance he had practically accomplished his task. At first the very completeness of the victory rendered it difficult for the Scots to credit the reports which came to their ears. It seemed incredible that no portion of the defeated army should have succeeded in effecting its return, and rumours 'of some good success of their forces in England' found ready credence (pp. 14, 17).

The progress of Monk's conquests was retarded by his own serious illness and by the paucity of his forces (pp. 14, 323, 337). But in October and November several new regiments of

---

¹ Five hundred is Monk's estimate in his letter of Sept. 1. William Clarke, in a letter dated Sept. 5, says, 'near eight hundred.'—Cary's *Memorials of the Civil War*, ii. 351, 366. Mr. Burton disbelieves the stories of the supposed massacre.—*History of Scotland*, vii. 42 ed. 1874. Mr. Gardiner also takes the same view.

horse and foot and a large number of recruits for the old regiments arrived in Scotland which enabled Monk to extend his quarters. The Marquis of Huntly signed articles of capitulation for himself and his forces on November 21, and Lord Balcarres followed his example on December 3 (pp. 21, 339, 340). Colonel Fitch occupied Inverness about the end of November (pp. 28, 342). Colonel Overton landed in Orkney about the middle of February and established a garrison there with scarcely any resistance (pp. 34, 36). The last castles which held out for Charles II. surrendered one after another. Dumbarton Castle capitulated at the beginning of January 1652. The Bass, which was summoned on October 27, 1651, surrendered in April 1652 (pp. 322, 333-335, *Commons Journals*, vii. 127).[1] On February 18, 1652, Monk left Scotland, and retired to Bath to try the effect of the waters in perfecting his cure. He was succeeded in command by Major-General Richard Deane, who carried out and completed the subjugation of the country. Brodick Castle, in the island of Arran, was occupied on April 6, 1652, by a detachment from the garrison of Ayr (p. 38).[2] Dunnottar Castle, besieged by Colonel Morgan, was surrendered to him on May 26, 1652, and with it fell the last place in Scotland which displayed the standard of Charles II.

Deane now had before him the more difficult task of pacifying the country, and reducing the Highlanders to obedience. The Mosstroopers, as the English termed generically all the little bands of mounted men who carried on a partisan warfare in the Lowlands, had been a source of great annoyance to the invaders ever since 1650. They infested the country round the English garrisons, intercepting the posts, cutting off small parties of men, and murdering stragglers (pp. 8, 28, 318, 332).[3] But now the cessation of warfare and the vigorous measures of

---

[1] *Several Proceedings in Parliament*, pp. 1838, 1847.
[2] Mackinnon, *Coldstream Guards*, i. 47 ; *Papers relative to the Regalia of Scotland*, Bannatyne Club, 1829.
[3] Cf. *Spottiswoode Miscellany*, ii. 95.

Deane put a stop to their activity, and until the rising of 1653 commenced little more is heard of them. The reduction of the Highlands, especially of the western portion, was a much more difficult business. On June 9, 1652, Deane appointed Colonel Robert Lilburne to command an expedition to march through the Highlands and to enforce their submission to the authority of the Commonwealth (p. 45). Deane himself with a second division of the army set out at the same time for Inverary. Some account of the incidents of his march and of its results is given in the letters from contemporary newspapers reprinted in the Appendix (pp. 360-367). One important result was a final and definite agreement with the Marquis of Argyll. For some months Argyll had attempted by every diplomatic artifice to maintain a neutral and independent position and to avoid committing himself to the acceptance of the English Government. During the siege of Dundee he had been reported to be raising forces for its relief, but it was subsequently asserted on his behalf that he had made no levies since Charles II. left Scotland (pp. 17, 20). After its fall on October 15, 1651, he addressed a letter to Monk proposing a treaty. 'I desire to know from you, as one having cheife trust in this kingdome; if it were not fit that some men who have deserved trust in both kingdomes may not meet to good purpose in some convenient place, as a meanes to stop the shedding of more Christian blood?' Monk curtly replied that he could admit of no such treaty without order from the Commonwealth of England (pp. 333, 335).[1] At the time when Argyll wrote, Chancellor Loudoun and the remnant of the Committee of Estates were endeavouring to procure the assembly of a Parliament, and that body had been summoned to meet on November 15 (pp. 19, 20, 26). Supported by its authority the Marquis evidently designed to treat with Monk, and the letter was meant to draw from him an implied permission for their

---

[1] The letter is printed in Balfour's *Annals*, iv. 316, and *Several Proceedings in Parliament*, p. 1702.

meeting. But the English Parliament was resolved not to recognise any kind of assembly which claimed to represent the Scottish nation, whether styling itself Parliament or Committee of Estates. On November 19 the Council of State had been ordered 'to prevent all public meetings of any persons in Scotland for the exercise of any jurisdiction other than such as is or shall be from the Parliament of England, or from such persons as shall have authority under them' (*Cal. State Papers, Dom.* 1651-2, p. 26). When Argyll sought to treat for his personal submission, the first condition imposed upon him was to prevent the intended meeting of the Scottish Parliament, or at least not to take part in it himself (pp. 19, 338). An interview was arranged to take place on November 19, 1651, between Argyll and two of Monk's officers; but when the day came the Marquis pleaded illness and postponed it (*Several Proceedings in Parliament*, pp. 1775, 1795). The relations between him and the new government were further complicated by the arrival of the Commissioners despatched by the English Parliament in December 1651 to treat of the union of the two nations. On March 18, 1652, the Marquis had a conference with the English Commissioners at Dumbarton, in which he renewed his old proposal that a number of select persons might be permitted to meet together for discussion, but was obliged to submit to the method of procedure preferred by the Parliamentary Commissioners (*Report on the MSS. of the Duke of Portland*, i. 635). After some further letters, in which he expressed a general desire to do all which with a safe conscience he might for the peace and union of this island, and to clear himself from any suspicions of a desire to raise fresh troubles, the correspondence dropped (pp. 37, 40, 42). On April 26 the deputy for the shire of Argyll accepted the tender of the union on behalf of its inhabitants, and engaged for them to obey the authority of the English Parliament exercised in Scotland (p. 42, cf. *Portland MSS.* i. 638, 644). His attitude is described in a letter from Edinburgh, dated April 27, and printed in *Several Proceedings in Parliament*. 'Arguill is now again seeking to come in, the pitcher goes often to the conduit, but at last is dasht in peeces. He solicites hard and sends letter after letter, and one messenger after another, using all the means he can through his best policy to obtain some singular act of favour. But I cannot understand that he will much advantage himself by his policy, for we are, I hope, sufficiently satisfied of his put offs and overreaching intentions, which will be a snare probably to himself. His curiosity in aiming too high will cause such delays, as will give us opportunity when grasse is more grown to fall to action. For we shal shortly be enabled to come upon him and the rest that stand out with a double infall; I hope we shall find no very great difficulty to reduce his country.' As expected, the march of Deane and Lilburne into the Highlands brought Argyll's hesitation to an end. He was obliged to declare his acceptance of the Union and his submission to the Parliament of England, which was at once published in the newspapers (p. 50). A week later, on August 19, 1652, an agreement was signed between Deane and Argyll (p. 48). In the speech in his own defence made by Argyll, April 9, 1661, he relates his dealings with Deane, and asserts that this agreement was extorted from him by threats (Wodrow, *Church History*, ed. 1828, i. 144). It was something between a treaty and a capitulation. Argyll, while generally accepting the English Government, was permitted to make certain reservations with regard to its religious policy and his own action concerning it. One clause stipulated that either himself or his eldest son should repair to England as a hostage, if summoned by the Parliament. Another clause allowed the establishment of English garrisons in Argyll's country, but as soon as Deane's troops withdrew three of the five garrisons he left behind were immediately surprised by the Highlanders. Argyll professed his disapproval of these acts, released the prisoners, and restored the captured posts (pp. 366, 368). In the end, however, they were not reoccupied, and the only places permanently held in his country by the English were Dunstaffnage and Dunolly. In a supplementary treaty it was agreed that 'except on some urgent occasions to march through the country for the peace of the island, or reducing some that are refractory,' no more forces should be brought into his country (pp. 55, 60; cf. *Spottiswoode Miscellany*, ii. 79, 81, 91, 93). He had therefore reaped some profit by the little outbreak of the Highlanders, and it is not unlikely that he had inspired it. The general result of all his manœuvres was that though forced to submit, and regarded with considerable suspicion by reason of them, he still retained some shadow of independence.

After the victory of Worcester the English Parliament seemed for a moment disposed to treat Scotland simply as a conquered country, and to annex it to England. On September 9, 1651, a committee was appointed 'to bring in an Act for asserting the right of this Commonwealth to so much of Scotland as is now under the forces of this Commonwealth,' and to consider 'how the same may be settled under the government of this Commonwealth.' An Act 'asserting the title of England to Scotland' was read a first time on September 30 (*Commons Journals*, vii. 14, 22). But it was eventually decided to adopt a more politic method of uniting the two countries, and on October 23 eight Commissioners were appointed to proceed to Scotland in order to settle the civil government of the country and to prepare the way for a union. The persons selected were Chief-Justice Oliver St. John, Sir Henry Vane, Richard Salway, Colonel George Fenwick, Major-Generals Lambert and Deane, Alderman Robert Tichborne, and Lieutenant-General Monk (*Commons Journals*, vii. 30). Their instructions, which were drawn up after many deliberations and with extraordinary precautions to keep them secret, were delivered to the Commissioners on December 18 (*ibid.* 44, 47, 49, 51, 53). The Commissioners arrived in Scotland by the middle of January, and on March 16, 1652, Vane was able to report to Parliament that the greater part of the shires and boroughs of Scotland had assented by their deputies to the tender of union (*ibid.* 105, 107, 110, 113).

The next step was the drawing up of a 'Declaration of the Parliament of England,' in order to the uniting of Scotland into one Commonwealth with England (March 25), followed by an Act for the incorporating of Scotland into one Commonwealth and free state with England, and for abolishing the kingly office in Scotland. This Act was read a first and second time on April 13, 1652. The completion of the Act and the settlement of the details were deferred till the twenty-one deputies of Scotland, summoned to appear in London by October 1, had been afforded the opportunity to set forth their views to the committee which the English Parliament had appointed to discuss the matter. These conferences, which began in October 1652, were continued till the dissolution of the Long Parliament in April 1653, and the deputies themselves remained in England till August 1653. The union was finally accomplished by the Instrument of Government in December 1653, which determined that Scotland should be represented by thirty members in the Parliament of the Commonwealth of England, Scotland, and Ireland, and by an ordinance of the Protector's dated April 12, 1654, for completing and perfecting the union which the Long Parliament had designed.

On the history of these lengthy and complicated negotiations the papers printed in this volume throw little light. There are occasional mentions however of different steps in the proceedings summarised above. The first letter of the English commissioners after their arrival in Scotland is printed on p. 31. Two newsletters contain accounts of the proclamation issued by the Commissioners for the abolition of the kingly power in Scotland, and of the parliamentary declaration concerning the union of the two nations (pp. 35-41). Colonel Lilburne criticises with severity the character of the deputies sent from Scotland to negotiate with the Parliament (p. 136). There is also a long narrative addressed by the Earl of Loudoun to Charles II. relating the procedure by which the consent of Scotland to the union was obtained, and dwelling on its illegality and invalidity (pp. 208-213).

The theory of the statesmen of the Commonwealth was that the union was so great a boon to Scotland that it ought to be thankfully accepted by the nation, and that it would be so accepted. 'This proposition of union,' writes Ludlow, 'was cheerfully accepted by the most judicious amongst the Scots, who well understood how great a condescension it was in the Parliament of England to permit a people they had conquered to have a part in the legislative power' (*Memoirs*, i. 298). This view is illustrated by the pained surprise with which the author of the newsletter describing the proclamation of the union at Edinburgh notes the absence of any sign of rejoicing amongst the auditors, and by the letter of Captain Hill to the gentlemen of Badenoch (pp. 41, 269). But in truth even those who had accepted the union acquiesced in it rather than welcomed it. It promised a certain amount of self-government instead of military rule, and it was well to choose the least of two evils. In the opposition to the union political and religious motives were combined. The desire to preserve the independence of the nation in its integrity was strengthened by a natural doubt whether the terms of the proposed incorporation would be fair to the weaker nation. 'As for the embodying of Scotland with England,' said Mr. Robert Blair, 'it will be as when the poor bird is embodied into the hawk that hath eaten it up' (*Life of Robert Blair*, p. 292). Both parties in the Church denounced the union in their official manifestoes on the ground that it meant the destruction of the freedom of the Church, and would open the door to unlimited toleration. In the declarations of Glasgow, Kirkcudbright, and other districts against the 'Tender' the religious objection holds an equally prominent place (*Report on the Portland MSS.*, i. 628, 630, 634).

On the other hand, with those who willingly accepted the union one of the guiding motives was hostility to the Presbyterian Church system. At first, therefore, the royalists showed themselves more ready than the Church party to submit to the new government, and so to accept the union. 'If any merit favour here,' said an English newsletter, dated January 1, 1652, 'it is those whom they call more malignant, who, as they are the most considerable party, soe have already done more reall and visible service than the whole generation of Presbyterians' (pp. 29, 339, 355). The most remarkable exposition of the views of this class is to be found in Sir Thomas Urquhart's ΕΚΣΚΥΒΑΛΑΤΡΟΝ; *or, the Discovery of a most Exquisite Jewel,* published in 1652. Urquhart's tract purported to be 'a vindication of the honour of Scotland from that infamy whereinto the rigid Presbyterian party of that nation, out of their covetousness and ambition, most dissembledly hath involved it.' In it he asserted that 'a malignant and independent will better sympathise with one another, than either of them with the presbyter.' He concluded by recommending the close union of the two countries, a union which should be 'not heterogeneal (as timber and stone upon ice stick sometimes together) bound by the frost of a conquering sword; but homogeneated by naturalisation, and the mutual enjoyment of the same privileges and immunities.' After quoting at some length Bacon's arguments on the subject, he urged on the English government the advisability of preferring 'rather to gain the love and affection of the Scots, thereby to save the expense of any more blood or money, than for overthrowing them quite in both their bodies and fortunes, to maintain the charge of an everlasting war against the storms of the climate, the fierceness of discontented people, inaccessibility of the hills, and sometimes universal penury, the mother of plague and famine; all which inconveniencies may be easily prevented, without any charge at all, by the sole gaining of the hearts of the country.'

The way to effect this was a union of such a nature that Scotland should possess 'the same privileges and immunities that Wales now hath . . . to enjoy everywhere in all things the emoluments and benefits competent to the free born subjects of England; and to this effect to empower that nation with liberty to choose their representatives to be sent hither to this their sovereign parliament, that the public trustees of England, Scotland, and Wales may at Westminster jointly concur for the weal of the whole isle, as members of one and the same incorporation.' . . . 'By which means, patching up old rents, cementing what formerly was broken, and by making of ancient foes new friends, we will strengthen ourselves, and weaken our enemies; and raise the isle of Britain to that height of glory, that it will become formidable to all the world besides. In the meanwhile, the better to incorporate the three dominions of England, Scotland, and Wales, and more firmly to consolidate their union, it were not amiss (in my opinion) that (as little rivers which use to lose their names when they have run along into the current of a great flood) they have their own peculiar titles laid aside, and totally discharged into the vast gulf of that of Great Britain' (Sir Thomas Urquhart's *Tracts*, Edinburgh, 1782, pp. 145, 153, 163-5).

The eight Commissioners of the Parliament, however, were not merely sent to set on foot the negotiations for the union, but also charged to settle the civil government of Scotland. Their proceedings in this part of the mission were reported to the English Parliament by Oliver St. John on 14th May 1652. On January 31, 1652, the Commissioners published a declaration abolishing all jurisdictions derived from the King, and stating their intention of appointing persons to administer justice for the time being until new judicatories and courts of justice could in a more solemn way be established. In pursuance of this plan they appointed seven Commissioners for the administration of justice, four of whom were Englishmen and three Scots. Their installation, which took place on May 18, 1652, is described in a newsletter of that date (p. 43).

For the last few months the administration of the law had been interrupted. 'Fra the incuming of the Englische airmy to Scotland to this very day, the last of December 1651, thair wes no supreme judicatories in Scotland, sik as Secreitt Counsell and Sessioun to minister justice, so that the pepill of the land for laik of the Scottis laws did suffer much' (Nicoll's *Diary*, p. 69). For a short time a kind of rough justice, both civil and criminal, was administered by a committee of English officers. A newsletter from Edinburgh, dated December 29, 1651, says: 'This day, according to custom, diverse Scottish suiters made their addresses to the honourable committee of officers at Leith, where all just expectations were duly satisfied with quick despatches in point of justice (whereas some suits before had hung 16 years without any period put to it in their old Judicatories), which doth much cheare up the Scottish people that they begin to read the Lord's dispensations of love and kindnesse towards them, in finding far more respect and justice from their supposed enemies than ever they did from their own countrymen' (*Several Proceedings in Parliament*, January 1-8, 1652). Nicoll, who copies this passage, also observes: 'In these tymes the Englische commanderis haid great respect to justice, and in doing execution upon malefactouris, such as theves, harlotes, and utheris of that kynd, by scurgeing, hanging, kicking, cutting of thair eares, and stigmating of thame with het yrnes' (pp. 69, 89). The appointment of the seven Commissioners put an end to these military tribunals, and substituted regular civil courts for them. The Commissioners began by imposing on the Writers to the Signet an oath of fidelity to the Commonwealth, and by issuing a proclamation that all legal documents should henceforth be drawn up in English (Nicoll's *Diary*, pp. 94, 96). Their justice is praised by Nicoll, who writes: 'To speak treuth, the Englisches wer moir indulgent and merciful to the Scottis, nor wes the Scottis to their awin cuntriemen and nychtbouris, as wes too evident, and thair justice exceidit the Scottis in many thinges, as wes reportit. They also filled up the roumes of justice courtes with very honest clerkis and memberis of that judicatory' (p. 104). The best account of the reforms attempted and the changes introduced in the administration of justice at this time and during the next few years is contained in Mr. Æneas Mackay's *Life of the First Lord Stair* (pp. 58-62). The orders of the Commissioners for the regulation of fees and the custody of deeds which are printed in this volume are from broadsides in Clarke's collection (pp. 276, 283).

Amongst the papers printed are a certain number of letters to the Commissioners from the commander of the English army of occupation, recommending the temporary suspension of legal proceedings against certain persons (pp. 77, 239, 262). Politically the severe impartiality with which the new judges enforced the law led to one evil consequence. During the long wars the nobility and gentry had incurred many debts, and they were now generally insolvent. As soon as peace was restored and the new judicatories established, their creditors began to press them hard and to put the laws in motion against them. It was held by the English officers that the too great rigidity with which the judges enforced the law in this matter of debt was one of the chief causes which swelled the ranks of the royalist rising headed by Glencairne (pp. 267, 289, 296).

The remainder of the work of the eight Commissioners may be more briefly summarised. A Court of Admiralty for Scotland was set up at Leith, new sheriffs were commissioned for all the counties in Scotland, and oaths of fidelity to the Commonwealth were imposed on the sheriffs, the magistrates of the boroughs, and other persons in public employment (pp. 35, 39; *Portland MSS.*, i. 629, 632; *Commons Journals*, vii. 106). The judges, visitors, and sheriffs appointed by the Commissioners were to hold office till November 1, 1652, but their term was subsequently extended, by an Act of Parliament, to May 1, 1653 (p. 135; Scoble, *Acts and Ordinances*, p. 210).

Besides organising the government by establishing judges and other magistrates, the Commissioners were empowered to settle the financial system of Scotland. The English troops were generally living upon free quarter, or upon roughly levied assessments on the districts in which they were quartered. Lambert and Deane, in December 1651, began the work of reducing and regulating these assessments. On February 18, 1652, the Commissioners ordered a general assessment of 10,000l per month to be levied on Scotland, authorising Major-General Deane to apportion the amounts to be levied on particular districts, and to make the necessary abatements for localities which had suffered during the war. But the total of the abatements made was not to excede £2000 per month. On October 26, 1652, Parliament approved the order of the Commissioners, and continued the assessment to May 1653. On May 3, 1653, the Council of State continued the assessment till the following November; and on November 12 of the same year, the Barebones Parliament extended it to June 1654 (*Commons Journals*, vii. 195, 350; *Cal. State Papers Dom.*, 1652-3, p. 303). Nominally the total of the assessment came to £10,016 per month. In practice, as arranged by the Commissioners of the different shires met at Edinburgh in July 1653, the total amounted to £8500 (p. 170). The valuation of the respective shires was based on earlier valuations made in 1629, 1644-5, and 1649 (p. 172.) A small quarto volume amongst William Clarke's collection, Number xxiii. in the catalogue of the manuscripts of Worcester College, gives the valuation of each particular parish. The table printed here on p. 170 gives the proportions at which the different counties of Scotland were assessed; whilst the second table on p. 174 shows the sums levied on the burghs included in the counties, with the abatements allowed, and the names of the collectors. Other papers show how disputed assessments were settled (pp. 173, 180, 219).

Respites were sometimes granted, and, in the case of Argyll, payment in kind allowed (pp. 204, 222). Two letters of Colonel Lilburne's are of special interest in connection with the assessment. In one he asserts the inexpediency and almost impossibility of raising the tax above £8500 per month. In another he enlarges on the difficulty of collecting it, caused by Glencairne's rising (pp. 287, 307).

During 1652 and 1653 the commander-in-chief of the English forces in Scotland was also the head of the financial administration. Major-General Deane, as has been stated, was the person specially charged with the original distribution of the monthly assessment. He had also the responsibility of determining the expenditure not only of that tax, but of other revenues. On 11th November 1652, the Parliament voted that all the public revenue of Scotland, arising by way of assessment, custom, late king's revenue, sequestrations, or otherwise, shall be issued forth by warrant, under the hand of the commander-in-chief in Scotland, until the first of May next. He was authorised to defray from these sources the salaries of the judges and other officials, and to spend a certain sum on fortifications; and also by way of loan upon account, for supply of the army and forces, for the preventing free quarter, and for carrying on other necessaries and public services in Scotland; and the remainder to be applied for payment of the forces in Scotland (*Commons Journals*, vii. 213). Lilburne, who succeeded Deane as commander-in-chief in December 1652, and held office till April 1654, exercised the same powers.

Of the sources of revenue enumerated in this order, the rents due to the late king and other public revenues were collected by the Auditor-General, John Thompson (p. 181). The sequestrations were under the management of three Commissioners, sitting at Leith: Richard Saltonstall, Samuel Disbrowe, and Edmund Syler (pp. 74, 152). These sequestrated lands formed the fund from which the services of English officers and officials were rewarded by Parliament. Major-

General Lambert was voted lands to the value of £1000 a year, Lieutenant-General Monk, and Colonels Whalley, Ingoldsby, Overton, and Pride, 500↑ a year a piece; Colonels Okey and Lilburne, 300↑; Mr. John Weaver, £250; Colonel Alured, £200. Major John Cobbett, who very nearly captured Charles II. at Worcester, obtained £100 a year from the same source; and the widow of Major Rookesby, killed at Dunbar, £300 a year (*Commons Journals*, vii. 14, 77, 132, 191, 247, 278).

In execution of these votes, Colonel Ingoldsby was given the manor and park of Hamilton (p. 74); whilst Whalley got the manor and lands of Liddington, and Monk, Kincale (*Portland MSS.*, i. 658). From the sequestrations also were derived the expenses incurred in building the citadels at Inverness, Ayr, and other smaller forts. There are a few references to these works amongst the papers now printed (pp. 17, 28, 36) Clarke's collections contain plans of the citadels, which it is hoped to reproduce in a later volume. Two thousand pounds a month was the amount which the commander-in-chief was empowered to spend for this purpose. During 1652 and 1653, however, the actual sum expended on fortifications came to between £4000 and £5000 per month (pp. 152, 288.) Contingencies and accidental expenses were charged on the same fund. On September 17, 1652, Parliament voted £1000 from the sequestrations for the relief of the poor at Glasgow, which had lately been devastated by a great fire (p. 359; cf. *Commons Journals*, vii. 183).

The cost of the army of occupation was only in part defrayed by the taxation of Scotland. The greater part of it fell upon England, and was paid by remittances from the English treasury (p. 111). The reports made to Parliament in September 1651 and April 1652, give the total cost of the army in England and Scotland, but are so stated that it is difficult to ascertain the cost of the portion of the army actually stationed in Scotland (*Commons Journals*, vii. 25, 127). In February 1652 there were in Scotland nine regiments of foot, seven regiments of horse, one regiment of dragoons, and a train of artillery. In June of the same year the regiments of foot had been raised to eleven; and by September there were five regiments of horse instead of seven. During the first four months of 1653, there were eleven regiments of foot, and five of horse, besides dragoons and artillery. But in pursuance of a plan of economy set on foot by the committee of the army in England, the number of men in the different companies and troops had been considerably reduced (pp. 53, 71, 80, 113-115: cf. *Commons Journals*, vii. 241). Before the reductions in August 1652, the pay of the army in Scotland had amounted to 36,000*l* per month, but by February 1653, this sum had been reduced to about 29,000*l*. In February 1653, when the reductions, not only in the number of regiments, but in the numbers of the rank and file in the various regiments, had taken effect, the strength of the army of occupation came to rather more than 12,000 foot, and about 2200 horse. When Glencairne's insurrection broke out, Lilburne found the forces at his disposal insufficient for the task of holding the country and maintaining order. The numbers of the cavalry in particular were quite unequal to the work before them; and his letters are full of complaints of his deficiency in this respect. In answer to his complaints, two regiments of horse and a regiment of foot were sent to Scotland in January 1654 (pp. 271, 273, 275, 286, 298, 305).

The discipline maintained in the English army during its occupation of Scotland is praised by Burnet, Nicoll, and others. Plundering, violence, or other misconduct on the part of the soldiers was rigidly punished (pp. 2, 15, 16, 323, 326). After the storm of Dundee the soldiers, in accordance with the usual custom in the case of towns taken by assault, were allowed to plunder for twenty-four hours, but as soon as that fixed period was over all licence was at once repressed. Monk's proclamations on the subject are given in the Appendix (pp. 324, 325). Amongst the proclamations issued by Colonel Lilburne in 1653 are orders against killing rabbits and pigeons, stealing cabbages and fruit from gardens, exacting money from persons who had not paid their taxes, and quartering soldiers an undue length of time in the same place (pp. 139, 142, 155, 162). Amongst William Clarke's papers is a small quarto volume containing reports of proceedings at courts-martial held at Dundee from September 17, 1651, to January 10, 1652 (Worcester College MSS., No. xxi.). It records the punishment of various soldiers for robbery, horse-stealing, and similar crimes, and also the trials of others for immorality. Illicit relations with Scottish women were visited with severe penalties. In January 1652 the Governor of Leith issued a proclamation that in respect much wickedness appeared in that garrison by the sin of uncleanness, chiefly occasioned by Scottish and English women and maidservants drawing and vending wine, beer, and ale, that no inhabitant of that garrison whatsoever retain or keep any Scottish or English women or maidservants longer than the second of February next, upon pain of paying 20 shillings sterling per diem for every day after that they shall so keep them (*Several Proceedings in Parliament*, p. 1875). Marriages were also very frequent, and an order was issued that no soldier of the garrison of Leith and Edinburgh should marry any Scottish woman without the leave of the governor or some other superior officer (p. 334). Other proclamations issued by the governors of Leith and Edinburgh fixed the price of bread and hay, and ordered the lighting and cleaning of the streets (pp. 344, 346-8).

The maintenance of strict discipline in the army was not only necessary for the sake of the army itself, but an essential condition of the success of the policy adopted by the Commonwealth. Its general aim was to reconcile Scotland to the union by evenhanded justice and good government. The statesmen of the Commonwealth trusted to gain the support of the lower and the middle classes by freeing them from the yoke of the clergy and the great Lords. 'Free the poor commoners, and make as little use as can be either of the great men or clergy,' was the advice tendered to the English Government in *Mercurius Scoticus* (p. 339). Similar advice had been tendered to Cromwell by one of his correspondents shortly after the battle of Dunbar. 'You have tried all brotherly ways to the Kirk and state, but without success. I humbly conceave that your honour hath not fallen upon the right way; for our best security and doing good to that poore and crafty people their bate must be freedome and proffitt, to which end wayes and meanes should be used to make that people, especially the common sort, to be assured that it will be for their freedome and proffitt to submit to or joyne with us, and that we will manumitt them, and mayntayn them in it, and acertayne there estaites and tenures freer and easier than to there Lords; if they shall not speedely come in and comply with us, they must expect the severity of warr to an obstinate people. This to be held forth to them in some particulars in print' (*Original Letters and Papers of State addressed to Oliver Cromwell*, edited by John Nickolls, 1743, p. 29). In the 'Declaration of the Parliament of the Commonwealth of England concerning the settlement of Scotland,' published on February 12, 1652, this policy was plainly set forth. While the estates of those noblemen and gentlemen who had taken part in Hamilton's expedition in 1648, or had fought for Charles II. in the late war, were to be confiscated for the use of the State, an amnesty was promised to the vassals and tenants whom the influence of their lords had led astray. If within thirty days they should put themselves under the protection of the Commonwealth of England and conform to the government it set up, they 'shall not only be pardoned for all acts past, but be set free from their former dependences and bondage services; and shall be admitted as tenants, freeholders, and heritors, to farm, hold, inherit and enjoy, from and under this Commonwealth, proportions of the said confiscated and forfeited lands under such easie, rents and reasonable conditions as may enable them, their heirs and posterity, to live with a more comfortable subsistance than formerly, and like a free people delivered through God's goodness from their former slaveries, vassalage, and oppression.' The Long Parliament was too much occupied with other business to carry out this scheme, and it was reserved for the legislation of the Protectorate to attempt it. But the military administrators of Scotland during 1652 and 1653 seem to have accepted the principle on which the scheme was based, and to have aimed at conciliating the people of Scotland as far as the necessities of their position permitted. Apart from national feeling, however, two causes prevented this policy of conciliation from succeeding. The first cause was the extremely burdensome nature of the taxation which the maintenance of so large an army in Scotland made necessary. Even under the Protectorate, when the development of the revenue from the customs and excise had rendered it possible to reduce the monthly assessment, officials of the English Government admitted that Scotland was more heavily taxed than England and had not gained pecuniarily by the union. The second cause was the opposition of the Church, which kept alive amongst the people the feeling of hostility to the government and to the union.

The policy of the English government in religious matters had been set forth by the Commissioners of the Parliament in a declaration published in February, 1652: 'We declare that for promoting of holiness and advancing the power of godliness, all possible care shall be used for the publishing of the Gospel of Christ in all parts of this land, and provision of maintenance made and allowed to the faithful dispensers thereof, together with such other encouragements as the magistrate may give, and may be expected by them, who demean themselves peaceably and becomingly to the government and authority by which they receive the same. As also, that care shall be taken for removing of scandalous persons who have intruded into the work of the ministry, and placing others fitly qualified with gifts for the instructing of the people in their stead. And that such ministers whose consciences oblige them to wait upon God in the administration of spiritual ordinances, according to the order of the Scottish Churches, with any that shall voluntarily join in the practice thereof, shall receive protection and encouragement from all in authority, in their peaceable and inoffensive exercising of the same; as also shall others who, not being satisfied in conscience to use that form, shall serve and worship God in other Gospel way, and behave themselves peaceably and inoffensively therein. We shall likewise take care, as much as in us lies, that in places of trust throughout this nation, magistrates and officers fearing God may be set up, who, according to the duty of their places, may be a terror to all evil-doers, and even to them whose licentious practices (though under pretence of liberty and conscience) shall manifest them not to walk according to godliness and honesty.'

Before this declaration was issued, the protection afforded by Monk and other officers to Sir Alexander Irvine of Drum against the Presbytery of Aberdeen, and Monk's general order against imposing oaths and covenants, had shown the policy which the new government intended to follow in dealing with the coercive jurisdiction of the Church. In the 'Epistle Liminary' to Sir Thomas Urquhart's *Discovery of a most Exquisite Jewel, etc.*, he mentions a Diurnal being brought to him which contained the relation of the irrational proceedings of the Presbytery of Aberdeen against Sir Alexander Irvine of Drum, together with his just appeal from their tyrannical jurisdiction to Colonel Overton.' The Diurnal referred to was evidently that entitled *Several Proceedings in Parliament*, for January 22-29, 165½, from which the documents reprinted in the Appendix have now been extracted (pp. 348-354). They supplement the papers printed in Whitelocke's *Memorials* and in the *Spalding Miscellany* on the same case.

The next important step in religious policy was the appointment by the Commissioners of the English Parliament of nine

Commissioners for visiting and regulating the universities and schools of Scotland, with power to remove scandalous ministers and decide causes concerning the maintenance of the clergy. The inaugural declaration of the Commission is dated June 4, and their first meeting took place on June 7 (p. 43). On August 2, 1653, the Commissioners issued a proclamation forbidding ministers to preach or pray for Charles the Second, and several persons were arrested for disobedience to the order (pp. 192, 222, 225). Their other proceedings are not mentioned in these papers. Baillie's letters, however, contain a long account of their dealings with the University of Glasgow.

More serious in its consequences was the prohibition of the meetings of the General Assembly of the Church, and the forcible dissolution on July 20, 1653, of that which had met at Edinburgh. Colonel Lilburne seems to have acted on his own responsibility, but his conduct was evidently approved by his superiors in England. He was half inclined to prevent the holding of provincial assemblies also, but hesitated to do so without definite orders, thinking, as he wrote, that 'the people are not well able to bear any more against their ministers' (pp. 161-3, 192). This was the more surprising, because in July 1652 the General Assembly had been suffered to sit and to deliberate without molestation (Nicoll, *Diary*, pp. 97, 99, 110).

At the commencement of the English occupation the English governors, viewing the dissensions which divided the Church of Scotland, had hoped to find allies in the Remonstrants. English officers and newspaper correspondents wrote with favour of the ministers who opposed the proceedings of the General Assembly, without inquiring too closely into the principles which dictated their opposition (pp. 317, 327). But the protests of the Remonstrants against the subordination of the Church to the State and against the toleration of sectaries guaranteed by the English army soon showed the groundless nature of these hopes (pp. 33, 108). Colonel **Lilburne** long continued to believe that 'the people in the west, who have always been accounted most precise,' would come round and accept the new régime, and reported that they professed to disapprove of the rising headed by Glencairne (pp. 127, 242, 271). In the end, however, he had to confess that even the Remonstrants shared the general antipathy of the Scots to their English rulers. 'Even in all these people there is a secret antipathy to us, do what we can to oblige them, unless in some few that are convinced, and those but a few' (p. 266). The attitude taken up by Mr. Andrew Cant was typical. 'Colonel Overton,' says a newsletter, 'at his late being at Aberdeen, hearing of some incivilities offered by some souldiers to Master Andrew Cant, went to his house, and told him he was sorry any injury should be done unto him, who he heard was a friend to us; to which Mr. Cant replyed in plain Scottish that he was a lying knave that told him so, for he neither respected him nor his party' (*Several Proceedings in Parliament*, December 18-24, 1651).

The declaration of February 12, 1651, had promised on behalf of the Commonwealth countenance and protection to those who preferred some 'other gospel way' than the Presbyterian. The propagation of Independency in Scotland was the earnest desire of many of the English officers. It was suggested that able preachers from England should be stationed in the great towns, 'which might convince the people to draw them off from the leven of their pharisaical and rigid presbyterian teachers' (p. 339). The Commissioners of the Parliament were empowered to take four chaplains with them on their mission, and three of the persons suggested, Mr. Caryll, Mr. Oxenbridge, and Mr. Lockyer, accepted the employment offered them (*Cal. State Papers, Dom.* 1651-2, p. 28; *Several Proceedings in Parliament*, April 29-May 6, 1652). The report of the Commissioners which Vane presented to the Parliament on March 1652 asked, that 'twelve or more ministers be speedily sent down to reside in the several garrisons and other convenient places in Scotland.' Parliament referred the proposal to the Council of State, which duly recommended it to a Committee, but no steps were taken to carry it out (*Cal. State Papers, Dom.* 1651-2, p. 191; *Commons Journal,* vii. 108; *Portland MSS.,* i. 632). However, the hopes of the officers in Scotland were from time to time raised by the willingness which many Scots showed to hear the army chaplains in private meetings, and by successful disputations between an occasional chaplain and a Scottish minister. If but few converts were to be made in the south, it was reported that in the north, in Sutherland, there was 'a very precious people,' and when Deane marched into the Highlands news came from his forces that 'some of the Highlanders have heard our preaching with great attention and groanings, and seeming attention to it' (pp. 31, 53, 364). In the end a few Independent congregations, or 'gathered churches,' were established in the Lowlands in the course of 1652 (p. 370). 'There are two eminent ministers in Scotland,' said a newsletter, written in April 1652, 'that were, one of them, of the Assembly, have already joined with gathered Churches, a great change, yet more there are that are going about the same work. This gives satisfaction to many (otherwayes averse) that gathered Churches in England chuse ministers for their pastors, and that Churches joyn in a public way of fellowship. But they like by no means to hear of such as gather Churches in private, without the approbation of other Churches, and have no pastors' (*Several Proceedings in Parliament,* 29th April-6th May 1652). Robert Pittilloh, in his *Hammer of Persecution,* published in 1659, enumerates the names of eight ministers who became converts to Independency about this period, and complains that they were not sufficiently protected and favoured by the government, and that after Cromwell became Protector they were even actively discouraged by his policy. 'Before this day there had been thousands in Scotland separated from the National Church, who would have jeoparded their lives for the godly in England, if they had met with that freedom and encouragement which justly they expected when first the English came to Scotland' (pp. 10-13). In the letters of Colonel Lilburne, written during 1653, a similar complaint is made, and he also points out that 'the poor congregated people' were the special prey of royalist plunderers (pp. 123, 127, 265).

By the end of 1652 Scotland seemed to be completely pacified. 'All things at present are in a strange kind of hush,' declared a letter from Edinburgh (p. 369). The English government felt itself able to release a number of important prisoners on parole, and also to set at liberty the ministers taken at Alyth, or for other reasons confined in England, pp. 9, 193, 342). But from June 1652 the royalists had been making preparations to take up arms once more, and in February 1653 the movements of the Highlanders began to attract the attention of Colonel Lilburne, who had just succeeded Major-General Deane as commander-in-chief in Scotland (pp. 79, 82, 85). During the first months of 1652 the hopes of Charles II. seem to have been confined to the retention of Dunnottar and to the safe transport of the regalia and the personal property which the king had left in that stronghold. 'In this castle,' wrote Hyde to Nicolas, 'besides the crown and sceptre, there are all the king's rich hangings and beds, plate, and other furniture, to so good value, that it is avowed by very good men, who are to be believed, that if all were at Amsterdam it would yield £20,000 sterling, and the king is pressed to send a frigate to bring all this away, which you will easily believe he very much desires to do, but knows not which way to compass it.' Charles also desired to send some provisions to the garrison of Dunnottar, in order to enable the governor to hold out. 'The preservation of this place,' explains Hyde, 'being the foundation of all the hope for Scotland; for there is room enough within this castle to receive an army, and it is in the very centre of the kingdom, so that as soon as the summer is over, any little succors or great supplies of men from Norway may be landed there, and there will be care taken to that purpose.' 'If you shall be able,' promised the king to the governor, 'to defend and keep the place till the beginning of the next winter, we make no question but that we shall transport such supplies to you as shall not only be sufficient to enlarge your quarters, but by the blessing of God to free your country from the tyranny of those rebels' (*Clarendon State Papers*, iii. 56, 60, 61). The king selected as his agent Major-General Vandruske, a Dutch soldier, who had served some time in Scotland, and charged him not simply to relieve Dunnottar, but to repair to the Highlands and consult with Glengarry, Pluscardine, and other royalists (*ibid.* pp. 69, 72; *Cal. Clarendon Papers*, ii. 124). But the difficulty of raising money to procure a ship and provide supplies prevented Vandruske from starting, and the fall of Dunnottar put an end to the scheme.

In the summer of 1652 the King's hopes suddenly revived. In May 19 took place the collision between Blake and Tromp in the Downs, followed a few weeks later by open war between England and Holland. If the Dutch chose to aid Charles with ships and men he might succeed in recovering Scotland. But, at all events, the war gave an opportunity for a successful insurrection in Scotland. About June there came a representation 'from diverse of the most considerable nobility,' giving Charles an account of the condition of Scotland, and urging him to action (p. 137). The King at once resolved to send an agent to Scotland to take the command of the royalists and manage the intended rising. For this purpose he selected Middleton, who, having been taken prisoner at Worcester, had escaped from the Tower and had joined his master at Paris. Besides his qualifications as a soldier and the soundness of his political views, Middleton had the advantage of being thoroughly in the confidence of Hyde and the English royalists. 'He is the soberest man I have met with,' wrote Hyde to Nicholas, 'and very worthy of any trust, having the greatest sense of the errors he hath formerly committed, and the best excuses for them that I have found from any' (*Clarendon State Papers*, iii. 56; cf. p. 53 *post*). On June 25, 1652, Middleton was commissioned as Lieutenant-General of the King in Scotland, and accredited to the Scottish nobles (p. 46).

In November Captain Smith, who had been despatched from Glengarry and other Highland chiefs in the preceding July, reached Paris with another appeal to the King. Charles replied by drawing up a commission to Glengarry and five others (Dec. 30, 1652), appointing them commissioners for the government of his forces in Scotland, and authorising them to choose a person to act as commander-in-chief till Middleton should arrive (pp. 65-70; cf. *Cal. Clarendon Papers*, ii. 158). Soon after Smith's arrival, and before he had left Holland for Scotland, there came two more messengers. One, Captain Strachan, came from the Earl of Glencairne, who offered to join the Highlanders in arms, and to raise levies of his own to join them. The King at once instructed Glencairne to take command of the forces raised in the Highlands till Middleton's coming, and gave him an absolute commission as interim commander-in-chief (March 14, 1653). But as it was important not to disaffect the Highlanders, Charles instructed him not to produce this commission except in the last resort, and provided him with a letter recommending the chiefs to elect him their commander (pp. 99, 103, 138). A little later came letters from Lord Balcarres and a messenger named Malcolm Roger. Finally, in September 1653, arrived Colonel Bampfield furnished with letters from Seaforth and Balcarres urging the King to trust the bearer, and setting forth his great services to the royalist cause in Scotland (pp. 97, 107, 120, 128, 130, 183). There were signs, however, that the religious dissensions and personal jealousies which had been so fatal to the royalist cause in the late war would be an equal hindrance to the success of the intended rising. Middleton was regarded as not Presbyterian enough to be thoroughly trusted by the Church party, and while the King had no difficulty in composing a singularly pious letter to the Moderator of the General Assembly, he found it impossible to draw up a public declaration which should satisfy the ecclesiastical party without alienating his other supporters (pp. 47, 106, 293). There was evidence of a certain jealousy between the Highland royalists and their allies from the Lowlands. It was hinted that Glengarry would not be commanded by Middleton in the Highlands and a suggestion was made that the command should be divided (pp. 139, 311). Glengarry desired to be rewarded by being created Earl of Ross, a demand which, if granted, would entail similar demands from others, and cause some heartburnings amongst other associates who deemed their services equally great (pp. 309, 310, 313). The selection of Bampfield as the agent of Glengarry and Balcarres was extremely distasteful to the King, who thoroughly distrusted Bampfield, and had gone so far as to send orders to Scotland for his arrest (pp. 94, 104, 310, 312). Glencairne and Balcarres were not on good terms with each other (p. 247). But in spite of his distrust Charles was obliged to receive Bampfield and listen to his proposals (pp. 287-9). All he could do was to warn his friends in Scotland not to trust Bampfield, and to urge Balcarres to co-operate cordially with Glencairne and Middleton. In the beginning of November he despatched three new agents to Scotland, Colonel William Drummond to Glencairne with special instructions to effect a reconciliation between him and Balcarres (p. 246); Colonel Norman Macleod to the Highlanders to induce them to accept Glencairne as their general (p. 250); and Captain Shaw to Loudoun and Lord Lorne (p. 253). They were charged to announce Middleton's speedy arrival in Scotland, and to give hopes that he would be followed by Charles himself (pp. 245, 249).

The necessity of Middleton's immediate presence in Scotland was evident, but many causes combined to delay his departure. In the autumn of 1652, soon after his arrival in Holland, he fell seriously ill (pp. 52, 60). He was charged to raise money to procure arms and war material for the Scottish royalists, but the King was scarcely able to send him money for his personal expenses (p. 60). There were hopes of obtaining a loan from the Princess of Orange, but the King's main reliance was on gifts from Scottish soldiers and merchants in foreign countries, or from well-disposed foreign princes (p. 51). Negotiations for these contributions took time and brought little into the royal exchequer. Middleton wrote to the Count of Oldenburg (p. 54), entered into a negotiation with the Count of Waldeck for transporting German troops to Scotland (p. 123), and applied to the States General of the United Provinces for arms and money (pp. 157, 233). Applications were also made to Scots in French, Swedish, or Imperial service (pp. 61, 157, 233). The King himself wrote to the Duke of Courland to engage him to further Middleton's appeal to Scots under his government (p. 78), and sent Lord Wentworth to negotiate in Denmark (pp. 106, 109, 246). The Earl of Rochester had been despatched, in December 1652, to negotiate with the princes of Germany and the Diet at Frankfort (p. 52; cf. *Clarendon, Rebellion* xiv. 55).

From these different sources Middleton laboriously got together a small fund for his intended expedition. General Douglas collected 5200 rixdollars in Sweden and sent them to Charles, whilst Sir James Turner raised about the same amount in Germany (pp. 54, 261). Rochester obtained a grant of about £10,000 from the Diet, but it was mostly consumed by the expenses of his mission (*Clarendon Rebellion*, xiv. 103). Well-affected Scots in Holland gave something, and something too was supplied by the Princess of Orange and by the province of Holland itself (pp. 61, 105, 238).

In Scotland the movements of Glengarry and the Highland chiefs began to excite the suspicions of the government in February 1653. Colonel Lilburne received information of their meetings from the Marquis of Argyll and from Sir James

MacDonald of Sleat (pp. 79, 82, 84, 85). At the end of May the Earl of Seaforth began hostilities by seizing some English sailors who had gone ashore at the island of Lewis (pp. 140, 148). Seaforth had opened communications with the King in the previous month, and had been added by him to the council which was intrusted with the control of the movement (pp. 127, 137, 200). About the middle of June Lord Balcarres and Sir Arthur Forbes wrote to Lilburne complaining that the capitulation made with them in December 1651 had not been observed, and declaring themselves released thereby from any obligation to the English government. This was practically a declaration of war, so far as they were concerned (pp. 146, 147). An important meeting of the royalist leaders took place at Lochaber in the beginning of July, and Glencairne, who now assumed the leadership, wrote to Middleton charging him to apply to the States of the United Provinces for assistance (pp. 144, 150, 157, 184). According to the English newspapers the King's standard was set up at Killin on July 27 (p. 186). One after another royalist Lords began to join Glencairne, and little bands of mounted men made their way from the Lowlands to the rendezvous in the Highlands. The Earl of Athol, who seems to have hesitated a little at first, now announced his adhesion in a letter to Charles, and endeavoured to rouse the gentry of Blair Athol (pp. 141, 150, 183, 193, 271). Lord Kenmore joined with a hundred horsemen, and was henceforth one of the most active leaders of the insurrection. He set to work to levy supplies, to raise recruits, and to force neutrals to take up arms for the King (pp. 186, 191-195, 205, 228, 231). The Earl of Roxburgh and Lord Newburgh wrote to Charles to promise their support and to protest their fidelity (pp. 190, 200). More important was the adhesion of Lord Lorne and the consequent division amongst the Campbells. The Marquis of Argyll himself remained firm to the government. He had informed Lilburne of the first symptom of the rising, and protested his disapproval of it (pp. 88, 161). Sir Robert Murray, however, assured

Charles that Argyll took this course merely from motives of self-preservation, and that if it could be done securely and effectively he too would appear for the King's service (p. 134). Lord Lorne, on the other hand, was 'invincibly constant and faithful' to the King, and resolved at any risk to draw his sword for his master (*ibid.*). In a letter, probably written in 1649, he had promised to serve the King even against his father, and he now kept his word.

> MADAME,—I am sorry there Maties have so hard thoughts of my father, who hath, and I am persuaded will be, ready at all occasions to approve himselfe a loyall subject and a very true and reall ser[vant] and well wisher of the King and his family, and if ther were no other thing to speake for him I conceive that first his declaration with the publique against the present proceedings in England and change of government, and againe his particulare oath given latly in Parliament against the calumnies laid upon him that he approved of the way was taken ther, may sufficiently justifie him in that point. Neverthelesse, that I may satisfie your La. desire more fully, I protest to you before God I am so farre loyall to his Matie that if I thought my father meant otherwise then he professes, and were, as some have beene pleased to call him, ane enemie to Monarchicall Government or the King's Matie, I would not only differ from him in opinion as your La. desires me, but allso quite all the interest I have in him rather then prove disloyall to my lawfull prince or to the goverment we have lived so happily under these many hundreth yearss, and for any further declaration then this I hope your La. will not expect it of me, for I am shuch a stranger to home that these two yeares I have but seldome heard of the state of my parents health. That which I desired was to have had the honour to kiss his Maties hand, and indeed I will take it for a great one if it be granted, and if otherwise, I shall no lesse then before wish and pray for the prosperity of there Maties familie. Now, for all the ties and obligations your La. hath beene pleased to lay upon me long since, and at this present, I shall take some more fit occasion then this to testifie my thankfullnes and to approve my selfe, Madame, Your La. most humble servant, LORNE.[1]

---

[1] *Clarendon Manuscripts*, xlvii. 409.

In April 1653 Lorne wrote to Charles protesting his inviolable fidelity (pp. 120, 254). In July he openly joined the insurrection, in spite of his father's curse and a letter of warning from the chief gentlemen of his clan (pp. 165-169). Campbell of Auchinbreck was his chief supporter amongst his kinsmen (pp. 169, 261). Campbell of Glenorchy, on the other hand, remained firm to the policy of Argyll, and suffered considerably for his adherence to the English government (pp. 197, 222; cf. *Thurloe Papers*, vi. 352). In October Lorne and Kenmore marched into Argyll's country and attacked the Lowland planters in Cantire (pp. 241-3). Argyll, who protested that his clansmen were unwilling to oppose his son, retired to Carrick (pp. 257, 261). Colonel Lilburne was half inclined to suspect him of 'juggling' in the matter, and to doubt the reality of his protestations.(pp. 243, 244). But the material assistance which Argyll gave to Colonel Cobbett in his expedition to the western isles was some evidence of his sincerity (pp. 221, 275).

The commander-in-chief of the English army in Scotland, Colonel Lilburne, had at first judged the royalist movement of little importance. He thought Glengarry was preparing to resist a possible attack rather than concerting a general insurrection (p. 79). When convinced that the design extended further than he thought, he believed that the victories of the English fleet over the Dutch had completely discouraged the party who were plotting against the government (pp. 122, 151). In June he reported his belief that the chief aim of the leaders of the movement was simply to make a demonstration which would give Charles more reputation abroad (p. 147). 'The people,' he wrote on July 12, 'are more apt to be quiet than they are able to provoke them to new troubles' (p. 160). By August, however, he was convinced of the reality of the danger, and in October he was writing urgently for reinforcements (pp. 190, 238, 265).

The measures by which Lilburne endeavoured to meet the

insurrection, and to combat the general disaffection which gave it strength, may be summed up as follows. He began by arresting Pluscardine, and Sir John Mackenzie, and ordering the arrest of other Highland chiefs (pp. 83, 140, 148, 153). He revised an old law requiring the chiefs of clans to give security for their peaceable behaviour, and issued proclamations against vagrants, and against all persons who helped or harboured the adherents of the rebellion (pp. 149, 155, 229). The dissolution of the General Assembly was accompanied by an order that its members should leave Edinburgh within twenty-four hours, and was intended to prevent any correspondence between the Assembly and the Highland royalists (pp. 163-5). He recommended to his superiors in England the immediate sequestration of the estates of the chiefs of the movement, and the offer of rewards to any person who brought them in dead or alive (pp. 149, 295, 303). At the same time, in order to relieve the country of the unemployed fighting men, who might otherwise join the royalists now in arms, he suggested that leave should be given to well-affected persons to raise regiments for the service of foreign princes in amity with England (pp. 227, 231, 295). In addition to this, he advised that legal proceedings for the recovery of debts should be moderated, or temporarily suspended, lest debtors should be driven to take arms by desperation (pp. 267, 289, 295). Moreover, the passing of the Act of Union, which was still under discussion, was to be accompanied by a general Act of Oblivion for the past, and a free pardon to all who laid down their arms and submitted.

Lilburne's military measures were hampered by the want of ships, of men, and of money. On the Earl of Seaforth's declaration for the king, Colonel Ralph Cobbett was ordered to reduce Lewis, Mull, and the smaller western islands, and to establish garrisons at Duart Castle, Eilcandonan Castle, and Stornoway (pp. 149, 186, 202, 221, 275). The English government feared an attempt of the Dutch to obtain possession of Shetland, Orkney, or Lewis, and ordered Lilburne to secure the islands by fortifications and garrisons. This fear was by no means ungrounded, for Glencairne and Middleton, with the full approval of the ministers of Charles II., were seeking to win Dutch help by offers of ports and fishing stations in any island they preferred (pp. 158, 236; cf. *Clarendon State Papers*, iii. 119). There was an English fort already at Kirkwall, and Lilburne proposed to establish another at Bressay Sound. But his difficulty was that he could not spare men enough for strong garrisons in the islands, while weak ones were of little use, and exposed to much danger (pp. 227, 231, 232). For the safety and supply of such distant ports, he needed a squadron of ships; but he had not enough for his ordinary needs, and was quite unable to prevent Middleton from sending supplies to the Scottish royalists. In spite of repeated appeals, the ships he demanded never came, no doubt because they were all employed by the necessities of the war with the Dutch in the Channel (pp. 238, 290, 308).

As soon as the insurrection began, Lilburne found his forces insufficient for the task of maintaining order over so large a country, and amid such general disaffection. The most serious weakness of his position was the deficiency in horse. Very many of the superior officers of his five regiments of horse were in England—of ten colonels and majors, only one was in Scotland (p. 241). From motives of economy the troops had been reduced to the lowest possible strength; and Lilburne asserted that there were not in all Scotland 'above 1200 or 1300 fighting horse' (p. 305). With this small number he had to prevent plundering raids by parties of royalists from the Highlands, to intercept the bands of horsemen who set out from the Lowlands to join Glencairne, and to keep down the mosstroopers, who began once more to infest the borders. His cavalry were worn out by the constant service required from them, and until the reinforcements which he urgently appealed for should arrive, Lilburne's only resource was to seize all the horses he could obtain and mount a portion of his infantry (pp. 274, 299, 307).

So far as infantry were concerned, Lilburne's eleven regiments were enough to meet any force which could be brought into the field against him, and his regiments were of excellent quality. But he had a very large number of garrisons to maintain, and as soon as the rising began he increased their numbers, and divided his regiments still more by occupying different houses and castles on the Highland frontier. These petty garrisons he held necessary, not only to protect the well-disposed from attack, but to prevent the ill-disposed from rising in arms (pp. 226, 240, 271). The result was that when he wished to collect a force for service in the field, he found himself obliged to choose between two alternatives: either he must denude Edinburgh and the south of Scotland of troops, or else by withdrawing his forces in the north, he must surrender that part entirely to the enemy. Unless reinforcements arrived, he thought of adopting the second alternative, and abandoning 'all beyond Dundee except Inverness' (pp. 271, 273, 305).

In the few encounters which took place in the course of 1653, the English had the advantage. A skirmish took place at Aberfoyle, which was claimed by Glencairne's partisans as a victory, but Colonel Reade, who commanded the English, reported his loss as only three men killed (p. 204; cf. *Military Memoirs of John Gwynne*, pp. 160, 200). In December Captain Hart routed a party of a hundred horse, under Sir Arthur Forbes, at Borthwick Brae, whilst Captain Lisle, about the same date, beat up Lord Kinnoul's quarters, and took a number of prisoners (pp. 303, 305; *Gwynne's Memoirs*, pp. 218, 221). But the real difficulty was to find the enemy. Lilburne made an attempt to pursue Lord Kenmore, and to force him to an engagement, but it was totally unsuccessful, for he found the ways 'impassable,' and the places to which Kenmore retreated 'unaccessible' (pp. 240-243, 256). As to the smaller parties, who carried on a guerilla war in the Lowlands and on the borders, Lilburne found it impossible to get any knowledge of their movements, 'they are soe subtle and cunning, and the country soe true to them' (pp. 270, 273, 287, 307). Though the royalist army was small, and had no great success to boast of, yet, wrote Lilburne, 'even this small appearance of this unconsiderable enemy heightens the spirit of the generality of people here, who have a deadly antipathy against us' (p. 271). If the royalists gained any real success, he expected that the rising would become general; 'undoubtedly upon the least advantage of this nature they would increase exceedingly, and probably drive us into our garrisons, doe what we can with these forces' (p. 283). Lilburne's position was undoubtedly difficult, and his difficulties were increased by the neglect with which his appeals and his proposals were treated by the home government. He complained that his letters were unanswered. The changes which followed the expulsion of the Long Parliament in April 1653, and the dissensions which led to the break up of the Little Parliament in the following December, seem to have disorganised the administration. With three different Councils of State in one year, no continuity of policy could be expected. Lilburne lost heart, and began to wish that some one else had the responsibility of a command for which he felt unequal. 'Being jealous of my own weakness, I am doubtful soe great affaires as are here to be managed may suffer for the want of one more fit to wrastle with them' (p. 302). Hearing that a commander-in-chief was to be sent to replace him, his only wish was that it should be 'such a one as may pay these people for their knavery.' 'Monk's spirit,' he suggested, 'would doe well amongst them,' and before long the Protector arrived at the same conclusion.

The papers printed in this volume are derived from four different sources. The bulk of them are from the manuscript collections of William Clarke, which are now in the library of Worcester College, Oxford. William Clarke, who was born about 1623, became in 1645 one of the assistants of John Rushworth, the secretary to General Fairfax and the New Model Army. He accompanied Cromwell to Scotland in 1650, and remained there as secretary to Monk in 1651. From 1651 to 1660 he was secretary to the different officers who succeeded each other in command of the English army in Scotland. He accompanied Monk to England in 1660, was knighted soon after the Restoration, was appointed Secretary at War on 28th January 1661, and was mortally wounded in the battle with the Dutch off Harwich on June 2, 1666. A life of Clarke is given in the *Dictionary of National Biography*, vol. x. p. 448, by Mr. Gordon Goodwin. Additional details respecting his career are contained in the preface to the two volumes of his papers, printed by the Camden Society in 1891-4. An account of his manuscript collections is given in Mr. Coxe's *Catalogue of Manuscripts in the possession of Oxford Halls and Colleges*, 1852, vol. ii.

The papers from Clarke's collection included in the present volume are printed from copies sometimes entered into letter-books, sometimes on loose sheets of paper. Many are derived from draughts full of erasures, and in other cases the letters seem to have been originally taken down in short-hand, and written out later. It is not surprising that errors and omissions of all kinds abound, and that mistakes about names are frequent. Most of the papers relating to the years 1651 and 1652 have been lost. For the years 1654 and 1655 the series is much more complete, but with the later years of the Protectorate the number of documents again diminishes.

To supplement the few papers relating to 1651 and 1652, and to supply the place of those missing, a few letters have been added from the *Tanner Manuscripts* in the Bodleian Library. The great collection of letters officially addressed to the Speaker of the Long Parliament was borrowed by Dr. John Nalson about 1680 from the office of the Clerk of the Parliament, and was never returned. Part of it is now in the possession of the Duke of Portland, and is calendared in the first volume of Mr. Blackburne Daniel's report on his manuscripts. Mr. Daniel traces the history of the collection in his preface (*Thirteenth Report of the Historical Manuscripts Commission*, Appendix, part i.). Bishop Tanner borrowed in Nalson's own fashion from the papers Nalson had borrowed, and left his spoils to the Bodleian Library. The Tanner Manuscripts in the Bodleian are the second source drawn upon in this volume. They contain several letters addressed by William Clarke to Speaker Lenthall during 1651 and 1652. Two of these were printed in 1842 by Mr. H. Cary in his *Memorials of the Civil War* (ii. 327, 366), and are consequently omitted here. Three letters of Clarke's, some communications between the Marquis of Argyll and the Commissioners of the Parliament, and several miscellaneous documents, have been inserted.

Of many of the letters addressed to the Speaker, and read in the House of Commons, the originals have not been preserved. Fortunately they were often printed in the official newspapers of the Parliament, and this third source has supplied five more letters from Clarke to Lenthall. Some letters from Monk and other officers have been also selected from the newspapers. To these there has been added a few extracts from the unique copy of the Journal called *Mercurius Scoticus*, which was published at Leith during the winter of 1651. It was probably edited by William Clarke, and is amongst his books in Worcester College Library. These previously printed letters have been relegated to the Appendix.

To represent the royalist as well as the republican view of events, and to furnish a more exact account of the movements and the plans of the King's party, a large number of papers have been drawn from the correspondence of Clarendon in the Bodleian Library. From the beginning of 1652, the management of the affairs of Charles II. was mainly in his hands, and the communications between him and the royalist leaders in Scotland give a more exact account of the origin and progress of the rising of 1653 than anything hitherto published. The part played by individual royalist leaders in that movement, and the reasons for its failure, are very clearly explained in these letters and reports.[1]

The Editor hopes to put together from the Clarke and Clarendon Collections, a volume relating to the history of Scotland during the Protectorate, which will continue and complete the present one. He desires to express his sincere thanks to Mr. T. G. Law and Mr. Alex. Mill for their assistance in the editing of the present instalment of those papers. The Index is the work of Mr. Mill.

---

[1] In the management of all business relating to Scotland, Clarendon's chief assistant was Lord Newburgh, who helped to supply his lack of local knowledge. The letter to the King, No. cxlix., which is attributed to Lord Newburgh in the indorsement on the manuscript, and in Mr. Macray's ' *Calendar of the Clarendon MSS.*,' ii. 250, is probably assigned to him by mistake. He was with the King in France at this time.

A NARRATIVE or DIARY of the Proceedings of the Forces under LT. GENERALL MONKE, after their parting from the Army. Aug. 4, 1651.[1]

Aug. 4.—Upon his Excellencies marching[2] with the greatest parte of the army from Kinros, about two miles from the towne, 4 regiments of horse, vizt. Col. Hacker's, Col. Okey's, Col. Alured's, Col. Grosvenour's, and three of foot, vizt. Lt. Generall Monke's, Col. Ashfield's, and Col. Reade's, with troopes of dragoones, vizt.   and the greatest part of the trayne of artillery, with the 2 companies of firelockes, were sent under the conduct of Lt. Generall Monke from the rest of the army towards Sterling, and quartered that night at   .

Aug. 5.—The Lt. Generall with his forces quartered at   .
Col. Hacker's regiment had orders to march from him towards the army.

Aug. 6.—Lt. Generall Monke came with his forces before Sterling. Upon his approach he summond the towne and Castle, promising freedome from plunder or violence to the persons of the inhabitantes. He had noe answere from the Castle, but the towne clarke came out to treat upon condicions [for those] in the towne, which after some delaies were agreed upon, he threatning to storme. Our men went in about one

---
[1] From the Clarke Manuscripts in the Library of Worcester College, Oxford.
[2] See Cromwell's Letter to Lenthall, Aug. 4, 1657, No. clxxx. in Carlyle's collection.

of the clock in the morning. The enimy that were in the towne retreated into the Castle.

Wee got over a poste [1] about 2 miles above Sterling, where never trayne marcht. One of the peeces fell downe a very high and steepe mountaine, but neither horse or man had any hurt.

Aug. 7.—This day the Lt. Generall began to raise platformes for batteries against Sterling Castle.

Aug. 9.—The platformes and batteries went on. The enimy shot very little out of the Castle.

10.—The 4 battering guns, and 2 morterpeeces were brought by water to Sterling, with other ammunition. The Countesse of Argile (being sick) went out of Sterling this day.

11.—Our men plaid hard upon the enimy out of the Kirke steepe, which was neare the Castle. The enimy plaid hard upon the batteryes and church; shot through the steeple, but did noe harme. One George Smyth, a gunner, was kild. Six of Col. Berryes regiment were condemnd at a Court Martiall for stragling and plunder, and one of them executed. Col. Okey's and Col. Berrye's regiment were sent to quarter in the west, and onely Col. Grosvenour's left in the toune. Col. Pinchbancke, whoe (according to Articles) came from Silly, acquaunted the Lt. Generall that he went as farre as Glasgow with the King's forces, but could have noe satisfaccion to goe further with him.

Aug. 12.—The platformes were begining to be made to play the morter peeces; the enimy discovering it, plaid hard against them with their great guns, but did not much spoyle. The morter peeces were drawne downe towards the evening. The Lt. Generall summoned the Governour of the Castle to surrender the same for the use of the Parliamentt of England. The Governour answered that he would keepe it as long as he could.

13.—The morter peeces were planted, and Mr. Hane, the engineer, plaid with one of the morter peeces twice. The second shot fell into the middle of the Castle, and did much execucion. Afterwards he plaid with the other great morter peeces and did execucion. The Governour being sent to about exchange of prisoners, refused.

---

[1] Passe?

14.—This morning betimes both great guns and morter pceces plaid very hard against the Castle, and both did execucion. After the playing of the guns and 24 granadocs shells sent into the Castle, which kild 2 or 3 of the enimy, the Highlanders and other souldyers fell into a mutiny, and one of them beat a drum for a parley. The Governour and other officers commanded them to cease, but they refused, and said they would not fight for their Countryes geare, but for their King and Country. Thereupon the mutinie not being to be laid, the Governour sent out a letter, wherein he desired a treaty: to which the Lt. Generall sent an answere, wherein he offerd him condicions to march awaye, himselfe, officers, and souldyers, with their armes, etc. That the Country should have their goods. The Governour sent out one Capt. James Coningham, and one Mr. Wright, with condicions to surrender, upon which they might treat. The Lt. Generall appointed Col. Grosvenour and Col. Ashfeild to treat with him. The treaty was held at the Marquesse of Argiles house, and after 2 houres debate, wherein they insisted much to have the records, they agreed upon the Articles following :—

' ARTICLES agreed upon betweene Col. Edward Grosvenour, and Col. Rich. Ashfeild, Commanders, on the behalfe of the Right Honourable Lt. Generall Monke, and Capt. James Conyngham on the behalfe of Col. Wm. Conyngham, Governour of the Castle of Sterling, for the rendition thereof.

' 1. That the Governour, and all officers and souldyers, shall have libertye to march with their horses (not exceeding six), armes, beat of drum, lighted matches, and what baggage belongeth to them, to any parte of this Kingdome, and to have a sufficient convey for 5 miles beyond any of the garrisons or guards belonging to the forces of the Parliamentt of England, and such of them which shalbe desirous to goe to their owne houses shall have libertye and passes for that purpose.

' 2. That all noblemen, gentlemen, and inhabitants of the towne of Sterling, whoe have goods in the Castle shall have 8 daies libertye to transport their goods to such place as they shall please, provided that noe bedding be removed out of the towne without order.

'3. That the Castle of Sterling, with all the ordnance, armes, ammunition, and other provisions of warre therein, be delivered unto Lt. Generall Monke, or whome he shall appoint, without any spoyle or imbeazlement, by ten of the clock to morrow morning.

'4. That all prisoners which are now in the Castle be forthwith released.

'5. That hostages be forthwith sent for the perfourmance of these Articles.

'*Aug.* 14, 1651.   EDW. GROSVENOUR.
                                                                                                                                 RICH. ASHFEILD.

'I doe hereby ratifie and confirme these Articles.

                                                                                    'GEO. MONKE.'[1]

This day, about 12 of the clock, Col. Wm. Coningham, with about 300 men, and which were a commanded party out of euerie regiment of the King's army, marched out of Sterling Castle, according to their condicions. Before they went out, Lt. Jones and about 35 other prisoners were delivered out. They had hard usage there. All that night the enimies souldyers went and plundered the goods, and everie man carried away as much as he could of pillage, having plundered many of the trunckes and coffers of the country people.

There was taken in the Castle 40 peeces of ordnance, vizt. 26 brasse peeces, 11 leather guns, 3 iron peeces, 26 barrells of powder, great stoare of match and other ammunition, great stoare of meale, and other provisions to have kept them many monthes, about 30 or 40 barrells of beefe and beare, and as many rundlets and vessells of claret wine, two coaches and a sedan, the Earle of Murris coronet and Parliament roabes, divers of the Kinges hangings.

There was over the Chappell this inscripcion: Nobis haec invicta miserunt Centum sex Proavi.

---

[1] Monk's letter to Cromwell announcing the surrender of Stirling Castle is printed in the Old Parliamentary History, vol. xx. p. 18. William Clarke's letter to the Speaker, dated Aug. 19, is printed in Cary's *Memorials of the Civil War*, vol. ii. p. 327. It repeats the facts contained in this narrative.

Col. Rede was appointed to take charge of the Castle and towne, and entered the Castle with his owne and Capt. Badger's company.

The morter peeces had defaced the Castle in divers places.

Aug. 16.—The inhabitantes continued fetching their geere out of the Castle. There was great stoare of goods, by which the souldiers got very good booty by helping to carry them out, and to guard them to their severall places, the inhabitantes receiving little or noe damage by any of their goods, but what their owne souldyers had plundered before they went away.

Aug. 17. The Lt. Generall and the forces continued in Sterling. Col. Okey came from the party of horse in the Westerne partes; he relates there was a regiment raising there for Col. Cockram, which the King had first given to Maior Generall Vanrosse,[2] but afterwards, upon the king's coming into England, he gave it Cockram. They sate about it at Paiseley, whereof the Colonel having notice fell upon them, tooke one Laird Osbaston, Mr. Alexander Kinsmart, Sir Sigismund Alexander, and one Mr. Hendson. Col. Cockram and the Laird Blantire was there with his troope the day before, but went from thence into the Highlands. Col. Okey alsoe apprehended 16 ministers, but upon a promise not to act against us they were released. Hee alsoe fined the toune of Glasgow 900†, Paisley 150†, and the Lord Rosse 50†.[1]

Aug. 18. The inhabitants continued to fetch their geere out of Sterling Castle. Orders were given for a march, 10 daies provision to be delivered out. Col. Fennick, Governour of Leith and Edinburgh, and Col. Hubbold came hither to visit the Lt. Generall.

Aug. 19. The waggons sent to Blacknesse. Intelligence that the Highlanders came downe in partyes of about 2 or 300 foot at a tyme, and drove away the countryes cattle, especially about Killmallock about 8 or 9 miles from Sterling.

Aug. 20. Wee had newes of some gathering togeather of the forces that came from Brunt Island, St. Johnstons and

---

[1] See Okey's letter of 14th August, printed in the Appendix.
[2] Vandruske.

Sterling Castle on the other side the river Tay, but their number not certainly knowne.

Aug. 21. Wee understood that Marquesse Huntley and the Gordons were gone back, but were within 3 or 4 miles of St. Johnstons, to which they came with 1000 men, having plundered the country.

This day the Lt. Generall marched out of Sterling with his forces, 3 battering peeces, and a morter peece to Dunblain, and quartered thereaboutes. Col. Grosvenour's and Col. Berryes regiment were in the van, Col. Ashfeild's of foot and then the trayne, and the Lt. Generalls of foot and Col. Okeys in the reare.

Aug. 22. The forces marched from Dunblain to Blackford. Appearance of about 60 Highlanders to fall upon our reare, but nothing done.

23. The forces marched from Blackford to   neare St. Johnstons, where they quartered that night in the feilds. The Lt. Generall came to St. Johnstons, where he had intelligence that the enimy had lately severall meetings about 8 miles from the Garrison, about raising of forces, but the old Generall Leven would not raise any unlesse he were Commander-in-Cheife, and Marq. Huntley he would not raise any upon the same account. The Earles of Atholl, Arroll, and especially Tulabarding were besie about raising of forces, but they could not effect it. Major Bourne, Commander of the *Speaker*, came hither this day. At his passage by Dundee he gave them severall shotes. Two vessels of their men of warre which were goeing out upon his coming with severall vessells and shallops, went back into harbour. He sent a summons to St. Andrewes, whither Col. Overton had sent before, and to all the country hereaboutes to resigne and submitt by the first of September next, or else to be taken as enimies. To which they answered, that they had received a summons before from Col. Overton, and that for the things desired by him they were not yet satisfied in conscience to comply with him. This day there came severall vessells laden with bisket and cheese and other provisions for the supply of the army in these parts.

The ministers in St. Johnstons and other partes hereaboutes

will not preach nor attend their ministerie unlesse they may pray for their King and the army in England. The Governour said hee would give them leave to preach the gospell of Jesus Christ, but it seemes that is not their businesse.

Aug. 24. The foot and a good parte of the horse got over on the other side of the river. The horse were forced for want of conveniencie of boates to swimme over, soe that wee had 3 or 4 men drownd and as many horse.

25. Five troopes of Col. Alured's regiment, and the five troopes of dragoones that were at St. Johnstons before were ordered to march over towards Dundee. Capt. Compton's troope was onely left for the toune. The Lt. Generall with Col. Overton went over the water towards Dundee, and marched to Beligarney, where they quartered that night. The Lt. Generall sent a summons this day from St. Johnstons to St. Andrewes requiring them to deliver up their armes, ammunition, and utensills of warre to him, promising them protection and a free trade.

Aug. 26. The 3 great guns and mortar peeces were put aboard the shallop to goe for Dundee, but the morter peeces broke the shallop, which staid the sending of them. A proclamacion made for all upon paine of death to repair to their colours both horse and foot.[1]

The last night there were bonfires and thanksgiving for the great successe of the Scottish forces in England, that they had kild about 10,000 of our forces, that Major Generall Harrison was kild, and the Lord Gray taken, with much to the like effect.

---

[1] On the 26th of August Monk summoned Dundee. See his letter of August 28, printed in Cary's *Memorials of the Civil War*, ii. p. 345, and also in *Several Proceedings in Parliament*, Sept. 4-11, 1651. This newspaper also prints the answer sent to Monk's summons by the Governor of Dundee.

'Wee received yours. For answer whereunto we doe by these acquaint you, that we are commanded by the King's Majesty, to desire you, and all officers and souldiers and ships, for the present in arms and opposition to the King's authority, to lay down their arms, to come in and joyn with his Majesties forces in this kingdom, and receive protection from them, conforme to the Kings Majesties Declaration sent you herewith, which if you will obey, we shall continue, Sir, your faithful friend and servant in the old manner, ROB. LUMSDAINE.

Dundee, 26th *August* 1651.
  For Generall Major Monke.'

The firelockes were shipt away with the great guns.

Aug. 27. This day wee understood that Col. Augustine was abroad with a partye of about 60 horse, that he had kild some of our men that were behinde the army, and 2 at Skoone.[1]

A letter was sent by Maior Borne to the toune of St. Andrewes.

Aug. 28. Wee are making of a very gallant trench on the west side of St. Johnstons, which being filld with water from the Mount will make the towne very strong, and as considerable as any inland towne in Scotland.

The ladders sent to Dundee which were prepaird for St. Johnstons.

Answere of the Magistrates of St. Andrewes to Maior Bournes lettre :—

'SIR,—Wee conceive that there is much reason, etc.'[2]

Aug. 28. A relacion of the taking of the Lord Generall Leven and others at Elliot.[3]

---

[1] Augustine is said to have been 'a High German,' who was 'purged out of the army before Dunbar Drove.' As a partisan leader he soon earned a great reputation. A Scottish rhyme quoted in *Mercurius Politicus* says :
  'Leslie for the Kirk and Middleton for the King,
  But deil a bit will any fight but Ross and Augustine.'
Mosstroopers was the name usually given by the English army to these partisans. A proclamation was issued by Cromwell against them on 5th November 1650, which is printed in Carlyle's *Cromwell*. A later one, issued by the Governor of Edinburgh, is printed in the Appendix to this volume. Two instances of the activity of the Mosstroopers about this time are supplied by *Mercurius Scoticus* :—

'We had intelligence that on Sunday last our letters in their passage between Leith and Barwick were, by Capt. John Humes and a party of 30 resolute Horse, intercepted. They slew one or two of the convoy in their stragling march, and took the rest prisoners, but sent home the post-boy.—*Mercurius Scoticus*, Tuesday, August 9, 1651.'

'Captain Hume, with about 60 Moss-Troopers, was again this day within very few miles of Edinburgh and Leith, and seised on two Merchants, and some few stragling soulders, of which soulders they wounded some, and took the rest prisoners. The Merchants were inlarged with their cloaths on their backs onely, engaging to pay them 40 pounds next morning, but it's hoped they will be prevented of their expectation; for a considerable Party under Captain Walley marcht immediately towards them, and scoured about a good part of the Country, but the Mossers too, too nimble, were presently disperst, so that our Men were forced to return with a *Non Inventus.—Mercurius Scoticus*, August 23.'

[2] Unfinished.   [3] Omitted. Elliot, *i.e.* Alyth.

A list of the prisoners taken at Elliot in Perth :—

Noblemen.

Generall Lesley.
Earle Marshall.
L. of Creith.
Earle Crawford.

Lord Ogleby.
Lord Bargenny.
Lord Humby.
Lord Lee.

Knights.

Sir Ja. Fowlis of Collington.
Sir Alex. Fothringham of Pawney.
Sir James Lockyer.

Gentlemen of Quality.

Col. Andrew Milnes.
Mr. Archibald Sedforth.[1]
The lord Hombye's sonne.[2]
Mr. John Crickbourne.[3]

Mr. Robert Nearne of Stratford.
Mr. John Manethes.
Mr. Hen. Crane.
Mr. Ja. Fleming.

Ministers.

Robrt. Douglas.
James Hamilton.
Mungoe Law.
John Smith.
Geo. Pittilton.

John Rattray [Ruttera].
James Sheipe [Sharpe].
Hugh Ramsey.
Andrew Care [Ker].

Country Gentlemen.

Mr. John Lawrence, Blaire.
„ Alex. Nearne.
„ Daniell Crocket.
„ Andrew Gray.
„ John Ramsey.
„ Wm. Lethan [Levinston].
„ David Duell [Duer].

Mr. Ja. Ogleby.
Andr. Wood, Captain.
Thome. Browne, Cornet.
With about 70 prisoners, souldyes, and servants to noblemen.[4]

Aug. 29. The platformes and batteries for about 10 guns which were brought from the ships, made ready and the guns

---

[1] Sidserfe. [2] Thomas Hepburn.
[3] John Cockburn of Ormiston.
[4] The names are hopelessly corrupt in the manuscript. The variations given in the footnotes or between brackets are from the printed accounts.

planted. The great guns and morter peeces came this night from St. Johnstons to the leaguer before Dundee.

30. A drumer of ours being sent into the towne about some cloathes for some of the prisoners, had this declaracion following delivered to him to bring to the Lt. Generall.

Aug. 30. This night the 3 battering guns and morter peeces were plaid against the towne; the night proved very wet and windie, which prevented our playing, and the not coming back of Col. Okey with his partye prevented the storming of the towne.[1]

This evening there came some Gentlemen from the towne of St. Andrewes with the letter following. The Lt. Generall returned them answere, that in regard they had stood out and refused his first summons, they would give 500† as a gratuity to the souldyers, and then he would take them into proteccion, which if they did not speedily comply, he would heighten their fine everie tyme they came to him.

'SIR,—Wee doe hereby accept of your first offerre to us, and tender our submission to your demaunds, humbly deprecating any mistake.'

Aug. 31.—This night the enimy in Broughton[2] Castle quitted it, and fled away. It lies upon a point upon the sea beyond Dundee; they left in it 4 peeces of ordnance, one barrell of powder with match and bullet, 19 barrells of salmon, and some other provision.

This evening Col. Okey and Col. Grosvenour returned to the head quarters. They had bin about 40 miles from the leaguer, and about 8 miles into the Highlands, they had notice that the enimye were at Helsmore, and coming thither about 4 in the morning, they found the enimy was drawne out the night before, fearing to be surprized as the great ones were the other day.

Their Commander in cheife being the Lord Belcarris, having about 250 armes that came from Swethland, armed about soe

---

[1] 'Thursday night Col. Okey was sent out with 5 troops of horse and dragoons to attend the enemies motion in the northern parts from hence.'—*Mercurius Scoticus.*   [2] Broughty Castle.

many of them, and told them that now they were soe well
armd as Cromwell's men, he hoped they would fight as well
as Cromwell's men.

Our partye having sight of them pursued them, there being
about 400 horse of them, and 4 troopes of horse, and 3 of
dragoones of ours; they fled over mountaines, and soe from
hill to hill til our men were tired in the pursuite, and they
in runing away, soe that they threw their armes one way and
turn'd their horses another way, and everie man shifted for himselfe on foot; our men were soe [weary] that they could not take
above an hundred of them, many of which they were forced to
let goe, having no horses to carry them along, nor could their
owne horses well returne, they had gone such a course after
them that both greyhound and hare were tired. Augustine
was with them but fled away in the van. On our returne wee
secured great stoare of meale which was provided for the
enimies army and laid up in a towne, to the value of 400𝑙.
They came to the Lord Spynee's house, wherein he was, and
some others, whoe at first refused to yeild, but upon firing the
gate, there being above 20 ladyes and gentlemen in the house,
which was very strange, they let them in. There was in it the
Lady Spynee, the Lady Crawford, and divers others. It's supposed the Lords were there, but they let them downe, while
our men were besy about the doore. He secured 20 or 30
horses, and 8 good coach horses, and 2 coach horses. Left
30 dragoones to secure the house.

Sept. 1.—About 4 of the clocke in the morning our great
guns began to plaie before Dundee round about the line. The
enimy for 2 or 3 houres answered us gun for gun, besides small
shot from their workes, til such tyme as large breaches were
made in two of their most considerable fortes. They shouted
and seem'd very high, calling our men dogges. Wee had a Commander and severall matrosses hurt by the hasty spunging of
a great gun. Mr. Hane the engineere plaid the morter peece.
There was 3 horses kild in Col. Okeys regiment in the west
side at one shot by a great gun.

Three hundred horse and dragoones, being 11 of a troope,
were appointed to fall on with the foot with sword and pistoll.
Our men were drawne forth in ambeskadoes by day breake to

fall on upon when breaches were made, and with them 200 seamen whoe had their postes assign'd, and 400 horse appointed to second them mounted. About 11 of the clocke the signall was given, and breaches being made into the enimies fortes on the east and west side of the towne, our men entred, and after about halfe an houres hot dispute, divers of the enimy retreated to the church and steeple, and amongst the rest the Governour, whoe was kild with betweene foure and five hundred souldyers and townesmen. When our men[1] got to the marquet place they gave quarter, and tooke about 500 prisoners, and amongst the rest Col. Coningham, Governour of Sterling, whoe was in the towne with many of his souldyers which marched thence. The souldyers had the plunder of the towne for all that day and night, and had very large prize, many inhabitantes of Edinburgh and other places having sent their ware and geere thither.[2] There was about 190 sayle of ships[3] in the harbour of 10, 6, and 4 guns, which were all prize, about 40 peeces of ordnance, many armes and stoare of ammunition. Capt. Hart led on the forlorne of Lt. Generall Monkes regiment on the west side, Maior Robinson the horse, and Col. Ashfeild's regiment went on the east side. There was kild of ours Capt. Hart and about 20 souldyers, and as many wounded. Capt. Ely led on the Pioneers whoe made way for the horse, and the Lt. Generall went in person. Our word was God with us, and the signe a white cloath or shirt hanging out behind. By the best testimony wee could get, the townes people were most obstinate

---

[1] MS. 'townsmen.'

[2] The following story is told in *Mercurius Scoticus*, under date of Sept. 3 :

'Many of the people in and about Edinburgh and Leith, now make it their whole Work to obtain leave to go fetch home their Goods from Dundee, which (not being granted) they are importunate for leave to go see the Place, which was the receptacle, and indeed their supposed Sanctuary, but what can stand in opposition against the Lord, where he goes on with a people conquering and to conquer: yet 'tis observable, the Men within that Place were so high as ever any were or could be, in confidence either of their Treasure or strength, that they presumed upon Summons from the Lieut. Generall, in stead of rendering a civill answer, to return a Summons to him, requiring him, and all under his command, with his Shipping, to yeeld to his Majesty (as they called him) and repent in time; but no doubt such terms are recompenced upon their own heads, it being this day generally confirmed, that the Place was taken by storm Munday last, and 800 slain, many prisoners taken, besides what escaped.—*Mercurius Scoticus*, Sept. 2-9, 1651.'

[3] Sixty sail according to Monk's letter.—Cary's *Memorials*, vol. ii. p. 352.

against a rendition upon termes, being confident of their owne workes and strength, having formerly beat out Montrosse, but they have now most sufferd for it, and paid dearely for their contempt.

Sept. 2.—Proclamacion was made by the Lt. Generall that the souldyers should forbeare further plundering, or rifling of the houses in Dundee, and order given to the inhabitantes to bury the dead carkases.

Slayne.

Sir Robert Lumsdale, Governour.
Lord Newton.
Capt. Forgisson.

Prisoners taken at Dundee.

Col. Coningham, late Governour of Sterling.
Sir George Melvill.
Lt. Col. Melvill.
Capt. Castle of North Leeth.[1]

Sept. 3.—An order given to Lt. Col. Gough, Maior Butler, and Maior Dorney to examine all such prisoners as were in Dundee, to the end that such of them which were strangers, and came upon their owne private affaires, and went not commissioned, nor were in armes, might be discharged and power given to them, or any 2 of them, to discharge accordingly.

---

[1] A better list is given in *Mercurius Scoticus* for Sept. 2-9, and is therefore added here:

Officers taken in Dundee the first of Sept. 1651.

Col. William Cuningham, late Governour of Sterlin.	Capt. John Sutherland.
Lieut. Col. Straughan.	Lieut. Tho. Johnson.
Major Colvill.	Lieut. Tho. Shaun.
Capt. James Cuningham.	Lieut. John Sutherland.
Capt. James Bennet.	Ensign Francis Butler.
Capt. John Caddell.	Quart. Will. Ferguson.
Capt. George Ogilby.	Sir George Melvil.
Capt. James Hamilton.	Lt. Col. Hen. Melvin.
Capt. John Robertson.	Sir Tho. Ferry, prisoner for debt 3 years and a half, now released.
Capt. Caustell.	

Slain in the Storm.

Sir Robert Lumsdale, Governour.	Capt. Ferguson.
The Lord Newton.	The minister of the Towne.

With many other Officers and Gent. of quality, whose names are not yet known.

Sept. 4.—Generall Leven and the rest of the Scotes prisoners went in Capt. [Marriot's][1] ship for England. Upon intelligence of the enimy intended to fortifie Monrosse, a port towne about 24 miles from Dundee, the Lt. Generall ordered a stronger party of horse and dragoones to goe thither, and sent a summons comanding them to surrender for the service of the Commonwealth of England, the partye ordered to be commanded by Col. Overton.

5.—There came a trumpeter from Aberdeene with a lettre desiring a list of the prisoners lately taken at Elliot, to the end they might send them provisions. Col. Okey and Col. Overton, with troopes of horse and dragoones under Col. Morgan, marched from Dundee towards Monrosse.

The Lt. Generall fell very ill.[2]

Newes of Sir John Brownes death, and that the enimy were gone from Aberdeene.

9.—Wee had the happy newes of the rowting of the King of Scots army on both sides Worcester by our men. 4000 kild in the place, etc.

Col. James Hay and some other Commanders came from Fife in order to an easing of their   and of their submission to the Commonwealth of England. At night orders were given for the drawing out all the foot to the lines, where, about 8 of the clock, they gave severall shoutes, and after that 3 severall vollies of small shot. There was discharged about 25 peeces of ordnance about the towne, and about 40 from the ships in the Roade.

10.—Wee had notice that our men were well entertaind by the inhabitantes of Aberdeene, whoe made a banquett for them. They staid there 3 nightes, and had very good quarters. They brought away 2 ships laden with armes and ammunition, fined the towne 1000ł for assisting of Huntley.

11.—Col. Overton and Col. Okey returnd from Aberdeene with the horse that went with them.

12.—A proclamacion was issued out to declare that the inhabitantes of Dundee should for the future be protected from plunder and violence, and have libertye to follow their trades

---

[1] See *Mercurius Politicus*, pp. 1075, 1096.
[2] See Clarke's letter of Sept. 11, printed in the Appendix.

and employmentes, as also to the people of the country to bring in their commodities and returne.

Col. Berryes regiment ordered to goe into the west to gather up straglers there.

Col. Fennick, Governour of Leith, etc., came to visit Lt. Generall.

Wee had notice that about   of our men were taken neare St. Johnstons, being of Captain Compton's troope, whoe went to gather contribucion in the Country, 300 men armd cap-a-pee came and surprized them. Mr. Jeffries and other Commanders came from Aberdeene about setling that towne.

Sept. 14.—There was a discourse betweene Provost Jeffries, and the other Commanders from Aberdeene, with the officers, at which they expressed their affeccion and readinesse of complyance with our partye, that they should not entertayne any forces of the enemy, unlesse they were overpowred, which gave the officers such satisfaccion, that they suspended the fine of 1000𝑙.

Sept. 15.—Upon informacion of the abuse of sutlers in taking of shops belonging to the townesmen and inhabitantes without giving them satisfaccion, the Lt. Generall published a proclamacion against it.[1] Col. Okey, Col. Alured, and Col. Morgan went out with severall parties of horse and dragoones, some towards Monrosse, some to the Clans (where some of our men were murthered), to scowre the coostes. Wee had notice of a Pirate ship that came into Aberdeene, which one intended to secure there.

17, 18, 19, 20.—Generall Court Martialls here in Dundee, where divers souldyers were tryed and sentenst for plundering the Country, under pretence for searching for armes, and taking away things that belongd to countrymen, though they were hid in the feilds.[2]

---

[1] Monk's proclamations on this subject are printed in the Appendix.

[2] The two following extracts from *Mercurius Scoticus* supply instances of this rigid discipline :—

'*Tuesday* [*Sept.* 23].

' This day at a Court Martial held at Dundee, two Souldiers of Colonell Berries Regiment were sentenced for robbing two Countrey-men neer that Town, and taking about seven shillings six pence from them, to be led with ropes about their necks to the Gallowes, there to be tyed up and receive 30 stripes a-piece;

Mr. Bilton came with the muckle somme 5000 ℔ to Dundee. A great dispute betweene the officers and Comm[issioner] Desborow about the disposall of the shipps taken at Dundee. He claymd them in right of the state, which they denied, and went on in the sale of them.

Sept. 21.—Wee had notice that at Aberdeene a souldyer and a Scotch man went forth and abused the Country, pretending themselves to be Augustines men, for which they were soundly whipt at the drawing up of our horse in the marquet place. The Scotch man of warre which fled into Aberdeene for succour, being required to be yeilded by our shipps from Aberdeene, [they] sent out word that they would neither protect them nor deliver them up; but that if they pleasd they might come and take her; whereupon some of our men were sent to secure the vessell, which they did, but the men fled out of her; shee had 6 peeces of ordnance, and stoare of wines, and other good comodityes.

Sept. 22.—Wee had intelligence that the Marq. Huntley was marched with his forces, being about 600 [horse] and 1000 foot, towards Lough Tay in the Highlands. Most of his men were much harassed. That the Lord Belcarris, upon the coming of our forces towards Aberdeene, went towards Lough Head, where the present Committee sets. He had about 250 horse. That a randevouz was [to be] kept the 3d of Oct., when the whole Country

then to ask forgivenesse to the Countrey-men upon their knees, and to be kept with bread and water in prison, untill they should restore four-fold for what they had taken away. Certainly this strict course will reduce the rude Souldiers to a better order, and much satisfie the Countrey.

'This day also the poor Fishermen and Masters of Vessels belonging to Craill, Anstruther, and Pettinweemes obtained leave from the Honourable Colonell Fenwick, Governour of Berwick, Edinburgh, and Leith, for to follow their Fishing trades, for main[te]nance of themselves and Families. Surely love and encouragement will win upon this People as much as any thing, they now beginning to see Providence sent us more to relieve them from slavery then bring them to misery.'

'Yesterday at a Court Martiall, two Souldiers were sentenced to ride the Wooden Horse, for carrying away a chest of goods buryed by a Countrey-man in the fields, under the pretence of prize (so severe is the Lieut. Generall and Officers against the Souldiers injuring the Countrey, to whom we endeavour to shew as much favour as may be (especially to the poorer sort) to convince them, if possible, of the slavery they have been under, and freedom they may now enjoy under the English.'

was to come in, under paine of rebellion and to be proceeded against as enimies. The Marq. of Argile is then expected with 4000 foot, which its thought he will hardly get togeather, having not above 300. The Marq. Huntly threatens to plunder and fire Aberdeene, which they are afraid that he will doe unlesse wee send some forces to secure them. In regard none of the Scotch forces that were defeated about Worcester are come into these partes, they will not beleeve that their army is routed, for they are confident their King hath a great army. They say that when Hamilton was routed in Lancashire, they had notice by severall parties that got away. Nay, wee heare that on Friday last, at Glascoe and Dunbarton, they made bonfires and shot of guns, for some good successe of their forces in England.[1]

Two companies of Col. Sylers regiment and the 2 Scarborow companies were sent to Abrobrothwick, a port towne 12 miles from Dundee, where they are fortifieing there an auncient Abbey, which will make a considerable strength when fortified. Col. Overton went thither to give orders for making of workes there. Capt. Kirkby, of Col. Grosvenour's regiment, who hath a troope of horse, is appointed Governour.

---

[2] I find the officers of the garrison, and others whoe were present at the taking it, much troubled that there should be

---

[1] A similar account is given in *Mercurius Scoticus* for Sept. 17, 1653:—

'*Wednesday [Sept.* 17]. From Boghall, thus:

'In my last I gave an Accompt of the stop of the new Levies in the West. Since that, the L. Johnston hath wrote two Letters to them, affirming that the squandering of the Scottish Army in England was false; for their King was Crowned in London, and had given a Defeat to our Army. There hath been great rejoycing, with shooting of their Cannon, and making Bonfires at Evandale for that Newes. This day they have a Randezvouz at Aire, and on Munday next at Evandale, if not retarded by some Scots that are now returned in a miserable low condition, who escaped the sword in England, and now declare all is lost on their Party. The Castle of Evandale is a great shelter for the Moss-Troopers, and Meetings of the Malignant Commisioners. But no doubt upon the approach of some of our Forces before it, it will be rendred; for 'tis presumed they will not, or cannot, hold it out.' See also *Mercurius Politicus*, p. 1105.

[2] This last page seems to be the draft of a letter from Monk to the President of the Council of State, and not properly part of the narrative, though it is appended to it in the manuscript.

resolucions above taken to dispose away the ships taken here, to be sold by the Commissioners, when (not to speake of the prize they were bought with) they had noe other prize, and the souldyours whoe had booty by the plundour of this towne wilbe in a better condicion then the officers, whoe are in a worse condicion here then any where else, having had but a fortnights paie this long tyme, soe that they have noe monyes to buy themselves cloathes and other necessaries.

I might alsoe adde that it might be more honourable to the State to gratifie these officers which had soe farre adventured for them, then to dispose of the ships otherwise, since I could never observe soe much benefit to arise to them out of the prizes that were taken in that nature. This I onely privatly hint to your Honours, that in case it lye in your way, the officers might be considered that stay here. And whereas generally those in England have little mind to come hither againe, you may judge how little encouragement any have to reside in this place from the place itselfe, and therefore needs the assistance of frinds.

I must alsoe advertise your Honours of what I have from good hands concerning Dunbarton Castle, a strong hold; as the Governour, Sir Charles Erskin pretends to hold onely for the Duke of Lenox, whoe is under your proteccion, I humbly offerre it to your Honour whether it were not necessary for him to write to Sir Charles Erskin to render the Castle for the use of the Parliament, which would save the State much charge in the reduceing that place, or else would leave it inexcuseable.

II

Mr. WILLIAM CLARKE to SPEAKER LENTHALL.

For the Right Honourable WIL. LENTHALL, Esq., Speaker to the Parliament of Eng.[1]

SIR,—On Thursday last, the 6 Instant, the Gentlemen of the

---

[1] From the Tanner Manuscripts in the Bodleian Library, vol. lv. f. 92. The letter also printed in *Several Proceedings in Parliament* for Nov. 13-20, 1651, where several clauses are omitted. A number of other letters by Clarke, taken from the newspapers of the period, are printed in the Appendix.

severall Counties of Fife, Perth, Merne, and Angus, met at St.
Johnstouns, where they agreed upon the inclosed Letter and
Commission to be sent to the severall Shires and Burroughs to
be signed by the Inhabitants for the appointing of four Commissioners from each shire to attend the comeing of the Commissioners from England. The Earle of Athols Tenants and
Vassals are come in to the Lieutenant Generall, and desire
protection from him. There was a meeting the last weeke at
Edinburgh of the Provinciall Synod for Edinburgh, where
Mr. Andrew Dixon was chosen Moderator. They had verey
much debate in relation to the late proceedings of the Generall
Assembly and last meeting, and some of them protested
against it, and entred their Protestation, so that the Clergy
are like to go together by the eares for priority and power.
There was also a meeting of the Province of Kirkowbry, where
they generally declared against the proceedings of the Assembly. And the like also at St. Andrews. The Ministers of
the Synod of Glasgowe were upon declaring against it, but there
being many Lay-Elders among them, they dissented from it.
The Earle of Weems and Earle of Linlithgow have been with
the Lieutenant Generall. They came from the Marquesse of
Argile, who much desires to have a meeting with the Lieutenant Generall, or whom he should appoint, at St. Johnstons;
upon which the Lieutenant General hath granted a Passe to
the said Marquesse to come with his servants, their horses, and
arms, to protect him from the violence of their enemies (his
servants not exceeding the number of 30), to St. Johnstons,
where Lt.-Col. Brayne and Major Peirson are appointed to
treate with him, in order to his comming in to submit to the
Commonwealth of England, the meeting to be on Wednesday
the 19th instant; Provided that the Marquesse take care to
prevent[1] the meeting of the Parliament at Kickillum, which
he will endeavour to doe, att least will nott be att itt in person,
which Parliament was called by about eight or ten Lords of
the Committee of Estates, viz., Argile, Loudon, Glencane, and
others, besides the severall Burgesses of that Committee, who

---

[1] The terms agreed upon between Monk and Argyle, dated Nov. 19, and
Argyle's letter to Monk, dated Oct. 15, are printed in the Appendix.

have power to call a Parliament, soe that what proceedings they had made there would be embraced for law amongst the people. Some persons of quallitie are alsoe come from the Marquesse of Huntly, who itts believed will come in to Col. Overton at Aberdeene, soe that in probability all the Highlands will be reduced to the obedience of the Parliament of England without the effusion of more blood. For the Lord Belcarres he hath endeavoured lately very much to ingratiate himself by punishing some troopers of his who lately tooke mony from some friends of ours at Monrose, and caused the mony to be restored. Col. Lilburne came to the Lieutenant Generall on Saturday last: his Regiment is quartered in Irvidale. That day also nine Companies of Col. Coopers Regiment landed at Dundee.—Sir, I am, Your most humble Servant,
WILLIAM CLARK.

Dundee, 9 Novemb. 1651.

The Earle of Weems affirms upon his honour that the Marquesse of Argile never made any leavies since their king went for England.

The Marquesse of Arguiles thirty servants and attendants are to be disarmed as they enter St. Johnstons.

III

Mr. WILLIAM CLARKE to SPEAKER LENTHALL.[1]

RIGHT HONOURABLE,—The Scotch Parliament mett the last weeke in some parte of the Highlands, where were present only the Lord Chancellor Lowdon, the Lord Ardrosse, and one Lord more, with some few Burgesses, but could not agree about their sitting nor adjourning the same, wheruppon they presently brake uppe without effecting any thinge. The Lord Belcarris is certainly disbanding of his forces, which were the most considerable partie that stood against us. Huntley will likewise follow the same course, and then I know of noe forces that will bee in armes against us—only some few highway robbers. There landed at Dundee the other night two companies of

---

[1] Tanner-Manuscripts, vol. lv. f. 95.

foote out of Col. Barkestead's regiment, and are now to be setled in Col. Overton's regiment.

The Lord Torphesen is come in, and hath engaged himself to the Deputy Governor of Leith, Lieut.-Col. Wilks, nott to act any thing prejudiciall to the Commonwealth of England. The Lord Chancellor Lowdon, the Lord Balfour (?), and others are comeing in.

Five Companies of Col. Overton's, and some parte of Col. Alured's foote regiments are come to Edinburgh, where the Commissioners are daily expected by the common people, who hope to have ease rather then burthen by the English conquest. —I am your most humble servant,

WM. CLARKE.[1]

Leith, 23o 9bris 1651.

Mr. Speaker.

IV

A BRIEF RELATION of the PROCEIDINGS of the COMMITTEE of ESTATES and AFFAIRS of SCOTLAND, since the King's Majestie went from thence to England.[2]

THE Governement of the Kingdome of Scotland under his Majestie was (in his absens) intrusted to the Committee of Estates in all matters civill, bot the militarie power for raising and commanding the forces of the Kingdome was so divyded as did incres and heighten the former differences and distempers, that many did withdrawe themselfes, their counsells and asistance from the meittings of the Committee, and their concurrence from raising any forces, when the condition of the King-

---

[1] The articles of capitulation agreed on by the Marquis of Huntley with Colonel Overton are dated Nov. 21; those between Lord Balcarres and Overton, dated Dec. 3, are printed in Balfour's *Annals* iv. pp. 345, 346. Some extracts from *Mercurius Scoticus*, illustrating the subjects mentioned in this letter, are printed in the Appendix.

[2] From the Clarendon Manuscripts in the Bodleian Library, vol. xlvi. f. 243. This narrative, written by the Earl of Loudoun, was received by Charles II. on Sept. 19, 1653, with two other papers, printed later in the volume. As this narrative relates entirely to the events of 1651 it seemed best to insert it here.

dome did stand most in neid of the united counsells and forces of the wholl nation, which proved verie prejudi[ci]all to Scotland. But those to whom such commissions wer granted finding a generall dislyk against the same, and that it was represented to them by some of the Committee of Estates, and by the Commissioners of the Generall Assembly, how inacceptable these Commissions wer to the wholl people, and how prejudiciall the same wold be to the King's service, they receded from their Commissions, at leist layd them asyd as that they wold not act by. And yet many of the Committee still schuned to meitt or joyn with these who hade the former Commissions and power given to them, which did soe weaken and divyd the Kingdome and the Committee (to their own and the Cuntries overthrowe) as their was noe effectuall conjunction of counsells or forces for defence and safetie of the Kingdome. The Lord Chancellor regraitting these miserable and unseasonable divisions, did his utmost endevour to compose and remove the same, and within few days after his Majesties going to England he went to attend the Committee in Angus, wher they wer for the tyme. And the Enemie being at that tyme verie active in prosecuting their victories and improveing the succes they hade gottin to the best advantage, St. Johnestoun being taken in and the Castle of Sterline besieged, the Chancellor did move and urge with all earnestnes at his meittings with the Committee of Estates, that all differences and animosities might be removed and layd asyd, and that the wholl forces of Scotland might presently with all speed be raised to stopp the Enemie, who with so small forces (wanting opposition) did take in the strongest holds, and rinne over the Kingdome; which motion was approved and secounded by such of the Comission of the Generall Assembly as wer with the Committee of Estates for the tyme, and was so farr taken hold one, that it was resolved that all the forces of the schyrs of Perth, Forfar, Mearnes, Sterlingschyr, and Dumbartane should be furthwith raised, and brought to randevouzes, and to march and joyn with the small remainder of the forces that wer on foot for relief of Sterling. Bot ther was such ane eager desire of recrootting some regiments that wer broken at Innerkeithen in Fyfe that it did for some daye forsloe the raising the forces of the Cuntrie for releif of Sterling Castle. And the Lord Chancellor and the Earle of Crawford wer appoynted to meitt with the Earle of Atholl for the more speedie raising the forces in these pairts, and the Chancellor (after meitting with the Earle of Atholl) went from Dunkell to rais the forces in the Braes of Pertschyr, bot the tyme which was spent and lossed in recrooting these few regiments did so retard and forsloe the Cuntries rysing in armes, that the Castle of Sterling (by the pusillanimitie and base cowardice of the sojours who wer in it) was lossed and taken in by the Enemie. And the Lord Chancellor haveing writtin to the Marquis of Argyle to meitt with him at Strafillane, wher he came, did expostulat with him verie much that he did withdrawe from the meittings of the Committee, and did not concurr with them by his counsell and power of such ane exigencie and tyme of danger for defence of the Kingdome. And haveing used all the motives and arguments he culd to perswad him to joyn with the Committee, at last he promeised soe to doe if the wholl forces of the Kingdome should be made use of and disposed upon for the gude of the King's service and defence of the Kingdome, and not be led and overruled by a pairtie who wold miscarie and dispose of all for their own ends, and they to have all the thanks of any gude culd be done, and others to bear the blame of all that wer amiss. Bot the Lord Chancellor, being most desirous to remove all misunderstandings, and to unite and strengthen all who should joyn for defence of the Kingdome, did for that end returne as soon as he culd to wait upon the Comittee of Estates in the discharge of the publick trust of his place, and was the length of the east end of Lochtay, within a dayes journey to the place wher the Committee was, and the Enemie (after takeing the Castle of Sterling), being upon their marche towards Dundie, did with a pairtie miserably surpryse the Committee of Estates and the Comission of the Generall Assembly at Eliott, and did take and carie a number of them away prisoners, and sent them to London. After notice of which sad disaster and bloe, the Lord Chancellor did immediatly writt to the Lord Balcarras, who hade escaped with some small remainder of his regiment, and of Sir Johne Brounes, then under the command of Sir Arthure Forbes, into the North; and did lykways writt to the wholl Members of the Comittee to meitt at Killin at the west end of Lochtay, a place safe for meitting in respect of the situation amongst mountains, Loches, woods, and strait passes, wher they culd not be surprysed, and neir the midst of the Kingdome, and of equall distance for all the members of the Committe[e] to repair to from the severall pairts of the Kingdome, to resolve speedily upon the best means for defence of the Kingdome, and discharge of that great trust committed to them by the King and Parlament. Bot some of the Committee in the North did writt to the Committee and to the Lord Chancellor, that they thought it not expedient to come, bot that the Lord Chancellor and the rest of the Committee should come North to them, and that they wer about the raising of forces in the North; bot the Committee (wher the Lord Chancellor was present, and to whose charge and place it doeth properly belong to call the meittings of the Committee of Estates and other publict judicatories and meittings and to presed in them) being a full quorum, and the farr greatter pairt of the Committee being unwilling to relinquishe their trust and abandone the power committed to them by the King and Parlament; and finding that ther goeing to the North at that tyme was in effect a relinquishing and giving over of the wholl rest of the Kingdome to the Enemie, did again writ to these members of the Committee in the North, to remove all mistakes and prejudices, and desired them with all earnestnes to come and joyn with the Committee of Estates, and meitt in Perthschyr in the midst of the Kingdome, wher the meittings and counsells of the Committee might be more frequent and unanimous, and wher the wholl forces of Scotland might come to stopp the prevalencie of the Enemie, which culd noways be performed by retiring to the remote pairts of the North; and at last (after much intreattie) these of the Committee in the North condescended to come with the remainder of these regiments they hade to Dunkell, with any other forces that they culd rais in the North. Bot the Committee of Estates haveing (before their receat of this answer) adjourned the next meitting of the Committee to be at Dunbartane, wher they did lykeways give order to some regiments that were in the South to march again the tyme of the meitting of the Com-

mittee, they wer glade these in the North hade condescended
to come southward the length of Dunkell in order to their
conjunction, and the Committee did resolve to bring such
forces as should come to Dunbartane, with such other forces as
culd be raised in the south and west, alongst with them to joyn
with those forces should come from the North. And the
Committee at that same tyme did dispatch letters with gentlemen to the severall schyrs of the Kingdome to be all in readines,
both horss and foott, with their best men and armes, upon
sex hours warning to march and joyn with the forces of the
Kingdome. After dispatch of which letters and messagers
immediatly the sad news of the defeat of the King's armie at
Worcester came, which did so much damp and discourage as
that all men almost everie wher lossed both heart and hand;
and the few forces that wer in the North wer so farr from
their former resolution of coming to Dunkell that upon capitulation with the Enemie they disbanded. And the regiments
in the south wer some of them dissipated and the rest disbanded, and the Committee finding the forces of the Enemie so
near Dunbartane that they culd not meitt ther with safetie,
did meitt at Rosneath, and (after two dayes consultation) did
adjourne their meitting to Rothesaie in the Yle of Boot, and
being desirous in tyme of such extream danger and difficultie
to be asisted with more counsell and strength they did writt to
the members of the Committee that wer absent, and to some
of the most considerable gentlemen of the next adjacent schyrs
to come to the meitting of the Committee at Rosa; and the
Chanceller (finding the meitings of the Committee grow dayly
weaker and thinner, and some of the Committee, especially the
burgesses, of whom ther culd hardly two be gotten to make up
a quorum in the former meittings, unwilling to goe to Rosae,
or to meitt at any place of farther distance) did move and pres
before the pairting of the Committee from Rosneath, that the
Committee then present, being a full quorum, wold, according
to the trust committed to them, at least renew their former
orders to all the schyrs in the Kingdome to be in readines with
all their forces to march as they should be requyred and receave
orders; and that (the tyme appoynted for the meiting of the
Parlament being then approaching, and the place of meitting

referred to the Committee of Estates) they wold adjourne the meitting of the Parlament to some convenient place, leist it should desert; bot all was delayed till the ensewing meitting at Rothesae, wher none of the burgesses did come at all, nor any of the gentlemen of the schyrs that wer writtin to, except some from Galloway, who came after the meitting was disolved, soe that ther was noe quorum at that meitting;[1] bot these who did meitt appoynted the meitting of the Parlament to be at Finlarge at the west end of Lochtay, and did writt letters to all Noblemen and to the wholl Commissioners of schyrs and burghes, desiring them most earnestly to keip the meitting of the Parlament, wher all such of the Comittee who wer then at Rosa promeised to be present; and the Chanceller went and keiped the tyme appoynted for the meitting of the Parlament at Finlarge, wher he appoynted the best accommodation for the Parlament that cuntrie culd afford, and did sett gards at the severall passes on all sydes, that the Parlament might meitt and sitt without danger. Bot none of the members of Parlament came thither bot only the Earle of Hoome, the Earle of Calander, and the Lord Cardross.

The Lord Burghley, who was Presedent of the Parlament, haveing come to the Laird of Glenurquhays sons of Balloche, tenn myles distant from Finlarge, did writt his excuse for his absens to the Lord Chanceller, that being come that length

---

[1] The following account of this meeting of the Committee confirms Loudoun's statement:—

'*Wednesday* [*Nov.* 5].—By other Letters thus: From the Isle of Boot, where the Committee of the Scots did meet with Argyle and the Chancellour, and divers other Nobles and Gentlemen, we hear that the result of their Meeting was, that the Chancellour was the man that pressed most the leavying a New Army, but was opposed by the rest, in respect that there was no considerable Places of this Nation to raise Men in that was not possessed by the Englishes; and though they had Men they wanted Money, Arms, and Victuals, and the Forces which they had already, being about 300 under Major Generall Sterling about Dunbarton, would not be commanded by them, they sending him Orders to command all his Souldiers to go home to their dwelling houses, till further Orders from the Parliament, which should meet the 12 of this instant at Killen and Finleyrig in Lochtay, from whence they might expect fuller Orders; but both he and they refused to obey their Orders, and at that Meeting they could not do any considerable thing, they not being a full number, there being only one Burgesse, viz., John Kennedy, Provost of Aire.—*Mercurius Scoticus*, Nov. 4-11, 1651.'

on his journey towards the Parlament he did fall sick, and was forced to returne home. The Marquis of Argyle, who was certainly expected, came not, bot writt his excuse to the Lord Chanceller, that he hade taken a pain of the stone or gravell, which made him unable to travell. Nether did any other of the Comittee of Estates that was at the former meitting at Rosae (except the Earle of Hoome) come to the appoynted meitting of the Parlament, nor send ther excuse, bot went all home upon passes from the Enemie without returne, soe that the Parlament deserted, and the Earles of Hoome, and Calander, and the Lord Cardros regraiting to the Lord Chanceller that all hade relinquished their trust and charge and gone home and given all over, they told [him] they culd doe noe thing bot returne and live at home, if they culd without engagements to the Enemie or taking oathes be permitted to stay at home, and that they did perceave the Chanceller was in verie hard condition, all haveing relinquished and leaft him alone, and that it was in vain for him to wrestle any more expecting any asistance from the Kingdome. All forces of Scotland being thus disbanded, the Committee of Estates refuseing to meitt, and the meitting of the Parlament being deserted, and the Lord Chanceller haveing assayed all just and possible means in discharge of his trust and duetie of his place to incite all men to stand to the defence of their Religion, Lawes, Liberties, King, and Cuntrie; and ther being so much division in Scotland amongst persons of all rankes, and such despondencie of spirit and consternation upon all men, as he culd gett noe concurrence, nor any to hazard for defence of the Kingdome, he culd doe noe more; bot in farther testimonie of his faithfullnes he did retire to the montaines in the Highlands to eschew the Enemie, wher he, his Lady, and cheildren did indure noe small hardship, being forced some tymes in the greatest stormes of winter to travell throwe the snowe in the night, and to wander in the desert and barren wildernes, wher for a long tyme they indured great trouble, sufferring with much patience the spoyling of ther gudes, plundering of their housses, and sequestration of their estate, choosing affliction rather then sinne. Which being a true Relation of the proceidings of the Comittee of Estates, and of the affairs of Scotland after the King went to England till the tyme that the King's armie was broken at Worcester, and that Commissioners wer sent from the pretended Parliament of the new usurped Comonewealth of England into Scotland, the Lord Chanceller referres his wholl deportment in relation to the publict trust of his place to be judged according to his actions and sufferings. And many passages which wold give clear evidence of his fidelitie and loyaltie are purposly passed over, least the same might any ways reflect upon others.

V

A NEWS-LETTER from DUNDEE.[1]

Dundee, New Yeares Day,
January 1, 1651.

SIR,—Since the last wee understand that Captain Augustine, the great robber and murtherer of our men, uppon the disbanding of Marquesse Huntley's forces, went into the Islands of Orknay, and from thence is shipp't to Norway. Mr. Hane, the Engineere, is return'd from Invernesse hither, and findes that Towne nott to bee fortifiable without a great deale of charges, nor tenable without a greater number of men then the Towne can possibly provide accommodacion for, for wheras a Regiment was intended for itt, there are now only 3 companies quarter'd there, and half of them want beds, and the rest of Col. Fitches Regiment quarter'd in great houses beyond the River Spey and Lake of Nesse. Steelhand the Mosser (who was nott comprized in the Articles with Huntley) hath dispersed his followers (which never were above 20), and is now att his Mother's house in the North Highlands, and some Gentlemen of qualitie have undertaken to bringe him in to the Lieutenant Generall within 48 houres, uppon his passe, which the Lieutenant Generall doth nott thinke fitt yet to grant, though itt bee alleaged in Steelhand's behalf that hee never was present att the killing of any of our men, nor ever tooke any of our men but only those 4 dragoones, and a foote souldier, which hee tooke about a fortnight since neere the Northwater Bridge. There

---

[1] Clarke Manuscripts, vol. xxii.

are about an hundred people of severall nations, call'd heere by the name of Egyptians, which doe att this day ramble uppe and downe the North Highlands, the cheifest of which are one Hause and Browne: they are of the same nature with the English Gypsies, and doe after the same manner cheate and cosen the country.

Captain Robyns of the Lieutenant Generall's Regiment lately died att Aberdene.

The Regiments heere are now very full. Col. Cobbett's musters 1183 souldiers besides Commission officers, and Col. Coopers 1146.

Friday last, the 26th of December, Captain Sergeant's Company (one of the Scarborough Companies) marched hence towards Aberdeene as recruites to Col. Ashfeild's Regiment, and Captain Skelton's (the other of them) are added as recruits to Col. Cobbett's and Col. Cooper's Regiments.

The ground of the last weekes intelligence from the Marquesse of Argile's country of the gathering together of some hundreds of Highlanders was only uppon occasion of his summoning the severall clans for to select 30 out of them to attend him to the Major Generalls and Lieutenant Generall, itt being usuall uppon such like occasions for a thousand or twelve hundred of them to come in, although hee makes choice of nott above 20 or 30 for his service, soe slavish are those barbarous creatures to his will.

The Presbyterian partie (seing themselves slighted, and having noe other way to ingratiate themselves but by some addresse to those imployed from the Commonwealth of England) are now endeavouring tooth and nayle to gett Commissioners to present some overtures to the Major Generalls, and doe cast all the aspersions they can invent uppon the malignant partie, and to bring their Commissioners who were first with much freedome elected into disrepute both with their owne Nation and with us; yet I suppose as neither of them will bee trusted much by the Commonwealth, yet these shall nott have more but rather lesse respect then the former, in regard they did nott make overtures till they found all other wayes of power or policie would doe noe good, and if any meritt favour heere, itt is those whom they call more malignant (for both of them deserve that title) who as they are the most considerable partie soe have already done more reall and visible services then the whole generation of Presbyterians are able to performe for many yeares, who, though they now cringe and bowe, yet will bee alwayes sowing sedition against the Commonwealth of England, unlesse they have their wonted power both in Kirke and State; yet that wee may a little guesse att what they intend, some great Presbyterians, att a meeting this weeke in Fife, they excepted against the late Commission subscribed by the severall Counties for three reasons, first, for that noe mencion is made of the Kinge. 2. That there is nothing said of the Covenant. 3. That one of their Estates, vzte., The Lords, are excluded.

On Tuesday last Major Generall Lambert and Major Generall Deane came to Bruntiland, and on Wednesday they lay att the Lord Craighall's, within 3 miles of Cowper in Fife. The Lord Craighall, Lord Hopton, and Laird Swinton came over with them. The last night they were att St. Andrews, soe that they are expected here Febr. 2, where they will bee much furthered by the Lieutenant Generall in their consultations about the publique affaires.[1]

VI

A News-Letter from Dundee.[2]

Dundee, January 8, 1651.

The Major Generalls having bin heere since Friday last, setled all the Northerne parts in a way for the taking off free quarter and ease of the Country in paying transeunt quarters, both which were very great burthens, for which purpose they gave the inclosed instruccions to the Treasurer. Col. Lilburne came hither on Munday last very seasonably, by whom they had an Account of the state of affaires, and accordingly they gave order for the repayring and making tenable the Marq.

---

[1] Unsigned: nor does the copy of this letter, printed in *Several Proceedings in Parliament*, p. 1875, give the writer's name. Compare *Mercurius Politicus*, pp. 1363, 1378.

[2] Clarke Manuscripts, vol. xxii.

Huntley's house in Invernesse, and for the alteration of quarters for the ease of the Country in Murrayland and other parts. They have reduced the Sesse, which was reduced in most places 2 Monthes and half of their former maintenance (and in some more) to one monthes Sesse and half, which the Country take for a great ease, considering how much they paid before. Mr. Jefferies, the Provost of Aberdene, was heere with them, and offer'd severall particulars in relation to that Towne, which, though one of the richest and best Citties in Scotland, yet complaine much of the burthen of one Regiment that lies uppon them. Captain Giffin was in the North with Col. Lilburne, and did good service. I perceive by Captain Empson and others that came from thence, that there is a very precious people who seeke the face of God in Sutherland and divers other parts beyond Invernesse, which, but that I had itt from soe good hands, I should have much question'd, considering how few all the Southerne parts have afforded; but the Spiritt bloweth where itt listeth, and though there were very few in any parte of this Nation where ever wee came that would bee present att any private meetings, yet the people in those parts will rather leave their owne Ministers and come to private houses where our officers and souldiers meete together.

Yesterday the 2 Major Generalls, having notice of the other Commissioners being uppon their way from London, hastened over the water towards Leith, and intended to bee last night att Bruntiland. The Lieutenant-Generall intends to goe over thither on Monday next.

VII

A Letter from the Commissioners of the Parliament in Scotland to the Speaker.[1]

Sir,—Since our first setting out from London, we have lost no time in our repaire unto this place, where through the gracious hand of our good God towards us, we arrived in safety on Thursday last.[2] Upon our coming hither we found free quarter in a hopefull way of being taken off, the better to

---

[1] Tanner Manuscripts, vol. lv. f. 118. [2] 15th January.

prepare the mindes of the people heere to the work you have entrusted us with, but hearing as yet no newes of the arrivall of the money for the pay of these forces, which was to be put on board the beginning of this moneth, to be transported hither, we doe very much apprehend the evill consequence of its delay, knowing how great a prejudice it will certainly be to your affaires heere, and could doe no lesse in duty then present the same to you. The next day after our arrivall at this place, we tooke into consideracion our commission and instructions, and as we shall make progresse therein, shall give you a frequent account.[1] Our resolucions are (through God's assistance) to apply our best endeavours for the effecting of the Parliament's comaunds with faithfulnesse and diligence, being very sensible by the experience we have already had, how great a charge this imployment will occasion, yf it be not expeditious; the successe whereof is onely in God's hand.—We are,

Your most humble and faithfull servants,

J. LAMBERT.   OL. ST. JOHN.   RI. DEANE.
H. VANE.   G. FENWICK.   RICHARD SALWEY.[2]
ROBERT TICHBORNE.

From Dalkeith, 17 January 1651.
Read. 23 *Jan.* 1651.

Addressed: *For the Most Honorable William Lenthall, Esq., Speaker of the Parliament of England.*

VIII

A NEWS-LETTER from SCOTLAND.

Leith, January 31, 1651.

I HAVE inclosed the heads of a letter[3] sent to Major Generall

---

[1] On their further proceedings, see Nicoll's *Diary*, pp. 79-87, and *Mercurius Politicus*, pp. 1387, 1406, 1423, 1438.

[2] These were the Commissioners sent by the Parliament to settle the government of Scotland and to treat of the union of the two nations. The documents concerning their mission are very numerous and deserve to be separately collected and reprinted. They are altogether omitted in Bruce's Report on the Union of England and Scotland, but might be collected from the Journals of Parliament, the newspapers of the period, and the *Domestic State Papers*.

[3] An abstract of this letter is given in *Mercurius Politicus* for January 22-29, p. 1378. See also *Several Proceedings in Parliament*, February 5-12, p. 1924.

Lambert, but intended to bee presented to his Excellency from the Lord Warreston, Col. Halkett, Mr. Samuell Rutherford, and other rigid Presbyterian Gentlemen, Ministers, and others, in the name of those who would bee call'd the Godly partie. You will perceive by itt the drift of their intencions, which is to exalt their Governement in the Kirke, and soe to bring all kinde of Governement into their owne handes *in ordine ad spiritualia*, to vilifie the proceedings of the Parliament of the Commonwealth of England, and scandalize the practice of the officers of the Army in their most religious performances, and to perswade both to lett them have a liberty to tyrannize both over the bodies and soules of the poore people under pretence of giving them liberty of conscience, which cannott stand with the principles of any who are lovers of true freedome either to their outward or inward man. The letter was brought to the Major Generall by Sir John Cheisley, Sir James Stuart, and one or two more.

IX

Mr. WILLIAM CLARKE to SPEAKER LENTHALL.[1]

SIR,—Though there bee noe materiall newes heere, yet I have presumed by these to send you the inclosed, which will bee published the next weeke. Lieutenant Generall Monke begins his journey for England on Munday next, and Major Generall Lambert a day or two after him.[2] The Commissioners of Parliament doe receive daily the Commissioners from the severall Counties of Scotland, and a good correspondence for the greatest parte is nott doubted, though in some places the Kirke partie only are chosen, uppon misapprehension that they alone are intended by persons of knowne integritie.—I am, Sir, Your most humble servant,   WM. CLARKE.

Leith, 14th Febr. 1651.

---

[1] Tanner Manuscripts, vol. lv. f. 135.
[2] Lambert had been appointed on January 29, 1652, to succeed Ireton as Lord-Deputy of Ireland. Monk was obliged to leave Scotland in consequence of his ill-health. See Nicoll's *Diary*, p. 85.

X

A News-Letter from Leith.[1]

Leith, 21 February 1651.

This weeke the Marquess of Argisle sent his steward, Mr. Campbell, as Commissioner from the County of Argisle, to treat with the Commissioners of Parliament att Dalkeith about the publique affaires. In his letter hee excuses his and the shires nott sending sooner, for that neither hee nor they knew anythinge concerning the Commissioners, nott soe much as their being in Scotland, as hee hopes his Commissioner will make appeare to them. That hee is confident when many other informations and particulars concerning him are rightly weighed, they shall bee found light in the ballance of righteous judgement, as in relacion to men, with whom hee sayes hee hath ever studied to walke uprightly, as the Lord was pleased to furnish him with light and direccion, which hee hopes for the time to come by his grace strengthning him, never to bee found otherwayes.[2] The Commissioners have sent a Messenger with a particular expresse to him, uppon whose returne itt's supposed the Marquesse of Argile will come in, or give some assurance that he will nott act against us, for now hee sees there is noe other way to secure himself.

From the North wee heare nothing since the landing of 2 Companies of Col. Cooper's Regiment in Orkney, where they were civillie entertayned by the Country. The Company which was driven back to Bruntiland, with Captain Robsons which came last weeke out of England, are to be shipt for Orknay in the *Tyger* and *Satisfaccion* frigotts.[3] On Wednesday

---

[1] Clarke Manuscripts, vol. xxii. f. 31.

[2] Argyll's letter is amongst the Clarke Manuscripts, vol. xxii. f. 26, but in a cypher or shorthand. See also Nicoll's *Diary*, p. 90.

[3] An earlier news-letter, dated Leith, Feb. 3, 1651, gives the following details on the expedition to the Orkneys:—

'The time of action being over, you must expect little from Military pens. Wee heare Argyle doth still continue to fortifie some places in the Highlands, yett probably in the Springe hee will bee able to give but a poore account of his winter's worke. Col. Cooper's regiment was to bee shipt from Montrose to Orkney the 28th past. Itt's hoped they were past the danger of the Seas before the last night, when there was the greatest storme there hath bin knowne for many yeares in these Northern parts.'

last the Commissioners of Parliaments Declaracion for anulling Kingly power and Prerogative Courts of Justice was proclaymed att the Markett place in Dundee by beate of drum and sound of trumpett.[1] The Magistrates shewed their respects by giving attendance during the time, and would have adorned the Crosse, if the Governour, Col. Cobbett, would have given way, which hee refused, in regard itt was never before used by them.

XI

HENRY WHALLEY to SCOUTMASTER GENERAL DOWNING.[2]

FREIND,—I received by the hands of Mr. William Thompson and Mr. John Mill, Deputies for Edenbrough, a commission to administer an oathe to the Provost and other officers as should be elected for Edenbrough, in pursuance whereof, and according to my commission, I have administred the oath unto them, vizt.,

Provost.
Archibald Todd.
Bayliffs.
James Ellis.
John Marjoribankis.
Thomas Calderwood.

The fourth Bayliff chosen, but by reason of his absence not sworne, is John Jossie.

Deane of Gild.
James Rucheid.

The Treasurer elected, but as informed refuseth to take upon him the imployment, is John Lawder.[3]

---

[1] The Proclamation dated Jan. 31, printed in *Mercurius Politicus*, p. 1306.
[2] Tanner Manuscripts, vol. lv. f. 102. Compare Nicoll's *Diary*, p. 88.
[3] A news-letter amongst the Clarke Manuscripts adds the following particulars:
'*Jan. 27, Leith*, 1651.—Yesterday Mr. Archibald Todd, provost of Edinburgh, and other inhabitants of Edinburgh, petitioned the Commissioners of the Parliament of England sitting at Dalkeith, that they might chuse a provost, 4 Bayliffs, a Deane of Gild, and a Treasurer, according to their ancient customs, rights, and priviledges. They were ordered to bring in their charters on Wednesday next.'

I leave the communication hereof to the Commissioners as to you shalbe thought fitt, remaining your very loveinge freind, HEN. WHALLEY.

Edenbrough, 9th of March 165½.

XII

COLONEL OVERTON TO GENERAL CROMWELL.[1]

MAY IT PLEASE YOUR EXCELLENCY,—Having setled and fortified our quarters both by land and sea in Orkney, and received assurance from the inhabitants of Shitland of their comportment and complyance with the English interest, I made my retreat to Edeneburgh, where I now am attending the Major Generall's returne from the West to receive such further comands as may tend to the discharge of my duty, and the doing such services as may be answerable to your Excellencie's commands, or the interest of God and my Country. Collonel Cooper doth only attend the Major Generall's returne, in order to the attainment of some accomodations which it will be requisite to take along with him for the accomodation of his regiment, as moneys, provisions, guns, etc., for the fort (under the comand whereof 100 sayle of ships may safely ride from the annoyance of any enemy), and the works, whereby we have taken in, and made teneable the Cathedrall Kirk of St. Maans, and the Earle of Morton's house, where we can upon occasion very conveniently and intirely lodge a regiment of men or more. The church and house are not within battery of any comanding ground, save one hill, which lyes within pistoll shott of the place, and there we have drawn forth a little fort, which, if your Excellency think fitt to continue a force in those Islands, will soon be finished. I had once thought to have sent a company over into Shitland, but having no comission from your Excellency or any other superior officer, I have hitherto in that respect respited it, though I humby conceive when the Major Generall returns from the West, though it be for nothing else but a preposession of the place, he will pass

---

[1] Tanner Manuscripts, vol. lv. f. 170.

over a party thither for the prementioned purpose. During my abode in Orkney, we had a fair comportment from the generality of the people in that place, save some little rising and falling upon our men in our out quarters; but (blessed be God) the assaylants were the greatest sufferers, for they were not only beaten into good behaviour, but thereby gave us a very good occasion to disarme the whole Island, which, as it is reported by some of the best affected inhabitants, are able to raise an Army of 5 or 6000 fighting men. Pardon, my Lord, my prolixity, and be pleased to accept this rude and hasty relation from him who unfainedly rests and remains in his best, most humble and hearty obedience, your Excellencie's servant ever to be commanded, RT. OVERTON.[1]

Edenburgh, March 22th, 1651.

XIII

THE MARQUESS OF ARGYLL to the COMMISSIONERS OF THE PARLIAMENT.[2]

RIGHT HONORABLE,—I doubt not but these noble Gentlemen of your number whom I had the honor to wait upon at Dumbarton, will lett you know my earnest desire to have cleared particulars, which doubtles your Honours would heare to my disadvantage, by some ignorantly, and others maliciously, yet both to my prejudice for their severall ends. And how desirous I likewise was to make knowne the ende I still aimed at (never being my owne perticuler interest), and the rules I walked by of conscience and dutie, but that the Parliament's Declaration had anticipat all I could propose for conjunct resolutions of best-principled men in this Kingdome for a lasting peace and union betwixt both Nations; howsoever, as it hath beene, so it is still my desire to shunn all occasions which may lead mee beyond my owne station and calling; I make it my humble desire therefore to your Honours that I may know what is required of mee, who shall be very willing to doe all

---

[1] A life of Robert Overton is contained in the *Dictionary of National Biography*.
[2] Tanner Manuscripts, vol. lv. f. 172.

which with a safe conscience I may for the peace and union of this Island. And I hope when I receive your Honours answer in this, you will allow mee to represent any other thing which may then occurr to mee as your Honours most humble servant,

A. ARGYLL.[1]

Inverary, 23 March 1651.

For The honorable the Commissioners of the Parliament of England.

XIV

A NEWS-LETTER from SCOTLAND.[2]

THOUGH there bee little considerable in these parts, yet I shall give you an account of what wee had this day by lettres from Aire. That Major Pounall having received a command from Major Generall Deane to send a commanded partie of 50 foote to the Isle of Arran to possesse the Castle of Bradick, the late Duke Hamilton's House, hee being alsoe Earle of Arran, accordingly the 6th instant, by 4 in the morning, a partie were ship't from Aire under the command of Captain Goldsmyth, who landed them att Cannemashe, [?] 5 miles from the Castle, and coming about 3 of the clock in the afternoone neere the Castle, having drawne uppe his men, summoned itt. They within granted admittance with these complements, That our men were very welcome, because they were not in a capacity to avoide itt, for they told them in plaine termes, that if they could have prevented itt, our men should nott have come in there, yet after about 2 hours stay, the cheif tenants in the Island came and were very civill to the Captaine and souldiers.

---

[1] A news-letter in the Clarke Manuscripts, dated March 2, says: 'The messenger of the Committee at Dalkeith is returned from the Marquesse of Argile, and bringes only an overture of his meeting our Commissioners at Dumbarton uppon 4 dayes notice, where hee doubts not but to give all due satisfaction; hee hath noe souldiery about his House at Innerara, nor any show of leavying an Army, his chaplin usually prayes for the King under the notion of a distressed prince. There are noe persons of quality with him, only his son (the Lord Lorne), his Lady, and 4 daughters.'

[2] Clarke Manuscripts, vol xxii. f. 70.

The Castle may bee made very tenable, and is of great consequence, in regard itt bringes the Island into subjection, which is 7 or 8 miles over, and 24 miles in length. The Inhabitants expresse much dissaffection to Argile, and itt's hoped the civillity of our souldiers will much engage them.

[*April* 1652.]

XV

AN ORDER by the COMMISSIONERS of the PARLIAMENT OF ENGLAND.[1]

By the Commissioners of the Parliament of the Commonwealth of England for ordering and managing affaires in Scotland. Aprill 9, 1652.

WHEREAS the said Commissioners have by Commission under their hands, bearing date the third day of March last, aucthorized and appointed the Neighbours and Inhabitants of the Towne and Burgh of Dunbarton to nominate and choose Magistrates and other officers for the Governement of the said Burgh, in which provision is made that the persons elected and chosen by virtue therof to any office or place should nott proceede to the exercise of the same untill the oath in the said Commission mencioned should bee administred to them. And, whereas, Henry Campbell, provost, John Conyngham, and   Alpine, lately chosen Bailiffs of the said Burgh, refuse to take the said oath, although Captain James Thompson, Governour of Dunbarton Castle, who is by the said Commissioner's warrant, bearing date the 24th day of March last, impowred to administer the same, hath tendred himself unto them for that purpose, as by a paper under their hands to us now produced, bearing date the 6th of Aprill instant appeares. Itt is therfore ordered, That the said Captain Thompson doe take an especiall care, that neither the aforesaid persons nor any other persons within the said Burgh doe take uppon them the exercise of any office or place within the said Burgh by

---

[1] Clarke Manuscripts, vol. xxii. f. 68. Dumbarton had surrendered on Jan. 5, 1652. Nicoll's *Diary*, p. 79.

colour of the said Commission untill they shall have first taken the aforesaid oath, according to the tenour therof.—Signed by order of the said Commissioners, Jo. Phelpes, *Secretary*.

XVI

A Letter from the Commissioners of the Parliament of England to the Marquess of Argyll.[1]

My Lord,—Wee have received your letter of the xxiiith of March, in which you express a desire to know what is required of you. For answer wee shall referr your Lordshipp to the Declaration of the Parliament of the Common-wealth of England concerning the settlement of Scotland, which hath beene lately published to the people of this nation, and whereof your Lordshipp's letter takes notice. In which Declaration the Parliament hath expressed what they expect from the people of Scotland in order to the settlement therein mencioned. And such as express complyance therein have opportunity with freedome to propound what they thinke fitt. Not having else at present, Wee remaine, My Lord, your Lordshipp's humble servants,   Ol. St. John.   Ri. Deane.
                  R. Salwey.   Robert Tichborne.
Dalkeith, ix*th Aprill* 1652.

XVII

The Marquess of Argyll to the Commissioners of the Parliament of England.[2]

Right Honorable,—I received your letter from Dalkeith the ninth April, and though it bee not so favorable as I had some reason to expect, yet I easily beleive that the Commissioners from this shire not giving you a positive graunt to your desire, with some other misreports, which I heare are abroad, might occasione the same. I have, therefore, desired the bearer, Mr. Archibald Campbell to bee at the paines to

---

[1] Tanner Manuscripts, vol. liii. f. 6.   [2] *Ibid.* vol. liii. f. 12.

waite on your honnors, for clearing the falshood of any such reports, and vindicating mee from the burdeine of other mens carriage. For I have still professed it is my desire that all occasiones of more trouble in those dominiones may bee fully removed, that (religion and righteousnes being the foundacion) the peace of them may bee perpetuated to all posterity. And I hope in the Lord's mercy it shall never bee found that I shall either bee a cause or give any just occasion to the contrair. I will not put your honnour to more trouble by a long letter, but remittes particulers to the bearer, and rests,—
Your honnors most humble servant,   A. ARGYLL.

Inveraray, 15th April 1652.

Superscribed.—*For the Commissioners of the Parliament of the Common wealth of England.*

XVIII

A NEWS-LETTER from LEITH.[1]

Leith, Apr. 24, 1652.

ON Wednesday last, the Declaracion of the Parliament of England for the union with Scotland, and their Eleccion of 21 Deputies to come into England in Order to their sending Members to the Parliament, was proclaymed with much solemnity att the Markett Crosse in Edinburgh by beate of drum and sound of trumpett and the Crosse adorned with hangings. Itt was read by Judge Advocate Whalley (a Guard of Horse and foote being drawne out during the time). There was a very great concourse of people att the proclayming of itt; after the reading wherof the souldiers gave severall shouts, as complying with the Parliament in their free conferring of liberty uppon a conquered people, but soe sencelesse are this generation of theire owne goods that scarce a man of them shew'd any signe of rejoycing. Though the most flourishing of their Kings would have given the best jewell in their crownes to have procur'd a vote in Parliament for their equall shares or staking in the Lawes of England.

---

[1] Clarke Manuscripts, vol. xxii. f. 80. On the Declaration referred to, see Nicoll's *Diary*, pp. 90-92. This letter is printed in *The French Intelligencer*, British Museum, E. 662, 3.

The Commissioners of Parliament att Dalkeith intend to begin their journey towards England on Wednesday next. There hath bin lately some further overtures from Argile, but what they signify or the Commissioners have done therein is nott publiquely knowne, yet wee hope hee will gett nothing by his juglings and dissembling devises, which are soe generally knowne.

XIX

A Letter from the Commissioners of the Parliament of England to the Marquess of Argyll.[1]

My Lord,—According to your Lordshipp's desire in your last letter, wee have heard from Mr. Archiball Campbell what he thought fitt to offer, and would have your Lordshipp beleive that the matter of our last to you was not grounded upon any misreports concerning your Lordshipp, but was intended by us onely in answer to the matter contained in your former letter. And whereas Mr. James Campbell, Deputy for the sheire of Argyle, hath accepted the tender of union on behalfe of th' inhabitants thereof, and hath also engaged for their living peaceably under, and giving obeadience to the authority of the Parliament of England exercised in Scotland; and having (amongst other things) offered some particulers concerning your Lordshipp, wee think fitt to let your Lordshipp know, that the same will be speedily communicated to the Parliament. Not having else for the present, wee remaine, My Lord, your Lordshipp's humble servants,

Ri. Deane. Ol. St. John.
Robert Tichborne. R. Salwey.

Dalkeith, 28th Aprill 1652.

---

[1] Tanner Manuscripts, vol. liii. f. 18.

XX

A News-Letter from Leith.[1]

Leith, May 18, 1652.

THE Judges mett this day in the usuall place of Session in Edinburgh, after they had heard a very excellent sermon preached before them in the High Church by Mr. Durant of Newcastle, which was very pertinent to the present occasion. The sermon being ended, the Judges, vzte., The Lord Craighall, Laird Swinton, Mr. John Marsh, Mr. Andrew Owen, Mr. Edward Moseley, and Col. Lockhart, being satt, their Commission from the Commissioners att Dalkeith was read before a very great concourse of people. After which Mr. Smyth made an elegant speech concerning the occasion of their meeting, and to take off some aspersions which were laid uppon the Parliament by the Ministers of Scotland, as to the tolerating and countenancing of heresies and blasphemies, wheras the Parliament of England had by severall Acts declared against all evills of that nature, and more particulerly against swearing, breaking the Sabboth, and the like, and gave direccions for the reading the Act of Heresies, etc. In the conclusion hee advis'd them to lay aside all prejudicate or malicious thoughtes against them, and they doubted not (through God's Blessing) they should faithfully discharge their duty to him, and answere the trust reposed in them by the Parliament of England, to which end they published a Declaracion of the Abatement of Fees in Courtes of Justice and other priviledges.

---

[1] Clarke Manuscripts, vol. xxii. f. 92. On the proceedings of the Judges, see Nicoll's *Diary*, pp. 93, 94, 96.

XXI

A Declaration of the Commissioners for Regulating the Universities.[1]

By the Commissioners for Visiting and Regulating Universities and other Affairs relating to the Ministry in Scotland.

The Commissioners of Parliament of the Common-wealth of England (being carefull to promote Piety and Learning, and to settle a godly and peaceable Ministery through this Nation, who may make it their onely work sincerely to preach the Gospel of Jesus Christ), Have Constituted and Appointed Richard Dean, Esquier, Major-Generall of the Army, George Fenwick, George Smyth, John March, Andrew Owen, Edward Mosley, Richard Saltingstall, Samuel Disbrowe, and Edmund Tyler, Esquiers, or any three, or more of them, to be Visiters of the Universities, Colledges, and Schools of Learning in Scotland; By vertue whereof, they do hereby Declare and Publish, That they intend (Godwilling) in convenient time, to alter and abolish all such Lawes in the same, as shall be found inconsistent with the Government of the Common-wealth of England, or the Union and Incorporation of England and Scotland, and to frame and make others in their room. And they do hereby Declare, That all Acts and Proceedings, since the fourth day of February last, made and done by any Persons, pretending to have power of Visitation in the same, are and shall be null and void: And that they will remove out of them such Person or Persons as shall be found scandalous in their lives and conversations, or that shall oppose the Authority of the Common-wealth of England, exercised in Scotland, and place others more fitly qualified in their rooms. And further, they shall and will remove all and every Minister and Ministers, through this Nation, from his and their Place and Places, that shall be found scandalous in his and their life and conversation, and take care that other fit Persons be put in his and their Place and Places; and in all other Places,

---

[1] From a printed broadside amongst William Clarke's collection.

that are, or shall be, vacant: And shall also hear and determine all Causes relating to the Maintenance of the Ministers or others, as aforesaid. And they do hereby further Declare, That for the better executing of their Power, according to their Commission, They intend (Godwilling) to sit on Monday the seventh of this instant June, at Edinburgh, in the Parliament-House there, and to continue their sitting every Monday fortnight following; where they shall be ready to receive all Complaints and to hear and determine all Causes concerning the Premisses: Of which they desire all good People of this Land to take notice.

Given under our Hands at Edinburgh, this fourth day of June 1652.

GEOR. SMYTH.	ED. SYLER.	JO. MARCH.
SA. DISBROWE.	A. OWEN.	EDW. MOSLEY.

Printed at Leith by Evan Tyler, *Anno Dom.* 1652.[1]

XXII

A DECLARATION by MAJOR-GENERAL DEANE.[2]

June 9, 1652.

WHERAS itt is thought needfull for the securitie and peace of this whole Isle, and the Inhabitants therof, that some forces belonging to the Parliament of the Commonwealth of England should march into the Highlands of Scotland for the ends aforesaid: And I having appointed Col. Robert Lilburne, with certaine Regiments of horse and foote, to performe that service by the way of Invernesse, have thought fitt to intimate soe much to the Cheif of Clans, Gentlemen, and Inhabitants of

---

[1] A news-letter, dated Leith, June 7, states:—'This day the Commissioners for uniting and regulating the Ministerie of Scotland (consisting of the English Commissioners for the administration of justice and the Commissioners at Leith) mett at Edinburgh, and settled severall thinges in order to their future proceedings, and intend to meet at Edinburgh every Munday fortnight.'—Clarke Manuscripts, vol. xxii. Compare Nicoll's *Diary*, p. 97.

[2] Clarke Manuscripts, vol. xxii. f. 103. An account of the expedition to the Highlands, undertaken in June 1652, is given in the letters from contemporary newspapers, collected in the Appendix.

Elgin, Nerneshire, Invernesse, Rosse, Cromarty, Sutherland and Caithnesse, and the Isles therunto belonging, desiring and requiring them to come in to the said Colonell, and give him their engagement for themselves and clans to live peaceably, and their best assistance in guiding him through and providing for him in their Country all such necessaries of grasse and other provisions as shall bee found needfull, wherby the souldiers may nott bee necessitated nor the Country wronged, but that all thinges may bee done with the greatest ease to the Inhabitants of those parts, and accomodacion of the forces appointed for the service, for which there shall bee due satisfaccion given, and nothing done to the prejudice of any who behave themselves peaceably and conformable to the Parliament of the Commonwealth of England and their aucthority exercised in Scotland.

Given under my hand att Aberdene, June 9, 1652.

RI. DEANE.

XXIII

A CIRCULAR LETTER from CHARLES II. to the NOBLES and GENTLEMEN of SCOTLAND.[1]

CHARLES R.—Trusty and welbeloved, We greete you well. We have received so good informacion of your affection and zeale to our service, that we are most confident you will most gladly embrace any opportunity to contribute your utmost endeavours to the advancement thereof, and to the recovery of your countrey from the oppression, misery, and dishonor it now groanes under, by the insolence and tyranny of our English rebels, who propose to themselves the absolute change of the whole Government thereof, and the extirpation of the ancient Nobility and Gentry of that our Kingdome, and the entire subjecting it to their arbitrary and lawlesse jurisdiction, which every true Scotchman must from his heart abhorre. And therefore we have appointed Lieutenant Generall Middleton (to whose fidelity and conduct we have committed the managery of that great affaire) to communicate our purpose unto you,

---

[1] Clarendon Manuscripts, vol. xliii. f. 178.

that we are resolved to leave no way unattempted on our part, whereby we may suppresse those wicked rebels, and relieve our good subjects of that Kingdome. For the better and more effectuall doing whereof, We desire you to give him your best assistance, in such manner, as upon conference with him, or with any person intrusted by him to you, he shall make appeare unto you to be most conducing thereunto; and whatsoever part you shall beare in this good worke, upon information given us, by our said Lieutenant Generall, We shall for the present acknowledge; and gratify and reward, assoone as it shalbe in our power. And so we bid you heartily farewell.

Given at the Louvre, in Paris, the 25th of June 1652, In the fourth yeare of our Reigne.

XXIV

A Letter from Charles II. to the Moderator of the General Assembly.[1]

I am well assured that you who have the conscience in this time of persecution to undergoe the place and the service you now are in, cannot be without the courage to be willinge to receave a letter from me, how dangerous soever our Common enemies have made it to you; and I could not give my selfe leave to be sylent at a time, when you may do God and your King so much service, without telling you how much I rely upon you, and am concern'd in you, and comforted by the constancy of your affections to me, which your greatest enemies acknowledg and reproach you with: The eyes of very many are upon you, to observe how farr the threats and violence of prophain and prosperous rebells can prevaile to make men weary of the conscience for which they suffer so much, and to introduce sacralidg, neglect, contempt, hindring and opposeing the worship and ordinances which God hath appointed: But I am most confident, that as you, and they who joyne with you, are your selves eminent examples of walking stedfastly in performeing of your duties, so you will leave no good means unpracticed to keep up the spirits of those who are ready to faint, and to

---

[1] Clarendon Manuscripts, vol. xliii. f. 226. To Mr. David Dick presumably.

encourage them to suffer with the goodnes of their cause; and not to be ashamed of it, or a shame to it, by uncomfortable, unwise, unfruitfull, and offensive walkeinge, or backslideing from it. Commend me to your fellow labourers, and assure them that I am not negligent in the discharge of my duty in endeavoureing all the probable wayes for their releife, of which I hope they will shortly find some effect. In the meane time God Almighty give us all grace to make the right use of, and to be the better and the wiser for, theis heavy afflictions with which he thinks fitt to exercise us, and that we may do as in his sight whatever we pretend to do in his service, which is the constant prayer of your very lovinge freind, C. R.

St. Germains, Aug. 5th, 1652.

Addressed:—*For the Reverend the Moderator of the Generall Assembly.*

XXV

ARTICLES of AGREEMENT betweene ARCHIBALD, LORD MARQUESSE of ARGISLE, on the behalf of himself and freinds on the one parte, And MAJOR GENERALL RICHARD DEANE on the behalf of the Parliament of the Commonwealth of England on the other side.[1]

1. Itt is agreed, and the said Lord Marquesse doth heerby oblige himself, that his Lordshippe shall neither directly, nor indirectly, act or contrive any thinge to the prejudice of the Parliament of the Commonwealth of England, their forces or aucthority exercised in Scotland, but shall live peaceably and quietlie under the said Governement, and shall use the utmost of his indeavours that his children and family shall doe the same. And if any walke otherwise his Lordshippe, uppon cognizance therof, shall forthwith make itt knowne to the cheif Officers of the next Garrison, or the Commander in cheif in Scotland. Itt being alwayes intended, that this shall nott hinder his Lordshippes good endeavours for the establishing

---

[1] Clarke Manuscripts, vol. xxiv.

religion according to his conscience. Provided itt bee nott by acting or contriving any way of hostility or force in the least manner against the aforesaid aucthority.

2. Itt is agreed, and the Lord Marquesse of Argile doth heerby oblige himself, that hee shall use the utmost of his endeavours, that the Inhabitants of the shire of Argile, and all others, either vassalls or tenants, that hold land of or have dependance uppon his Lordshippe, shall deport themselves conforme to what his Lordshippe is engaged for himself in the preceding Article.

3. Itt is agreed, and the Marquesse of Argile doth heerby oblige himself, that either his Lordshippe or his Eldest sonne the Lord of Lorne (whether of them the Parliament shall thinke fitt) shall, uppon notice given to his Lordshippe, repaire into England to such convenient place as the Parliament or Councell of State shall appoint, and nott remove from thence without leave: Provided they bee nott confined to lesse then 20 miles compasse, and may have leave to waite on the Parliament and Councell of State, as their occasions shall require.

4. And in consideration of the premises, Major Generall Deane doth heerby oblige himself in the name of the Parliament of the Commonwealth of England, That the said Lord Marquesse of Argile shall enjoy his liberty, estate, lands, and debts, and whatever duty belongs unto him, free from sequestration or molestation from the Parliament of the Commonwealth of England, or any by aucthority for them. Provided alwayes that this shall nott extend to the freing of the said Lord Marquesse or his estate from paying Assesse or other publique burthens proportionable with other the good people under the Parliaments protection, nor any of his Houses from Garisoning if there shall bee neede, except Inverary and Carrick, which shall nott bee garrison'd but uppon extraordinary necessity.

> In confirmation wherof wee have severally and interchangeably obliged our selves as abovesaid, witnesse our hands and seales this 19th day of August, one thousand six hundred and fifty-two.

Memorandum, before the signing and sealing of this itt is agreed, that after notice given, there shall bee a monthes time att least allowed for the Lord Marquesse of Argile, or his son the Lord of Lorne, to prepare for their journey into England.

Ri. Deane.
A. Argyll.[1]

XXVI

Charles the Second's Instructions to General Middleton.[2]

Instructions for our trusty and welbeloved Lieutenant Generall, John Middleton.

Aug. $\frac{2}{12}$. 1. Since we have committed the whole conduct of our affaires with reference to our kingdome of Scotland to your discretion and managery, and soe have left the time and season of making any attempt there, and what is to be done preparatorily in order thereunto, entirely to your wisedome, we must rather expect such particular advertisements from time to time from you as may enable us to give you future direccions, then for the present give you any particular and positive instruccions, other then that you use your best diligence in keeping correspondence, and getting intelligence with our subjects of Scotland, and that you soe manage your publique and private negociacion upon the severall letters we have committed to you, that if it be possible this Winter may not be passed over with out endeavouring to releive our subjects of that Kingdome from the oppression they groane under.

---

[1] The newspaper entitled *Severall Proceedings in Parliament*, for September 2-9, 1652, publishes Argyll's formal acceptance of the Union of England and Scotland.

A Declaration by the Marquis of Argyle.

'My duty to Religion, according to my Oath in the Covenant always reserved, I doe agree (for the Civill part) of Scotland being made a Commonwealth with England, That there be the same Government without King or House of Lords derived to the people of Scotland, and that in the mean time while this can be practicable I shall live quietly under the Parliament of the Commonwealth of England and their authority.

August 12, 1652. *Sic subscribitur*, Argyle.'

[2] Clarendon Manuscripts, xliii. 249.

2. When you come into Holland, and resort to the Haghe, you shall conferr with Secretary Nicholas, and understand from him (whom we will direct to communicate freely with you) the state of affaires there, and though it be not yet time for any thing to be directly offer'd by us, or proposed to those States in our Name, yet you shall advise together, how in a secret way they may be taught to know what vast advantages they may receive by us in our Kingdome of Scotland, and if any particular person of the States, whom you shall understand to be wel-affected to us, shall desire to speake with you for his better informacion in that point, you shall, as of your selfe, deele freely with him, in presenting the benefitt that might accrew to them, and of the facility of putting them in possession of that benefit, still reserving your selfe from entring into any particular treaty till applicacion be first made to us, and our approbacion and commands be knowne therein.

3. You shall direct any of those letters we have entrusted you with to any particular wel-affected person of our Scotch subjects, or to any corporacion or community of them, and you shall use your utmost power to perswade them to assist us with the loane of moneys, or with ammunicion and armes, whereby we may be enabled to free their Country from the servitude and dishonour it suffers under, and you shall assure them from us, that noe part of the money they shall soe lend or disburse to that purpose, shall be employed otherwise then to that service. And to that end, if either our subjects from Scotland, or any considerable part of them in any forraigne parts, shall desire to appoint treasurers for the receipt and yssuing thereof, you shall gratify them therein, and when they have nominated such persons to you for that service, whom you doe approve of, you shall by vertue of the power we have given you, grant them such commissions as are necessary.

4. You shall acquaint such of our subjects of that Nation who live under the proteccion of Forraigne Princes and States, how farr it will be from that affection and duty which they owe to their King and Country, if they shall in this time, wherein they both suffer so much, absteyne from assisting them in a liberall proporcion towards their restauracion. You shall informe them how liberally that Nation, living under the King

of Poland, did by the direction of that Prince supply us the last Summer, and that we make noe question but we could procure the like orders from other Princes and States, but that we chuse rather to proceede with them in this manner by your solicitacion, and to depend upon their owne voluntary affeccions. And you shall particularly let those of Sprusia, under the Marquis of Brandenburgh, know that we doe not looke for the lesse complyance from them, for our not pressing them upon the former order from the King of Poland, which was, and still is, in our power to doe.

5. You shall, upon the experience your self have had of their good affeccions and inclinacions to our service, or upon the testimony of such whose integrity is knowne to you, or upon their expressions of their present readynesse and disposicion to serve us, give those proteccions we have entrusted you with to Marchants of that Nation, who trade for Scotland or other places, by which meanes we hope you will still have good intelligence from that Kingdome, and likewise receive other advantages.

6. Whereas we are now sending an Ambassador into Germany in hopes to procure an assistance of men and money from thence, we would not that you should treat for money with any Princes of the Empyre, otherwise then as the same is to be raysed by and amongst our Scotch subjects, nor that you endeavour to make any publique leavyes of men, by the license of any of the Princes, least any overtures of that kinde prejudice the negociacion of our said Ambassadour.

7. You shall employ such persons whom you judge fitt to those Princes, to which you cannot conveniently resort yourselfe, and give them such instruccions upon the matter of those we have given you, as you thinke requisite, all which they are to observe as punctually as if they received them under our owne signe manuall, and you shall deduct out of such moneys as shall be collected for our service, and to our use, all such charges as you shall be at, whereof you shall keepe a true account to be presented to our self only. And you shall likewise out of the said moneys make such allowances to the persons you imploy, and to all other messengers, as in your

discrecion you thinke reasonable. For all which this shall be your warrant.

Given at St. Germains the 19th day of August 1652.[1]

XXVII

A News-Letter from Leith.[2]

Leith, October 16, 1652.

For Newes wee have nothing considerable that I can give a particular accompt of. Something hath beene lately done by Capt. Mutlo, and the ships that wente to him with releife, on the Highlanders, which in generall is, that Capt. Mutlo sallied out of Dunstafness after his men were refreshed with the supplies sent them, and fell uppon the Highlanders who beseiged them, and tooke and kill'd diverse of them. The ship that brought the supplies landed some men in an Island neare Cantire, and burnt the Highlanders corne and howses in it. They yet beseige Dunstafness and Dunollie, though at a farther distance, and releive their number once a month. There hath beene some disputations betwene som ministers of regements heare and some Scotch Ministers, which may tend to the discovery of truith. There was a dispute began in Couper in Fife, on Tuesday last, betwene one Mr. Browne, Chapline to Coll. Fairfax Regiment, and one Mr. James Wood, a Scotch

---

[1] Middleton is described by Hyde to Nicholas, August 23, 1652, as the most trustworthy of Scots. 'He is as worthy a person as ever that nation bred, of great modesty, courage, and judgment. . . . He is the person to whose conduct his Majesty commits the entire conduct of all his hopes of and in Scotland, and upon my word is worthy of any trust.' 'He seems to be,' answered Nicholas, 'indeed a very modest and discreet person, such as I have not yet met with of his nation;' but at the same time expressed his belief that 'Glengarry will not take it well to have any man be put to have a superior command to him in the Highlands, he having with his party and friends kept it so bravely hitherto against all the forces of the rebels of England.' Hyde retorted that Glengarry himself was scarcely fit for supreme command. 'All who know that man believe him honest and stout, but neither a soldier, nor a wise man, nor indeed a man of interest, there being many in those parts, and some who are now in arms with him, of more power and authority' (7th December 1652).—*Clarendon State Papers*, vol. iii. pp. 91, 122; *Nicholas Papers*, vol. i. p. 319.

[2] Clarke Manuscripts, xxiv. 34.

Minister. Many people were present, but the discourse was referd till Thursday following, uppon these 3 heads, viz.: whither Addam by his sinn contracted uppon mankind a temporall death only, or a spirituall and eternall death; 2, whither infants babtisme be gronded uppon the word of God or noe. 3, Consernin universal Redemption. Thurday last they againe mett, where 2 of these points, viz.: Accompte of death of Addam, and universall Redemption, were more calmely discoursed uppon, and all though the Disputers were not convinc't, yet it's hoped a good seed is sowne which will sprout foort[h] in such of the Auditors who ar enquirers after truith. Yesterday the Commissioners for Administration of Justice sat at Edenburgh about prepairing thing[s] for theire sitting uppon Criminall Matters the 20° instant.

XXVIII

Lieutenant-General Middleton to the Count of Oldenburg.[1]

Oct. 18. Monseigneur,—Ayant receu une letre du Roy de la Grande Britagne, pour vostre Excellence, J'avois l'intentione d'avoir eu l'honneur moy mesme en la presentant de baiser tres humblement les maines de vostre Excellence, mais ayant estè surpris par une maladie extraordinaire, m'a rendu si foible que Je suis du tout incapable de faire un voyage, par cette reason J'ay pris la hardiesse, faire mon excuse en ces peu de mots, et envoyer a son Excellence cet Gentilhomme Collonell Turner[2]

---

[1] Clarendon Manuscripts, xliii. 347.

[2] In Sir James Turner's *Memoirs* (p. 107) he states that he came to Middleton at Breda about September 1652, and found him very sick of a tertian fever. 'Within a month he was in a capacitie to make dispatches, and I was sent with a commission from him, and many letters from the King, to some places in Low Germanie, to seek the assistance of such Scotch gentlemen as I had formerlie been acquainted with in the German warre. . . . I began my journey the first of November 1652. . . . In Februare next I returned to the Generall, bringing with me fifteene hundreth dollars. In Aprille 1653, I was sent back to some other places; and that summer I ressaved three thousand foure hundreth dollars, which I sent to the Generall by bill of exchange, retaining for my charges so much as he was pleasd to allow me. What I had done encouraged him to send his brother-

avec les lettres du Roy, et en tant qu'il y a a cette heure plusieures des fideles sujets Escossoises de sa Majeste en armes contre les rebelles, lesquelles ont envoyè tout maintenant un expres au Roy, tesmoigner leur fidelitè, aussi monstrant le grand manquement qu'ils ont d'armes ammunition et autre necessaires pour la guerre, le soin de la quelle y trouver des remedes m'estant recommendè par le Roy Je me trouve obligè les communiquer a vostre Excellence, comme a un de ses plus favourables et plus puissantes amis, en toutes chosès que vostre Excellence desirera de sçavoir touchant les affaires du Roy, donnez credit au porteur, il vous en informera pleinement, aussi luy donnant telle responce aux letres du Roy, que semblera bon a vostre Excellence, et Je me tesmoigneray tousjours en tout sort de gratitude et humilitè, Monseigneur, le tres humble et tres obeysant serviteur de son Excellence,

Jo. MIDDLETONE.

Breda, le $\frac{18}{26}$ d'octor. 1652.

Addressed: *Au tres Illustre et tres Excellente Prince Monseigneur Le Count d'Oldenburg et Delmenhorst, Signeur de Jever, et Kniphausen.*

XXIX

AN AGREEMENT made betweene MAJOR GENERALL RICHARD DEANE in the name of the Parliament of the Commonwealth of England on the one part, And ARCHIBALD, LORD MARQUESSE of ARGILE, in the behalf of the Gentlemen and Inhabitants of the shire of Argile on the other parte. This 27th day of October 1652.[1]

1. That the Gentlemen and people of Argile, with their Complices and Adherents, doe sett at liberty the English Officers and souldiers now in their custody, and make restitu-

---

in-law, Durhame, to Sueden; where our countrymen contributed for the King's assistance about seven or eight thousand dollars, besides what was got in Holland from well-affected Scotsmen there, and five thousand guldens which the Princesse Royall advanced.'

[1] Clarke Manuscripts, xxiv. 41.

tion of what was taken from them, as alsoe, That they restore the garrisons which they surprized with the horses, armes, ammunicion, and provisions, except such provisions as have bin expended on the souldiers, and such horses as were dead before the signing of this, as alsoe such ammunicion and armes as were spoyled att the surprizing the garrisons.

2. That they lay downe armes, returne to their respective homes, and live quietly for the future.

3. That they pay Assesse according to their ability, proportionable to the rest of the Nation, which said Assesse for the shire of Argile shall nott exceede one Hundred pounds sterling per Mensem, untill a new and common valuacion, and is to begin the first day of July, Anno Domini 1652. And the first payment to bee made the second day of February ensuing $165\frac{2}{3}$, and the times of payment heerafter first of August and 2d of February.[1]

4. In consideration wherof, The Gentlemen and people of the shire of Argile, with their Complices and Adherents, both within and without the shire, shall bee free of all challenge or any prejudice to their persons or estates for their late ariseing in armes against the garrisons and forces of the Parliament of the Commonwealth of England, or for being gather'd and making some stoppe att Glencro [?] of their forces.

5. That noe more garrisons shall bee planted in the shire of Argile then Dunstaffnesse and Dunolly, nor any more forces brought to stay within the said shire of Argile soe longe as they live peaceably, nor march though the said Country without urgent necessity for the peace of the Island, nor make any leavies of men without their consent.

6. That wee shall bee very willing, uppon their future good deportement and peaceable living, to quit the said garrisons that yet remaine in possession, if itt shall appeare advantageous to them; and in the meane time the souldiers shall live quietly and meddle with nothing of the peoples of the Country without paying for itt att such rates as they are usually sold

---

[1] The Sixth Report of the Historical Manuscripts Commission, p. 618, contains four letters from Sir Dugald Campbell of Auchinbreck to the Marquis of Argyll, refusing to take any part in paying the assessments to be levied for the English Government under this agreement.

amongst themselves. And that wee shall not bringe any greater quantity of forses into the garrisons of Dunstafnes and Dunolly then what belong to them att present, being about 120 foote and 12 horsemen, with their officers.

RI. DEANE.
A. ARGILE.[1]

An additional article concerning Loch Heall and Clan Leon.

Wheras there is a clause in the 3d Article of a former Agreement made this present day betweene the Lord Marquesse of Argile, in the behalf of the Gentlemen and Inhabitants of the shire of Argile, and Major Generall Deane, Commander in cheif of the Parliaments of the Commonwealth of England's forces in Scotland, That the Gentlemen and Inhabitants of the said shire of Argile shall pay one Hundred pounds sterling a month Assesse from the 1st of July 1652 forward, untill a new valuacion bee taken, itt is heerby declared, That Clan Leon, nor Loch Heill their nott payment of their proportionable part of the said Assesse of the said shire shall nott bee accompted as a breach on the parte of the said shire, the Major Generall or the Commander in cheif being alwayes free, notwithstanding any clause in the former agreement, to march what forces shall be thought fitt through the Country of Argile and plant what garrisons shall bee needfull in those parts that are refractorie.

Signed the 27th October 1652. RI. DEANE.

XXX

AGREEMENT between MAJOR-GENERAL DEANE and the MARQUESS of ARGYLL concerning his guns.[2]

ITT is agreed betweene Archibald, Lord Marquesse of Argile, and Major Generall Deane, Commander in cheif of the Parlia-

---

[1] A letter from Charles II. to the Marquis of Argyll, dated Oct. 14, 1652, is printed in the Maitland Club's volume of *Letters to the Argyll Family*, 1839, p. 43. From its contents, however, the letter seems to have been written in October 1651, immediately after the escape of the King from England. In that case the date, 'Haghe, this 14 of Oct. 1652,' must be wrong.

[2] Clarke Manuscripts, xxiv. 45.

ments forces in Scotland, this 28 day of October 1652, as followeth.

That the said Lord Marquesse shall cause 16 brasse guns which hee hath in his possession in the Highlands, to bee forthwith putt on board such shipp as Major Generall Deane shall order.

Uppon performance wherof, and receipt produced from the Commander of the said shippe that shall have the said guns aboard, Itt is concluded, That the Lord Marquesse shall receive one shilling, fower pence sterling for each English pound weight of brasse that the said guns shall weigh, and that the said Lord Marquesse shall receive the like for such guns of his as were received by the Major Generall his order out of the House of Carick. And itt is further agreed, That the said Lord Marquesse shall cause to bee putt aboard the aforesaid shippe five Hundred musketts, for each of which musketts soe deliver'd whole and sound hee shall receive eight shillings sterling, and if any shall bee deficient abatement shall bee made according to reason.

The payment for the aforesaid guns and musketts to bee made on this manner, vizte.: one thousand pounds sterling uppon the guns and musketts landing att Aire (or certaine knowledge of their miscarriage), if the said guns, by the Master of the shippes receipt that receiveth them aboard, shall bee judged to weigh soe much as may amount to such a summe or more.

And the remainder to bee paid on the 2d day of February next ensuing $165\frac{2}{3}$. In witnesse wherof wee have sett our Hands and Seales to two of this tenure. Ri. Deane.
A. Argile.

XXXI

Major-General Deane to Captain Mutlow.[1]

Sir,—I desire you will give passes to such persons for trading or passing to Ireland as shall bee desired by the Lord Marquesse of Argile, his Lordshippe having engaged to mee for

---

[1] Clarke Manuscripts, xxiv. 42.

such as [he] shall mention to you to that purpose. And for soe doing this shall bee your warrant, from, Yours, etc.,

R. D.

You are to frame your passes according to the forme inclosed.
Dalkeith, 29 *October* 1652.

Indorsed :—*To Capt. Mutlow, Governour of Dunstaffenage, to give passes to the people of Argile that trade in Ireland.*

XXXII

GENERAL DEANE to the MARQUESS of ARGYLL.[1]

MY LORD,—I have appointed Capt. Weddall and his Lieutenant to receive the garrisons of Lochhead and Tarbott, according to the first Article of our Agreement, made the 27th of this instant; as alsoe I have aucthorized them to receive into possession, and take an accompt of all the armes, horses, amunicion, and provisions, which, according to the said Article, are to bee deliver'd or restored. My desire being, That your Lordshippe will please heerby to take notice of the same, And that the said garrisons may accordingly bee deliver'd uppe to them, and likewise the armes, horses, ammunicion, and provisions aforesaid, with a full account therof, according to our agreement and my instruccions to them in that behalf.—I am, Your Lordshippes very humble servant,   RI. DEANE.

Dalkeith, 29 *October* 1652.
To the Lord Marquesse Argill.

Indorsed :—*To the Marq. of Argill to deliver the armes according to Agreement to Capt. Weddall.*

XXXIII

MAJOR-GENERAL DEANE to the MARQUESS of ARGYLL.[2]

MY LORD,—I have received your Lordshippes from Edinburgh of this day, and that your Lordshippe may perceive how

---

[1] Clarke Manuscripts, xxiv. 43.   [2] *Ibid.* xxiv. 46.

willing I am to give all satisfaccion that may bee, and to take away any occasion that might raise the least scruple, I doe declare, That the meaning of the 5th Article of the Agreement lately made with your Lordshippe, bearing date the 27th of October last, is, That soe longe as the people of the shire of Argile live peaceably and performe what they are bound to on their part in the said Agreement, wee shall bringe noe more forces att all into the said Country but what is agreed to bee in the garrisons, except on some urgent occasions to march through the Country for the peace of the Island, or reducing some that are refractory. The reason why I added reducing those that are refractory is, I should else debarre my self of what is agreed on in the case of the deficiency of Clanleon and Lochheall paying their part of the Assesse due from them in the shire of Argill. RI. DEANE.

Dalkeith, November 6, 1652.
To the Marquesse of Argill.

Indorsed :—*Nov.* 6, 1562.—*To the Marq. of Argile, in explanacion of a 5th Article of the late Agreement of the 27th of October betweene the shire of Argill and him.*

XXXIV

CHARLES II. to LIEUTENANT-GENERAL MIDDLETON.[1]

Paris, Nove. 16.

Nov. 1⁶⁄₈.

MIDDLETON,—I receaved not yours of the 24 of Oct. till the 6 of this month, nor doe I yett heare of the expresse from Scotland, which much troubles me. You will beleeve that I have bene very sorry for your sicknesse, since you know how much it imports me that you have your health. You will find I hope when you come to the Hage, that some care is taken for your necessary supply, which you may be sure I will contineue as much as shall be in my power, and when you know (which you would not thinke) that I have scarce receaved two hundered pistols since you went from me, you will not beleeve that it is my faulte that you have not bene releeved, which trust me

---

[1] Clarendon Manuscripts, xliv. 32. In the King's own hand.

hath troubled me as much as it hath you. Secretary Nicholas will tell you much that is fitt for you to know, and I presume you will quickly finde a way to send reliefe to our frinds : and for God's sake thinke of what is more to be done, for my harte is more sett upon that worke then you imagine, therfore lett me heare constantly from you how it is advanced. All the dispatches you desire shall be speedily sent to you, though the Chancelour will tell you my feares, that some of them will produce little effect, and therfore it may be you will forbeare making use of them, which I leave wholy to your discretion. My Ld. Newbrough will informe you what I have written to Scottland, and I hope you have settled good correspondence there. I longe to be gone from hence, and excpect every day a good occasion to remove, which will be most wellcome to Your constant assured frind, CHARLES R.

Addressed :—*For Lieut. Generall Middleton.*

XXXV

CHARLES II. to LIEUTENANT-GENERAL DOUGLAS.[1]

GENERALL DOUGLASSE,—I have heard from severall persons Nov. $\frac{6}{16}$. so much of your good affection to me, that I cannot but tell you my selfe, that I very much depende uppon it, and will rewarde it when I am able. I know not how the affections of that place wher you are now stande towards me, and therfore cannot well tell how to apply my selfe, or what I may expecte from thence, and therfore I have directed Lnt. Generall Midleton to guyde himselfe by your advice, and to desyre your assistance in what concernes my service, and the redeeminge your Country from the servitude and dishonour it grones under. I pray helpe him, or any who shall come to you from him, all you may, and give me such adverticement and councell as you judge necessary for my affayres, which shall be alwayes very acceptable and wellcome to Your, etc.

Paris, 16 *Nov.* 1652.

---

[1] Clarendon Manuscripts, xliv. 34. Lieut.-Gen. Robert Douglas, who was in the Swedish service. *Calendar of the Clarendon Papers,* vol. ii. pp. 156, 186, 255, 256. This letter is printed from Hyde's copy.

XXXVI

CIRCULAR LETTER from MAJOR-GENERAL DEANE to the COMMANDERS of the ENGLISH FORCES in SCOTLAND.[1]

SIR,—I have received orders from the Councell of State for my speedy repaire to London, as alsoe authority and positive commands from his Excellency the Lord Generall to make all possible hast, and leave the charge of the forces in Scotland with such as are present uppon the place. And in obedience therunto I have appointed Col. Robert Lilburne to take the charge and command of all the forces in Scotland, wherof I thought fitt to give you the intimacion, desiring that you will observe and follow such orders and instruccions as you shall receive from the said Col. Lilburne in my absence accordingly, untill my Lord Generall shall send a Commander in cheif uppon the place to give further order therin. And heerof I desire you will nott faile.—Your loving freind, R. D.

Dalkeith, 12*th Dec.* 1652.

To the Colonells of the severall Regiments and Commanders of the severall Garrisons in Scotland.

XXXVII

COMMISSION from MAJOR-GENERAL DEANE to COLONEL OVERTON.[2]

SIR,—Wheras his Excellency the Lord Generall Cromwell hath laid commands uppon mee to make all possible speede to London, and to leave the forces heere in the best posture I can, I doe, in pursuance of the said order, and according to the aucthority given mee, heerby constitute and appoint you to command all the forces in the West parts of Scotland round

---

[1] Clarke Manuscripts, xxiv. 71. Deane had been summoned to England by order of the Council of State (Dec. 4) in order to serve as one of the generals at sea in the war with the Dutch. He was killed in the battle of 3rd June 1653.

[2] Clarke Manuscripts, xxiv. 86.

about, quartering in the shires of Dumfreeze, Wigton, Kircowbright, Galloway, Aire, Lanerick, Peblis, Renfrew, and Dunbarton: That is to say, The Regiments of Col. Okey, Col. Alured, Col. Rede, with your owne Regiment, and the troopes of dragoones of Col. Morgan that quarter in those parts: The which you are to order and dispose the most convenient way for securing of the country, preserving the peace, and the Parliament's interest. The severall officers and souldiers of the said Regiments, troopes, and companies, being heerby required respectively to observe your orders from time to time, and your self is desired to follow such directions as you shall receive from Col. Robert Lilburne. And for the better manageing and regulating the aforesaid forces under your command, you are heerby aucthorized to call Councells of Warre, consisting of the Commission officers of the Regiments above mentioned, or soe many of them as you shall see cause to call together, and with them to proceede to give sentence uppon any malefactor according to the lawes Martiall allowed by Parliament, and to cause execution to bee done accordingly. And for the premisses this shall bee your warrant.

Given under my hand and seale att Dalkeith the 30th day of December 1652. R. D.

The like Commission for Col. Morgan to command the forces on the North side Tay.

XXXVIII

Instructions for Col. Overton.

1. You shall receive heerwith orders to command all the forces in the West parts of Scotland, vzte.: your owne Regiment, Col. Okey's, Col. Rede's, Col. Alured's, and the Troopes of Dragoones quartered in those parts which assoone as you have, I desire you will repaire thither, and take the charge and care of them accordingly.

2. I desire, That you will nott draw any of the forces out of Aire, but leave them to the Governour, Col. Alured's direction, Except uppon extraordinary occasion.

3. You shall heerwith receive orders to dispose of all shippes

and vessells that shall come into Dunbarton-Fryth belonging to the State, as you shall finde most for the service of the Parliament of the Commonwealth of England, which you are heerby desired to doe accordingly.

4. Wheras you have made knowe unto mee your extraordinary occasions for your repaire into England for to follow some businesse of your owne, you shall heerwith receive a passe for your going thither some six weekes or 2 monthes hence, or when the affaires heere will permitt you; and when you shall conceive itt a fitt time or season soe to doe, I desire you will acquaint Col. Lilburne with itt, who is aucthorized to take care of all the forces in Scotland untill my Lord Generall shall appoint a Commander in Cheif, that he may take a more particular care of those Garrisons in the West in your absence.

Dated att Dalkeith the 30th of December 1652.   R. D.

XXXIX

Instructions for Col. Morgan.

1. You shall heerwith receive a Commission to command all the forces on the North side the River Tay, which assoone as you have, and that you have deliver'd an account of the businesse you are imployed on att present to Col. Overton (if he come into those parts where you are before your returne), as alsoe to Col. Lilburne (who hath the charge of all the forces in Scotland, during the absence of a Commander in Cheif), you are to repaire into the Northerne parts, and take the best care you can that the said forces bee lodged and quartered as safe as conveniently you may, and to that purpose you are to repaire to Col. Lilburne before your going, to have his directions and advice concerning itt.

2. You are from time to time to give to Col. Lilburne an accompt of all your proceedings in these parts, and observe such further orders as you shall receive from him.

3. I desire you will have a speciall care of Invernesse in the absence of the Governour, and that you draw none of the forces out of that place, except uppon emergent necessities, but bee assisting and helping to them in what you may.

4. For your better inabling to travaile to and fro in this your charge you shall receive a warrant from Col. Lilburne, signed both by himself and me, directed to the payment of contingencies to pay unto you 6s. 8d. a day for as many dayes as you shall continue in this employment untill a Commander in Cheif shall arrive on the place and further order given. Given under my hand att Dalkeith the 30th day of December 1652. R. D.

XL

A Commission from Charles II.[1]

Charles R.

Charles by the grace of God King of England, Scotland, Dec. 22 France, and Ireland, Defender of the Faith, etc. To our trusty and welbeloved Sir James Macdonald Laird of Sleite, Angus Macdonald, Laird of Glengary, John Cameron, Laird of Lougheil,   Macdonald, Laird of Cappoche, Fraser, Laird of Foyer, Donald Gorme Macdonald and to every one of them Greeting. Whereas We are informed that divers of our good and welaffected subjects of our Kingdome of Scotland out of their duty and affeccion to Us, and

---

[1] Clarendon Manuscripts, vol. xliv. p. 223. The Commission is written on vellum. The reasons for its sending are thus explained by Hyde:—'The messenger, Captain Smith, who came from Scotland, is at last come hither, and we shall dispatch him as soon as possible, and all his commissions and other matters shall be sent to the Lord Lieutenant-General, that if he likes he may deliver them, if not, suppress them. The method we intend is to send so many commissions of Colonels, in every one of which there shall be a reference of obeying such orders as they shall receive from Middleton, and because it will be impossible for them to keep together or do any great matter, if they be all of equal authority, and it may be Middleton will not be willing to send them any positive orders till he go himself, I am preparing a commission to the Chiefs of the Clans (who are up in arms) constituting them a Council of War, and authorising them to choose a person to command in chief upon all expeditions in the absence of Middleton, and to perform anything else which shall be requisite for the service, with such instructions as may prevent all factions; this is the best way we can think of, and if Middleton does not like it he may suppress it.' Hyde to Nicholas, Nov. 22, 1652, *Clarendon State Papers*, vol. iii. p. 119. On the strength of the rising in the Highlands and the desires of its leaders, see *Nicholas Papers*, vol. i. p. 314.

their tender zeale and respect to the interest and honour of their Country, now groaning under the heavy yoke of Oppression and Tyranny by the strength, power, and successe of the cruell and bloody Rebells of our Kingdome of England, have put themselves in armes, and drawne into a body, and with notable courage have opposed the said Rebells, and forced them to retire from severall places, whereof they were possessed, and that many other of Our good subjects are willing and ready to joyne with them to the same good end and purpose, if they may be encouraged thereunto. And whereas We have appointed Our trusty and welbeloved subject and servant Lieutenant Generall John Middleton (who, We are well assured, for his knowne and tryed fidelity to Us, and his approved skill in martiall affaires, is most acceptable to all Our well affected subjects of that Our Kingdome, of what quality and condicion soever), to repayre thither, and to governe, leade, and conduct the said forces, as soone as such supplyes can be provided as are necessary, and as We intend to send with him; And in the meane time We have thought it fitt and requisite for Our service to depute and appoint some discreete and able persons to take care and charge of those who are already in armes, and to give them authority to doe all such things as are in order to the advancement of Our service, and preparing and carrying on soe good a worke. Now know yee, that We, reposing spetiall trust and confidence in the affeccion, wisedome, integrity, and courage of you the said Sir James Macdonald, Laird of Sleite, Angus Macdonald, Laird of Glengary, John Cameron, Laird of Loughcil,   Macdonald, Laird of Cappoch,   Fraser, Laird of Foyre, Donald Gorme Macdonald

And of every of you, have made, constituted, and appointed, and doe by these presents make, constitute, and appoint yee Our Commissioners for the ordering, governing, and disposing the said forces, which now are, or hereafter shall be drawne together for Our service, And We give full power and authority to you, or any three of you (during the absence of the said Lieutenant Generall Middleton, and untill he shall land in that Our Kingdome of Scotland), to make choice of any one Person whom you shall judge to be most fitt to command the said forces in cheife, and to conduct them against the enemy, and to execute to all purposes the office of Commander in Cheife, And We require all persons to give such obedience unto the said Person who shall be soe chosen by you (untill the said Lieutenant Generall Middleton shall arrive) as if he were chosen and nominated by Us, that soe Our service may be advanced, and the Rebells as much damnifyed as is possible, And We doe hereby likewise give you full power and authority during the time aforesaid to make such Orders for the leavying of men, raysing of money, seizing upon, and securing the persons of those who are disaffected to Our service, and who keepe intelligence or correspondence with the Rebells, without leave from you or the major part of you, as you judge requisite for Our service, and to make choice of, and to establish a fitt number of good and able officers, as a Councell of Warr, to proceede in all cases according to the knowne Articles and Custome of Warr, upon such occasion as shall happen and aryse proper for the same, Provided that in all things you observe such instruccions as We now send, or hereafter shall send to you, And that this Our Commission shall be determined as soone as Lieutenant Generall Middleton shall give you notice of his being landed in any part of that Our Kingdome, from which time you are punctually to observe all such orders and directions as you shall receive from him. Given at the Palais Royall in Paris the 30th day of December 1652. In the fourth yeare of Our Raigne.

Indorsed :—*Dec.* 30, 1652.

Commission to Sir James MacDonald, etc.

XLI

Instructions to the Commissioners[1]

Charles R.

Instructions for Our trusty and welbeloved Sir James Macdonald, Laird of Sleite, Angus Macdonald, Laird of Glengary, John Cameron, Laird of Logheil,   Macdonald, Laird of

---

[1] Clarendon Manuscripts, vol. xliv. p. 225.

Cappoche, Fraser, Laird of Foyre, Donalde Gorme Macdonald.

Commissioners appointed by Us for the present governing of the Forces now in Armes for Us in the Highlands in Scotland, and for advancing Our service in that Our Kingdome.

1. Since you cannot but looke upon the heavy persecution and great calamityes which that Our Kingdome of Scotland, and Our subjects thereof, at present groanes under, as an effect of God's just anger against Us all, for all our sinnes and offences against him, we must in the first place require you to demeane your selves with that humility, piety, and devotion, and to exercise that true repentance towards God Almighty in all your actions, that may render him propitious to you, and drawe downe a blessing from him upon the great worke you goe about, and that by striking terrour into the prowde hearts of your Enemyes, he may make you, as his chosen People, the instruments to abate and destroy their tyranny, and to restore your Country to its antient honour, happynesse, and prosperity.

2. Since you cannot undertake any notable service against the Enemy, except you drawe all your Forces into a Body, nor then, except you unite them by good disciplyne under the government and command of some one Person, who may lead and conduct them, and whose orders they must precisely obey, therefore you shall meete all together, if with conveniency you may, and make choice of some one Person to be Commander in Cheif of all the Forces (during the absence, and untill Lieutenant Generall Middleton shall arrive in that Kingdome) whom all the rest shall obey, and you shall put that power of Commander in Cheife into his hands, either for one particular expedition, or for a prefixed time, or indefinitely, untill the comming of Lieutenant Generall Middleton, or further orders from Us, as you shall judge to be most fitt for Our service; and whosoever the said Person shall be, We presume he will always take the advice and councell of you our said Commissioners, aswell in the forming any designe, as in all other affaires of moment; and though any act done by any three of you shall be as good and valid, as if it were with the consent and approbacion of all, yet We desire that you should be all present at the Election of such Commander in Cheife, and at the delibera-

cion of all matters of great importance, if you may be soe with conveniency, however, that all have notice to be present when that or any transaccion of moment is intended to be done.

3. You shall proceede in all your actions without any faction and personall animosityes, suppressing all antient grudges and differences which may have been formerly, and be heartily united with and to all who heartily desire to advance Our service, and to free your Country from the servitude it now suffers under, which being the common cause, is to be only and zealously intended, remembring that your enemyes will not make lesse use of any divisions and differences which shall happen amongst your selves for your owne destruccion, then of their armyes, and hope to compasse it sooner by the former then by the latter.

4. Because We have not a full informacion of the present state and condicion of that Our Kingdome, and know well that very many of Our wel-affected subjects there, are for the present compelled to submitt to the power of the Rebells, and to live in their quarters, and yet nevertheless We doubt not will be very ready as soone as an opportunity shall be offred, to engage themselves in Our service, and may in the meane time be of great use to it, in keeping secrett intelligence and correspondence with you, or some of you, and because it may be very dangerous to any to have their names inserted in this, or any other Commission from Us, who are not actually engaged in armes with you, and soe in a condicion to secure themselves, and many may be in armes with you since We heard last from you, whom We would joyne with you in this Our Commission if We were assured of the same. Therefore Our pleasure is, that you first, and as often as new occasion shall require it, by the comming in of any persons of principle, quality, and interest to joyne with you, make choice of such persons, whom you thinke fitt to be joyned with you in this Commission, and upon such choice made by you, or the major part, such person and persons shall be held and reputed Our true and lawfull Commissioners with you, to all intents and purposes, as if he or they had been nominated and inserted by Ourselfe in this Our Commission.

5. Whereas we have sent severall Commissions for Colonells,

Lieutenant Colonells, Serjeant Majors, and Captaines, with blancks for the names of the persons, We do intrust and authourize you in the manner aforesaid to make choice of fitt and able persons for the said severall commands, and having soe done, to insert the names of the men soe chosen by you in the said Commissions according to the quality of the command which you assigne to them, and thereupon to deliver Our Commissions to them; In the choice of which persons We presume you will proceede with justice and equity, according to their meritt, experience, or interest; all which We doe referr to your discretion.

6. Whereas nothing can be more advantagious to you in many respects then the resorting of shipps of warr to your harbors and coast, and We have adviced many Captains who have Our Commissions, and have likewise invited the men of warr of the States of the United Provinces, to visit the ports of Scotland, which are out of the power of the Rebells. You must be very carefull and industrious to give all encouragements to them; And if any Captains of shipps shall desire in respect of the prizes which are to be taken upon those Seas, to settle and fortify any Island or Port of those Our dominions, you shall doe well to consent to any reasonable priviledges and immunityes they desire, and what you shall doe therein We shall confirme and ratify.

7. You shall keepe intelligence with Lt. Generall Middleton, to give him informacion from time to time of your condicion, which you are likewise to doe with Our right trusty and right welbeloved Cosen the Lord Viscount Newburgh, who being with Us, shall let Us know your advices and desires, and shall transmitt Our pleasure to you by all such opportunityes and conveyances as shall be offred.

8. You shall observe such further instruccions as We shall hereafter finde fitt and seasonable to send you.

Given at the Palais Royall in Paris, the 30th day of December 1652. In [the] fourth yeare of our Raigne.

Indorsed:—*Dec.* 30, 1652.

Instructions to Sir James M'Donald, etc.

XLII
A Letter from Col. Lilburne.[1]

Honoured Sir,—These late orders for remanding of prisoners and reducing the souldiers come very thicke [and] something unseasonable uppon mee: and though I had never soe great abilities to act what I am required, [it will] bee impossible for mee to dispatch itt within that time appointed, nor I thinke can the accounts bee compleated in att least a fortnight or three weeks time; and how hard a thinge itt is unto the poore souldiers, especially those that lie farre North and have noe arreares due to them, to disband after they are mustered, which now they will bee before my orders can reach them (though I have sent to stoppe the muster), and have noe consideration att all thereuppon, nor any thinge to beare their charges in their travailes, you cannott your selfe but bee sensible of itt; and though providence hath freed you from that clamour that might fall out in these hard conditions putt uppon them, yet I hope you will both sympathize with them and mee soe farre as to improve your interest in the poore souldiers behalfes in procuring a fortnights pay, or some small allowance more, towards their charges homeward. I know nott whome to direct my lines to that can or will bee soe sensible of these thinges as your self, and were I nott very confident of your candor heerin I should nott presume to give you this trouble, but however, whether there bee a possibility of prevayling or nott heerin, which I hope there may, either out of contingencies or some way, I intend, God willing, to observe those instructions I have received as farre as I am able with all possible expedicion; and what you have desired concerning your owne troope (if you had nott said a worde to mee in your letter) I should nott have forgotten what you formerly hinted unto mee concerning them, nor forgett those obligations laid uppon, Sir, your reall and most humble servant.

Postscript.—I have acquainted his Excellency with these particulars, and hope hee will befreind the poore souldiers heerin.

---

[1] Clarke Manuscripts, lxxxvi. 4.

I hope before this overtake you, you and your good Lady and all your good companie are safelie arrived att London, which I should rejoyce to heare, to whom I desire to present my very kind respects and service.[1]

I desire further instructions concerning the quarterment of draught horses, and the number of waggoners and horses that are to bee disbanded heere, and how the horses shall bee disposed.

XLIII

Col. Lilburne to the Lord General Cromwell.[2]

May itt please your Excellencie,—I am in some straightes wherin I humbly intreate your Excellencies further command, whether itt shall bee Lt. Generall Monke's Company or the Comptrollers that must bee disbanded, that your Excellencie will bee pleased to signify your pleasure heerin with as much expedition as may bee. In the interim I have issued out orders to reduce one hundred of the souldiers out of both Companies. And further I humbly intreat to know your pleasure, whether a Colonell of foote's Company and the Feild officers of a Regiment of foote shall have noe more men in their Companies then a private Captaine, which in my poore judgement I thinke would bee best, and there will bee something saved to the State in itt, for then the Feild Officers Companies will neede noe more sergeantes or corporalls then a private Company. I must humbly intreate your Excellency further (which I have already writt to your Excellency about) to signify your pleasure concerning some further allowance after the 10th of January for the reduc't men, the want of which will bee a very sad thinge, and I feare of ill consequence, for itt will bee about 3 weekes or a month before Col. Saunders men, Col. Fitche's men, and some of my owne can come to Leith to have their accounts stated, though orders were issued out the

---

[1] Probably written to Major-General Deane, who had just left Scotland to take command of the fleet. He left Dalkeith on 28th December 1652. Lilburne's letters are printed from rough draughts in a letter-book, unsigned and full of corrections and alterations.

[2] Clarke Manuscripts, lxxxvi. 7.

day after I received them. Pardon mee, my Lord, if again I begge of you your cordiall favour and assistance in the poore souldiers' behalf, and that itt may nott slippe out of your memory, some of them having neere 400 miles to travaile and nott one penny in their purses.[1]—I remayne, your Lordshippes most faithfull and humble servant.

Dalkeith, 8 January.

XLIV

COL. LILBURNE to the COUNCIL of STATE.[2]

MAY ITT PLEASE YOUR HONOURS,—Receiving this inclosed account from Mr. Sandilands,[3] who I finde very diligent in the inquirie after those woods in this Nation that may be usefull to the Commonwealth, and in finding out a way to promote the worke, something that hee reports I know to bee very true, and I thinke the thinge may bee very feasible if artists had itt in hand that understand those things. I have endeavour'd to gaine an estimate of the charge from him, and to bringe the thinge to some certainty, that if you have occasion to use pitch or tarre, or masts or such thinges you might know exactly what every particular would stand you in, but in this hee falls shorte att present, yet is endeavouring to gaine a more exact account, the which if you thinke fitt to incourage, and to send mee your commands I shall study to improve all opportunities to my duty as Your most faithfull servant.

Dalk. 15° Jan. 1652.

I suppose Major Generall Deane is able to advise a little in this businesse.

Since I writt this I understand there are some officers of the army that desire to buy the Faulcon frigott att Leith, and to send her out as a man of warr. I doe conceive itt may bee the

---

[1] See *Cal. S. P. Dom.*, 1653-4, pp. 107, 114, for the response to this request.
[2] Clarke Manuscripts, lxxxvi. 9.
[3] An account of Andrew Sandelands is given in Masson's *Life of Milton*, vol. iii. pp. 487-494, v. 227, 706; and references to his plan for utilising the woods of Scotland for the benefit of the navy of the Commonwealth are to be found in the *Calendar of the State Papers*, 1652-3, pp. 241, 453. A longer letter of Lilburne's on the subject of his proposals is contained in the same volume, p. 178.

best way soe to dispose of her, but shall humbly submitt to your further commands about her, which I intreate I may receive assoone as may bee, for I thinke they will give more for her then any other will.

XLV

The Commissioners at Leith to the Speaker.[1]

Right Honorable,—In pursuance of an order of Parliament to us directed, bearinge date the fourteenth of May last past, for the settinge forth five hundred pound per annum of lands of inheritance of the confiscated and forfeited estates in Scotland to Coll. Ric. Ingloseby,[2] wee have caused to bee surveyed the Manner Howse, the Parke, and part of the land of the Barony of Hamilton, late part of the inheritance of James Duke of Hamilton, which survey being retturned to us uppon oath, wee have further, according to the said order, and in obedience thereunto, sett the same out to Coll. Ric. Ingloseby, and have sent the said survey here inclosed to your Honour to bee presented to the Parliament.—Wee are, Right Honorable, Your Honours most humble and faithfull Servants,

Ri. Saltonstall.   Sa. Disbrowe.
                   Ed. Syler.

Leith, 18 January 16$\frac{52}{53}$.

Addressed:—*For the Right Honorable Wm. Lenthall, Esq., Speaker of the Parliament of the Commonwealth of England.*

XLVI

Circular Letter from Col. Lilburne to the Commander of the Army in Scotland.[3]

Sir,—The Gentleman (whome these inclosed proposalls concerne) being recommended from divers of the Councell of

---

[1] Tanner Manuscripts, liii. 202.

[2] Lands were voted on the same day to the value of £500 per annum to Colonels Richard Ingoldsby, Robert Overton, and Thomas Pride. But out of the said £500 a rent of £100 was reserved to the use of the State.—*Commons Journal*, vol. vii. p. 132.

[3] Clarke Manuscripts, lxxxvi. 8.

State, as alsoe from the Councell of the army att Whitehall to Major Generall Deane, and by him by reason of his suddaine remove referred unto mee; and being very sensible of the great fruites and emolument that may bee deducted from a worke of such publique importance, both to the present and after ages, mutuallie reflecting both on the honour of the armie and whole nation, I am therfore desirous to recommend the consideration therof to your selfe and officers of your Regiment; as well for furnishing him with such military passages as have come under your or their cognizance or observation in this last expedition, as alsoe unanimously to afford him such free and liberall encouragement as may inable him to carry on this historie, in pursuance wherof hee hath taken this longe journey. And forasmuch as 'tis like to bee an elaborated peece requiring much paines and some time, hee hath promised to continue amonge us, and nott leave Scotland before hee hath given you and the world a full account of this consummated history, which when imprinted is intended to bee taught throughout all the free schooles of England, to the end that future ages may acknowledge and stand amazed att those miraculous providences of the Almighty exhibited to view, in which your selves have bin instrumentall.

Dalkeith, January 21, 1652.

XLVII

PETITION of MAJOR FISHER to MAJOR-GENERAL DEANE.

To the right honorable MAJOR-GENERALL DEANE and the Officers of the Army under His Command and Conduct.

The Proposalls of MAJOR FITZPAINE FISHER.[1]

WHEREAS it hath pleased the indulgent goodnesse of the Almighty with a propitious providence miraculously to Blesse

---

[1] An account of Payne Fisher is given in the *Dictonary of National Biography*. Except a facility in writing Latin verses, he had no qualifications for the task he proposed to undertake, and the history he was 'determined to write' seems never to have been written. The petition is from a printed broadside amongst William Clarke's collections.

this Commonwealth with such unparallel'd victories and successes, both at home and abroad, that shee is like in all probability to become both the Envie and wonder to all Nations. And forasmuch as it might be deemed an Injury to Posterity to conceale those late Mercies and stupendious successes of your armie in Scotland, in so suddenly and beyond all imagination so neere reduceing that Place, your servant therefore, through the late encouragement from the Councill of State, the Generall astipulation [1] of divers learned and well affected persons, together with that sense of duty he owes his Country, is determined to write and faithfully transmitte to Posterity the transactions and matchelesse atcheivements of your armie in this last expedition, as well thereby to inculcat a reverentiall observance in the present, as to kindle the noble sparkes of æmulation and vertue in succeding ages.

To the end therefore that hee may write (as well to the satisfaction of the Councill as of the whole world) the exact truth of those transactions, and Compile them in such a Piece as may in all points become his pen and your Honors patronage, hee hath heereto annexed these proposalls:

1. That being a meere stranger in these Parts, he desires that some competent quarter be assigned him, as well for his present accomodation during his short stay, as the conveniency of his studdies.

2. That it might please the right honorable Major-generall Deane to send out and give orders to every regiment to draw up a compendious abstract of all the military remarkable passages that have Occurr'd in each respective Regiment, from their first advance in this Country to this instant.

3. That a list of all the Commanders be had, as well of those that have deserted as those that still continue in the service, to the end that their names may be perpetuated to posterity, being fixed either in the frontispice or reare as an Appendix to the History, as the right honorable the Lord Whitlock and the rest of the Councill shall appoint.

4. That from every Regiment a topographicall description be drawn (either with ink or black lead) of the most eminent

---

[1] The action of agreeing to a proposal; agreement; bargain.—*New English Dictionary.*

Castles, Cittadells, forts, with their severall situations, as also a slight draught or representation of the chiefest battailes; to the end that they may be afterward more lively ingraven in Copper, to be placed twixt the divisions of each Idilia or section, that thence the History may be illustrated with more perspicuity, being soe set forth and made visibly obvious to all spectatours.

5. Lastly, your servant, in Compensation to his great jorney, paines, perill, and expenses, desires that from every respective Regiment consideration be had, and such an allowance be assigned him, as the said respective officers thereof in discretion shall think meet, and the weight of so great a worke may merit.

XLVIII

Colonel Lilburne to the English Judges in Scotland.[1]

Right Honorable,—Although I am very tender in troubling you with any matters relating to the law, yet being certainly informed of the former faithfull services and sufferinges of Thomas Ker, Laird of Mersington, and having observed his carriage to bee very civill to our force uppon their coming into Scotland, staying att his owne house in the times of the greatest danger, when most others fled and tooke parte with the Enemy, I am induced to represent his condition to you, and desire that you will vouchsafe him all possible favour that lawfully you may, in the granting his desires in the inclosed peticion (the like respect having bin showne to others, and his condition being as sad as any), there seemeing to be very much equity in it, which is the greatest reason of this boldnesse in your very humble servant.

Dalkeith, 28 *January* 1652.

For the right honorable the Comissioners for administracion of justice these, Edinburgh.

---

[1] Clarke Manuscripts, lxxxvi. 14.

XLIX

Charles II. to the Duke of Courland.[1]

Jan. 29.
Feb. 7.

Mon Cousin,—Je ne doute point que vous ne soyez particulierement informé que mes bons sujets en Escosse travaillent à se delivrer de l'oppression tyrannique des rebelles d'Angleterre, et à m'y restablir en mon authorité Royalle ; mais comme leurs forces ne sont pas assez suffisantes pour executer ce juste dessein, ils ont besoin d'estre renforcez d'un bon et puissant secours de gens de guerre, d'armes, de munition, et d'autres choses necessaires pour le mettre en execution ; et comme il y va de mon interest de leur donner toute l'assistance possible pour ce renfort ; je me trouve obligé pour cet effect d'avoir recours non seulement à mes bons amis, mais aussi à tous mes fidelles sujets qui sont affectionnez et interessez à mon restablissement et à la conservation de mes Couronnes : et comme je suis asseuré de la bonne volonté que vous avez tousjours portée à l'avancement de mes affaires, m'en ayant donné des marques signalées en plusieurs rencontres, j'ay estimé que je pouvois bien prendre cette confiance de vous prier et requerir de me vouloir assister en cette occurrence ; c'est pourquoi j'ay donné charge au Sieur de Middleton, mon Lieutenant-General en mon dit Royaume, de faire cet office en mon nom, et de traitter avec mes sujets Escossois qui vivent sous votre jurisdiction, et des autres Princes voisins, pour le dit secours et renfort ; me promettant un heureux succez de sa negotiation pour les grandes preuves qu'il a rendues en plusieurs charges honorables où il a esté employé pour mon service de sa prudence, bonne conduite, vaillance, fidelité, et affection au bien d'iceluy ; je vous prie de le vouloir assister de votre authorité, faveur, et protection en cette affaire, et en son absence celuy qui y sera employé de sa part ; et de croire qui je reconnoistray cet effect de vostre amitié, estant veritablement, Mon Cousin, Vostre bien affectionné Cousin,   Charles R.

À Paris ce 7me de Fevrier, 1653.

Addressed :—*A mon Cousin, Monsieur le Duc de Curlande.*

---

[1] Clarendon Manuscripts, xlv. 56 ; *cf.* Clarendon State Papers, iii. 142.

L

Colonel Lilburne to the Lord General Cromwell.[1]

May itt please your Excellency,—Since the former intelligence which I sent by the last expresse, I have had some further account of affaires in Fife from another hand, and I perceive that the contracting of our quarters and recalling of prisoners doth nott only amuse them, but hath begotten great cause of jealousie amongst themselves. I am alsoe told, both from thence, and some letters from Col. Morgan in the north, that there is some kind of agent come from young Charles, that was putt on shoare in Fife by a Dutchman and one of Middleton's brothers, which I am endeavouring to discover aswell as I can. I could nott meete with that red-haired man that the letter made mention of. I have alsoe somethinge from Invernesse, which tells mee that Glengary had a meeting in the Highlands about Straglasse. I perceive hee hath bin tampering [?] with all the cheifs of Clans in and about Loughaber, in the Isles and Northward, but they seeme to bee cautious, and nott to give him any further incouragement then, if hee can prevaile with any of their clans to serve him, to looke through their fingers att him, soe as my intelligence tells mee hee intends to raise 1500 or 2000 men to bee in readinesse uppon a small warning, either to assist a forraigner, or to oppose us if wee undertake a march uppon their confines this Springe. I doe conceive itt is meerly necessity that putts Glengary uppon any of these actions.[2]

Dalkeith, 5 February 165$\frac{2}{3}$.

---

[1] Clarke Manuscripts, lxxxvi. 12.

[2] About this time the English government seems to have received the first intimation that a new war was brewing in the Highlands. Glengarry's suspicious movements are mentioned in *Mercurius Politicus*, under date of Feb. 5 and Feb. 12, 1653. 'About three days agoe,' says a letter from Edinburgh, dated Feb. 12, 'the Marquis of Argile was with Colonel Lilburn, and yesterday he sent him a letter signifying the great and frequent meetings of Glengary with the other Highlanders and Islanders; but what the intent of their meeting may be, he saith he knows not.'—*Mercurius Politicus*, p. 2248; *Spottiswoode Miscellany*, ii. 102. But as early as December 27, the English government had suspended

LI

Col. Lilburne to the Lord General Cromwell.[1]

MAY ITT PLEASE YOUR EXCELLENCY,—I received your Lordshippes letter, and before that came an order from the Councell of State about disbanded souldiers, most wherof were dispatch't before they came, and such as had noe arreares, and were in want of monie to beare their charges home, had 14 dayes pay allowed them for that purpose; but I was in good hopes that those that lie soe farre north, and cannott bee dispatch't till 5 weekes after the 10th of January, might have had some consideration for that time, which I dare nott take uppon mee to give any order in, because I finde noe instructions from your Excellency or any to that purpose; however, I am glad that your Lordshippe has sent advice to Mr. Hatter to take care of those men that come by Yorke, which I doubt will nott bee many, though I am confident abundaunce are gone hence that begges their bread in their way homeward, and hath nott a groate in their purses to live uppon, which mee thinkes does much reflect uppon the honour of the Commonwealth, and somethinge I feare uppon your Excellency and the cheif officers of the army.

Concerning the traine horses, and that quarter (?) that is to bee reduc't, according to your Excellencies instructions I have give order to the Comptroller to performe itt.

Col. Overton sends mee worde, that Glengarry is busy, and hath seized of the Lord Argile's frigott and guns; but I hope itt is nott soe, because I heare hee is more northerly amongst Seaforth's people.

---

the discharge of the Scottish prisoners then in England, and ordered the Commander-in-chief in Scotland to secure all prisoners discharged on bail.—*Cal. S. P. Dom.* 1653-4, pp. 55-6. *Mercurius Politicus* for March 3-10 contains a letter from Dalkeith, March 1, and one from Leith of the same date, intimating that the success of the English fleet against the Dutch had put a stop to the intended rising in Scotland for the present.

[1] Clarke Manuscripts, lxxxvi. 15.

LII
Colonel Lilburne to Colonel Okey.[1]

Sir,—There came to my hands by the post on Saturday last a large packett of printed letters, signed by the appointment of the generall meeting of officers att James's,[2] but the letter signed by your self and Lt. Col. Mason (by some miscarriage) nott coming to mee till this evening, I had noe directions for their disposall. I shall now take care for the speedy dispersing of them to the severall regiments and garrisons, and shall desire that the Lord may direct your Councells, that they may bee to his glory and the good of all men.—I remayn.

Dalkeith, 8 *February* 1652.

Addressed :—*Col. Okey.*

LIII
Colonel Lilburne to Mr. Rowe.[3]

Sir,—I shall nott say very much to you att this time in answer to yours untill I receive that account you intend to send mee the next post, but I conceive itt is something strange that your self and Mr. Smythesby should take uppe such resolutions att this time to quitt that imployment, which is soe necessary for the promoting of the publique service heere, and leave mee (that am but a stranger as yett unto these affaires) without that necessary assistance, which itt seemes your self is sensible there ought to be; and if that bee soe that the Major Generall's power bee ceas'd, itt putts mee yet to a greater dilemma, and leaves mee and the affaires heere in a very strange posture, my aucthority being but derivative from him, and I nott knowing how longe itt may continue cannott

---

[1] Clarke Manuscripts, lxxxvi. 18.

[2] A circular letter from the army in England is printed in *Mercurius Politicus*, Feb. 3 to 10, 165⅔, and said to have been agreed upon at a meeting of officers held on Jan. 28.

[3] Clarke Manuscripts, lxxxvi. 19.

come to soe cleare a resolution in many thinges as otherwise I would; but concerning provisions I thinke I shall goe neere to finde a way to supply us with biskett much cheaper then from Londen, nor shall wee neede any wheate or such kind of graine, which wee finde exceeding chargeable to the poore souldier, but yett cannott bee without supplies of cheese, shoes and stockings, and such thinges, for which I know nott to whom to apply my self to prepare them; though I could wish that seing your self and Mr. Smythesby understand the businesse you would nott yett decline itt, att least untill some fitt person may bee thought on to supply that charge, or untill a Commander in cheif bee uppon the place to appoint whom hee thinkes fitting.

For the 150 beds for Invernesse, if you please to provide them, and send notices to whome the mony shall bee paid, itt shall bee return'd from hence as formerly.

To Mr. Rowe.

LIV

Sir James McDonell to Colonel Fitch.[1]

Right Honourable,—Pray know, that I am informed, that the Laird of Glengary and some other Highlanders are drawne to an head, and intend to disquiett the peace of the Country; and least itt should bee told your Honour that I or any of mine have any such intention, I have taken the boldenesse as by these lines to assure your Honour, that none shall bee more carefull to keepe the peace of the Country then I shall bee, and that I shall nott bee wanting in doing anythinge that your Honour layes to my charge, soe farre as lies in my power, for preserving peace in these Feilds wherin I live. I am already threatned by those who are drawne to an head, soe that I humbly crave your Honour's advice how to behave myself if I bee invaded by these people; your Honour may expect on your advertisement what I can learne of their intentions or Resolutions. And if I bee a sufferer, I trust your Honour will

---

[1] Clarke Manuscripts, xxiv. 117.

consider itt as done to him who alwayes resolveth to behaev himself as becometh, Right honorable, your Honour's affectionate freind and humble servant,

JAMES McDONALL of Sloat.[1]

Dunvolme (?), *15 Feb.* 1652.

To Col. Fitch, Governor of Invernesse.

LV

COLONEL LILBURNE to COLONEL COOPER.[2]

SIR,—I have inclosed these orders[3] that you may see them, and if you aprehend my inconveniencie therein, I desier you to recktyfie it, because att this distance I can not so clearely judge what may be best for all partyes. [From] the sence I have of Captain Farmer's danger in regaurd of those clouds that are gathering and threatening some disturbance, and that he can not be releived att that distance, nor com of when he pleases, I though[t] meet to determine to remove all with as much speed as conveniently he can; som thing elce I have to ofer as to the secureing the cheife of clanns: and desier [you] to advise with Ltt. Col. Bluntt and others privately about the doeing of it, and returne your thoughts speedyly unto your very affectionate servant,   R. L.

Dalkeith, 14 Feb. 1652.

If any thing be necessarie to be don about the [chiefs of] Clanns speedyly, I desier you to putt it [in] execution, but I conceave the best way will bee to send for them in a faire way for makeing the least noyse.

---

[1] ? Sleat.

[2] Clarke Manuscripts, lxxxvi. 23.

[3] The orders in question were, that a company and a half should be sent to Castle Sinclair, and half a company to Thurso, and that Captain Farmer should march his troop of horse to Cromarty, and put half of it in the house there, and the other half at Brawl (?), and send the foot at present there to Inverness. Captain Hope was to withdraw his troop to Inverness.

LVI

COLONEL LILBURNE to the LORD GENERAL CROMWELL.[1]

MAY ITT PLEASE YOUR EXCELLENCY,—I have severall times given your lordshippe an account of what intelligence came to my hand, and by the last sent 2 letters inclosed to Mr. Downing that hee might waite uppon your Lordshippe with them; and I finde the designes of the wicked heere going on, I hope to their owne destruction, I haveing an account from severall hands that their plotts doe ripen, especially amonge the mountaines; and undoubtedly one from young Charles has bin with Glengary with Comissions from him, which hath putt a great deale of life into these kinde of cattell, and itt is to bee read in many of their countenances what they shortly intend, which makes mee contract quarters in severall places; but, my Lord, I am afraid if wee have occasion to draw into the feild, wee shall want those necessary supplies as are fitting, for Mr. Rowe, whom I lately writt unto to send us downe those new provisions that were now expected, tells mee of an account hee is preparing to give in of all the provisions hee hath sent, and that hee intends assoone as that is done to quitt himselfe of that charge and trouble: by which meanes I doubt the businesse of provisions may bee much neglected, or att least retarded, and will bee wanting when wee may stand in neede of them, the consequence wherof your Lordshippe very well knowes; and itt seemes Mr. Smythesby intends alsoe to give over his charge, nott being aucthorized to issue out any mony now, the aucthority given him by Major-Generall Deane ceasing; which if soe, my Lord, mine being but derivative from him, there will bee want of some body to command in cheif heere that may bee sufficiently impowred to doe all such thinges as are necessary, and to take a timely care that such supplies may bee laid in heere as are fitting for the accomodating the forces this summer, which now drawes neare.

Dalkeith, February 15, 1652.

---

[1] Clarke Manuscripts, lxxxvi. 19.

LVII

COLONEL LILBURNE to the MARQUIS of ARGYLL.[1]

My Lord,—Meeting with a confirmation of what your Lordshippe both told and wrote to mee, I am apt to beleeve some thing is intended by Glengary and his accomplices. I am informed that Macheldee (?) the tutor of Maclaine, Mac Clende, and Mac Donald, with severall others of your Lordshippes acquaintance and freinds, neerly related to you and whom you have power of, doe meete and are likely to engage with Glengary, but withall am further informed, that Mackaldee and some others, uppon whom your Lordshippe hath a powerfull influence, would willingly receive your Lordshippes commands nott to obey any of those summons from Glengary or others of his confederates. I doe nott presse your Lordshippe to any thinge, a word being sufficient to the wise, nor doe I value much all that can bee done against us by such a rable, yet should bee glad noe more bloodshed might bee amongst us, nor that any wise or discreete men that incline to goodnesse would imbodie themselves, patronize, or connive att such transactions as are conceived are now amongst those desperate people.

I lately sent your Lordshippe 2 or 3 lines, with a list of some of the particular losses of Captain Weddall, since which this inclosed copy is come to my hand, to which, as to the former, I intreate your Lordshippes answer unto. My Lord, your Lordshippes most humble servant,   R. L.

Dalkeith, 18 *February* 1652.

To the right honorable the Marquesse of Argile.[2]

---

[1] Clarke Manuscripts, lxxxvi. 20.

[2] By 'Mac Clende' Macleod is probably intended, and for 'imbodie' in line 17 'imbroile' should probably be read. These letters contain numerous verbal errors due to the fact that they are derived from hasty copies probably originally made in shorthand and written out later.

LVIII

COLONEL LILBURNE to COLONEL ALURED.[1]

SIR,—Hearing that Col. Overton is gone for England, and that there may bee a want of some to take care of those forces in the West, I desire you to take the charge of them in his absence, or untill Col. Okey come uppon the place, and to take this inclosed into consideration, and to doe something therin, tending to the better security of his regiment, and the officers of the severall regimentes are heerby required to observe such orders as they shall receive from you.—I remayne, Your affectionate servant,   R. L.

Dalkeith, 19 *February* 1652.

To Col. Alured.

LIX

COLONEL LILBURNE to the LORD GENERAL CROMWELL.[2]

MAY ITT PLEASE YOUR EXCELLENCY,—Such intelligence from time to time as comes to my hands I have communicated, and thought meete to send you these inclosed. I formerly intreated your Lordshippe to dispatch those officers hither that are att London; I suppose your Lordshippe cannott but bee sensible, that itt is but necessary they were heere with their charges, nott knowing ere longe what neede there may bee of them, and I could wish your Lordshippe would make some of them examples, having outstaid their passes for many monthes.

In my last I gave your Lordshippe an account of our want of provisions, and uppon inquiry I finde there will nott bee above 2 weekes or a monthes provision for any more then 6000 men; if these thinges bee wanting while the charge lies uppon mee I shall suffer for itt, and yet know nott how to helpe itt. I doe therfore intreate your Lordshippe to consider these thinges and the condition that wee may bee in in case of want

---

[1] Clarke Manuscripts, lxxxvi. 21.
[2] *Ibid.* lxxxvi. 26.

of supplies, and to lay your commands uppon Mr. Rowe or some other to provide for us a reasonable quantity to bee heere with all expedition; for if wee bee putt to draw into a bodie, wee are nott able longe to keepe together. Your Lordshippe knowes these thinges very well, and I am confident you will bee pleased to remember your poor servants in this strange country, and pardon this boldenesse in, My Lord, your most humble and faithfull servant, R. L.

Dalkeith, 19 *February* 1652.

I desire that an Adjutant Generall of horse and another of foote may come downe, there being nott one in Scotland, as alsoe some body to looke after intelligence: I desire Mr. Downing[1] would appoint a couple, one to lie att Sterling and the other att the Blaire of Atholl.

LX

Col. Lilburne to the Lord General Cromwell.[2]

May itt please your Excellency,—I still thinke itt my duty to communicate what intelligence I have unto your Lordshippe, and therfore have sent this inclosed. I doe heare from another Island, that Sir George Monroe is newly started pretending to goe towards Orknay to take shipping for Sweden, [and] hath taken his progresse towards Loughaber. I am informed that there is one James Boyde, a Scotchman in the North of Ireland, that is imployed as an Agent by the Lord Glencairne and Glengary to stirre uppe factions in those parts, and to boate over as many men as hee can to those Westerne Islands. Peradventure that Boyde might bee taken, if notice were given to Col. Venables, which cannott well bee done from hence, because there is nott that passage. Since my last I have heard nothing from Col. Morgan, nor from the North. I hope they are in a safe posture there, but, my Lord, I must humbly

---

[1] The Scout-master General, George Downing.—*Cal. S. P. Dom.*, 1651-2, p. 439.

[2] Clarke Manuscript, lxxxvi. 28. There is a long letter of the same date from Lilburne to the Council in *Cal. S. P. Dom.*, 1652-3, p. 178, concerning masts and tar.

intreate you again to cause some provisions to bee dispatch't to us speedily. I had a letter from my Lord Argile this day who seemes to bee much a stranger, and protests his ignorance uppon my sending him word I heard some of his people were engaged in this businesse. Hee promises to use his endeavour to his utmost power to preserve peace, and uppon his returne from Castle Camell, which will bee very shortly, hee will send for some of these new engagers, and try if hee can convince them of their follie.—I remayne, Your Lordshippes most humble servant.

Dalkeith, 22 Feb.

I hope your Lordshippe remembers there are many officers wanting heere.

LXI
Letter to Sir James M'Donell.[1]

Sir,—My Colonell being absent your letter of 15° instant came last night to my hands, wherin I understand you have nott bin in conjunction with Glengary and others who have bin actors in the late disturbance in the Highlands : I am glad to heare a Gentleman of your worth can free yourselfe from those Commotions, and I shall bee more glad to finde you continue in a true obedience to the Governement which God hath evidently sett over you, when itt is well considered how remarkably in the continued passages of his providence, and in an evident concurrence of successe nott only in breaking many and great powers, overthrowing deepe plotts and conspiracies, but by blessing the Councells and forces of those which have bin imployed for the settlement of the just rights and priviledges of the people of the 3 Nations united under one Governement, and that the Governours therof have given ample testimonie to the world, that in the prosecucion of their undertakings they have indeavoured an equall distribucion of Justice, and doe desire and will protect all persons in their borne Rights (they nott forfeiting the same by indirect practises) and will that every man may enjoy his

---
[1] Clarke Manuscripts, xxiv. 120.

lawfull patrimonie, and whatsoever more he hath gott by just labour; I say when these thinges are fully consider'd I hope in time all honest men will see their owne happinesses, and willingly sitt downe under that power which the policie and strength of Man hath not bin permitted to overthrow (though indeavours therin hath nott bin wanting to the utmost) and nott to soile their fingers and venture their interests with a Companie of discontented, malicious men, who harbour and support to their power those persons that live by the goods which other men have gott by their honest labour, and by force of Armes detayne the Right of such, which the disposer of all thinges in time will vindicate. Sir, what you doe in the preservation of the peace of the Country and keeping your owne people in the obedience which becomes good men, and what further you shall make knowne to the service of the State concerning the intentions and resolutions of those discontented persons relating to any disturbance, as well as what you now have done, shall bee declared to the Commander in cheif in this Nation; and you may be assured will bee both acceptable and esteemed, and as by those in highest command, soe alsoe by him which desires to shew himself, Sir, your reall freind and servant,

R^t. B.[1]

Invernesse, Febr. 24.
For Sir James Mac-Donall of Sloat.

LXII

Sir Edward Hyde to Lieutenant-General Middleton.[2]

Sir,—I doubte by your writinge seldome, and your writinge Feb. 25. shorte, that you are not cheerefull, and the truth is Roterdam March 7. is not a place to make a man in the best humour, therfore I heartily wish you had taken your leave of it. I have seene your letter to my Lord Newburgh, and perceave you are not throughly satisfied with the dispatch which was provyded for

---

[1] Probably from Lieut.-Col. Blount.
[2] Clarendon Manuscripts, xlv. 128.

Capt. Smith, which is still in your power to mend, and any thinge shall be reformed you advise, and to that purpose and for the reasons I shall tell you afterwards, the Kinge hath writt the inclosed letter to Capt. Smith, of which I send you the copy. But I am of opinion, that when you have carefully looked over the Commissyon and the instructions and the letters (of which you have copyes) you will thinke that they may be fitly sent, and may do much good, and can doe no harme, if they will conforme themselves to his Majestyes pleasure, and if they will not, it is no matter what he sends. I must remember you that the next weeke after Capt. Smith came, and the Kinge had considered upon perusall of his instructions and the desyres of those who sent him (all which you your selfe had reade) what was to be done, I sent you by his Majesty's order an accounte of what was then thought fitt, accordinge to the modell wee have since followed, and desyred you would send your advise concerninge any particulars which you thought fitt to inserte, and you returned me an answer that you liked well the course wee resolved to take; so that you are to be chidd if all be not well, for I persued punctually the way I informed you of. In the consultation upon the matter it was considered: whether the Kinge would heare nominate a person to commande in chiefe till you arryved ther; and it was thought best, and least lyable to exception to leave it to themselves: then, whether they should be requyred to observe your orders before your comminge into that Kingdome; and it was concluded, that, as it was not easy for you at a distance, and upon so ill information as you must have of the state of the affayres, to derecte them what to doe, so they would pretende that they were restrayned by it, and that if they had bene left at liberty, they would have done wounders: then, whether they should be referred to you, for ther Comissyons; and to that, it was one of ther desyres in writinge to have Pattents for officers under the King's owne hande, and both the Kinge and my Lord Newburgh were of opinion that ther is somewhat in the nature of that people, which would not be satisfyed with lesse. You see cautions, derections, and comands the Kinge hath given to the Comissyoners, in his instructions, and in his letters to the particular persons, which do provyde against all the mischieves wee could foresee. Now the questyon is, whether upon the dispatches which wee have since receaved by Capt. Straghen, and the other which is upon the way by Roger, ther be cause to alter any of the former councells, and of that the Kinge makes you the sole judge, and hath commanded me to tell you, the prospecte which wee have made of the whole. You will first consider, whether it be not very necessary that the Highlanders should heare from the Kinge, and know his pleasure, and have some authority and derections to proceede, as soone as may be, and the rather because of Bampfield's beinge amongst them, who no doubte is sent thither to corrupt and perplex them; and therfore you finde by the King's warrant inclosed what remedy his Majesty hath provyded for that mischieve, which I wish should be in ther hands with all imaginable hast, for that fellow is cunninge, and diligent in all his designes. It hath bene considered, whether it might not be fitt to give Capt. Smith posityve orders to goe immediately to the Earle of Glencarne, and to shew him all his dispatches, and to follow his advice for the delivery or not delivery of them, because if he himselfe will goe amongst them, the charge and comande may be immediately conferred on him, till your arryvall; but then to this ther occured two objections; the one, the delay that must be by that meanes, before the officers ther be derected what to doe; the other, the greate hazarde and danger, that both the messenger and the dispatches may fall into the Rebells power, the Earle liveinge so farr from the Hills; besydes that it may be, he would be very unwillinge to trust any person in a matter of such importance, but the messenger himselfe hath sent; and it is as possible, that if those in the Highlandes should know, that ther authority and power hath bene considered and upon the matter referred to any man, it may displease ther haughty spiritts, and make them the more jealous and humorous; and it is believed, that the expedyent proposed may cure any inconveniences which may flowe from the sendinge Capt Smith presently to the Highlands with all those Comissyons and letters he hath with him, and with such others as you thinke fitt to send by him. That is, that Capt. Straghen make what hast he can to my Lord of

Glengarne, to whome his Majesty hath writt in such manner as you see, and that you sende to him the copy of all the dispatches which Capt. Smith hath carryed to the Highlandes; and for your more easy procuringe those to be provyded I have writt to Secretary Nicholas to lett his sunns write out any dispatches you shall desyre, and I will give you my worde, they will do it with greate secrecy, and in very good handes. If upon perusall of them, and the intelligence he is sure to have of ther condicion the Earle thinkes fitt to goe himselfe amongst them, he shall have a letter from the Kinge to the Comissyoners to choose him into the number, and to commende him to them as the fittest person to conducte them untill your comminge. He shall likewise have a Comissyon absolute from the Kinge to take charge and commande of them as commander in chiefe till you come, which beinge of a later date determines thers. When the Earle hath both these in his handes, he will best judge whether it be best to deliver the letter, and so to come amongst them upon the matter by ther owne election, or to assume the authority immediately by virtue of his commissyon, and to burne the letter, and the Kinge is confident he will judge best which is the best way, and will persue it accordingly; and now I have told you this, I tell you agayne, you are to give such order to Capt. Smith as you thinke best. Ther are likewise severall blanke comissyons signed by the Kinge, for Collonells and inferiour officers of horse and foote, which you are to sende to my Lord Glengarne, that he may make himselfe as considerable as he can by his owne leavyes, as well as by the strenght he shall finde ready reysed to his handes: all which Commyssions, and whatsoever I mention in this letter, which comes not now to you with it, you will receave for the savinge of charges by an expresse which will be with you in very few dayes after this post. If you finde the dispatches so full as you desyre, you cannot send Capt. Straghen away to soone; if otherwise, you must send us particular directions, or himselfe hither, which would be avoyded for his sake, if it may, without mischieve to his busynesse. I know he will take all care for his security, and, it may be, it would not be amisse that he leave the commissyons and the bulke of his dispatches in some secure place after his landinge, and goe himselfe and acquainte the Earle with them, rather then venture to carry them so farr into the country. I do not thinke that it will be fitt to deferr the sendinge away ether Capt. Smith or Capt. Straghen, till wee know what Roger's errande is, for besydes that it will take up so much tyme (for it will be at least 3 weekes before you can receave an accounte from hence of it, he beinge yett at Antwerpe), and putt the poor men who stay to an unreasonable expence, nothinge he can say will change the Kinges minde in what he hath resolved in these particulars, except you advise him to change. Ther is greate reason to believe that Roger, if he be honest, is cozened by some crafty fellowes ther, and if wee finde him fitt to be trusted, he shall be quickly dispatched backe to you, otherwise he shall do no harme; and you shall quickly know, what is to be done w[itha]ll. One worde now to your selfe, and I have done: you see how necessary it is that you were upon your winge, and that you gett into Scotlande as soone as may be, for that would putt an ende to all differences which may aryse upon commande; which may be more then you yett apprehend, for if Marquis Huntly be likewise gone to the Hills, as wee have cause to believe he is, or may shortly be, how will he like to be commanded by any body but your selfe whome all honest men will obey? If you could take Sweden in your way, I have more reason to expecte good from thence then we have had of late, and heare is an honest gentleman heare, who will shortly be with you, and would I thinke be good company for you, and do you some service. The Kinge hath writt to his sister to assiste you with some mony, and derected Secretary Nicholas to attende her aboute it, who I know will do his parte. You must not be angry at the summ (beinge but 100l) God knowes the Kinge had rather give you 1000l, but if he should desyre more, shee would not be able to procure it, this I hope may be gotten; and I hope you may by some of your letters gett some Scotts Marchant to helpe you, particularly Mr. Davyson of Amsterdam; if you knew the necessityes all men undergoe heare, you would not thinke your frends negligent of you. I shall say no more at present, but that I am very heartily yours, etc.

Indorsed:—*Myne to Lt. Generall Middleton.* 7 *March* 1653.

LXIII

CHARLES II. to CAPTAIN SMITH.[1]

Feb. 25.
March 7.

TRUSTY, etc.,—Though we doe not in the least degree doubt but that your owne inclinacion and discrecion will lead you to observe and obey all such direccions as you shall receive from Lt. G[enerall] Middleton, which shall in any degree relate to your carrying on our service in our Kingdome of Scotland, since you know that we have committed the whole conduct thereof to his care : yet We have thought fitt hereby to signify unto you that our pleasure is, That you observe all such direccions as he shall give you, as well for the delivery, or not delivery of those dispatches which We have already committed to your charge, as for any thing els he shall appoint you to doe in that Our Kingdome, or before your going thither : and in that you hold a constant correspondence with him, and give him full advertisements of all that occurs there, and that you use your utmost endeavours when you come there to prevent any misunderstanding or differences which may aryse amonge those who wish well to our service. And soe not doubting of your diligence in whatsoever We have, or shall entrust to you, We bid you farewell.

Mar. 7.
Capt. Smyth.

LXIV

WARRANT for APPREHENDING COLONEL BAMPFIELD.[2]

Feb. 25.
March 7.

TRUSTY, etc.,—Wheras wee are informed that Coll. Bampfeilde hath transported himselfe out of Hollande into our Kingdome of Scotlande, and is now with you, pretendinge much affection to our service, and alleadginge that he is sent to you by us, Wee have thought fitt heareby to signify unto you, that wee were in no degree privy to his journey, nor are satisfyed of his good affection to us, but on the contrary looke on

---

[1] Clarendon Manuscripts, xlv. 130.   [2] Ibid. xlv. 131.

him as a person trusted and imployed by our enimyes, or by those of whose integrity wee have no assurance, and therfore wee advise and requyre you to looke on him as such, and strictly to examyne him by whome he was sent, and with whome he corresponds, and if in truth he hath informed you that he was sent and in trusted by us, you have the more reason to conclude his purposes are not honest, and to proceede with him accordinge to his meritt; however putt no trust in him, nor lett him be at liberty amongst you. And so wee bid you farewell. Given, etc.

March 7, 1653.

To our trusty and wellbeloved subjects, the principle officers who are at present in armes for us in the Highlands of Scotland.

LXV

COLONEL LILBURNE to the LORD GENERAL CROMWELL.[1]

MAY ITT PLEASE YOUR EXCELLENCY,—You will perceive by these inclosed that the former I sent by the last post had something of truth in itt, and itt is confirm'd unto mee by divers hands that they had a Randezvouz in Glengaryes Bounds, and were a considerable number, but are now dissolved. My intelligence tells mee further, that Major Generall Monroe was amongst them, which I did beleeve before, uppon that account I had of the mannour of his going from home; but I am something more confident then I was that their designes will prove very ineffectuall to them, and they will hardly venture uppon any of our quarters hearing of that watchfulnesse and posture that wee lie in, which I hope is much safer then formerly. I intend to gratifie the Badgenorth people (because they are very considerable) with the abatement of a monthes sesse, because I know nothing will encourage them more then their owne particular advantage.—I remayne, your Lordshippes most humble servant.

Dalkeith, 26 *February* 1652.

---

[1] Clarke Manuscripts, lxxxvi. 28.

The Generall Assembly is sett downe att Edinburgh. There is great expectacion of the Act of favour intended by the Parliament.

LXVI

Colonel Lilburne to Mr. William Rowe.[1]

Sir,—I am very glad that itt is now under consideration of the Councell of State to putt thinges into such a way as the forces in this Nation may bee conveniently supplied and accounts sett straight, and that itt is referr'd to your self, Captain Blackwell and Captain Deane, to offer your thoughts concerning the best method for doing out, because all of you understand itt soe well. Concerning the particular you write of relating to your self, wherin you seeme to blame mee for misrepresenting of you in my letters, I assure you itt was farre from my thoughts to injure you in the least, nor can any such conclusion, I am confident, ingeniously bee drawne from any of my expressions in any of my letters to any body concerning you; what I said was but out of a sence of that duty I owe to the publique to bringe thinges to a good passe, and unlesse I should have bin silent altogether I could nott well say lesse, which was noe more then a account of the state of affaires as they stood, and as they were likely to bee in, in case of an infall of the enemy, which did sufficiently threaten us att that time; which now I hope in God is otherwise qualified and allayed, and those wilde people dispers't to their severall habitations after about 2000 of them was mett together to attempt some mischeif in some place or other uppon us. I thinke if all these accounts about provisions here once sett straight, and thinges putt into such an order and method as you mention in your letter, and left to the Commander in cheif to manage itt, would bee best satisfaction to the forces, and most ease and lesse charges to the State, for I perceive itt is and has bin noe little trouble to you in particular in that thanklesse office you have bin in : and if any thinge were added therunto by my meanes, I am sorry for itt, but I assure you, as I said before, I had nott

---

[1] Clarke Manuscripts, lxxxvi. 28.

the least intention of misrepresenting of you, or doing you the least prejudice, but beleeve if you had bin in the like condition as I was, you would have writt as much your self as I did. I have sent you this inclosed account of the Falcon frigott, which was viewed by 2 honest men, and by what I can gather from all hands, itt will bee best to sell her, though I thinke the State more able to repair her then any other, and guns and such thinges may bee sent hither to furnish her, shee being a very swifte goer, and therin exceeds all that shee comes in companie with, and might bee of great use for scouting, and carrying letters, and such thinges.—I remayne, your very affecctionate humble servant.

Dalkeith, 1 *March* 1652.
To *Mr. Rowe.*

LXVII

CHARLES II. to LORD BALCARRES.[1]

THOUGH I was very gladd to heare from you by an honest man who left you aboute the 9 or 10 of January, yett I cannot tell you how sorry I am for your indisposicion of health, which I perceave for the present will depryve me of much good service I should have had from you, though I doubte not the goodnesse and wisdome of your minde will upon all occasyons contribute your necessary assistance, which your body is not able to doe. I heare ther is a man upon his way hither, who pretends to come from you, but I suspecte from some discources he letts fall, and from some persons he mentions to be sent from, that he hath not seene you, and then it may be others may derecte him to speake ther owne sense as yours, knowinge how much I depende upon your judgement in all my concernements. Give no creditt to any thing you heare out of Flaunders or Hollande, excepte you are sure it comes from Middleton, for ther are still some busy, who have hitherto never done any thinge well. I have desyred G[lencairne] to bestirr himselfe, and I know I neede not bespeake you to assiste him with your

March 4.

---
[1] Clarke Manuscripts, xlv. 151.

councell, and any other way you thinke best. But I charge you no otherwise to imploy your owne person, then as is consistent with your health and your more speciall convenience, and believe me to be unalterably, Yours, etc.

Ld. Balcarris.

LXVIII

Sir Edward Hyde to Lieutenant-General Middleton.[1]

March ⚹.

Sir,—The expresse I told you in my last would go from hence towards you, by whome you were to receave the commissyons and other dispatches for Coll. Straghen, is still heare; and truly I thinke if he had gone, my Lord Newburgh and I should hardly have trusted him to have carryed those thinges to you, since wee finde that you were not thought worthy to be trusted by him, or by those who sente him when he came hither; you know it is a Doctor of your owne Country, who does not desyre we should know when and which way he goes. You will now receave in this and from my Lord Newburgh, all the dispatches wee can thinke necessary for Capt. Straghen; and if you like them, I do heartily wish that both he and Capt. Smith were gone, and it may be they may goe best togither. I finde Capt. Smith expects letters from hence, that might procure him some supply of mony, which alasse is not possible if, by the Queene of Bohemia's meanes, Sir William Mackdowell be not perswaded to furnish him, and Secretary Nicholas is derected to moove her Majesty to endeavour.[2] I longe to heare of your owne confirmed health, and that you have any hope shortly to moove your selfe, which is the only way to putt life into the busynesse of Scotlande, which will elce be destroyed by factions and emulations amongst themselves. Wee heare not yett of Roger, nor can any thinge he bringes meritt the pawse of an howre in executinge any resolucion that is taken. God

---

[1] Clarendon Manuscripts, xlv. 148.
[2] Cf. Clarendon State Papers, iii. 144, 149, 150, 181.

preserve you, I am very faythfully and heartily, your most affectionate humble servant.

Lt. Gen. Middleton.

14 of March.

Indorsed:—*My letter to Lt. Generall Middleton, 14 March 1653.*

LXIX

INSTRUCTIONS to LORD GLENCAIRNE.[1]

UPON the accounte his Majesty receaved from 6 or seven of the Heades of the Clans, of ther being in armes for him, and of the assurance they had that the rest would joyne with them, if his Majesty sent his Comissyon and authority, by which they might be governed, and wherewith they seemed to make little question but that they should make a considerable impression upon the enimy; the Kinge considered what Commissyon to send them, untill Lt. Generall Middleton, who was then very sicke, and not like in many respects to be speedily with them, should arryve. And knowinge well the humours and natures of that people, and how difficulte a matter it would be for him to name a person, (especially since he knew not who was yett joyned with them, and foresaw that others might dayly resorte to them of equall quality and interest) who would be generally acceptable to them, and whose commands they would be all ready to obey, his Majesty thought it best to inable them to choose one themselves, for a particular engagement, or for a shorter or a longer tyme, and annexed such instructions to the Comissyon, as beinge punctually observed by them, would provyde for all contingencyes which might happen, and prevent all mischieves and inconveniences which he could foresee in any degree like to fall out. A copy of which Commissyon, Instructions, and letters which he likewise writt, you will receave.

What progresse they have made, since they sent that expresse to the Kinge, or what course they may have taken upon

March

---

[1] Clarendon Manuscripts, xlv. 149.

the receipte of the Commissyon, is not yett knowne heare, or whether they are in any posture to do greate businesse, or only ready to come togither when they shall judge it convenient; nor doth his Majesty know whether they have armes and ammunicion enough soberly to engage in any notable attempte. If they are only in small partyes and devyded, they will be the more capable of councell and advice how they may make themselves considerable; but if they are in a considerable body, and united under any commander, especially if they have had successe upon the enimy, they must be the more warily handled, and dextrously treated with, that they may take no disguste.

In both cases his Majesty knowes that you can well handle them, and that with reference to their natures, and humours, and inclinations, you will proceede that way which may most advance his service; and therefore he armes you with those expedients which are most naturall for any temper they can be supposed to be in, and relyes intirely upon your wisedome and dexterity in the applyinge of ether.

If you finde that they may be dextrously ledd to doe that of ther owne choyce which will be best for themselves, and yett more acceptable to them because ther owne choyce, you may cause the letter to be given to them (if you like it), of which you have a copy, and so receave the charge as a trust and honour from them.

If you finde them well united amongst themselves, and that they are disposed into order and government like to produce some good effects, and would be troubled or humorous upon any alteration, you will proceede with the more care, and helpe them at a distance, or by conjunction with them, in that manner as they are best inclined to admitt, and by makinge what leavyes you judge necessary, and any reasonable attempte in any other parte of the Kingdome.

But if you finde that by the unaptnesse and unskilfulnesse of the understandinge, or obstinacy and perversenesse of the humours, or by factions and differences amongst themselves, they cannot be induced and wrought to submitt by any agreement and election of ther owne to such methode and order of commande, as may probably be succesfull, you will then produce your absolute Commissyon, and assume the command over them till L^te Generall Middleton come, and the tyme and waye of doinge this the Kinge intirely referres to your wisedome and discrecion, and will approove what you doe, and thinke it best to be done; his Majesty committinge the whole so absolutely to your jndgment that this memoriall is only to your self, and not communicated to any other, save to Middleton only; nor shall any else know any thinge of it.

You have a copy of what his Majesty writes to B. to the end that you may judge of it, and cause it to be delivered or not delivered as you judge fittest; and you have the copy of a warrant which is sent to take of all confidence from a person who is understood to be in the Highlands,[1] and of whome you may see what opinion the King hath, that you may be sure to prevent any mischieve his crafte and activity may hope to bringe to passe.

LXX

CHARLES II. to the HIGHLAND CHIEFTAINS.

TRUSTY, etc.

GENTLEMEN,—We receave information so rarely of your condicion (havinge never had any expresse from you since Capt. Smith) that We know not whether you are only in a readynesse and disposicion to ryse, or in a body togither able to make any attempte upon the Rebells, or what correspondence you have, or what persons of honour or quality from more remote partes are ready and willinge to joyne with you; but in all cases, if you observe the Commissyon and instructions which We have sent to you, We doubte not but all differences and unseasonable emulations amongst your selves will be prevented, and the publique service be well enough conducted, untill the arryvall of L^nt Generall Middleton, who We hope will not be longe from you. In the meane tyme, We have endeavoured to perswade some persons of honour, of whose affection and fidelity to Us neither We nor you can doubte, to rayse forces in the Lowlandes, and to corresponde and joyne

March 4/14.

---
[1] Colonel Bampfield. See p. 94.   [2] Clarendon Manuscripts, xlv. 150.

with you, that so you may togither with the more successe
attacque and destroy our common enimy. And if agreably to
our wish, the Earle of Glengarne (whose wisdome, courage, and
zeale to our service you cannot be ignorant of) shall resorte
to you, and be ready to engage himselfe, his frends, and interest with you, wee do recommende him to you, as a person
fitt to be chosen by your selves, accordinge to the authority
wee have intrusted you with, for your Commander in Chiefe,
untill the arryvall of L^{nt} Generall Middleton; since it is not
possible to succeede in any greate designe, without a perfecte
union under one commande of all those who have the same
good purposes for our service, and We know he is a person so
generally acceptable and trusted by all well affected persons,
that he will be able in severall respects to advance very much
our service, and will comply with all your desyres.

LXXI

Charles II. to the Earl of Glencairne.[1]

I am much satisfyed with the newes I have lately seene from
you, and with the assurance that you continue your old zeale
and affection to me, which I never doubted, though ther have
bene many chaunges since wee parted. I hope our affayres
will shortly mende in all places, and you may be very confident
(though you heare little of any stirringe) that I omitt nothinge
that is within my power to mende the condicions of us all.
You will finde a shorte accounte of what I have designed and
wish to be done in your partes, in the inclosed relation, under
an honest hande, which you well know, through whose I shall
be gladd to receave frequent advice from you. I suppose
Middleton will give you a larger relation, and will not be
longe from you; in the meane tyme you see how much I
depende upon your affection, interest, and conducte, of which
you will make use at such tyme, and in such manner, as in
your judgment you finde best for any occasyons. I neede not
advize you to consulte with B. if you can with convenience,
to whome you will convey the inclosed letter. The Bearer[2] is

---

[1] Clarendon Manuscripts, xlv. 152.   [2] Captain Strachan.

a person of greate honesty and courage, and I have not bene able to rewarde him so much as for his journey. You must, with the helpe of our other frends, take care that he be not only no looser by such good services, but that he be upon any good occasyon preferred to a charge worthy of his experience and mettle, which I know he will exequte very well. Whatever discources you heare, be confident I am the man you wish me to be, and very heartily Your constant and affectionate Frend.

Kinges letter to the E. of Glencarne, 14 of March.

LXXII

Sir Edward Hyde to Lieutenant-General Middleton.[1]

Sir,—That you may know, that commendinge is as much in my nature as findinge faulte, I cannot forbeare to tell you that the Kinge is abundantly pleased with your letter by the last post to my Lord Newburgh; and indeede if you will alwayes write such letters, and advise us perticulerly what is best to be done, it will be oure faulte if you have not satisfaction in whatsoever you desyre, wheras if you leave us to our selves, who have so many misrepresentations made to us of thinges and persons, it will be no wounder if wee mistake often; for who could have thought that after so much discourse of an army in the Highlandes, which had taken Innernesse, and would quickly dryve all the English out of that Kingdome, if they were but supplyed with armes and ammunicion, ther should indeede be no men ther, but such who lodge in ther owne bedds, and only projecte what they will doe when they are able. Your excepcion to the Commissyon is consented to, and it is renewed, with the instructions as you derecte, to those persons you name in your letter, and to no others; only as you forgott to tell us the Christien names, and my Lord Newburgh, with all his correspondents amongst your country men, cannot informe us, so ther are blanks left for them, which

March 11.

---
[1] Clarendon Manuscripts, xlv. 176.

is not materiall, since the persons are sufficiently denoted. I had now sent you the Commissyon and instructions reformed, for they are engrossed and ready, but upon lookinge over your letter agayne, I finde you desyre wee would first heare and consider Roger's message and dispatch; and therefore though I am confident it will not produce the alteration of a worde in those, or in any thinge the Kinge hath resolved, I do satisfy you, and forbeare sendinge them till the next post, before which tyme I presume Roger will be heare; and I do consent that it will in one respecte indeede be necessary that he be heard before the Commissyon be sent away, that they may know that all this resolucion is taken after the Kinge hath considered what he hath receaved by him, wheras otherwise they might possibly looke for some alteracion, and so be the lesse united for the present. All the argument for hast is, the preventinge the mischieve which Bampfeild will every day doe, therfore I wish that warrant against him were in ther handes, I meane in such handes as would exequte it, and I have now inserted it in the instructions; and I doubte not but as soone as this dispatch shall come to them my Lord Balcarris will quickly decerne how much he hath bene seduced, and the Kinge will never indure a conjunction with those men; but I do not wounder that a confident offer from the good Earle of a shipp with armes and ammunicion should make impressyon upon a man, who had prejudice enough to him, and who will abhorre him much more when he discovers all those offers and undertakings to be meere mountebankry. My mistake that my Lord Glencarne lyved so farr from the Hills, proceeded from what I thinke Capt. Straghen wrote in his letter to my Lord Newburgh, or I am sure I saw it in some other letter, that he was at his house neere Leyth.—Ther is no doubte, as your goinge home would infinitely advance the service, so no man can wish you should goe without proper supplyes of what will be ther wanted; and when I mentioned your goinge to Sweden, which was purely of my selfe, it was only out of hope that it might be the most likely way to procure both men, armes, and ammunicion; and if it be not like to do that, I would never advise you to go thither. The Kinge bidds me tell you that my Lord of Rochester hath greate assurance that he can rayse men, and it may be upon correspondence with him he may give you good advise to that purpose; therfore I pray write very particularly to him, and propose any thinge which you thinke fitt, for ther must be men gotten, or elce ther will be no greate matter done, and truly methinkes it should not be harde to procure double the number you mention. Secretary Nicholas will convey any letter from you to my Lord Rochester, and it is very necessary you hold intelligence with him. I send you as many letters you propose as could now be made ready, the rest you shall receave by the next. The letter which you have for L^{nt} Generall Douglasse would serve very well, beinge all with the King's owne hande, and as kinde as is possible, and therfore he would not take it ill if he had a lesse title then were dew to him, wheras in truth he hath a greater, L^{nt} Generall beinge more then Generall of the Horse, and the addicion of Lord upon any forraigne title is not proper for the Kinge, at least for a letter under his owne hande. However, you shall have another to use as you please. I send you the letters for Generall Major Forbes and President Erskin with the copyes, which I thinke fitter to be in French then Latine, since this way the titles are avoyded, which would not be well in Latine, and in Latine the titles must be as well in the insyde as the outsyde of the letter. I had some reason to mention Mr. Davyson of Amsterdam to you, because to my knowledge others have desyred a letter to him, which I stopped, and I will ether now or by the next send you a letter for him, which you may use as you thinke fitt; and if he be willinge to do no more, because he hath once done well, he should be putt to declare that temper, and not be reserved to contribute to factions and designes of other men. This is all the trouble you shall receave at present from, Sir, Yours, etc.

I cannot doubte the disbursinge that 100ł by the Princesse, since shee hath writt to the Kinge that she will do it, and I am sure the Secretary will sollicitt it.

Indorsed:—*Myne to Lt. Generall Middleton, 21 March* 1653.

LXXIII

SIR EDWARD HYDE to LIEUT.-GEN. MIDDLETON.[1]

March 18/28.

Sir,—I have receaved yours of the 20, and am gladd you are at Hague with the good Secretary, who will helpe you much more in the dispatch of your busynesse then your silly Sir William, who indeede does nothinge but promisse and undertake, and performes nothinge. Roger is not yett come, so that the Kinge is resolved not to deferr his busynesse for him, nor to alter his resolucion upon any thinge he can say. The Earle of Diserte sent the Kinge this weeke a letter, which my Lord Balcarris writt to him by Roger; it contaynes nothinge but commendation of Bampfeild, to which his Majesty hath returned this answer, the copy wherof I send you, so that you see the King's constancy, as well by that as by the Commissyon and Instructions, which he will have dispatched to you without further delay; and all the letters which I did not sende to you by the last post you will now receave, so that ther remaynes nothinge upon my hands which you demaunded. Conferr with the honest Secretary aboute getting of men and shippinge, of which I have writt a lyne or two to him in cypher; and in my opinion it is necessary that both Smith and Straghen, or at least one of them, be sent away as soone as may be, for they cannot but be in payne to heare from the Kinge. His Majesty intends to sende the Lord Wentworth very speedily into Denmarke. I believe he will be at the Hague before you departe from thence, and he will be instructed to give you all assistance that shall be in his power. I am not without hope that wee shall be shortly gone from hence, and then wee shall prosper accordingly. This I will assure you, that rather then ly still heare and dreame out his tyme, nay, if he finde he can no other way give the Rebells worke, our Master will keepe you company in the Highlandes of Scotland.[2] I feare you are not Presbiterian enough, for I do not finde any of that trybe who are ther have any confidence in you, excepte it be, that they thinke you to kinde to such malignants, as is, Sir, your, etc.

Lt. Gen. Middleton.

---

[1] Clarendon Manuscripts, xlv. 193.
[2] Cf. Clarendon, *History of the Rebellion*, xiv. 149.

I thought it necessary to send the inclosed letter to Capt. Smith, least he may have the old Commissyon and instructions in his handes, which you shall do well to leave with Secretary Nicholas. I know no reason why he may not still deliver all his other letters to the Commissyoners, to Glencary, and to the Heades of Clans, which contayne nothinge but what should be sayd to them.

LXXIV

Charles II. to Lord Balcarres.[1]

I have seene your letter to the Earle of Diserte of the 24 of January, at which I should wounder more, but that I perceave it is in answer to some undertakinge of his to send a shipp with armes thither, which, trust me, will never come to you by his meanes or interest. I must conjure you not to hearken to his councells, to which I am in no degree privy, and for what you desyre concerninge Bampfeild it is not possible for me to repose any confidence in him, nor shall you, if you will be advised by me, since I know more ill of him then any body can know good. Therfore the safest way for you and those who have communicated with him, is to proceede accordinge to the warrant and instructions which I have signed concerninge him. I neede say no more to you of my affayres, havinge writt often to you of late, and now send you a dispatch in which you will know all my designes, and I am sure Middleton will informe you at large of what he intends, and I hope you have the same confidence in him, whatever others say, which you have alwayes had. I am confident you will alwayes continue the same I left you, and you may be as confident ther is no alteration in, yours, etc.

Margin: March $\frac{18}{28}$.

28 *March*.
Ld. *Balcarris*.
Indorsed :—*The Kinge to my Ld. Balcarris*, $\frac{18}{28}$ *March* 1653.[2]

---

[1] Clarendon Manuscripts, xlv. 195.

[2] An intercepted letter from Charles II. to Balcarres, answering a letter from Balcarres dated Aug. 9, is printed in Thurloe, i. 495; see also p. 503. In it the warning against Bampfield is repeated, and jealousy against Glencairne deprecated. Hyde's copy of this letter is dated Sept. 30, the one given by Thurloe, Oct. 2.—*Cal. Clarendon Papers*, ii. 258.

LXXV

Address to Col. Lilburne [1]

Right Honourable,—The God of the spiritts of all flesh having (after a search of our owne sins, and the sin of our land) putt itt into our hearts to speake the impressions of our spiritts unto these of the English Nation that are in power and place, in order to their actings and transactions anent this Land; wee did conceive itt to bee incumbent to us to communicate the same unto your Honour, that you might nott only, after prayer and supplication unto God, ponder these things in your owne heart, but alsoe communicate the same unto others imployed in places of power and trust, and speciallie to such as have bin or are uppon the search of their sin and duty in these times. And itt is our very humble request that, as you desire to regard the advancing of the Kingedome and interest of Jesus Christ in these parts and in these Nations, you would bee pleased to bee instrumentall that the thinges represented may bee heard without prejudice, and with humble seeking of God apart and together bee communed uppon, and weighed in the Lord's ballance, which only can returne the true weight therof to such as would judge of itt. Our hearts doe beare us record that wee have nott intended or falne uppon this with a purpose to provoke or to heighten differences, but with a better spiritt. Our soules desire is, soe farre as wee are therunto called of God, nott to suffer sin uppon our neighbours, and if wee cannott take out of the way, yett to indeavour the discovery of these stumbling blockes that doe offend soe many gracious hearts in this land, and to testifie for the most light unto the consciences of those with whom wee have to doe in the behalf of truth and righteousnesse, nott that wee justifie our selves, while wee call uppon others to take will[?] guiltinesse. As

---

[1] Clarke Manuscripts, xxv. 14.—This document is entered in Clarke's letter-book under April 28, 1653, though dated March 17. It is accordingly inserted at the end of March. It is followed by a 'Brotherly and Christian Exhortation and Warning to those of the English nation who have been authors of the late or present actings,' which fills about thirty pages, but is not of sufficient interest to reprint. On the proceedings of the Remonstrants, see *Mercurius Politicus*, pp. 2325, 2352, 2368, March and April 1653.

wee have searched our owne sin and the sin of our Land, soe
have wee published itt unto the world to bee a record for the
Lord his Righteousnesse in all his sad dispensations to this
nation, and to stirre uppe others who with us have had a hand
therin to inquire why God contends; and wee have heerwith
transmitted a coppy of the same unto your Honour, that wee
may, soe farre as the Lord doth inable us, therby provoke unto
Repentance.¹ Wee desire to entertaine such perswasions concerning your Honour, that seeing these thinges doe in sim-
plicity of heart proceede from such as wee trust through grace
have obtayned mercy to bee amongst those who belonge to the
bodie of Jesus Christ, that they shall bee entertained with
tendernesse and love, and that though wee bee poore and
afflicted, yet our counsell shall nott bee despised. And in this
persuasion wee rest.

Subscribed att the desire, and in the name of many Ministers
and Elders and professors of the Gospell of Jesus Christ, mett
att Edinburgh the 17th of March 1653. By

Your Honours in the Lord,

A. JOHNSON.	Mr. ANDREW CANT.
Jo. CHEISLIE.	„ SAMUELL RUTHERFORD.
D. WEMYS.	„ JAMES GUTHRIE.
R. HALKET.	„ RO. TRAILL.
Mr. JO. INGLIS.	„ EPHRAIM MELVILL.
	„ JOHN NEVAY.

*To the much honour'd Col. Lilburne, Commander in Cheif of
the forces in Scotland.*

LXXVI

CHARLES II. to LIEUT.-GEN. MIDDLETON.²

CHARLES R.,—Trusty and welbeloved We greet you well.   April ⁵⁄₁₅.
We have sent the Lord Wentworth our Ambassador Extraordinary to our good Brother the King of Denmarke, and have

---

¹ This refers to the 'Causes of the Lord's wrath against Scotland manifested
in his sad late dispensations. Whereunto is added a paper particularly holding
forth the Sins of the Ministry. Printed in the year 1653.' Its publication is
mentioned in *Mercurius Politicus* for April 7-14 of that year.

² Clarendon Manuscripts, xlv. 237.

imparted unto him the great trust and confidence We have reposed in you for the raysing and transporting of soldiers into Our Kingdome of Scotland, and conducting Our forces in that Kingdome as Our Lieutenant Generall, and have given him direccions to assist you therein, and to doe all such good offices for you to that King as you shall desire, for the advancement of that Our service, and for the procuring the freedome of his Portes, and loane of shipps for the transport of soldiers into Scotland, and to assist you in any leavyes to be made there. And therefore We would have you to communicate very freely with him in whatsoever may concerne Our service, and the carrying on the worke in hand, and to receive his advice and assistance in whatsoever may conduce to the same, and which will neede the countenance or connivance of that King; and that you communicate all Our intelligence with him, that he may be thereupon the better able to councell and assist you, which We are very well assured he will very diligently doe, out of his particular affeccion to, and esteeme of you, as out of his duty to Us, and zeale to Our service. And besides other important advantages We hope for by this Embassy, We doe promise Our selfe much fruite from it in advancing and promoting the buisinesse which We have committed to your charge, and upon which We soe much depend. And soe We bid you heartily farewell. Given at the Palais Royall in Paris the 15th day of Aprill 1653. In the fifth yeare of our Raigne.

Addressed :—*To Our trusty and Welbeloved Servant Lieutenant Generall Middleton.*

LXXVII

The Earl of Loudoun to Charles II.[1]

Most Gracious Soveraigne,—After I hade resolved to dispatch ane expres to your Majestie I hade occasion by the meanes of a true and faithfull servant of yours to meit with this trustie bearer, whose indefatigable paines and actions ar more reall evidences of his affection to your Majesties service

---

[1] Clarendon Manuscripts, xlv. 267.

then any thing I can writt. And with him I thought fitt to send ane expres, who (after your Majestie shall seriously consider that which I doe humbly conceave I ame in duetie oblidged to represent) may returne with your Majestie's answer. And that God who hath saved yow from many dangers may be pleased still to preserve your Royall person, and may so direct and blis your counsells as may be most for his honour, the establishment of your thron, and the prosperitie of your people, shall be the earnest prayer of your Majesties most faithfull Loyall subject and humblest servant

LOUDOUN.

8th of Appryl 1653.

Addressed :—*To the King's most excellent Majestie.*

LXXVIII

EXPENSES of the ENGLISH ARMY in SCOTLAND.[1]

Accompt of Monie received for and paid to the 10th of January 1652, by George Warre, vizt. :—

On accompt of 3 *monthes pay, viz.* :—

Receipts.

Out of the Lawrell frigott, Captaine Tailor, Commander, . . .	60000 00 00
By bills charged on the said Treasurers, ...	34500 00 00
From Commissioners for Sequestrators in Northumberland,	05000 00 00
From the Commissioners for Sequestrators in the County of Durham, . . .	03000 00 00
From the Commissioners for Sequestrators in Cumberland,	00500 00 00
From the Commissioners for Sequestrators in Yorke, .	0500 00 00
	————
	108000 00 00

---

[1] Clarke Manuscripts, xliii. 5.

On accompt of a 2d 3 monthes pay, vizt. :—

By waggons conducted by Mr. White,	30000 00 00	
Charged by bills on the Treasurers,	24279 00 00	
Monie paid to Mr. Gauden for provicions,	11191 17 10	
Monie paid to Lt. Col. Mason and Lt. Col. Mitchell for recruites to Col. Fairfax and Major Gen. Deane's Regiment of Foot,	02000 00 00	
From Ralph Rymer, Receivour Generall of York	00600 00 00	
From the Commissioners for Sequestrators in Yorke	00600 00 00	
From Alderman Ledgard att Newcastle,	06000 00 00	
		080070 17 10

On accompt of a 3d. 3 monthes pay, vizt. :—

Charged by bills of the said Treasurers,	79853 17 05	
From Alderman Dawson of Newcastle,	05000 00 00	
From Mr. Rymer, Receivour Generall of Yorke,	05146 02 07	
		090000 00 00

[On accompt of a 4th 3 monthes pay, vizt. :—]

By waggons conducted by Mr. White,	40000 00 00	
Charged by bills,	41541 09 08	
From Mr. Rymer, Receivour of Yorke,	04134 00 04	
From Alderman Ledgard,	01024 00 00	
From the Commissioners of Sequestrators of Northumberland,	02500 00 00	
From the Commissioners of Sequestrators of Cumberland,	00800 00 00	
		090000 00 00
		368070 17 10

EXPENSES OF THE ENGLISH ARMY [1653

Coppy of the Accompt sent to Captain Blackwell to bee communicated to the Committee for the Army, 26 February 1652, per G. B.

To the Army in Scotland, from the 23th of February 1651. Bilton, Deputy,' to William Leman and John Blackwell, Esqrs. Treasurers att:—

Payments.

28 daies pay for 9 Regimentes of Foote, 7 Regimentes of Horse, 1 Regiment of Dragoones, and trayne of Artillery—muster 9° February 1651, to commence the 23th of the same, ...	037911 17 06
42 daies muster, 22° March 1651, . .	056607 14 11
28 daies muster, 3° May 1652, . . .	032459 03 06
28 daies muster, 31° May, ...	032133 15 10
28 daies pay for 11 Regimentes of Foote, 7 Regimentes of Horse, 1 Regiment of Dragoones, and trayne of Artillery—muster 28 June 1652, ...	036072 02 02
28 daies muster, 26 July, ...	035899 10 10
28 daies muster, 23 August, . . .	036079 09 06
28 daies muster, 20 Sept., for 11 Regimentes of Foote, 5 Regiments of Horse, 1 Troope of Horse, 1 Regiment of Dragoones, and trayne of Artillery, ...	032338 08 08
42 daies muster, 18 October, . . .	047555 19 03
42 daies muster, 29 November, . . .	047567 03 09
Paid to Lt. Col. Mason and Lt. Col. Mitchell for recruites, ...	002000 00 00
Paid to Generall officers, ...	005816 01 00
Governours of Garrisons, fire and candle, .	000995 17 00
	403437 03 11
Paid more than received,	035366 06 03

Examinatur per G. B.

Memorandum.—Besides this there hath bin issued forth about 50000 ł out of the Assesse of the Country for the carrying on the Fortifications, and other contingent charges for the forces there.

Memorandum.—That the 22th of March last I charged uppon the said Treasurers to compleate 90000ᵗ assigned for the first 3 monthes pay, ... 09929 02 02

Rests in arreare 25437 03 11

Examinatur, G. Bilton.

Deliver'd in to Col. Lilburne
9° Aprill 1653.[1]

LXXIX

EXPENSES of the ENGLISH ARMY in SCOTLAND.[2]

An Accompt of Three Monthes pay for the Feild Forces and Garrisons in Scotland, commencing 10 January 1652. And determining 4° Aprill 1653. Exclusive, viz.,

For 11 Regimentes of Foote, 5 Regiments of Horse, 4 Troopes of Dragoones, Trayne of Artillery, etc., vizt.,

42 *daies pay on the muster of the* 10*th of January* 1652, *viz.,*

	Officers.	Souldiers.	£	s.	d.
Major General Deane's Regiment of Foote,	114	1050	2478	07	00
Col. Fairfax's Regiment,	115	1000	2404	17	00
Lt. Generall Monck's Regiment,	113	0996	2341	17	00
Col. Overton's,	114	0995	2392	12	00
„ Alured's,	113	0994	2380	03	00
„ Fitch's,	114	1050	2478	07	00

---

[1] An estimate for a month's pay for the army in Scotland, dated March 2, 1653 (Clarke Manuscripts, lxxxvi. 39), gives the strength of the regiments as 1000 men for the foot, and 300 for the cavalry, not including the officers. It adds four companies of dragoons, consisting of sixty men each.

[2] Clarke Manuscripts, xliii. 7.

	Officers.	Souldiers.	£	s.	d.
Col. Cooper's,	113	0993	2380	00	00
„ Reade's,	113	1000	2381	15	00
„ Cobbett's,	115	1000	2404	17	00
„ Daniell's,	114	1000	2390	17	00
„ Ashfeild,	113	0990	2370	18	00
Col. Lilburne's Regiment of Horse,	72	0300	2607	17	00
„ Okey's,	70	0297	2547	06	00
„ Twisleton's,	72	0300	2607	17	00
„ Sander's,	72	0300	2607	17	00
„ Berrie's,	70	0300	2593	17	00
Troopes of Dragoones,	55	0240	1516	04	00
Traine of Artillery, with with one Companie of Firelocks,	10	0100	1354	15	03
			42240	03	03

42 daies pay on the muster of the 21th Febr. 1652,—

	Officers.	Souldiers.	£	s.	d.
Major Generall Deane's Regiment of Foote,	100	0998	2370	18	00
Col. Fairfax's,	109	0998	2368	02	00
Lt. Generall Monck's,	108	0992	2312	02	00
Col. Overton's,	109	0997	2366	17	00
„ Alured's,	109	0980	2336	19	00
„ Fitche's,	109	1000	2374	08	00
„ Cooper's,	108	1000	2375	16	00
„ Reade's,	106	0996	2341	17	00
„ Cobbett's,	110	1000	2388	08	00
„ Daniell's,	108	0999	2370	04	00
„ Ashfeild,	109	0998	2364	09	00
Col. Lilburne's Regiment of Horse,	72	0300	2607	17	00
„ Okey's,	70	0293	2526	06	00
„ Twisleton's,	72	0298	2597	07	00
„ Sander's,	72	0300	2607	17	00
„ Berrye's,	71	0296	2566	11	00
4 Troopes of Dragoones,	55	0240	1516	04	00

	Officers.	Souldiers.			
Traine of Artillery, with one Companie of Fire-			£	s.	d.
locks, . . .	10	0100	1328	17	03
2 Sergeants, 3 Corporalls, and 100 Souldiers, in the Garrison of Dunbarton, . . .	05	0100	0189	07	00
			41909	16	03
		Brought over,	84149	19	06

For severall Garrisons, viz.,
Garrisons established, viz.,

Leith—		£ s. d.	
Fire and candle, . . .		033 12 00	
Edenburgh—			
Deputy Govornour, .	12 12 00		
fire and candle, .	08 08 00		
		021 00 00	
Insgarvey—			
fire and candle, . . .		008 08 00	
Linlithgowe—			
Governour, . .	025 04 00		
fire and candle, .	008 08 00		
		033 12 00	
Dunbarton—			
Governour, . .	012 12 00		
fire and candle, .	006 06 00		
		018 18 00	
Sterling—			
Governour, . .	025 04 00		
fire and candle, .	021 00 00		
		046 04 00	
Brunt Island—			
fire and candle, . .		006 06 00	
S. Johnston—			
Governour, . .	25 04 00		
fire and candle, .	21 00 00		
		046 04 00	
Dundee—			
Governour, . .	25 04 00		
fire and candle, .	25 04 00		
		050 08 00	

	£ s. d.	
Invernesse—		
Governour,	42 00 00	
fire and candle,	42 00 00	
		084 00 00
Orknay—		
Governour,	42 00 00	
fire and candle,	42 00 00	
4 gunners,	42 00 00	
12 matrosses,	56 16 00	
		182 16 00
		531 08 0

Officers in Garrisons not established, viz.,

Tamptallon Castle—		
fire and candle,		06 06 00
Basse Island—		
fire and candle,		06 06 00
Inskeith—		
fire and candle,		08 08 00
Linlithgowe—		
storekeeper,		04 04 00
Dundee—		
storekeeper,		21 00 00
Invernesse—		
storekeeper,		21 00 00
Orknay—		
storekeeper,		10 10 00
Aberdene—		
fire and candle,		42 00 00
Ruthven in Badinoth—		
Governour,	08 08 00	
fire and candle,	08 08 00	
chyrurgeon,	10 10 00	
storekeeper,	04 04 00	
		31 10 00
Brae of Marre—		
Governour,	08 08 00	

		£ s. d.
fire and candle, . .	08 08 00	
chyrurgeon and storekeeper, . . .	10 10 00	
		31 10 00
Blaire in Atholl—		
Governour, . .	04 04 00	
fire and candle, . .	08 08 00	
storekeeper, . .	04 04 00	
		16 16 00
Dunkell—		
fire and candle, . .	06 06 00	
S. Johnston—		
storekeeper, . .	10 10 00	
Sterling—		
storekeeper, . .	10 10 00	
Dunbarton—		
storekeeper, . .	04 04 00	
Ayre—		
fire and candle, . .	25 04 00	
storekeeper, . .	21 00 00	
		46 04 00
Brodrick Castle—		
fire and candle, . .	07 00 00	
storekeeper, . .	04 04 00	
		11 04 00
Donnottyr Castle—		
Governour, . .	08 08 00	
fire and candle, . .	08 08 00	
storekeeper, . .	04 04 00	
		21 00 00
Dunstaffenage—		
Governour, . .	08 08 00	
fire and candle, . .	10 10 00	
storekeeper, . .	04 04 00	
chyrurgeon, . .	14 00 00	
		037 02 00
Dunnolly—		
Governour, . .	04 04 00	

[1653] EXPENSES OF THE ENGLISH ARMY   119

		£ s. d.
fire and candle,	10 10 00	
storekeeper,	04 04 00	
	018 18 00	
	365 0 8	

	Brought over,	85046 15 06
Ten Gentlemen of the Lord Generall's Life Guard attending on the Commander in cheif for Scotland,		00210 00 00

For Generall Officers, viz.,

Major Generall of the Foote,	084 00 00	
Commander in Cheif for Scotland,	504 00 00	
1 Adjutant Generall of Foote,	050 08 00	
1 Adjutant Generall of Horse,	067 04 00	
Assistant to the Quarter Master Generall,	042 00 00	
Scoutmaster Generall,	168 00 00	
3 Deputy Mustermasters, att xviijs. per diem,	075 12 00	
Advocate and his Clarke,	077 00 00	
Deputy to the Marshall Generall and 10 men,	130 04 00	
A Phisitian,	042 00 05	
Apothecary and 2 men,	056 00 00	
Chyrurgeon, 2 Mates, and his chest horse,	061 12 00	
Commissary of provisions, 1 Deputy and 2 clarkes,	112 00 00	
		01470 00 00
Incident charges for the Traine of Artillery,	00300 00 00	
Charge of Fortifications, and other contingent charges of the Army, for the Three Monthes past from the 10th of January,		12500 00 00
		99526 15 06

Examinatur per Geo. Bilton.

Deliver'd in to Col. Lilburne,
    Aprill 9° 1653.

LXXX

Colonel Lilburne to the Speaker.[1]

Mr. Speaker,—In regard the power formerly granted by the Parliament to the Commander in cheif in Scotland for raising and leavying the Monthly Assesse expired by the first of May next, and there being some inconveniencies likely to fall out by giving out of orders soe late for the assessing the same, I presume to intreate that you will please to move the House to give speedy order for the timely assessing and leavying the Monthly sesse heere, in such manner and ways as to their wisedomes shall seeme most convenient for the service of the Common wealth, which presumtion I hope you will pardon in Sir, your, etc.

Dalkeith, 9 Aprill 1653.

LXXXI

Lord Lorne to Lord Wilmot.[2]

My Lord,—I intend to send one to his Majestie from my selfe, but finding the occation of this worthy gentleman I have intrusted what I had to say for the present to him, and by this I desire to plead the continuance of your Lo[rdship's] favoure, and that you would remember of me as one most desirous to approve my selfe to his Majestie, and that is with a greate deall of reality.—My Lord, your Lo[rdship's] most humble servant, Lorne.

Inveraray, Aprile 14, 1653.

[Addressed—] *For The Rt. Honble. My Lord Viscounte of Wilmote.*

LXXXII

Lord Lorne to Charles II.[3]

May it please your Gratious Majesty,—The difficulty of passage is such that none can promise to them selfes or any

---

[1] Clarke's Manuscripts, lxxxvi. 42.
[2] Clarendon Manuscripts, xlv. 286.   [3] *Ibid.* xlv. 288.

they would send a certaine occation, and finding this worthy
gentleman who hath beene very active and diligent to further
your Majesty's service in these parts, I would not let slipe the
occation without assuring your Majesty of my constant loyalty
and affection to your Majesty's Royall persone, family, and
goverment, and my desirs to doe your Majesty service according
to my power, and in case ane expresse whom my Lord Chancellor
and I have dispatched gette not so ready passage as this
gentleman, your Majesty will learn from him all we can say,
except it be a more particulare accounte of what hath passed of
late in this Kingdome and of the condition of this shire, which
your Majesty may expect by him we send; but for what concernes your Majesty's affairs in generall the bearer can give
your Majesty a perfect account of all, and to him I reffer every
thing I needed to trouble your Majesty with at present, and
taking leave I humbly rest, Sir, your Majestys most Loyall and
most obedient subject and servant, LORNE.[1]
Inveraray, the 14 *of Aprile* 1653.

LXXXIII

THE EARL of LOUDOUN to the EARL of ROCHESTER.[2]

MY LORD,—I thought it a necessarie pairt of my dutie (after
so great Revolutions and changes as have by God's providence
and permission bein in Britane) to give the King a true accompt
of the posture of affairs of this Kingdome of Scotland, and I
have a most earnest desire to knowe his Majestie's condition,
that I may be the more enabled to be servicable to him in this
tyme of trouble, and have sent this expres to that effect; and
knowing your constant affection and faithfullnes towards his
Majestie, and haveing found so many proofes of your former
favour, I have taken the boldnes to intreate your Lordship
most earnestly that yow wold be pleased to countenance and

---

[1] An Answer from the King to Lorne is abstracted in the Calendar of the Clarendon Manuscripts, vol. ii. p. 410, and a second letter from Charles dated Dec. 30, 1654 is printed in the Sixth Report of the Hist. MSS. Com. p. 613. Amongst the Clarendon Manuscripts is also a letter from Lorne calendared under Feb. 1654 (vol. ii. p. 318) which was probably written in Feb. 1649.

[2] Clarendon Manuscripts, xlv. 290.

asist this gentleman, and to interpose the power and credit your Lordship has with his Majesty to take the busines for which he is sent into serious consideration, and that he may be returned as speedily as may be with such answer as his Majestie shall (in his Royall wisdome) think fitt to give. And as your Lordship's favorable asistance theirin may be a speciall and powerfull means for promoting his Majestie's service so it will lay an obligation of perpetuall thankfullnes upon, Your Lordship's most humble servant, LOUDOUN.

Apryle 15*th*, 1653.

Addressed :—*For The Right Honoble. The Earle of Rotchester.*

LXXXIV

COLONEL LILBURNE to ———.[1]

DEARE AND TRULY HONOURED SIR,—That you should please to remember soe unworthy a freind att soe great a distance, and send mee soe large expressions of your respects unto mee, I cannott but acknowledge itt as a very great adition of your exceeding civilities unto mee from time to time, and am much refresh't to heare of [the] health and well faire of one I soe truely honour as your selfe, and should bee heartily glad a way of correspondence might bee found out wherby I might have an opportunity more frequently to tender my due respects and service.

Of late there was some meetinges in the Highlands amongst those wilde people where some papers were offer'd from Charles Stuart, and faine they would have begun some new designe, which was nott only sett a foote there but through out this whole Nation, and reach't as farre as the North parts of Ireland, if noe farther, but that great mercy and deliverance that the Lord was pleas'd to give us att sea hath given checke very much to all those thinges that was intended, and att present wee are in a very peaceable posture, and I hope our adversaries att their witts end, though those Ministers of the Assembly partie cease nott to blowe the trumpett to prepare the people for something

---

[1] Clarke Manuscripts, lxxxvi. 37.

they themselves doe nott well understand; though on the other hand the Lord is pleas'd to open the eyes of many to draw them out of their old formes into a neerer communion with those that truly feare God amongst us, and divers are become Members of Churches, and many more would if meanes were nott wanting amongst them. I have told divers officers that you were pleas'd to remember them, who much rejoict to heare of you, and returne you many thankes. My wife alsoe desires to returne you humble thankes for your kinde remembrance of her, and shee and I desire to present our very humble service to yourself and good Lady, and I remayne, Your most cordiall humble servant.[1]

Dalkeith, 16 *Aprill* 1653.

LXXXV

The Count of Waldeck to Lieut.-Gen. Midleton.[2]

Monsieur,—Je vous envoy isy joint les articles que m'avez demandé pour la levée de mil cinq cent hommes, affin de les communiqu[er] à Mylort Wentwort et autres que treuvères à propos, mais sur tout faut il tenir cette affaire en secret et ne point faire esclatter, qu'aucune levée se fera pour le Roy d'Angleterre si autrement nous y voulons reussir à nos souhaits, le prétexte que j'en prenderay sera le service du Roy de Dennemarc pour la défence de son pays, mesme, je trouve à propos que on ambarquera les troupes sous prétexte de les conduire en Norwège, car autrement les Anglois en pouront avoir advertissement par leur Resident de Hamburg, et nous empescheront le passage en envoyant une flotte à l'ambouscheure de l'Elbe, sa Majesté de Dennemarc se treuvant affectione au Roy de la Grande Bretagne il sera aisé de la disposer à donner permission que lesdites[3] trouppes s'assemblent à Gluckstat et y soient embarquées, estant un lieu qui dependt absolument de sa d[ite] Majesté et ne regarde point l'Estat de Dennemarc, me pro-

---

[1] Possibly addressed to Major-General Lambert.
[2] Clarendon Manuscripts, xlv. 299. The ends of some of the words have been cut off.   [3] MS. 'led.'

mettant qu'elle aura assez de bonté de donner quelques vaisseaux, provisions de bouche et guerre et autres necessitez pour le dit embarquement, le quel led[it] Mylort Wentwort saura mesnager selon sa prudence et bonne conduite. J'en attenderay vos sentimens et response demeur[ant], Monsieiur, Vostre tres humble et tres affec. serviteur,

WOTRADT COMTE DE WALDECK.

Culenbourg ce 27 *Avril An* 1653.

Indorsed:—*Copie de la lettre de Mons. le Comte de Waldeck au Lieu^t. General Middleton le* 27me *d'Avril* 1653.

LXXXVI
Memorial from the Count of Waldeck.[1]

Mémoire pour Monsr. le Lieut.-Général Midleton

Monsieur le C[omte] de W[aldeck] ayant tesmoigné de tout temps l'affection qu'il a pour le service de sa Majesté Br[itannique], ne recerche que l'occasion de la pouvoir mettre en effect, et puisque son dessein ne se peut encores former si avant qu'il séstoit proposé, et que la levée de mil cinq cent hommes seulement se treuve nécessaire pour mettre le dit dessein en train, il soffre de faire cette levée en Allemagne et mener les trouppes jusques à Gluckstat, ou ils seront embarquez pour faire voile en Eccosse, moyennant les conditions suivantes:—

1.

Les despenses qu'il convient de faire pour cette levée seront reiglées à Gluckstat, à mesure de la quantité de gens que l'on y aura mené, et le Roy s'obligera de les faire bon, ou en argent contant, ou en gages et cautions, ou bien en obligations et promesses valables.

2.

Et des qu'ils y seront arrivez, les dits gens seront hors de la despense de Mon dit Sieur[2] C[omte] et de ceux qu'il y pourra employer, et leur entretenement aussy bien que l'embarquement

---

[1] Clarendon Manuscripts, xlv. 300.   [2] MS. 'Mondssr.'

se fera aux fraiz de sa M[ajesté] Br[itannique] ou bien de sa M[ajesté] de Dennemarc, si on l'y peut disposer, comme l'on espère qu'il se pourra faire.

3.

Pour ce faire il sera à propos d'envoyer un exprez au Roy de Dennemarc, et proposer à sa M[ajesté] le dessein que l'on a formé pour le service de sa dit M[ajesté] Brit[annique] affin de s'asseurer et de la d[it] place d'assemblée, et des navires qui embarqueront les d[its] trouppes, sans quoy l'on ne voit pas que ce dessein pourra reüssir.

4.

Il sera dans la disposition de Mon dit Sieur C[omte] de faire un ou deux regiments des d[it]es trouppes, et y employer des Colonnels et officiers, qu'il trouvera affectionnez et capables de pouvoir reüssir dans la d[it]e levée.

5.

Les dites trouppes ayants heureusement fait descente en Escosse, le Roy s'oblige que le havre, dont ils se pourront rendre maistre en aprez proche d'Edinbourg, lequel seroit de consequence et ou l'on pourra aborder commodement, sera gardé par les gens de Mon dit Sieur C[omte], et le commendant sera obligé au Roy et à luy.

6.

Affin que le secours que l'on y pourra mener soit d'autant plus assuré d'y pouvoir entrer, et treuver des gens à leur poste, comm aussy que les dites trouppes seront par là tousjours assuré d'un lieu de retraitte, et de seureté, ce qui animera les autres d'y aller avec d'autant plus de courage et d'allegresse.

7.

Les dits gens ne seront commandez en l'absence de Mon dit S[ieur] C[omte] que de Monsr. le lieut.-géneral Midleton, lesquels a l'arrivée du premier rentreront sous son commandement, selon les conditions que l'on en fera cy aprez.

8.

Et puis qu'il faudra employer une bonne somme d'argent

pour faire la dite levée, il sera à propos que le Roy fasse avoir
à Mon dit Sieur Comte quelque sept ou huit mil Rixdals pour
subvenir aux fraiz et advances qu'il conviendra de faire d'abord,
et de donner aux officiers de part et d'autre, lesquels mesmeme
[*sic*] pour la risque qu'ils courront en chemin à revenir sans rien
faire, voudront estre assuré de quelque recompense à leur retour.

9.

Le Roy pourra donner ordre que les gens qui ne se treuve-
ront pas armez le puissent estre à Gluckstat.

10.

Les gages et traittements des officiers et soldats seront payez
selon les conditions qui en seront faites par le dit Comte avec
eux, dont la ratification de la part de sa M[ajesté] Br[itan-
nique] se fera par le dit lieut.-general Midleton, avant que les
troupes seront embarquées au dit Gluckstat.[1]

LXXXVII
A Letter from Colonel Lilburne.[2]

Honoured Sir,—Your civilities are more then I can expect
or meritt, and therfore you neede nott apologize any thinge att
all, I am only sorry that my owne inability and the barrennesse
of these parts affords nothing worthy your view. Had any
thing offer'd itt self considerable I should nott have needed now
to excuse my silence for the time past, nor indeed have I any
thinge att present to present you withall in any measure
proportionable to the dimension of what I undeservedly receive
from you; what I have to observe to you att this time is only
a generall silence and stillnesse: a great inclination I finde in

---

[1] Charles II. had written to the Count of Waldeck on March 7, 1653, thank-
ing him for his good offices. This was done at the suggestion of Lord Norwich,
and led to the proposal printed above. The Count wrote to Charles on May 13,
professing great devotion to his service; and the king replied again on June 6.
Pöllnitz, one of the agents of the Elector of Brandenburgh, acted as an inter-
mediary in this negotiation.—*Cal. Clarendon Papers*, vol. ii. pp. 180, 197, 203, 207,
211. George Frederick, Count of Waldeck (1620-1692), was at this time one of
the most influential councillors of the Elector. See Erdmansdörffer, *Deutsche
Geschichte vom Westfälischen Frieden*, vol. i. p. 171.

[2] Clarke Manuscripts, lxxxvi. 43.

the commonality to acquiesce and submitt to the present Governement, and were itt nott for some Ministers that blowes the trumpett I thinke very little would bee heard from the Lowlands that might any wayes bee considerable or offensive; nor doe I perceive any such forwardnesse in the Highlands as of late, their greatest designe being by what I can gather from the best intelligence to bee uppon a defensive posture in case of our marching into their bounds. There is an increase of good people who daily some way or other are sweetned towards us, and become more united in their affections and judgements, only there wants some meanes to lead many into a clearer light that are waiting for it; and I could wish this were nott soe much neglected by the State as it is. The people in the west, who have bin alwayes accounted most precise (though att this time seemingly att greatest distance with us) had a meeting on Wednesday last, and are againe on Thursday next to meete to draw uppe something by way of apology and tending to compliance with the present Governement, which by some messenger of their owne (as I am informed) they intend shortly to present unto the Parliament; and doubtlesse if these people could bee gayn'd or brought over to you I thinke they would bee the most confiding people in this Nation: and therfore if they doe appeare in any handsome dresse, though they doe nott answer your expectacions fully, yett I hope they will meete with a benigne aspect, with soe much tenderness as may answer att least their Christian expectation.

Dalkeith, April 19, 1653.

LXXXVIII

The EARL of SEAFORTH and the HEADS of the CLANS to CHARLES II.[1]

SIR, MAY IT PLEASE YOUR GRACIOUS MAJESTY,—According to our duety and in obedience to your Majesties commaunds, wee your Majesties loyall subjects in the Highlands and Iles have all been carrying on your Majesties services with all possible diligence and celerity. And wee hope it will be very acceptable

---

[1] Clarendon Manuscripts, xlv. 322.

to your Majesty, and usefull to your affaires to know the present condition of things amongst us, and what is to be said from hence. Therefore that your Majesty may have a more full and exact account of all matters then any letter can beare, wee thought it most expedient to employ this noble gentleman Collonell Bampfylde, your Majesties most faithfull servant, to waite upon your Majesty for that effect. There is nobody can give your Majesty so perfect an information of all things as hee. For hee hath been so incredibly active and industrious in your Majesties service, sparing no labour how difficult and toylesome soever in going through all our Country, exciting considerable persones, and working out an unanimous conjunction of all such as may at present be usefull to the bussinesse, that there is nothing wherewith hee is not most intimately acquainted, as having been exceedingly instrumentall in carrying on your Majesties service. And withall hee is fully instructed with all [that] is to be said of our proceedings, our intentions, our humble desires, and our opinion in what relates to your Majesties affaires. Your Majesty will finde by what hee hath to say, that there is yet in this your ancient Kingdome a very considerable number of loyall subjects that are most ready and willing to spend their lives and fortunes in your Majesties service against your enemies; not doubting but your Majesty leaves nothing undone that may tend to the recovering of your just rights from their usurpation, and freeing of your Kingdomes and all that is precious in them from the confusion, miseries, and ruines that they have brought upon them. What lyeth in us to doe towards these shall not be wanting. And it is our most earnest prayer to God to blesse all with happy successe, and send us the happinesse to see your Majesty quickely settled upon your Thrones. And now wee do humbly beg your Majesty may be pleased speedily to send your commaunds to us, and looke upon every one of us as personnes that account ourselves bound by many indissoluble tyes to live and dy, Sir, your Majesties most humble, most loyall, and most obedient servants and subjects,   SEAFORT.

In the name and presence of the cheifes of clanes and families of the Highlandes assembled in a councell of war at Glenelgg, 22 of Apr. 1653.

LXXXIX

A Letter to the Council of the Army at Whitehall.[1]

May itt please your Honours,—Having perused your Declaration intituled, A Declaration of the Lord Generall and his Councell of Officers shewing the grounds and reasons for the Dissolution of the late Parliament, and the same through God's mercy altogether tending to the weale of the Republique, and doubtlesse to the great satisfaccion of all godly persons and well wishers to these Nations; wee therfore conceived itt our duties to make knowne unto you, that wee through the Lords assistance shall stand and fall with you in your further proceedinges of what you have begun, against all opposers

---

[1] Clarke Manuscripts, xxv. 38. On April 20, 1653, Cromwell had forcibly dissolved the Long Parliament; and on April 22 there was published 'A Declaration of the Lord General and his Councell of Officers shewing the grounds and reasons for the Dissolution of the late Parliament.' Old Parliamentary History, vol. xx. p. 137. The Army in Scotland approved of the action of Cromwell and the Army in England. The letter given above was probably from the garrison of Leith. *Mercurius Politicus* contains a letter similar to this in its terms, but shorter, said to be signed by the Judge Advocate and other general officers, the Comptroller, and the rest of the officers of the train resident in Edinburgh (p. 2417). The official answer of Lilburne and the general council of officers of the forces in Scotland, dated Dalkeith, May 5, is printed in the Old Parliamentary History, vol. xx. p. 145, and is to be found in Clarke's Manuscripts, lxxxvi. 53. *Mercurius Politicus* prints also (p. 2475) a second letter, of May 17, from the officers of the army in Scotland to those of the army in England. Other documents on the subject are contained in vol. xxv. of the Clarke Manuscripts. A letter from Cornet Baynes to Captain Adam Baynes, dated May 7, 1653, gives the following account of the feeling in the army:—'Here is an universal concurrence with your transactions. You will find the Army here with much freeness and truth represented their adherence to his Excellency and the Council, and truly I hope (since there is such a oneness and harmony of spirit throughout the Army, and all honest minds besides) that things will go on now with more speed and more righteousness than hitherto. Those that now [*sic*] will have opportunities and power in the hands to distribute justice and mercy equally, if they come short of their duty as did those who have fallen before them, let them not think to escape; nay I am afraid their judgment will be more examplary, but I doubt not their wisdom and fidelity; they cannot but learn both by observing the design of God throughout the world. I pray God sit in council with them, and be their all in all.'—*Letters from Roundhead Officers*, p. 54. Bannatyne Club.

whomsoever (if any such shall bee), nothing doubting but that the Lord who made you happy instruments in purging, will alsoe owne you in dissolving that Parliament, for the just reasons and grounds in your Declaration expressed. And [we] cannott but take notice of your sweete breathinges of spiritt for those who professe their feare and love to the name of God; [and of your desire for them] to bee instant day and night with the Lord on your behalfes, which wee trust the Lord will minde us of, being made sensible through the mercy of our God, that those glorious Dispensations, which wee observe and expect by faith to rise higher and higher, are nott brought about by might, strength, or the wisedome of the flesh, but by the spiritt of the Lord, which spiritt wee desire from our soules may bee your guide, that noe difficulties may bee too hard for you. The Lord teach us all to walke humbly, meekly, and beleevingly, that soe wee may bee used as instruments in the hand of the only wise God, with whom wee leave you all, and remayne, Your Lordshippes and Honours humble servants.

Leith, 30 *April* 1653.

XC

SIR ROBERT MORAY to CHARLES II.[1]

MAY IT PLEASE YOUR MAJESTY,—The last expresse sent by my Lord Balcarress brought all needed or could then be said. His name was Malcome Roger; he sailed as I remember the 8 of Feb., and wee hope your Majesty hath receaved long agoe from Sergeant-Major Retorfort and Sir W. Ballenden all they were intrusted with from your Majesty's true servants there. By this bearer Collonell Bampfylde Your Majesty will now receive all that is to be said, and most and greatest things will be represented by him at length, yet I shall most humbly beg leave to trouble Your Majesty with a long letter, and to say things as they occurr. My Lord Balcarress hath been exceeding ill of a disease that hath kept him unavoydably in his chamber at Balcarress these ten weekes past, else he had been long ere now in the North about Your Majesty's bussinesse;

---

[1] Clarendon Manuscripts, xlv. 324.

neither can he possibly make use of this occasion to write to your Majesty. It was by his encouragement, with the unanimous advyce of others of Your Majesty's faithfull servants, that the bearer C[ollonel] B[ampfylde] (who came hither to Scotland to employ his labour and lyfe in some attempt to do your Majesty service) went about the bussinesse that he hath now brought to all the perfection it could as yet possibly be driven to in the Highlands. And though the advyce and direction and concurrence of others hath not been wanting, yet the truth is the carrying on of things in the manner they have been, and bringin[g] them to what now they are at, ought cheifly to be attributed to the indefatigable industry and conduct of Coll. Bampfylde. If my Lord Balcarress could now have writt to your Majesty he said this much more truely then I can, but your Majesty cannot possibly question the truth of it seing it is so very evident, and I being fully acquainted with My Lord Balcarress mak [?] your Majesty he knowes [?] will esteem of all I say (he doubts not) as come from him.

Your Majesty then may be pleased to give entire trust to the compleat relation Coll. B[ampfylde] will make of all particulars, and what he represents as the desires of those that have been advised to entitle their meetings a councell of warre to give them the more authority and reputation, expecting from your Majesty as soone as possible an ample commission to establish it under that name, as C[oll.] B[ampfylde] will shew. All know of it think it most expedient, and the whole dispatch is drawne and ordered by the advice of some of your Majesty's most faithfull servants. And not doubting but your Majesty will at first reflection see the weighty reasons that do evince the necessity of settling here a Councell of warr during your Majesty's pleasure, I shall leave all further enlargement of them to the bearer, if your Majesty need enquyre after it.

Neither will it be needfull to insist upon the expediency, yea necessity, of sending one hither speedily to commaund in cheif, seing your Majesty cannot but apprehend it; were ther none other reason but order, secrecy, and taking away difficulties, in diferences amongst those that are all most willing to the service, but will never cede to one another, nor receve orders from one another. It is knowne your Majesty hath already intrusted Lieutennant-Generall Middleton with that charge, and the farre greatest part both of Noblemen and Gentlemen that are already engaged, or are about to engage, will be exceedingly satisfied with him, and nobody will show the least aversnesse to it; therefore it is most necessary and most earnestly beg'd your Majesty may send him alone to mold and order all things against the time that forces come from abroad, and it be fitt to think of appearing in the Low lands against the enemy.

All possible industry hath been used to have some attempt made upon Invernesse but could not be effected, as C[ollonell] B[ampfylde] will deduce at length, though every body be sensible of the expediency of it.

But since that hath fail'd hitherto, though it be still thought upon, we hope that what now comes by Co[llonell] B[ampfylde], the bond of union and declaration, will supply the failing of acting much, and give a high reputation to your Majesty's affaires abroad, and it is all could hitherto be by any imaginable industry wrought out. For the resolution is layd down for a defensive warre till some attempt be probable, which is all can now be done, and in the meane time, as the bearer will show, the union is so going on, that when any part of the Highlands shall be infested or invaded by the enemy, every body may be helpfull to his neighbours, and all be ready to ryse unanimously whensoever the Lord shall send your Majesty hether, whether the forces you bring be as considerable as is wish't, or not; and if it be possible for your Majesty to send or farre rather bring over a sufficient body of horse, with armes, etc., for foot, with artillery, there is [no] body but is confident your Majesty will quickly get such a body of foot as better cannot be desired, but horse are not at all to be here expected, seing course is taken by the enemy to sease all able horses, and the whole Lowlands are quite disarmed. But to get a perfect conjunction of all the Highlanders without any exception there is nothing so necessary as to have some such number of warre shippes on the west coaste as may secure them and the Iles from the ennemy, which is most heartily beg'd may be your Majesty's study to effectuate. Now to this end wee doubt not but your Majesty will endeavour with the Hollanders, by offring them such advantages as C[ollonell] B[ampfylde] will represent, to keep off their agreement with your Majesty's enemies and engage them more heartily to owne your interests. And to gaine time asmuch as may be the Councell of warre have made an adresse for ships and armes to the King of Denmark, and to the States of Holland by the mediation of your Majesties Royall sister, whereof C[ollonell] Bampfylde will give your Majesty an exact account.

Hee will also repeate what I hope your Majesty knowes already from two or 3 other handes about the sending of a letter of your Majesties to Glengarry, and enlarge particulars.

It hath also been more then twyce desired your Majesty may write letters to many eminent persones and others of your subjects, C[ollonell] Bampfylde will repeate the names, and say somewhat of the strain of some particulars.

Your Majesty hath also been informed of the ministry that are not against the late Assemblies are without exception most loyall to your Majesty. C[ollonell] B[ampfylde] will enlarge what others have already represented of their thoughts to your Majesty, neither is there any thing can be represented to your Majesty by my L[ord] Balcarress, or any other of your Majesties faithfull servants here, by way of advyce in your Majesties affaires, but Bampfylde is perfectly acquainted with it.

Hee hath seen and hath letters to your Majesty from the Chancelor, and narrowly mist the seing of my Lord Lorne, who have long been thinking of sending an expresse to your Majesty, which they now do to testify their respect, and return with your Majesty's commaunds, but every thing is at full communicated to Coll. Bampfilde, as your Majesty will finde.

The Chancelor hath never to this houre taken passe or protection from the enemy. He is conversant in all [that] is done here for your Majesties service, is most faithfull and loyall to your Majesty, and ready to receave your Majesty's commaunds and so to be assisting to your bussiness. I see him often, and I beg your Majesty's letter to him have [?] a ressentment of his faithfull carriage with encouragements and your Majestie's commaunds.

All I shall say of My Lord Argyle, that with how great disadvantage soever he may be represented to your Majesty, and whatever grounds of jealousy there may possibly be against him, the course he takes is meerely for self-preservation, his country being much more obnoxious to the enemy, specially by sea, then most of the very iles are. Hee thinkes men and things are not yet rype enough to appeare here in armes, alledging that it will cum to nothing but the ruine of the Lowlands, and the Highlands are to be destroyed by sea; whereas if it were done, or could be done securely and effectually in his judgement, he would certainly appeare for the bussinesse that is now carrying on for your Majesty's service. C[ollonell] B[ampfylde] will enlarge this and say matters of fact.

But my Lord Lorn, as your Majesty will find by his letters, hath ever been without the meerest shaddow of complyance of any kind most invincibly constant and faithfull to your Majesty's service and interest, will most fully, heartily, and actively joyne with those that appeare here for your Majesty, as they all know that, and should it cost him all he values most on earth. So will his brother and his frends, and how considerable this is to your Majesty's bussinesse C[ollonell] B[ampfylde] will say at length, and give your Majesty an account of my coming to stay in these parts.

I shall now most humbly beg pardon for this tedious importunity, remitting every thing else to C[ollonell] Bampfyld, and shall onely add that no creature alyve hath more fidelity, affection, and humble respect to your Majesty then, Sir, your Majestie's Most humble, most loyall, and most perfectly obedient subject and servant,   R. Moray.

XCI

Colonel Lilburne to Major-General Lambert.[1]

Truly honoured,—In regard of the suddaine dissolution of

---

[1] Clarke Manuscripts, lxxxvi. 42.

the Parliament and Councell of State, and of the necessity there will be heere for supply of monies for fortifications and other contingencies, as alsoe for pay to the forces, and that I doe nott know whether any course bee taken heerin, though I understand Mr. Rowe hath acquainted you with the substance of these inclosed copies; conceiving itt my duty to give an account of these things unto my Lord Generall, though by reason of the multiplicity of businesses att this time lying uppon him I forbeare to give his Excellency this trouble, yett [I] thought itt meete to recommend these thinges unto your consideration, that you will bee pleas'd to doe something therin as in your wisedome you see fitt. I am nott willing to trouble you with more lines because of your more emergent occasions, but desiring the Lord to direct you in your great undertakinges, that they may tend to the refreshment of all good men.—I remayne, Your most assured faithfull servant.

Dalkeith, 30 *Aprill* 1653.

For the right honourable Major Generall Lambert.

XCII

COLONEL LILBURNE to GENERAL CROMWELL.[1]

MAY ITT PLEASE YOUR EXCELLENCY,—Finding that the Commissions given to the Judges and Sheriffs in this Nation were but temporarie, and now expired, and that notwithstanding the Declaration sett forth by your Excellency and the army those Magistrates aforementioned are nott free to act without a further continuance of their aucthoritie (though they are willing to concurre (for ought I can perceive) with the late proceedinges of your Excellencie and the armie) I could nott but thinke itt my duty to give your Excellency an account heerof, that something may bee speedily done for their satisfaction; only I humbly conceive that as the Lord hath putt itt into your heart and the officers to appeare of late soe eminently against corrupt men and thinges, if you would nott establish any such thinge heere longer then necessity enforceth, that is to say, My Lord,

---

[1] Clarke Manuscripts, lxxxvi. 51.

that those High sheriffes heere that are any way corrupt may nott bee longer comissionated; and indeed I could wish with all my heart, for the satisfaction of the most godly in this Nation, your Excellency and your Councell might finde out a way to rid your hands of those Commissioners from hence, who are notoriously corrupt, and is that which doth most especially gravell [?] and hinder the concurrence and coming in of better men: who now begin to pluck uppe their hearts a little in confidence of a better Reformation and settlement then they could promise themselves, or hope to have incouragement for from many of those Commissioners that are now with you, for I am afraid whatever agreement you come to with them that are now with you, itt will bee but as untemper'd morter, but I doubt I trespasse too much heerein. Desiring the Almighty to direct, and councell, and to establish your heart in true righteousnesse and understanding in those weighty thinges I hope the Lord hath call'd you unto, and wherin I trust hee will yett make you more eminent, which shall bee the hearty prayer of Your unfaned servant.

Dalkeith, 3 *May* 1653.

For his Excellency the Lord Generall Cromwell these att Whitehall.[1]

XCIII[2]

SIR,—Haveing formerly writt to you to preserve the breede

---

[1] After the dissolution of the Long Parliament, and the Council of State appointed by it (April 20, 1653), the Army published a declaration (April 22) setting forth its motives, and ordering all sheriffs and other officials to continue to act (Old Parliamentary History, xx. 137-143). This is referred to by Lilburne in the opening lines of his letter. On April 29th a new Council of State, consisting chiefly of officers, was appointed, which on May 3rd ordered that the Scottish assessments should be continued till November 1st next, and that the commissioners and other officials employed there should continue to perform these duties till the same date. A Committee for Irish and Scottish affairs was appointed, consisting of Colonels Ingoldsby, Barkstead, Philip Jones, Goffe and Smith, and Lieutenant-Colonel Salmon, with Messrs. Ralph Harrison and John Upton.—*Calendar of State Papers, Dom.* 1652-53, p. 304. See also pp. 416, 417. The 'Commissioners from hence' are those sent from Scotland to treat of the Union of the two countries.

[2] Clarke Manuscripts, lxxxvi. 63.

of hawkes neere Dunnottyr Castle, I desire you to give order to the man that climbes the rockes that hee doe nott dispose or give away any of the hawkes to any person whatsoever, without particular direction from your selfe, and that you cause him to preserve them for me, and that you will doe me the favour to send to the Lord Arbothnotts Fawkner to come for them about that time they are readie, that he may bring them unto your very true friend.[1]

XCIV

MEMORANDUM on the RISING IN SCOTLAND.[2]

Scotlande.

1. A representation made about June or July last by an expresse from diverse of the most considerable Nobility to his Majesty of the condicion of Scotlande, with advices what was to be done.

2. Hereupon a Commissyon given by the Kinge to Lte. Generall Middleton, etc., authority given to him to treate with any of the Scotts Nacion in forainge partes for the loane of moneyes, armes and ammunicion, to be imployed for the reliefe of that Kingdome, and letters to severall Princes in whose dominions most of that Nacion inhabitt, to countenaunce the sayd Lte. Generall in desyringe that contribucion, and to permitt him to leavy and transporte souldyers for Scotlande, etc. An accounte returned by the same expresse to those who sent him of what was done and resolved, etc., they with the Lt. Ge[nerall] to appointe Treasurers to receave such monyes, etc.

3. An officer sent from Glengary, and 5 or 6 other Lords of the Highlandes, to informe the Kinge of ther resolucion to oppose the Rebells, to desyre Commissyons and armes, and that Middleton might be sent to them, etc.

4. A Commissyon sent to those Lords to governe the affayres untill such tyme as Middleton could come to them, with power to levy men, to choose a Commander in chiefe *pro tempore*, and Instructions how to proceede, etc., a letter to the Heades of

---

[1] From Lilburne to the officer in command at Dunotter?

[2] Clarendon Manuscripts, xlv. 370.

the Clanns to joyne with and assiste them, etc., power to inlarge the number of the Comissyoners by election of such persons as shall come to joyne with them, etc.

5. Whilst the officer who was to returne with this Comissyon and Instructions was in Holland, in expectacion to carry over armes and ammunicion, ther arryved togither two officers, the one sent from the Earle of Glengarne, to hasten Middleton's comminge thither, and in the meane tyme offringe his owne service to goe to those of the Highlandes and joyne with them, and to make other leavyes, and to conducte them till Middleton's arryvall, etc. The other from Balcarris, with the notice of Coll. Bampfeild's beinge ther; of his havinge gotten creditt with Bampfeild, and by his meanes with Glengary, etc., with desyres concerninge Bampfeilde, etc.

6. Upon the view of the dispatch from Glengarne, and the advice of Middleton therupon, the former Comissyon was stopped, and the same renewed with the Instructions, and derected to Glengarne, Balcarris, Seaforte, Pluscarden, and the former Comissyoners, without any other alteracion but of the addicion of the names, and of one Instruction for the apprehension of Bamfeilde, and disclayminge his havinge bene imployed by the Kinge. The other messenger from Balcarris was not yett come to [the King].

7. All this dispatch was sent to the Earle of Glencarne, togither with a letter to the Commissyoners to make choyce of him for the Commander in chiefe till Middleton should lande, and also a Commissyon to himselfe for that purpose, his Majesty out of his confidence, in his discrecion and affection to him, referring it absolutely to his judgement, whether he would deliver the Commissyon to the Commissyoners, and that letter for the election of himselfe by them, or whether he would suppresse both those, and execute the King's Commissyon to himselfe; his Majesty concludinge that he would do that which would be best for his service.

8. Blanke Commissyones for Coll., Lt. Coll., and Captaynes.

9. Since this, Roger is arryved from Balcarris, with instructions from Glengary to Bampfeild, (1) earnest sollicitacions from Balcarris on the behalfe of Bampfeild, as intrusted with all that concernes them; (2) intimacions as if Glengary would

not be commanded by Middleton in the Highlands; (3) proposicions to make Glengary Earle of Rosse, etc.; (4) desyre of letters to Lorne, and Argyle himselfe, etc.; (5) intimacion of Dunfarmelins purpose to come hither, etc.

10. Balcarris intrusts Roger with particulars which are not written, and amongst them disswades the makinge of Glengary Earle of Rosse, at least in the manner he proposed, etc. Bampfeild was sent over by the Earle of Diserte, with promise of a shipp with armes, etc.

The dispatch of Roger to be prepared, etc.

Indorsed:—*Summ of the Scotts businesse, May* 18, 1653.

XCV

PROCLAMATION by COL. LILBURNE.[1]

WHERAS I am informed severall complaints have lately bin made that souldiers doe stragle att great distance from their colours with their musketts, and kill and destroy rabbitts belonging to warrens and house-pigeons, contrarie to the lawes of this Nation and dishonour to the discipline of the army, and that some mischeif was like to have bin committed betweene souldiers and countrymen for the injuries done as aforesaid.

These are therfore to require all souldiers whomsoever, that after publicacion heerof they presume nott to shoote, kill, or any wayes destroy any rabbitts or pigeons aforesaid, as they will answer the contrarie under severe punishment att the discretion of a Court Martiall to bee held att the Head quarters [of the] regiment wherof they are or shall bee then Members, and all Officers of the Army are to take care to see the same duly putt into execucion. Given under my hand and seale att Dalkeith the 27th day of May 1653.[2]

RT. LILBURNE.

To bee proclaymed att the head of each Troope, and Companie, and in each Garrison.

---

[1] Clarke Manuscripts, xxv. 59.
[2] For other instances of the discipline maintained in the army of occupation, see *Mercurius Politicus*, pp. 2399, 2424.

XCVI

Summons to the Captain of the 'Fortune.'[1]

Being incited nott only by Conscience and Honour to stand firmely to the principles of Loyaltye, but alsoe disdaininge even in rationall interests to stoope to such a wavering servile power as now ruleth, I have laid hold on these men come on shoare as promoting the same. Wherefore I summon you to deliver your vessell for his Majesties service. And being perswaded that all or the most parte of you are with greife of heart employed in such service, I doe assure you that all that will voluntarily shunn the necessary effusion of [blood] by that surrender, shall have such faire quarter as is fitting for mee to grant and your severall condicions do require. And according to your demeanour herein you may expect to finde mee your frind accordingly,   Seaforth.

For the Captain, Souldyours, Master and Marrinours of the 'Fortune' these.

May 29th, about one a clock in the afternoone.[2]

The Answer.

My Lord,—I finde neither Conscience nor Honour ingaging mee to the performance of what you require. My men went nott ashoare with any intention of injury, and sithence you pretend to honour I desire you to send mee them aboard,

---

[1] Clarke Manuscripts, xxv. 61.

[2] Seaforth's letter is printed in *Mercurius Politicus*, June 23-30, 1653, and the *lacunae* of the version given in the Clarke Manuscripts have been supplied from that source. The newspaper gives the following account of this incident:—
'There being a privat man of war belonging to Capt. Brassie and commanded by one Capt. Edwards, who coming from Aire, anchored at the Lewis Island, and sent his lieutenant with 7 or 8 men ashore for some fresh meat, which was promised him by some of the gentlemen as he saith, that came on board of him; but the inhabitants made stop of all with his boat. And when he made signs from off a board, for the boat to return they sent him a summons, a copy whereof is here enclosed. The country people say that the Lord Seafort is broke out and declared for the King. The Lord of Pluckedy, and the Lord of Tarbut, his friends and curitors, with some others, are prisoners at Inverness, till they produce the liberty of the seamen taken in Lewis Island.'

otherwise you will constraine mee to make use of that power which itt hath pleased God to putt into my hands.—Yours as in Honour,   E. E[dwards].

For the Earl of Seaforth.

XCVII
Glengarry to the Earl of Athol.[1]

My Lord,—I am sorrie your Lolands receive such prejudice from those towards their feilds, but for restoring of these cows which are taken away, I must freely declare to your Lordshippe, that since your lands pay sesse to the Kinges enemies, and comes under contribution to them, these heir will nott thinke themselves obliged to any good neighbourhood; soe that qhat is taken from your people you may expect but little mends soe longe as they continue in that course, soe my opinion is your people looke the better to themselves, qhich is the further advice of, Your Lordship's humble servant,

Donald Glengarie.

Ranoth, June 7, 1653.

For the right honourable the Earle of Atholl these.

XCVIII
Proclamation by Col. Lilburne.[2]

By the Comander-in-Cheif of the Forces in Scotland.

Whereas there have bin many complaints come unto mee of late concerning the souldiers forwardenesse to take advantages against countrymen that are somewhat deficient, and doe make a common practice to exact monies without any order of their officers uppon such as they pretend are deficient. These are to require all souldiers whatsoever to forbeare to proceede in any such kinde to take any consideration for any deficiencie

---

[1] Clarke Manuscripts, xxv. 67. Atholl was between two fires. His lands were plundered by the one party for paying assessments, and his cattle seized by the other for not paying them. *Cf. Letters of Roundhead Officers*, p. 57.

[2] Clarke Manuscripts, xliii. 27.

from any inhabitant whatsoever, without consent and order from the cheif officer of the regiment and troope, uppon paine of punishment att a Court Martiall. Given under my hand att Dalkeith the 9th day of June 1653. RT. LILBURNE.

XCIX

COL. LILBURNE to the LORD GENERAL CROMWELL.[1]

MAY ITT PLEASE YOUR EXCELLENCY,—Upon the receipt of your Excellencies I did imediately examine our stores, which I found much short of what your Lordshippe seem'd to expect, there being nott above 700 barrells of powder in all the garrisons stores in Scotland, wherof I have spar'd 420, being as much as in reason or with any safety I could part with, and have appointed Capt. Allen to hasten away with them, as your Excellency will understand by the inclosed: but I doubt itt will bee Saturday night before hee can gett hence, by reason of our sending to Sterling and Dundee for some quantities from those places. I humbly intreat your Excellencies supply of these particulars according to your promise, as alsoe of such necessaries as have bin formerly desired for the traine and garrisons in Scotland, together with monie for the forces. Likewise that your Lordshippe will bee pledged with the Commissioners for the Navy for a store of victualls to bee laid in heere for furnishing such shippes as shall come into those parts; for through want therof such shippes as are sent to attend these coastes are many times incapable of doing any service, being constrained to goe away for victuall in a shorte time after their coming hither, and soe mispend their time to the great disservice of the State. That little baffle which was putt uppon the Highlanders by Col. Daniells partie[2] hath

---

[1] Clarke Manuscripts, lxxxvi. 59.

[2] Col. Daniel's success is the skirmish thus described in *Mercurius Politicus*, p. 2516:—

' From Col. Lilburne at Dalkeith in Scotland, June 7.—Last week a party of horse and foot being sent forth from St. Johnstons towards the Highlands, in Athole, to arrest the collector; the Lord Mac-Knab, one of the greatest Montrossians, with his whole clan did rise upon our party; and comming to them, after some little parley (we having got some of their cattel together) they offer'd our party free quarter, if

much discourag'd them, and was very seasonable unto us, there being att that time in those very parts divers great Lords and others complotting mischeif who since are discovered to us, and I hope to have some of them by the craigs; yet your Lordshippe may beleeve that many of them are in soe desperate a condition that they would bee glad to lay hold of the least opportunity to disturbe us.

Dalk. 9 *June* 1653.

C

A LETTER from the EARL of GLENCAIRNE.[1]

SIR,—His Majesty having sent hither ane commission for conducting his affaires in the Highlands of Scotland, soe many of the Commissioners as are heere mett have thought fitt to desire you in his Majesties name to come to Moy in Loghaber the first of July next precisely, where the Commissioners and Heads of Clans are to bee att that time to give their advice and concurrence in the carrying on his Majestie's affaires, according to the guid opinion his Majesty hath of the loyalty and affection [you bear] to his service, and your willingnesse to imploy the power and interest you have in the Country to advance his Majesties service and the guid of this kingdome. The assurance wee have of your tender respect to his Majestie's service (wherin is included the guid of Religion and the releef of our distressed country) makes us confidently expect you will nott faile to bee att that meeting: wee doe likewise earnestly desire that in the meane time you may take such course amongst your freinds and followers that they may uppon 24 houres advertisement bee in readinesse to rise and act as the Commissioners att the next meeting shall appoint, or in case of invasion before that time, to come to such Randezvous, and att such time as the Lairds of Glengarie and Loghyell sall name, they being by this meeting aucthorized for that purpose.

---

they would lay downe armes and return in peace. But our men, not willing to be so affronted, stood upon their defence; which the Highlanders perceiving sent a flight of arrows and a volley of shot among them: and ours letting fly again at them, killed Mac-Knab, the great chieftain of that wicked clan, with four more, and fell in upon them, and routed them all.'

[1] Clarke Manuscripts, xxv. 69.

Signed in presence by the appointment of his Majestie's Commissioners mett att Loghyell by your affeccionate servant,

GLENCAIRNE.

Loghyell, 13 *June.*
For the Guidman of Skellitor.

CI

To Sir Arthur Forbes.[1]

Ile of Loghyell, 14 *June* 1653.

DEARE ARTHUR,—By the letter to Scelitor you will see that this meeting hath only resolved to call ane other mor frequent,[2] and withall to desire that all may bee in readinesse uppon the advertisement which will bee sent in case of ane invasion betwixt [now] and then. If you have any considerable number with you, such as you cannott leade, you may advertise mee, and you shall have a further advice, but my opinion is rather that by any meanes you keepe the meeting, where you will see what may bee expected, and what may bee undertaken; anythinge that may tend to horsemen's security, either light able foote men, or horses you may have, but of this more att meeting. If you had any thing to say to mee betwixt [now] and then, your letter may bee sent to Glengarie, for I meane to stay in this Country 8 dayes, then I goe to Glengarie, and from thence to see my Lord Seaforth att Kintaill. If I can come back in time to the meeting you are allowed to informe Scelitor of all, but tell him promise secrecie, and by any meanes keepe the

---

[1] Clarke Manuscripts, xxv. 70. From Lord Balcarres?

[2] From Scotland, June 15.—' We had intelligence, that on the last day of May, at the Kirk of Killin, near the Laird of Glennochie's house, there was a meeting of severall considerable persons, viz., the Lord Balcarres, the Lord Lorne (Argile's son), the Earle of Glencarne, the Lord Loudoun, Sir Arthur Forbes, with many more. It's reported they have a commission from Charles Stuart, and are bound in a bond of secresie, and are sworn to stand to one another. They are gone to Glencarry, or thereabout, to put their design into execution.'

A second paragraph adds that Lorne and Loudoun were there by proxy and not in person.—*Mercurius Politicus,* p. 2536; see also p. 2546, where a meeting is said to have taken place at Rannoch, on June 3 and 4.

meeting. I am tormented with the worme [?] and can say noe more, but that I am, yours, A. B.

For Sir Arthur Forbes.

To bee left att Scelitor.

CII

An ENGAGEMENT of the GENTLEMEN of BLAIR, etc.[1]

WEE the Gentlemen and heritors of the parishes of Blaire, Donlye, Dull, Weeme, Logyerate, Kirkmichill, and Mullin, whose names are subscribed, doe hereby engage ourselves to save, defend, and keepe all such as [subscribe this from any harm that] may come to them by any of the Highlanders, or any other person or persons of . . . And further, wee doe engage our selves that neither directly nor indirectly to act or doe any thing against the present government, or against any officer or souldyour of the Englishe army, but shalbe ready and willing with our lives and estates for the preservacion of them, and the peace and quiet of the Commonwealth. In testimony whereof wee have hereunto subscribed our names this 15th day of June 1653.

ALEX. ROBTSON of . . .
DONALD ROBTSON of Kincragie.
JA. ROBTSON of Castrainervack.
JOHN STUART of . . .
ALEX. ROBTSON of Calbroore.
Alex. GORDON of the Manour of Blaire.
PATRICK ROBTSON of Blarefetly.
GEORGE STUART of Castrainervack.
JOHN STUARD of . . .
WM. STUART of Archinthall.

PATRICK STUART of Tultaft.
SHERIFF MEARE.
ALEX. STUART in Duart.
DUNCAN ROBTSON of Augleix.
JOHN STUART of Duart.
ALEX. STUART of Durghilbey.
ROB. ROBTSON of Faskallie.
PAUL ROBTSON in
JOHN STUART in Ballitine.
DONALD STUART in Behespick.
MR. JA. STUART.
JOHN STUART of Glasse.

---

[1] Clarke Manuscripts, xxv. 70. Very illegible, the names evidently baffled the original transcriber.

CIII

Lord Balcarres to Colonel Lilburne.[1]

Loghaber, 16 June 1653.

NOBLE SIR,—Give mee leave by these to shew you, that I have found my self and others comprehended in the Capitulation I made att Elgin[2] very unfairly dealt with, in regard that some of the most important Articles of it are broken to us. Our houses have bene searched by order, and our armes and goods seized on; the estates of some are kept from them; and withall both you and Col. Overton have bene pleased to declare of late in your answere concerning Sir Arthur Forbes, that the Capitulacion protected our persons, estates, and goods from the violence of the souldiery onely (a glosse which you never so much as hinted at whilst I was treating with you, and with noe equall judgement can rationally fix upon it), and that notwithstanding thereof they are still lyable (as you are pleased to expresse it) to the justice of the Commonwealth, by whome you say they may be either forfeited or sequestred; whereas wee had reason to expect our proteccion from them, seeing any assurance that was desired from mee was in reference to them, and not to the Army or souldyery from whence truly I never apprehended the danger of forfeiture or sequestracion; and besides I have bin at severall tymes and from severall good hands informed that my person was to be seised on by your order. All which have oblieged mee (notwithstanding of the extreame indisposicion of my body for travell) to retire my selfe somewhat further out of the way, where I may have some more hope of freedome then I had reason to expect where I was, and soe with tranquillitye of spirit waite upon the Lord's pleasure either to restore my selfe, or liberate mee from this mortall tabernacle. Having heard that there has bin some inquirye made after mee since I came away, I have thought fit to give you this account of my resolucion. Having noe further at present to saie but that I am, Your very humble servant, BELCARRES.

For Col. Lilborne, these.

---

[1] Clarke Manuscripts, xxv. 97.
[2] For the articles, see Balfour, *Annals*, vol. iv. p. 345.

CIV

SIR ARTHUR FORBES to COL. LILBURNE.[1]

NOBLE SIR,—After many addresses made by mee to your Commissioners in Ireland, where I expected the enjoyment of my estate by vertue of the Articles made betwixt my Lord Belcarris and your selfe, my answere was their resolucion to perfourme what soever Col. Overton and your selfe should conceive to bee the sence of them, which was all I did there desire, not doubting to have obteyned what was formerly granted to others, and which the sence of these Articles not being wrested clearely lead mee to enjoy; but in the contrary, after my earnest desires to your selfe and a returne from Col. Overton, I not only found my selfe denuded of all pretensions to my estate and livelihood, but alsoe obnoxious tto imprisonment, or what worse [those] acting by the authoritye of your Commonwealth should conceive expedient; wherefore I must beg pardon to shew you that I am not resolved any longer to live under your proteccion, and likewise declare my selfe to bee in reference to your party as I was before the making of these Articles. Soe having noe more but to adde my selfe, Sir, your humble servant, ARTHUR FORBES.

Lochaber, this 18th of June 1653.
For Col. Lilborne these.

CV

COL. LILBURNE to the LORD-GENERAL CROMWELL.[2]

MAY ITT PLEASE YOUR EXCELLENCY,—I perceive there has bin greate combinations amongst the Highlanders all this Springe to disturbe the peace of this Commonwealth, and all or most of the great ones have bin engag'd in itt. I gave your Lordshippe an account something to this purpose lately, and that I was in hope to have apprehended some of the greatest of them, but they are gone to the Hills, their cheif designe that I can learne being to gaine some reputation[3] abroad that there is yet

---

[1] Clarke Manuscripts, xxv. 98.   [2] *Ibid.* lxxxvi. 65.
[3] MS., 'regulation.'

the face of an army in the Highland, that young Charles by that meanes may gaine some assistance. There is come to my hand just now unexpectedly these inclosed copies, which I thought itt my duty to acquaint your Lordshippe withall.[1] The shippe is Capt. Brassie's. Uppon the receipt heerof I have sent orders to Lt. Col. Blount to seize and apprehend the Tutor of Seafort, and as many of the Cheif of that clan about Invernesse as can bee gott hold of, and shall humbly offer itt to your Excellency (if you see itt meete), that something might bee attempted upon my Lord Seafort and that Island, which is a very considerable place. I intreate that Col. Fitch and Col. Cooper may bee sent away with all speede, as alsoe two men of warr more to assist us in that service; and I doubt nott but what wee may bee able to doe uppon that Island will soe startle the whole Highlands and Islands that wee shall nott bee much troubled with them in such like cases heerafter. Undoubtedly to make the Lord Seaford and his Islland (called the Lewes) exemplary will bee a very great advantage to the peace of this Nation. I must humbly intreate alsoe a speedy supply of such a quantity of powder and shott as was lately sent from hence, with further supplies in convenient time according to the particulars formerly sent to the Councell of State.

Dalk. 18 *June* 1653.

CVI

Col. Lilburne to the Lord-General Cromwell.[2]

May itt please your Excellency,—By the inclosed you will perceive the temper of the Highlands, and I thinke itt may bee necessary (though the season have bin exceeding wett) to march a dayes march or two into the Highlands to see what temper the people are in, and whether wee can bringe them to enter into Bond for their good behaviours, for their subscripcions I doubt are but inconsiderable, though they promise never soe fairly; and heerin I intend to make use of the Civill aucthority, and of those acts of Parliament concerning

---

[1] See No. xcvi.   [2] Clarke Manuscripts, lxxxvi. 32.

the Cheifs of Clans giving security for keeping the peace and
making their appearance every yeare, wherby their mouthes
can bee lesse open'd against us, by reason these lawes of the
Nation are but putt in execution, and that there is nothing of
force uppon them but what is necessary, and which they
cannott except against. Uppon the Lord Seaforth's securing
these men in Lewis Island which I gave your Lordshippe an
account of in my last, his tutour, and some of the Cheif of
his Clan who are dangerous men, and have bin much suspected
by us to have an hand in the present contrivements against
us, are apprehended, and will bee secured till wee have some
good account of the Lord Seaforth of those men hee detaynes.
And truly I thinke itt a very good opportunity, if the State
thinke itt fitt, that uppon his late declaring for the King that
his estate might bee sequestred, and that Island, which is very
considerable and would bee of great advantage to our Nation,
might bee secur'd for the States service, and a garrison putt
into a Castle which is in itt, which would bee of good concernement, and an exemplary peece of justice tending to the
quieting and awing of all otheir Islands in those parts; for the
better carrying on wherof (if your Excellency approve of itt)
I intreate the assistance of 2 more men of warre, either uppon
this or the westerne coast. Wee are quite out of money in
the Treasury, and must either run uppon free quarter or our
souldiers must live uppon biskett and cheese, and yett the
Treasurers will nott allow Mr. ¦Bilton to returne any mony. I
beseech your Excellency to consider how unseasonable itt may
bee to run uppon free quarter in this juncture of time, as alsoe
that there is neere uppon 60000ł (of what was intended) due
to us, as Mr. Bilton gives mee an account, and without supply
the fortifications cannott goe one: butt of this I have said soe
much already that I shall forbeare any further; only in regard
that through the want of an agent wee have nott those necessary dispatches att London as the service heere requires, I
would humbly offer itt to your Excellency, and intreate that
5s. per diem may bee allowed out of the Scotts contingencies
to one to looke after our businesse att London, and the
officers heere will bee willing to contribute some thing for such

a mans better incouragement.—I remayne, your Excellencies most humble servant.

The little 'Faulcon' frygott hath this day brought in 2 Dutch prizes, and Col. Atkins hath brought in a 3d worth 1000l.[1]

Dalkeith, 21 June 1653.
Lord Generall.

CVII
A LETTER of INTELLIGENCE.[2]

MAY itt please your Honour to take notice, that I arrived att that place of the Highlands where the water of Earne issueth out uppon Sunday last, whence I sent out a man to search out Gerard Irvine, who mett mee on Munday about 12, with Sir Arth. Forbes, att an alehouse 8 miles within the hills. After wee had refreshed our selves they carried mee out to the hills 4 miles off, and having att large discoursed of our businesse in Ireland, which I pretended the reason of my coming to them, wee began to their intentions.

They told mee, That the men who were with them were the Lord Chancellour, the Earles of Glencairne and Atholl, Balcarras, Sir Robert Murray, the whole Highland Clans, and the Isles men.

2. There was many more ready to come out if they had opportunity.

3. The Highlanders would have entred in blood ere now, but they were hindred by Glencairne and Sir Ro. Murray till forrenners should come.

4. The 25th of this month they all meete about Loquhaber, where they open their Kinges Commission directed to them; they then chuse their officers, and will send a Commissioner to Holland for assistance.

5. They expect Middleton to bee Commander in Cheefe with some forces from abroade; they call them 2000 horses and 4000 foote.

---
[1] On the captures made by Atkins and others, see *Mercurius Politicus*, pp 2468, 2540, 2549, 2547.

[2] Clarke Manuscripts, xxv. 75. Addressed to Lilburne; undated, but written about June 25.

6. I found by them the defeate of the Hollanders had much discouraged nott only themselves but the Highlanders alsoe, soe that I really beleeve they will nott stirre, and [the man] I sent for assured mee of itt privately; yet they will indeavour to gett the Highlanders once to enter in blood with us, and then they know they will never capitulate, because they will never trust us after, for that is their disposition never to trust those they have once wrong'd.

CVIII

Colonel Lilburne to Mr. John Rushworth.[1]

Sir,—I have severall times consulted with officers heere about an agent to manage our businesse att London, and finde a great inclination in them to desire you to undertake that worke, for which wee are contriving to make the sallary as good as 200t. a yeare; if this can bee done, and that you will bee pleased to undertake the businesse I shall intreate your speedy answer unto, Your, etc.

Dalk. 21 *June* 1653.

Mr. Rushworth.

There are 3 prizes this day brought into Leith, one of them (being Col. Atkins) worth 1000t.[2]

CIX.

The Earl of Seaforth to Lieut. Col. Blount.

Sir,—I had fullie resolved to sett those prisoners att liberty before I received your letter or knew of your unjust imprisonment of my unkle, which did nothing att all accelerate my purpose to free them, neither did itt alter itt, for uppon that account I should nott have released one haire of their head,

---

[1] Clarke Manuscripts, lxxxvi. 34. Rushworth seems not to have accepted the post. There were also agents in England employed by different Scottish towns to manage their business with the Parliament and Council of State. Gilbert Mabbot was agent for Leith (*Cal. S. P. Dom.* 1652-3, p. 376), and William Thompson for Edinburgh (p. 333).

[2] *Ibid.* xxv. 77.

since by itt I conceive you doe your self a great deale of prejudice, but none to mee who am, Your servant, SEAFORT.

26 *June* 1653.
For Lt. Col. Blount,
 Governour of Invernesse.

CX

COLONEL LILBURNE to Mr. THURLOE.[1]

SIR,—This inclosed order seemes to bee soe far short of what is necessary for the carrying on of that worke which is begun heere that I could nott but returne a copie unto you to compare with the originall, and intreate you to returne mee an answer, whether the Councell of State intends 2000l. only, or 2000l. per Mensem.[2] If either of them itt will bee farre short of what will bee expended, which must bee laid out if the fortifications goe forward, for I have sent an account already to the Committee for Scotch and Irish affaires of the monthly charge of those fortifications, which does amount to 5000l. per Mensem for these 10 or 11 monthes, and will rather bee more then lesse till this Summer bee over, soe that unlesse the State see fitt to reimburse those monies which were sett apart for fortifications, and paid out for the pay of the forces, those fortifications cannott bee carried on to any purpose. I conceive alsoe there is some defect in that order, wherin 'tis said that the Commander in Cheif bee authorized to give order for the issuing out of monie, etc., but doth nott say that hee is therby aucthorized; and therfore itt seeming to relate to another order that is to bee granted, I doubt the Commissioners att Leith will scruple the raysing of monies uppon this aucthority. I thought meete rather to acquaint you heerwith then to trouble the Councell heerin unlesse you see itt necessary.—I remayne, Your humble servant, R. L.

Dalk. 28 *June* 1653.

---

[1] Clarke Manuscripts, lxxxvi. 67.

[2] On June 16th the Council had authorised Lilburne to expend not more than £2000 on fortifications in Scotland. The chief work in hand at the present moment seems to have been the fortification of Inverness.—*Cal. S. P. Dom.* 1652-3, pp. 355, 369, 416.

CXI

COLONEL LILBURNE to the LAIRD of PLUSCARTY.[1]

SIR,—Notwithstanding I have heard nothing wherin you have acted publiquely against the Commonwealth, yet having information that both your selfe and divers of your Clan have had correspondence with those that are indeavouring to disturbe the peace, and as you are Tutor to the Lord Seaforth who hath lately declar'd against the Commonwealth, I cannott but thinke itt both Lieutenaunt Col. Blounts dutie and mine to secure you till wee have further account from the Lord Seaforth concerning those prisoners hee soe unworthily seiz'd uppon. I am really sorry for your particular, but the publique safety doth soe farre require my diligence and care, that I must desire you to excuse mee att this time in giving noe further answer unto yours, and in doing that which is expected by those above mee, from Your very humble servant,   R. L.

Dalkeith, 30 *June* 1653.

CXII

COL. LILBURNE to the LORD GENERAL CROMWELL.[2]

MAY ITT PLEASE YOUR EXCELLENCY,—I received your commands concerning the Lewis, and intend to bee very diligent therin, conceiving itt a great opportunity to proceede against the Lord of itt, from whome as yet I have heard nothing about those men hee hath prisoners, notwithstanding his Tutor, the Laird of Pluscarty, and Sir John Mackenzie[3] are both secur'd. For the better managing of this worke I must intreate your

---

[1] Clarke Manuscripts, lxxxvi. 68.   [2] *Ibid.* lxxxvi. 34.

[3] Sir John Mackenzie was speedily released as the following letter from Lilburne to Colonel Blount, written a few weeks later, testifies:—

'Sir John Mackinzie haveing bene with me I have desired him to finde caution for his appearance, and acting nothing prejudiciell directly or indirectly against the Commonwelth, and in regard he pretends he cannot doe it conveniently here, hath moved me that he may give you securyty in the North, and because I am not willing to dischardge his former bond untill new be given, I have sent you the inclosed that it may be signed, which being done you may deliver in his former bond, and keepe this untill further order, and to give me an accompt speedily what you doe herein.'—Clarke Manuscripts, lxxxvi. 93.

Excellency to give order to the Treasurers that wee may charge bills, and soe have some monie return'd unto us, for our stock is att present very lowe, and itt seemes to bee something strange why the Treasurers should hinder the returne of mony, and putt the State and souldiery to that charge and trouble of bringing on 't from London or Yorke in waggons, when itt might bee almost every groate received heere uppon bills.

I must further humbly intreate your Excellency to send order to Lt. Col. Mayers to lett us have that powder, as alsoe that the quantity I sent unto the Navy with further supplies, according to the paper I formerly sent uppe to the Committee for the army, may bee speedily return'd unto us, for wee have but very little if there should bee any occasion of service; and further, that your Excellency would bee pleased to order Col. Cooper and Col. Fitch to hasten hither, together with other officers that have bin a longe time from their charges; and in particular Mr. Hane, the Engineer, of whome wee have an exceeding great want, and I doe wonder hee should neglect this duty soe much as hee does, his absence being the losse of some hundreds to the State, and if wee should have any occasion to make use of a morter peece without Mr. Hane, there is noe body to undertake that businesse that is fitt for itt. If the shippes bee nott come away, I intreate that your Excellency would appoint one of them to call att Berwick for that powder to bringe itt alonge with them. I intend Col. Cooper to command the partie if hee come downe in any time, and hope to have all thinges in readinesse against hee come. There being nothing considerable att present to acquaint your Excellency with, I cease to trouble you further, but remayne, Your Excellencies most humble servant, R. L.

Dalk. 30 *June* 1653.

Lord Generall.

CXIII

A Proclamation by Col. Lilburne.[1]

These are to require all souldiers whatsoever to forbeare to breake into any orchards, gardens, and yards of the people of

---

[1] Clarke Manuscripts, xxv. 80.

this Nation, or to plunder any fruites, cabbage, or rootes there growing, to the prejudice of the owners. They are alsoe to forbeare to gather any greene pease or beanes in any of their feilds, uppon penalty of undergoing such severe punishment as to a Court Martiall held for the quarters or regiment (wherof they are members) shall bee thought fitt. And all officers are heerby required to take care they see the premisses putt in execution. Given under my hand and seale att Dalkeith, the 4th day of July 1653. R. L.

CXIV
A Proclamation against Beggars.[1]

By the Commissioners Appointed for Administration of Justice to the People in Scotland.

Forasmuch as multitudes of Vagabounds, masterfull Beggars, strong and idle persons, are to the great dishonour of God, and eminent prejudice of the Inhabitants within this Nation, suffered to wander up and down aswell in Burghs as in Landwart, many whereof pretending to have been in the late Scots Armies, do not only beg, but also commit many Insolencies, Mischiefs, and Robberies, under pretext thereof: which, as it is not to be suffered in any wel-ordered and governed Commonwealth, so it is expresly against many Statutes and Acts of Parl. of this Nation, whereby it is ordained, That none be permitted to beg, but only sick and impotent persons tollerated so to do, according to several Acts of Parl. in that behalf made and provided, and that within the bounds of their own Parishes allanerly. And all other strong and idle Beggars to be put to work, or sent to the Parishes where they were born, or had their last residences. And if they refuse, then to be punished by scourging, imprisonment, burning on the cheek or ear for the first fault, and as thieves for the second, as the 74 Act of the 6 Parliament of James the sixth more particularly containeth; which Act doth also relate to severall other Acts of Parliament made in the times of James the first, James 2, James 4, and James the 5, concerning punishing of strong and

---

[1] Clarke's Papers, G. 5, 7. Proclamation against masterfull Beggars.

idle Beggars and Vagabounds. Whereby all Provests, Bailiffs, Sheriffs of Shires, within their severall jurisdictions, are ordained to put the said Acts in execution, under certain pains therein contained. These are therefore to command all idle persons, masterfull Beggars or Vagabound Souldiers, not actually imployed about some lawfull Calling, but wandering and begging, whether in Burghs or Landwart, within any part of this Nation: That they repair to the Parishes where they were born, or had their last residence, within the space of twenty-one dayes after publication hereof: With certification, that who thereafter shal be found wandering and begging, shall be punished conform to the Acts of Parliament abovementioned, made for punishing such kind of persons. And for that effect all Provests, Bailiffs, and Officiars within Burghs, and Sheriffs within Shires, are required to take notice of the said Vagabond Souldiers, etc., and put the foresaid[1] Acts of Parliament in execution against them, under the pains contained in the Acts of Parliament, to be inflicted on all those who are remisse or negligent in their foresaid respective duties.

Given under our Hands at Edinburgh, July the fourth, 1653.

HEN. WHALLEY, Advocate Gen. in Causes Criminall.

GEO. SMYTH.

AND. OWEN. JO. MARCH. ED. MOSLEY.

Printed at Leith, 1653.[2]

CXV

COL. LILBURNE to the LORD GENERAL CROMWELL.[3]

MAY ITT PLEASE YOUR EXCELLENCY,—The James and the other 2 frigotts are now safly arrived heere, and wee are loading as

---

[1] ['foresaids' in broadside.]

[2] From a printed broadside amongst William Clarke's papers. *Mercurius Politicus* for Aug. 11-18, 1653, p. 2649, contains a second proclamation by the Commissioners for the execution of certain Acts of James VI., 'for the suppression of sorners, broken Highlanders, Borderers,' etc., ordering a number of noblemen and heads of clans to come in and to give security for the peaceable behaviour of themselves and their dependants. This is reprinted in the *Spottiswoode Miscellany*, ii. 117.

[3] Clarke Manuscripts, lxxxvi. 68. Compare *Mercurius Politicus*, p. 2597.

fast as wee can, and hopes to saile about Saturday next. The
60 barrells of powder is come from Berwick; I hope your Lordshippe is sending us more according to my former papers.
This inclosed is a coppy from the Lord Seaforth, wherin you
will perceive hee hath sett those 8 men att liberty. Hee is
yett resolute for the Kinge, and is fortifying a small Island
neere Sternway. There is an Englishman with him from the
Kinge, who goes by the name of Crawford, a black proper
man; and when Captaine Bressies shippe came first in sight,
Seaforth and the rest tooke itt for granted that itt was from
Charles Stuart, and thought hee had bin come for that Englishman. Seaforth hath sent to advise with his freinds, and wee
conceive is jealous of himselfe and his Island, by reason hee is
taking his guns from Kintaile to strengthen his Island. Your
Lordshippe will alsoe perceive by the inclosed coppies from
the Earle of Glencairne what they have bin about in the Hills,
knowing wee cannott this yeare come att them by reason of
wett, and hee with other Lords are yett in those parts about
Loquhaber(?). I beseech your Lordshippe once more to send
away the Colonells, but especially Mr. Hane, and to thinke of
some mony for us.—I remayn your Excellencies, etc.

Dalkeith, 5 July 1653.

CXVI

The EARL of GLENCAIRN to LIEUTENANT-GENERAL MIDDLETON.[1]

SIR,—You being our fellow sufferer and a deepe sharer in
these our Calamities, we shall not afflict you with a sad re-
hearsall of those things, to which you are noe stranger. As
we are most confident that the cry of our blood hath reached
Heaven, soe we doe not at all doubt, but the extremities of the
Earth are acquainted with the horrid actings of those men of
blood (ennemyes to Government and all humane society) under
whom we suffer. If those things had bene done amongst
infidles (who know nothing of God but by pure nature), we

---

[1] Clarendon Manuscripts, xlvi. 55.

dare say it had not bene unrecented to this day; but that which infinitely encreaseth our sufferings, and addeth to our afflictions is, that men and nations (for the promoting of whose interest we have not spared our best blood) should not only bring a curse upon themselves in not helping the Lord against the mighty, in not delivering us who are reddy to be drawne to death, but likewise by applications to, and unlawfull associations with, those murtherers, are pulling downe upon themselves the wrath of Heaven, not considering that of Solomon,[2] 'He that sayeth to the wicked thou art righteous, him shall the people curse, nations shall abhorr him :' O that men would forbeare to meddle with them who are given to change; and with-draw from the tents of those wicked men, not touching any thing of theirs, that doing soe they may not be consumed in their sinnes. As wee have just grounds to complayne that servants have ruled over us, and that there is none that doth deliver us out of their hands; soe we have likewise great matter of prayse, that the Lord hath bene pleased to encourage all rancks of people in this land with a fixed resolution, rather to perrish nor submitt to a sinfull compliance with those men, and that he hath bene pleased to stirr up soe mighty a people as the States of the United Provinces to withstand their tyranny; we looke to God's hand in this, and we trust that God will by those States deliver us his people; and honour them as rebuilders of his almost ruyned Sion in these three Kingdomes of Scotland, England, and Ireland. Therefore we desire and require you to addresse your selfe to the high and mighty Lords the Estates of the United Provinces, and lay downe before them our sad condition, which we are sure they looking upon at soe neere a distance cannot but reade in great charracters; you are likewise to represent to them what great advantages will redound to them by assisting us, and how able we are to promote there interest, by making a diversive warr, and how willing we are that the King our Soveraigne should posses them with any places or sea-ports which they shall desire, to be possessed by them for ever, for the securing of their fishing and commerce. We doubt not his Majestie will consent to this or

---

[1] Proverbs xxiv. 24.

any thing else which may conduce to the advancement of his service in our hands. We are not ignorant at what vast charge the Estats are in carrying on a sea-warr, soe that we should not, at soe unseasonable a time, demand any assistance from them, were it not for the promoting as well of their as our owne interest. We shall not take upon us to propose any particulars relating to our supply, but leave that totally to themselves and your managing. We shall only add one thing, that if our sad estate and condition be looked upon by them at this time, they must either conclude us to be monsters and not men, or expect the greatest returnes of thankefullnesse that ever were performed by ane obliged people. In the meane time we shall not cease to implore a blessing from Heaven upon all their undertakings, neither shall we be wanting in action against the common Ennemy. Wishing you a speedy and succesfull home-coming, we rest, Your very affectionate friends,

GLENCARNE, I.P.D.C.[1]

From Buchanan, July 5th the old stile.

Indorsed.—*Scotlande the 5 of July. A copie of the Earle of Glengarnes lettre to Lt. Grall Middleton, he being President of the Councell of the King's party in Scotland.*

CXVII

WARRANT from COLONEL LILBURNE.[2]

I DOE heerby desire and aucthorize you, or any three of you, to meete att Edinburgh the 12th of this instant July, with such Gentlemen as are or shall bee appointed, and sent as Commissioners from the severall counties for regulating the valuacions, and from time to time to receive such propositions and overtures as they shall bringe in concerning the same, and after debate theruppon to report your proceedings and opinions

---

[1] 'Most worthy Mr. Chanrs. perusall,' is the note added by Secretary Nicholas.

[2] Clarke Manuscripts, xliii. 4.

therin unto mee.   Given under my hand att Dalkeith the 11th
day of July 1653.   RT. LILBURNE.

*To Col. Edmund Syler, Col. Berry, Lt.-Col. Cotterell, Lt.-
Col. Wilkes, Lt.-Col. Talbott, Lt.-Col. Goughe, Judge Advocate
Whalley and Auditor Generall Thompson.*

CXVIII

COL. LILBURNE to the LORD GENERAL CROMWELL.[1]

MAY ITT PLEASE YOUR EXCELLENCY,—Our party is now going under the conduct of Col. Cobbett, and I hope will very shortly bee att the Lewis, from whence the Lord Seaforth is gone to the Mainland towards Loghaber to a great meeting there of the Kinges Commissioners, as they call themselves, who intend to doe something if they could tell how, but I perceive their hopes are exceedingly frustrated, and the people more apt to bee quiett then they are able to provoke them to new troubles, and Seafort's owne Clan are as sensible of his late folly as may bee, and decline him. Before hee came from the Lewis hee dispatch't away Crawford, the Kinges agent, for France, with his owne and many Lords and the Cheif of Clans subscripcions to younge Charles to send them supplies according to his promise, and of their readiness to doe him service. Hee alsoe brought over those men of ours hee had detayn'd, wee having apprehended his unkle and Sir John Mackenzie, who (notwithstanding our men are releas't) till wee have setled the Lewis I thinke itt nott fitt to discharge. The Lord Balcarris (being one of the great sticklers in the Hills) the other day had 2 of his best horses stolne by the Highlanders in Loghaber, and 'tis conceiv'd the next newes wee shall heare of him and some others of them will be their flight beyond seas (though att present they are endeavouring to doe what they can to disturbe us); and I am informed Mr. Robert Douglas is the principall man in their plott, and has his correspondence with divers presbyter in England. Marquis Huntley and Argyll had a

---

[1] Clarke Manuscripts, lxxxvi. 70.

meeting lately about settling of Huntley's estate, and both of them sent mee letters to intreate a proteccion for Huntley for 3 monthes to come downe to Edinburgh to advise with his Councell about ratifying that agreement betweene his unkle and him, and in regard both of them pretends peace towards us (upon advice with the Judges) I intend to give Huntley that liberty, which I conceive may tend to our advantage. I intreate your Lordshippe to remember Mr. Hane, and supplies of ammunicion and mony, as alsoe a tendernesse towards the prisoner[1] soe neerly related unto, My Lord, Your Excellencies most humble and faithfull servant,   R. L.

Dalk., 12 *July* 1653.

Postscript.—The Generall Assembly of the ministers being to meete the next weeke att Edinburgh, in regard of the fiklenesse of the times, and present designes that are amongst many, I would humbly intreate your Lordshippes direccions whether I should prevent that meeting or nott; because the late Councell seem'd to take offence att the nott hindering their former meeting.

CXIX

Col. Lilburne to the Marquess of Argyll.[2]

My Lord,—Wheras information is given mee, that severall Lords and Gentlemen are drawne together in the Highlands, and in combination to disturbe the peace of this Commonwealth, I desire your Lordshippe to keepe the shire of Argyll as free as you can from any commotions, and to suppresse any in itt whom your Lordshipp shall know to bee fomenters or concurrers any way in such combinations; and to oppose any who shall offer to invade the said shire of Argyll, or come into itt from other places of the Highlands, Isles, or Lowlands to disturbe the peace thereof; and to cause to bee apprehended and taken all suspitious and dangerous persons whatsoever,

---

[1] Lieut.-Col. John Lilburne, the writer's brother, then about to be tried for returning from banishment without leave.

[2] Clarke Manuscripts, lxxxvi. 91.

which I intreate your Lordshippe to secure untill you have signified soe much unto, My Lord, Your most humble servant.

Dalkeith, 15 *July* 1653.

Marq. of Argyll.

CXX

ORDER by COLONEL LILBURNE.[1]

WHERAS by reason of the constant quartering of souldiers in the houses where they are first placed, other houses are exempted, especiallie in Edinburgh, and other places of great receipt. These are therfore (for the prevention of the like inconveniencies for the future) to order and declare, that the Quartermasters in the City of Edinburgh and suburbes theroɪ shall have power, and are heerby aucthorized to remove souldiers, horse or foote, from one place of the citty to another, for the preventing their being too burthensome in any one place; provided that the officer in cheif of the Regiment, Troope, or Companie have notice of such removall, and that the companies bee nott intermixt one with another. This course to bee taken till further order. I doe alsoe heerby require, that all souldiers whatsoever doe forbeare to vitiate, abuse, or counterfeitt the ticketts given them by the said Quartermasters, uppon paine of being proceeded against and punished att the discretion of a Court Martiall. Given under my hand and seale att Dalkeith, the 20th day of July 1653.

RT. LILBURNE.

CXXI

COL. LILBURNE to the LORD GENERAL CROMWELL.[2]

MAY ITT PLEASE YOUR EXCELLENCY,—Having some intimation that the present Meeting of the Ministers of the Generall Assembly att Edinburgh tended to a further correspondence with those mett in the Highlands, I thought itt my duty, for the prevention of any thinge that might be to the disturbance

---

[1] Clarke Manuscripts, xliii. 32.
[2] *Ibid.* lxxxvi. 71.

1653] THE GENERAL ASSEMBLY DISSOLVED 163

of the publique peace, to dissolve their Assembly; for which purpose I ordered Lt. Col. Cotterell and Capt. Hope to repaire to Edinburgh with directions for dismissing of them, which they did yesterday. After 2 sermons, preached by Mr. David Dick and Mr. Robert Douglas, who prayed for the king, the Assembly going to meete in the usuall place Lt. Col. Cotterell came into the place, demanded of them whether they satt by virtue of any auctority from the present power, which they denying hee dismist them, himself going before them brought them out att the West Port, in order to their repaire homeward. The people generally doe conceive this was excused by the Remonstratours, though it was onely resolved on amongst ourselves upon the consideracion of preventing further designes, which I understand depended upon this meeting. I have allsoe dismis't by proclamacion all other Ministers and Gentlemen that are not call'd about their perticuler affaires, or the publique meeteing lately appoynted about the sesse.[1] The Remonstratours seeme very joyfull at the dissolution of the assembly, and had prepared a protestacion against them, as it appeared upon their riseing, yet itt's conceived they would have agreed, and both Mr. Dick and Mr. Duglasse [consent]ing tended to union and reconsiliacion.

The winde hath proved soe contrarie since the going forth of the shippes with provisions and necessaries for the forces designed for the Lewis, that they are scarce yet at Aberdene.

---

[1] An account of the dissolution of the General Assembly is given in Baillie's *Letters*, iii. 225; *Mercurius Politicus* for July 21-28, contains the following description :—

From Edinburgh, July 21.—' We have here a very remarkable accident fallen out yesterday; which is a dissolution of the General Assembly of the Kirk, and a dispersion of all its members. As soon as sermon was done, and they'gone to the Assembly-house, and entred upon their business, Lieut.-Col. Cotterel went in to them, and, standing upon a bench, with a loud voyce proclaimed, that no Judicatory ought to sit that had not authority from the Parliament; and so causing them to depart, he conducted them with a troop of horse, and a company of foot out at the West-port ; and then bidding them to close round in a circle, environing them with his horse and foot, he blamed them for their bold meeting, took in their commissions, required them not to meet 3 together in a company, and that by 8 a clock this morning they should all quit this city, and repair to their several homes, or else to suffer as enemies of the Commonwealth ; so there is an end of the Kirks grand Assembly, which hath bin an engine so formidable in Scotland.'

I heare the Lord Seaforth and Balcarres are returned from Loughaber towards Lewes, with some other G[entlemen], where they dayly expect some shipping. I am not throughly perswaded that Middleton is yet come. The Lord Argill seemes very readie to oppose those people in Loughaber.

Our want of money at this time seemes to be an incouragement to our enimies, who conceives we are not able to subsist long at the vast charge the Commonwelth is at; the foote eate biskett and cheese on Pentland hills, and hath not money to buy them other refreshments, being now 2 months and above in arreare, and our fortificacions readie to stand still, and the workemen giveing over will not easily be gott together, nor doe I know where to gett 100 t in the treasury; this hath bene often represented above and hinted to your Excellencie, and if supply come not, I feare it may be of greater disadvantage, and the reputacion of the Comonwelth much hazarded, all which I once againe humbly leave to your Excellencies consideracion, and beggs your Lordshipp's mindfullnes of us.—I remaine, My Lord, Your Excellencies most humble servant.

Dalk., 21 *July* 1653.

CXXII

Proclamation by Colonel Lilburne.[1]

Wheras there is information given, That there are frequent meetinges in divers parts of this Nation tending to the disturbance of the peace of this commonwealth, and that att this time many are conveened att Edinburgh in more then an ordinarie manner from all parts of the Nation without any publique order, These are therfore to require all Lords, Gentlemen, Ministers or any others who are nott inhabitants in Edinburgh, nor have any publique call to bee there, or suites of law presently depending to depart the said Citty by 8 of the clock to-morrow morning, being the 22th of this instant July, and to repaire to their severall habitations without further delay, uppon paine of being imprisoned and proceeded against

---

[1] Clarke Manuscripts, lxxxvi. 72.

as enemies to the peace of the Commonwealth. Given under my hand and seale att Dalkeith the 21th day of July 1652.

To bee proclaymed by sound of trumpett att the Mercatt Crosse of Edinburgh.

CXXIII

THE MARQUESS of ARGYLL to COL. LILBURNE.[1]

RIGHT HONOURABLE,—I have not seene my servant James Cambell whome I sent to your Honour after my meeting with my nephew. I sent the last weeke one lettre to him wherein I desired him to acquaint your Honour with Mr. Mackpherson's retorne to ane House of his within 2 miles of this place with Sir Arthur Forbes, one Capt. Gerard Irwine (whoe was taken at Worcester, and released since), and some others whereupon I have taken some men into my company for defence of my owne person, which God knowes is not soe much worth. But that Christian duty in using lawfull ordinary meanes is not to be neglected. And I have not lesse ground but more to increase my jealousie, for at my returne hither I desired to know if I was cleare in my owne family, whereupon I cal'd for my eldest sonne, that I might put him to it (as I did) to declare to mee if he was free from engagements with these people now stirring, and that he would assure mee he would never engage with them. He declared that he was not resolved to engage with them but would not[2] declare on the negative, though he said to some in private he resolv'd not to joyne with them, however imediately after his goeing out of my sight hee tooke horse and went to Glenurquhy[3] where it seem'd he appointed a meeting with Auchinbreck, Mac Nachtane, Sir Arthur Forbes, and such as are of that crew; but imediately after I knew of his resolucion I caused my last warning come to his hands, whereof the inclosed is a copie, soe what resolucion he takes on it I know not, for hee went but from this upon Munday after 12 a clocke. This much I declare unto your

---

[1] Clarke Manuscripts, xxv. 102.   [2] Manuscript, 'now.'
[3] Manuscript 'Glyngerry.'

Honour, that what I doe in this is sincerelye done, as in the Lord's sight before whome I must answere one day for all I doe otherwaies. And if I had not some apprehension that my presence here might hinder their designes in a great measure I had come my self to your Honour upon any hazard, and if your Honour require it, let mee be protected from violence of creditours and I shall waite on your Honour where you please, they have not one man togeather but their ordinary servants, and I beleeve without very great violence they will get very few. Sir James M'Donald came here on Munday whome I finde most inclineable to peaceable and quiett, but he wants not threatnings for it. I shall strive with the Lord's assistance to doe my best to hinder the country people here from raising men, which I doe finde them very inclineable to obey. And I pray God the guilty may finde their owne weight, and that the innocent[1] sufferr not with them. I can say noe more til I heare from your Honour but that I am, Your very humble servant, J. ARGILE.

Its the way of all that take them to such courses as this people are upon, to make lies their refuge. They haunt the common people with them, either for stirring them up or disaffecting them as it makes for their purpose.[2]

CXXIV

THE MARQUESS of ARGYLL to LORD LORNE.[3]

SONNE,—Hearing you are upon a course for disturbing the quietnes and peace of country in generall, and drawing new

---

[1] Manuscript, 'ignorant.'

[2] Of these four letters the originals of two, viz., cxxiii. and cxxvi. are amongst the archives of the Duke of Argyll. At present, however, they are in the keeping of Sir William Fraser. It was intended to compare the copies given amongst Clarke's papers with the originals, but it proved impossible to obtain access to them. However, the two letters are calendered in the Sixth Report of the Royal Commission on Historical Manuscripts (p. 617), and the abridged versions given there have supplied corrections of two or three obvious mistakes in Clarke's versions. These corrections are pointed out in the footnotes. The originals of the letters numbered cxxiv. cxxv. are not in the Duke's collection.

[3] Clarke Manuscript, xxv. 101.

troubles upon this shire, and my family in particular, whereupon there may follow soe much guiltinesse and prejudice. Therefore if there be in you either feare of God, or respect to his law in your obedience to your Parents, or any feare of the curse pronounced in God's word against the setters lightly of either father or mother, or if you desire not their curse to follow you in all your waies, These are requiring you as you will answere for it one day before the Throne of God, and as you desire to be free of all the guiltinesse and prejudice which will follow such waies, and as you desire to enjoy any thing that is mine, or would eschue to deserve my curse, that you will hearken to my counsell[1] to forbeare such courses; and if yet for all this God harden your heart to your owne destruccion and tryall or trouble of others, Then let all the guiltinesse and prejudice that may follow such waies fall on your selfe, and cleave to you and your adharents and noe other belonging to you; And let all the curse and judgements pronounced in God's word against disobedient children to parents come upon you and pursue you til they overtake you, and let nothing you take in hand prosper, for you are a crosse (I may say a curse) to your father and heavinesse to your mother, if you continue in your waies. But if you repent and returne, God will have mercy, you shall escape the miserye, and I shall remayne Your loving father, ARGILE.

CXXV

LETTER to LORD LORNE.[2]

My LORD,—Having received lettres before your Lordshipp's to attend your Lordshipps father in this place at ane meeting wee cannot conveniently waite on your Honour, but hearing of your Lordshipps goeing from this with the way of it, and your Lorshipps resolucion to goe to Lochaber for rising in armes, give us leave to saie it, wee conceive it our duty to let your Lordshipp know, that wee thinke your Lordshipps course in

---

[1] The position of this clause has been altered. In the Manuscript it follows 'trouble of others.'

[2] Clarke Manuscript, xxv. 101.

this nott onely imprudent but many waies of very ill consequence. Therefore wee have sent the bearer, Doughall Cambell of Logge, to waite on your Lordshipp, and to tell our minds more fully in this. We exhort your Lordshipp to returne, which if your Lordshipp will hearken to, wee shall not be wanting to assist your Lordshipp with our best councell, in every thing that may concerne your Honour or happinesse. If otherwise, wee are free in exonering ourselves, and shalbe sorry that your Lordshipp sett light by our advise, and disables us whoe are very desirous to obey your Lordshipp in all lawfull commands. As for your Lordshipps letter dated the 20th of this moneth, where your Lordshipp desires us to avoid any unlawful engagement, wee shalbe most willing to obey it by God's assistance, desiring and wishing your Lordshipp to doe the like, and not to engage without your frinds approbacion, which is the expectance of My Lord, your Lordshipps affectionate frinds and cousins to serve you.

Innerara, 21th July 1653.

CXXVI

The Marquess of Argyll to Col. Lilburne.[1]

Right Honourable,—I finde the proverbe true that experience may teach fooles, and that itt is the ordinarie practice of such as have followed or doe follow malignant courses to be expert in lyeing and dissembling, for though (as I writ in my former lettre to you) my sonne professed that he intended not to joyne with the Highlanders, yet since his partiag from this I feare he hath resolved the contrary. And soe your Honours informacion concerning him hath bin better then mine, for after the writing of this other lettre (which the Bearer carries) my servant James Cambell came home, with whome I received your Honours lettre, and has gotten any certainty that I have of my sonnes resolucions after that, likewise that I may assure your Honour for any thing that I know there is not any at all that concernes this shire that countenances him in his present course and present resolucions, except

---

[1] Clarke Manuscripts, xxv. 100; Hist. Manuscripts Comm. vi. 617.

Achinbreck, M'nahtone, Gdoquhire,[1] Ardchattane, for the whole rest of the gentlemen of the shire are here with mee at present, professing their dissatisfaccion of this way, which they are to make knowne to himselfe this day; and though I dare say nothing positive in this world, yet I am very hopefull with the Lords assistance they shall get very little concurrence from this shire in any of their desperate designes. Since the writing of my last lettre likewise Sir James M'Donald tels mee that he is to write to your Honour, and to desire the same favour which hee obtained from Gen. M. Deane; and indeed I doe really thinke he deserves it, for soe farre as a Christian and a gentleman's expression can bee beleeved I am perswaded he is resolved to live peaceably, and indeed he is considerable in the Highlands and Isles. I finde the gentlemen in this shire very inclineable to doe their duty concerning the Sesse, and I am confident if they had present mony, it would be instantly satisfied. And though it be never soe considerable as is to be had in mony it shalbe received, and obligaunts [?] under their hands for payment of the rest at a certaine day, whereof your Honour shall have an account soe soone as I can, for hearing that your Honour was remooving from Dalkeith I have onely sent a gentleman with this to find you out where ever you are, that upon Advertisement where you are certainly to be found I intend to send ane expresse to waite uppon your Honour; for in every thing I desire with the Lord's assistance to walke uprightly, and I shall remaine, Your Honour's very humble servant, J. ARGILE.

21*th July* 1653.

For the Right Honourable Col. Lilborne, Commander in cheife of the forces in Scotland, these.

---

[1] 'Straquhurre.' Hist. Manuscripts Comm.

CXXVII

THE VALUATION of SCOTLAND.[1]

ROLL for dividing of ninetie Thousand pound Scotts, condescended unto by the Commissioners of shires mett at Edinburgh. 22 July 1653.

Shires.	The severall shires proportions of the 90000$^{lib.}$ in Scots monie.	The severall shires proportions of the 90000$^{lib.}$ in English monie.	The valuations of shires att 48^s Scotts uppon ilk 100^l Scotts.	The proportions of the Assesse in English monie with an addition of ij^s viij^d in pound more per mensem.		
Orknay and Zetland,.	1625	0135 08 04	067700	0153	09	06
Caithnesse, . .	894	0074 10 00	037250	0084	08	08
Sutherland, . .	500	0041 13 04	020834	0047	04	06
Innernesse and Rosse,.	3868	0322 06 08	161168	0365	06	02
Cromartie, . . .	100	0008 06 08	004170	0009	09	00
Nairne, . . .	413	0034 08 04	017209	0039	00	00
Elgine, . . .	1580	0131 13 04	065834	0149	04	06
Bamff, . . .	1700	0141 13 04	070834	0160	11	02
Aberdene, . . .	6088	0507 06 08	253670	0574	19	06
Kincardine, .	1466	0122 03 04	061084	0138	09	02
Forfar, . . .	4888	0407 06 08	203644	0461	12	10
Perth, . . .	7521	0626 15 00	313379	0710	06	04
Fyff, ...	7521	0626 15 00	313379	0710	06	04
Clackmannan, . .	524	0043 13 04	021733	0049	09	10
Kinross, . .	200	0016 13 04	008334	0018	17	09
Stirling, . . .	2618	0218 13 04	109044	0247	05	02
Linlithgow, . .	1896	0158 00 00	079045	0179	01	04
Edenburgh, . .	4751	0395 18 04	197964	0448	16	02
Haddingtoun, . .	4151	0345 18 04	172964	0392	00	09

[1] Clarke Manuscripts, xliii. 12.

THE VALUATION OF SCOTLAND

Shires.	The severall shires proportions of the 9000lib. in Scots monie.	The severall shires proportions of the 9000lib. in English monie.	The valuations of shires att 48s Scotts uppon ilk 100l Scotts.	The proportions of the Assesse in English monie with an addition of ijs vijd in pound more per mensem.		
Berwick, . . .	4200	0350 00 00	175000	0396	13	04
Roxburgh, . . .	5501	0458 08 04	229214	0519	10	09
Selkirke, . . .	1350	0112 10 00	056550	0127	10	00
Peibles, . . .	1564	0130 06 08	065169	0147	14	02
Lanerick, . . .	4727	0393 18 04	196964	0446	08	09
Aire, . . .	5777	0481 18 04	240714	0545	12	02
Dumfreize, . .	4050	0337 10 00	168750	0382	10	00
Wigton and Stewartrie,	4000	0333 06 08	166669	0377	15	06
Renfrew, . . .	2020	0168 06 08	084169	0190	15	06
Dumbarton, . .	1140	0095 00 00	047500	0107	13	04
Argyll, . . .	2907	0242 05 00	121169	0274	11	00
Bute, . . .	460	0038 06 08	019212	0043	08	10
		7500 00 00		8500	00	00

CXXVIII

Order concerning the Valuation of Scotland.[1]

The Comissioners of shires conveened att Edinburgh in July 1653 for regulating the valuations and accomodating differences amongst themselves having taken into consideration the valuation made in the yeare 1629 for payment of the tenth and twentie pennie, and the rule of tax and loane (which was conforme to the retours, with some deductions and additions) and the valuations of rents given in the yeares 1644 and 1645, and perfected in the yeare 1649, and having had severall meetinges. According to their owne knowledge, and best information they could attaine, all parties interested being heard to the full, they doe uppon mature deliberation condescend uppon the Roll above written as the Rule of Division amongst shires for payment of ninetie thousand pound monthlie, and to bee a Rule for all common burthens: onlie itt is to bee understood that this Rule is agreed uppon without consideration had to the decay of casuall rents, and the devastations made in many shires through the calamities of warres, which is humbly desired to bee taken into consideration by the Commander in Cheif. And in regard some very few shires have dissented from this present agreement, notwithstanding the reasons given by them have bin heard att length, and answers therunto returned, and such case allowed unto them as may give satisfaccion. Therfore itt is humblie desired, that in case any of the Commissioners of these shires which have dissented shall make application to the Commander in Cheif, and give reasons against this Rule now agreed uppon, that noe alteration bee made therin, unlesse all the Commissioners of shires which have condescended to this Rule bee heard to give answers to the reasons of the dissenting shires: and in testimonie of our agreement wee have given warrand to Sir James Learmonth

---

[1] Clarke Manuscripts, xliii. 12.

of Balcolinie, our present preses, to signe and subscryve thir presents, written att Edinburgh the 22 day of July 1653.

Signed att command of the Commissioners be mee.

JA. LERMONTH.

CXXIX[1]

WEE whose names are subscribed being appointed Commissioners by Col. Lilburne, Commander in Cheif in Scotland, to meete with Commissioners from the severall shires to consider of an equall proportioning of the publique burthens amonge the said shires, and having received a paper heerunto annexed signed by their Praeses, Sir James Lermonth, wherin the severall shires are proportioned, to which proportions they all agreed and assented, except the shires of Dumfreize, Wigton, Orknay, Invernesse, and Aberdene, who have given their reasons of dissenting in writing (heerunto alsoe annexed), and uppon full hearing and debating of the said matter, wee cannott finde any reason to change or alter the rates agreed unto by the generalitie; therfore wee doe humblie give our opinion and desire, that the said paper signed by the said praeses may bee allowed as the Rule, by which publique burthens may bee heerafter laid. Dated this 23th day of July 1653.

JA. BERRY.   WM. BRAYNE.   JNO. THOMPSON.
The assesse.

---

[1] Clarke Manuscripts, xliii. 11, 6.

CX

The Assesse laid uppon Scotland for the 4

Shires.	Shires and Burghes.	Laid on Shires and Burghes.	Abatementes.
Orknay and Zetland	Orknay .	153 09 06	040 00 00
Caithnesse . .	Caithnesse .	084 08 08	004 00 00
Sutherland . .	Sutherland .	047 04 06	005 00 00
	Dornock .	002 05 00	000 15 00
Invernesse and Rosse	Invernesse and Rosse .	365 06 02	045 06 02
	Invernesse Burgh .	037 10 00	037 10 00
	Tayne . .	007 10 00	002 00 00
	Dingwell .	001 10 00	
Cromerty . .	Cromerty .	009 09 00	001 09 00
Nerneshire . .	Nerneshire .	039 00 00	009 00 00
	Nerneburgh .	003 00 00	001 00 00
Elginshire . .	Elginshire .	149 04 06	019 04 06
	Burgh . .	010 00 00	002 00 00
	Forras . .	004 10 00	002 10 00
Bamfeshire . .	Bamfeshire .	160 11 02	010 00 00
	Burgh . .	004 10 00	
	Cullen . .	002 05 00	
Aberdeneshire .	Aberdenshire .	574 19 06	040 00 00
	Burgh . .	100 00 00	025 00 00
Kincardinshire .	Kincardin .	138 09 02	008 09 02
Forfarshire . .	Forfarshire .	461 12 10	025 00 00
	Dundee Burgh	105 00 00	105 00 00
	Aberbrothoick .	006 15 00	001 00 00
	Forfar . .	003 00 00	000 10 00
	Monros . .	030 00 00	002 00 00
	Brechin . .	009 00 00	003 00 00
Perthshire . .	Perthshire .	710 06 04	040 00 00
	Burgh . .	060 00 00	060 00 00
	Culros . .	006 15 00	003 15 00

[1] Clarke Manuscripts,

XX

monthes of July, August, September, October 1653.

Cleere Assesse.	Collectors Names.	Regulators Names.
113 09 06	Col. Cooper	Col. Cooper or Lt.-Col. [ ]
080 08 08	Capt. Lawr. Dundasse	Gent. of Caithnesse
042 04 06		E. of Sutherland and
001 10 00		Gov. of the shire
320 00 00	Idem. (18t pr. guards and the rest for wasted lands; 18ti for Rosse and 2t wasted lands) and Ro. Monroe, Laird of Fowlis	Col. Fitch, Lt.-Col. Blount, Major Birde, Capt. Mon[ ], Capt. Cleare, or any 2 of them
005 10 00		
001 10 00		
008 00 00	ijdem	Col. Fitch and Lt.-Col. H. Pl.[ ]
030 00 00	Mr. Jo. Hay	Col. Morgan, Col. Fitch, ut infra
002 00 00		
130 00 00	14ti for Guards	Col. Morgan, Col. Fitch, Col. Blount, or any of them
008 00 00	Mr. Jo. Hay	
002 00 00		
150 11 02	10ti to the Guard Mr. Tho. Hamilton	ijdem
004 10 00		
002 05 00		
534 19 06	30t watch, 10t wasted lands, Mr. Ro. Ker	ijdem
075 00 00		
130 00 00	Sir Alexander Wetherburne, 8t for the guard	Col. Cobbett and Lt.-Col. [ ], or either of them
436 12 10	20t for the Guard	
005 15 00	Idem	ijdem
002 10 00		
028 00 00		
006 00 00		
670 06 04	25t watch 15t wasted lands Mr. Ro. Andrew.	Col. Daniell.
003 00 00		

Shires.	Shires and Burghe.	Laid on Shires and Burghe.	Abatements.
Fyff and Kynros	Fyff	710 06 04	002 00 00
	Kinroshire	018 17 09	
	S. Andrewes Burgh	050 00 00	007 00 00
	Dysert	021 00 00	003 00 00
	Kircaldy	036 00 00	008 06 08
	Cooper	016 10 00	000 10 00
	Anstruther East	012 00 00	006 00 00
	Petten wemb	010 00 00	
	Dumferlin	012 15 00	006 15 00
	Creele	016 10 00	
	Kinghorne	006 15 00	
	Anstruther West	004 10 00	002 10 00
	Innerkethen	007 10 00	005 00 00
	Kilrenny	002 05 00	
	Brunt Island	016 10 00	004 10 00
Clackmannanshire	Clackmannansh.	049 09 10	009 09 10
Sterlingshire	Sterlingshire	247 05 02	033 00 00
	Burghe	016 10 00	
Linlithgowshire	Linlithgowshire	179 01 04	010 00 00
	Burghe	027 00 00	013 10 00
	Queensferry	006 15 00	005 15 00
Edinburghshire	Edinburghshire	448 14 02	088 14 02
	Eden Burgh	540 00 00	340 00 00
Haddingtonshire	Haddingtonshire	392 00 09	040 00 00
	Burgh	027 00 00	005 00 00
	Dunbarre	016 10 00	006 10 00
	Northbarwick	003 00 00	002 00 00
Roxburghshire	Roxburghshire	519 10 09	
	Jetburgh	013 10 00	
Barwickshire	Barwickshire	396 13 04	016 13 04
	Lauther Burgh	005 05 00	001 10 00
Selkirkshire	Selkirke	127 10 00	005 00 00
	Burgh	004 10 00	
Peblisshire	Peblis-shire	147 14 02	010 00 00
	Burgh	007 10 00	001 00 00

1653] THE ASSESSMENT OF SCOTLAND 177

Cleere Assesse.	Collectors Names.	Regulators Names.
708 06 04		
018 17 09		
013 00 00		
018 00 00		
027 13 04		
016 00 00		
006 00 00	Mr. Glover	Col. Fairfax
010 00 00		
006 00 00		
016 00 00		
006 15 00		
002 00 00		
002 10 00		
002 05 00		
012 00 00		
040 00 00	Tho. Conhead	Col. Tho. Reade
214 05 02	Mr. Ja. Sterling	Col. Reade his Lieut.
016 10 00	20t for a guard	Col. or Major
	13t wasted lands	
169 01 04		
013 10 00	Mr. Wm. Dundasse	Gent. of the shire
001 00 00		
360 00 00	Mr. Ro. Sympson	Gent. of the shire
200 00 00		
352 00 09		
022 00 00	Mr. Ja. Cockburne	Gent. of the shire
010 00 00		
001 00 00		
519 10 09	Mr. Ja. Donne	The Gent. of the shire
013 10 00		
380 00 00	Capt. Jo. Hume	The High Sheriffe
003 15 00		
122 10 00	Mr. Ja. Donne	*ijdem*
004 10 00		
137 14 02	Mr. Alexander Bennett	*ijdem*
006 10 00		

Shires.	Shires and Burghes.	Laid on Shires and Burghes.	Abatements.
Lanerkshire	Lanerickshire	446 08 09	030 00 00
	Glasgowe	097 10 00	040 00 00
	Lanerick Burgh	009 00 00	
	Rutherland	003 00 00	
Ayreshire	Ayreshire	545 12 02	010 00 00
	Burgh	021 00 00	
	Irwin	015 00 00	
Dumfriezeshire	Dumfreizeshire	382 10 00	020 00 00
	Burgh	025 00 00	
	Zamher	009 00 00	006 15 00
	Lochmaben	009 00 00	006 15 00
	Annan	009 00 00	006 15 00
Wigtonshire	Wigtonshire	377 15 06	005 00 00
	Burgh	010 10 00	002 10 00
	Kircudbright	012 00 00	001 00 00
	White	003 00 00	
	Galloway	000 15 00	
Renfrewshire	Renfrewshire	190 15 06	
	Burgh	006 00 00	
Dumbartonshire	Dunbartonshire	107 13 04	003 00 00
	Burgh	009 00 00	
Argyll	Argyllshire	274 11 00	
Bute	Bute	043 08 10	
	Rothsea	004 10 00	000 15 00

Cleere Assesse.	Collectors Names.	Regulators Names.
416 08 09 057 10 00 009 00 00 003 00 00	Major Weare and Matthew Flemyng	Col. Reade, his Lt.-Col. and oldes Captaine or either of them with the Governour
535 12 02 021 00 00 015 00 00	Capt. Wm. Giffen	Col. Alured, Lt.-Col. Talbott, Major Pounall, Capt. Hublethorne or eny 2 of them
362 10 00 025 00 00 002 05 00 002 05 00 002 05 00	Mr. Thomas Mackhume	Gentlemen of the Shire
372 15 06 008 00 00 011 00 00 003 00 00 000 15 00	Mr. Jo. Eadger	Gentlemen of the Shire
190 15 06 006 00 00	Capt. Jo. Greene	
104 13 04 009 00 00	Mr. Howstoun	
043 08 10 003 15 00	Capt. Jo. Greene	Provost and Bayliffes of Rothesay

CXXXI

WARRANT for LEVYING the ASSESSMENT.[1]

THESE are to aucthorize and appoint you to give notice to the Heritors and others liable to the payment of sesse within the County of   , to meete and conveene att   , uppon the   day of August next, and there to nominate and make choice of such a number as they shall thinke convenient, nott exceeding   , to bee a Committee for rectifying and revaluing of the rents in the said shire, and that therin a speciall care bee had that some of that number bee of each Presbytery, or each parte of the shire, which Committee soe dulie chosen and sworne are heerby impowred to meete att such places and times as they shall thinke fitt from time to time for the purpose aforesaid, and to call before them such person or persons as shall bee judg'd necessary for giving information to them concerning the severall rents of the Heritors of the shire aforesaid, and that they proceede impartiallie, without respect to themselves or relations. Given under my hand and seale att Dalkeith, the 23th day of July 1653.

RT. LILBURNE.

To the   Collector of the shire of   .

CXXXII

WARRANT for LEVYING the ASSESSMENT.[2]

THESE are to aucthorize and appoint you to give notice to the Heritors and others liable to the payment of sesse within the County of   to meete and conveene att   , uppon the   day of   next, and there to nominate and make choice of such a number as they shall thinke convenient, nott exceeding   (wherof   to bee a quorum), to bee a Committee to proportion the sesse of your shire equallie uppon all persons whatsoever who have any free rent within the said shire, and for certifying and revaluing the

---

[1] Clarke Manuscripts, xliii. 11.   [2] *Ibid.* xliii. 12.

rents within the said shire; and that therin a speciall care bee had, that some of that number bee of each parte of the shire, which Committee soe dulie chosen and sworne are heerby impowred to meete att such places and times as they shall thinke fitt from time to time for the purpose aforesaid, and to call before them such person or persons as shall bee thought necessary for giving information to them concerning the severall rents of the Heritors of the shire aforesaid, and that they proceede impartiallie without respect to themselves or relations; provided that if this course give nott satisfaccion to the generallity of the Heritors and rentallers, and that there bee any just exceptions against the proceedinges of the said Committee in this particular, then   or   is to examine the justnesse of the complaint, and to order therin as shall bee most agreable to justice and equitie. Given, etc.

RT. LILBURNE,

To   *Collector, etc.*

CXXXIII

WARRANT for LEVYING CONFISCATED REVENUES.[1]

WHERAS John Thompson, Esq., Auditor Generall, is appointed to take care of the collecting and gathering in of severall feu duties, rents, and other dues belonging to the late Kinge and other publique Revenues in Scotland, now confiscated to the Commonwealth of England: For the better inabling him, or whome hee shall appoint for the collecting and bringing in the same for the publique use: you are therfore on sight heerof to bee assisting to the said Mr. Thompson, or whome hee shall appoint, with such parties of horse and foote as hee shall under his hand desire for the purpose aforesaid, and to quarter uppon the persons refusing to pay the said rents or duties untill they shall make payment of the same.

John Thompson's men.

---

[1] Clarke Manuscripts, lxxxvi. 67.

CXXXIV

Sir Edward Hyde to Lieut.-Gen. Middleton.[1]

Sir,—I have receaved yours of the 1 of this moneth, and though your not writinge to me can never make me suspecte your frendshipp, yett really I desyre to heare as often from you and as particularly as may be, for you have yett leasure enough, and many thinges must necessarily occurr to your thoughts, which do not to ours, and all communication is necessary for the greate worke in hand. I pray inlarge your selfe in that matter of the armes and ammunicion, and lett me know upon what grounde the States have proceeded in that unfrendly manner with the Kinge, and what defence was made, for to me it seemes a worse kinde of usage then any wee have before receaved from them. I am of your minde ther will be no peace betweene the Rebells and that people, and I hope ther Comissyoners are by this tyme come from thence, and then they will proceede another way in ther makinge warr. Ther must have fallen out some considerable misfortune to the Rebells in Scotlande, that hath putt them into so much disorder at London; the particulars wee shall know in good tyme. Wee are devisinge all manner of wayes to draw men out of Irelande into Scotlande, towards which somewhat is already derected, and other expedients are in projection, of which I hope to be able to give you a farther accounte shortly; in the meane tyme, if any Irish officer sends to you out of Flaunders to give him a meetinge, you will do it, and I shall not neede to advise you, that in any such treatyes you use your utmost dexterity to remoove all apprehensions of any ill purposes in the Scotts against ther religion, it beinge impresed into them, that when they have done all they can to inable the Scotts to do ther owne businesse, they will be therby only made the abler to roote ther religion out, beinge irreconciliable enimyes to all Catholiques.

I suppose it very possible, by what my Lord Wentworth writes, that before this comes to your handes, Collonell Bamp-

---
[1] Clarendon Manuscripts, xlvi. 137.

feilde may be come into Hollande, and I believe he will have the discrecion to apply himselfe to you; however his Majesty hath derected Mr. Secretary Nicholas that he derecte him so to doe, that so nothinge may be done but in order to what you desyre, though all the world can never persuade the Kinge to trust him in any degree, nor, I believe, to admitt him to his presence, yett no prejudice to his person must give any interrupcion to the businesse he pretends to come aboute; and therfore you shall do well to learne what you can from him, but be sparinge in communicatinge any thinge of moment to him, for our adverticements from London give us cause to suspecte that he is not without correspondence with the most powerfull ther. If he is intrusted with monyes for the provydinge of armes and ammunicion, it were to be wished that it might be putt out of his power as soone as is possible to betray that trust, which will not be harde by those gentlemen's meanes who are sent from the Highlanders with him, who, I suppose, have equall authority, and whome you will easily governe. My Lord Wentworth writes that all ther instructions are for the hasteninge you to them, and that they are unanimous in ther desyre to obey you. I hope you corresponde weekely with my Lord Wentworth, that you may know how that Courte[1] is disposed, for when they are ready to declare, it will be tyme for you to be ther to make the right use of ther affections. Some good newes from Sweden would be very seasonable. I wish you all happynesse, and am very heartily, Sir, yours etc.

Indorsed.—*Myne to Lt. Ge. Middleton,* 8 *Aug.* 1653.

CXXXV

The Earl of Athole to Charles II.[2]

May it pleas your Majestie,—I shall most humbly crave pardon for my silence untill this tyme, and beg earnestly that no doubtfull impressiones of my affection may therby take place in your Majesties gracious thoughts. I shall make it my

---

[1] Denmark.
[2] Clarendon Manuscripts, xlvi. 126. Indorsed as received, Dec. 16, 1653.

studie to deserve to be rekened amongst the number of thos who endevour to performe their dewtie in actiones rather then expressiones. It is possible also that I may be misrepresented to your Majesty in this present conjuncture of affaires, and blamed for slownes in contributeing to the advancement of your Majesties service, but I shall in all submissione supplicat your Majesty to be assured that it is both upon good grounds, and by the speciall advyce of some of the principall persones intrusted with the management of your affairs, that my name is not noysed abroad in publicke with the first that appear in the field for your Majesty's service. But when opportunytie may be improved, I shall now as formerly not declyne the adventure, though it should prove accompanied with greatter difficulties then any thing hither to undertaken. The bearer is a noble Gentillman of such worth and so weall knowen to your Majesty for his faithfullnes that I shall forbear to give him the character of his meritt, he can give perfect informatione of every bussines in thir partts, and therefor I remitt particulars to his trust, and shall kis your Majesties hands with confidence still to be esteemed.—Your Majesties Most faithfull subject and most humble servant. A. ATHOLL.[1]

Atholl, July 28, 1653.

CXXXVI

A LETTER of INTELLIGENCE.[2]

THE Highlanders had two meetinges, att the first the Kinges commission was opened and read, Glencairn appointed Governour, and that under his name all letters should bee sent to severall places in the Highlands and breas to command their presences att the next meeting, being the first Munday (as I heard) of July. The claus of the commission concernein the Commander in cheife was, they should chuse whome they would Middleton being content with him, therefore 'tis thought that

---

[1] The King's answer, which was intercepted, is dated Nov. 2, and is printed in the Thurloe Papers, which contain also a letter from Middleton to Athole, dated Dec. 17 (i. 553, 617), and from Balcarres to Athole (p. 586).

[2] Clarke Manuscripts, xxv. 103. Undated. Written in July 1653.

Midleton will be chused cheife of their modell. Midleton, in Holland, had shipped before this last bout with Holland armes for 10,000 men, but the Hollanders tooke them out againe; but they have gott intelligence they are restored, and att the comeing forth of the Holland's fleete he will come to what men and armes he can by the coast of Norway, where the King of Denmarke will give him ships for convoy, and other things for his jorney and designe.

They have by Collonell Drummond some demands to the Hollandres, the cheife is they would give their assistance, and they will pawn the Iles at Skie, Lewes, and other places to them that may be most for the advance of their fishing, and for the releife to their ships comeing[1] be the North Sease, and to bring the warre unto our dores. There is landed [a] vessell in the Lewes all ready with officers and munition, one Forester is the man that is most named in her. There is another vessell come to Argyles bounds, out of Ireland with sundry desperd officers, some of them I know who have free quarters appoynted them as the Lowlanders have in the Highlands. I asuer your Honour the greatest designe Lowland Lords have, is to make themselves soe strong as is possible of Lowland men [and] of strangers that they may thereby not onely secuer themselves from the barbarous cruelty and treachery of the Highlanders, but likewayes they may keepe them in awe and . . . rag more as Montrose did, whose forme of warre they intend to follow, and therefore entertaine his officers willingly.

They intend nott to truble us till September att soonest, and never to fight us but with parties, and that att passes or by infals. Since their last intelligence from Holland they seeme to be somthing raised in their spirits which warre droopeing before, and some of the Popeish preists being come from Flanders, puts them in hope the Spanyard and French will agree, and then they will gett assistance; but for all the faire flourishes the Lowland Lords make before the Highlanders they would gladly be att home if they knew how to live secuerly from his and their debters. Their theeves are very bussie in the breas, and have stollen many goods off my Lord Brodies lands,

---

[1] Manuscript, 'for the reliefe and their ships to comeing, etc.

and there are some terrible murthers committed amongst them, and they have cutt out some men's tongues.[1]

CXXXVII

Colonel Lilburne to Colonel Cobbett.[2]

Sir,—I am informed that many of the cheife of the inhabitants in the Lewes are alreadie fledd, and the Lord Seafort on the Maine land, that you are not likely to have any opposicion there; wherefor I desire you if this come to your hand before you goe from Orkney, that you will insteede of Major Bird's companie, leave one of the 3 of Col. Cooper's regiment designed for to attend you, because I have ordered Lt.-Col. Sawry to send one companie to a Castle in Scotland, for securing a Castle and Harbour there which is of greate use to the Dutch. But if you be gon from Orkney before this come, then I desire you forthwith to send away one of Col. Cooper's companies to Orkney. And when you have put Major Bird with 4 or 5 companies into a reasonable saife condicion to defend him selfe, I then desire you to saile with the rest of your men towards Kintaile, the Lord Seafort's land, and there to put in a companie into his Castle called, I thinke, Ellendonald; and then if the season and your time will permitt I desire

---

[1] The rising began in earnest about the end of July, as the following extracts from the newspapers will show:—'*From Edinburgh, August* 14.—We have now certain intelligence that on the 27 of July Charles Stuart's standard was set up at Killing. On that day 40 horsemen well mounted, with swords and pistols, went by the house of Donne (6 miles from Sterling) towards the Highlands. And on the 28 Sir Mungoe Murray went thither in the night, and Kenmore with 100 horsemen crossed the water of Clyd, and went by Dundreth towards Killin, and is returned into the south to raise more forces; for they intend speedily to attempt against us. On the 30 Glencairn was at Maggrigors house in Loth Kennoth, and listed three men there, to each he gave 2s. 6d., and sent them for the Lowlands, there to be in readiness, and return upon notice. All possible care is used to receive him if he comes into these parts. Bohauty is a place of no strength, but the best of the three ways out of the Highlands. On the 31 of July in the night divers horsemen went through Stratherne by the house of Oadoth into the Highlands.'—*Mercurius Politicus, Aug.* 18-25.

[2] Clarke Manuscripts, lxxxvi. 73. Evidently addressed to Col. Ralph Cobbett as later letters show, and written about July 20, 1653.

you to saile with the rest to the mouth of Louchabber and
Mull Island, and ride there at ancor untill you send to
Captain Muttloe, Governour of Dunstaffnage, to speake with
you, and to advise about takeing in the Isle of Mull or Mula;
and you may allsoe send for the Governour of Dunolly, to
both whome I shall give advertisement of your comeing, and
there to put in a companie into the cheife Castle of that Island,
called, as I thinke, Douart Castle, and secure as many of the
cheife of that Island as you can get, they being very active
against us; as allsoe cause 40ℋ to be restored and paid to
Captain Drew (who I shall send with another shipp and one
companie of men to meete you att Dunstafnage) that was
taken from an honest maister of a shipp that was driven in
thither by ill weather (his name was William Olive), and was
much abused by the chiftan of that clan; which being done, I
pray send me word to Ayre what supplyes are wanting, and I
shall take care therein, and returne with your party to the
Lewes, and there to see what condicion they are in, and then
to repaire to Dunde as fast as you can. If you can gett all
this done it wilbe of very greate advantage, and save the state
noe little charge, and shall not have any more such sumer
workes. If the Castle in Mull Island will hold above one companie then you may take the garrison out of Dunolly, and put
them to Mull to strengthen it; and to be the better able to
keepe the Island in awe, I shall advise you to leave 2 companies
of Col. Cooper's at the Lewes, together with Major Bird's and
one of your owne, which I conceive may be sufficient, and if
you goe to Mull lett Col. Overton's Captain be there, or one
of Col. Allured's that I intend to send, and for Kintale lett
them cast lotts, or as you thinke fitt; and in your passage
from the Lewes to Mull, you may summon those Ilands that
ye neare you to come aboard you, and give security for the
peace, and for this end it wilbe necessary to take some natives
from the Lewes to send into the other Ilands with your commaunds. Which being done and makeing a compleate conquest,
upon your returne I shall wish you may be crowned with more
then a lawrell. I have sent you 30 tun of beere more, which
I desire you to husband for the best advantage to the state
and souldiers, it stands in 2ℋ per tun. I pray lett me heare

from you speedily, and lett your men of warre while you stay at the Lewes goe abroade 2 or 3 days if they may conveniently, peradventure they may catch an East India Dutch man that may be worth their labour. I am very sorry the wind was soe crosse that hindered our shipps from comeing to you sooner. I shall send 2 little men of warre after you, but heareing of many guns and ancors that ly hid at Shetland I have given them order to goe and take them up, and put in a garrison into that Island. I desire you assoone as you have landed att Lewis that you will keepe only 2 of the men of warre with you, and send the others to sea to see if they can light of any prizes.

Sir James Macdonald of Slate, in Skie Island, I heare refuses to joyne with the Hylanders, and hath sent for proteccion, but shall advise him notwithstanding to shew him selfe unto you; to whome I pray be civill, yett keepe him or some of his freinds with you as hostages for the peece of their Cuntry till you returne to Lewes, if you dare not trust him, but doe it that he may not be discouraged.

CXXXVIII

Colonel Lilburne to Captain Drew.[1]

Wheras I am informed, that there are certaine great guns lye att Knapdrale [2] betweene Swin Castle and Rosse, These are therfore to require you with your owne, and the other man of warre att Ayre (whose Captaine is heerby ordered to receive orders from you), to take with you one other vessell laden with coales and other things, and to saile with all possible expedicion to Dunstafnage Castle, and to take aboard your owne and thother shippes that are to goe alonge with you one hundred souldiers of Col. Alured's regiment with their officers and other necessaries; and haveing delivered the coales and other necessaries at Dunstaffnage, you are to repaire to Knapdrale above said, and to take up all such gunns as you can find or shalbe discovered unto you, and to keepe them

---

[1] Clarke Manuscripts, lxxxvi. 79.   [2] Knapdale?

aboard your shippe till your returne to Dunstaffenage; and that the Governour have sent a partie to Loughaber to apprehend certaine Lords and others mett there to disturbe the peace of the Commonwealth, and to bee assisting to the Governour, with boates for the landing such men as hee shall send; and in case Col. Cobbet with other shippes doe nott come uppe to you by that time, I desire you either to saile towards the Lewis or Kintale, the Lord Seaforth's bounds, to bee assisting unto the said Colonell in some service hee is order'd uppon, or otherwise to stay neere unto Dunstaffenage till such time as Col. Cobbett come uppe thither, unlesse you scout abroad to meete with any boates coming from Ireland, or pyrates or others who disturbe those coasts which you are to seize and take: if you meete with any passengers therein to keepe them prisoners; and assoone as Col. Cobbett has done that service hee is commanded uppon you are to returne to Aire with the guns that you shall finde, and to deliver them to the Governour there, as alsoe to bring back the men you carry thence, unlesse Col. Cobbett shall dispose of them otherwise. Dated att D[alkeith] the 1st day of August 1653.

In case Col. Cobbett doe nott come in convenient time, that you cannot stay longer to attend uppon him for the season of the yeare or other emergencies, in such cases I must desire you to doe the best for your owne conveniency with due regard to the service of the Commonwealth. I desire you to send your boate [to the sheriff of Bute] to assist you with a guide to the place where the guns are, which hee will bee ready to do.

To Capt. Drew
Commander of

CXXXIX

The Earl of Roxburgh to Charles II.[1]

Sessfoul,[2] the 3 of Agust 1653.

Madame,—Iff by my services I could evidence that deutie I ou your La[dyship], it wold have apeared by my actiones

---

[1] Clarendon Manuscripts, xlvi. 148. [2] Cessford?

befor this what my desyres doth so much long for. I shall not hear trouble your La[dyship] with any further confirmatione of the sinceritie of my intentiones. Only Lord prosper me in this lyff, and hear me in my greatest need, as I have (ever since I hade the honour to knou your La[dyship] been and shall continue faithfull to the last periode of my lyff to your La[dyship] in all your interests, and tho ther be such tyes upon me as its not in my pouer to choose what best wold please my self, yet I shall pray your La[dyship] may injoy and have the greatest mach the world can bestow, and the blissings of the right and left hand of God may accompany you in it and all your other deseinges [sic]. Ther ar I doubt not many false calumnies suggested to your La[dyship] against me, by thos who ar my ennimies. Bot be pleased, Madame, to hear my Cusing, who was ane ey wittnes to som of thame, and concluid what he will promise in my name I shall make good to the last drop of my blood, for your La[dyshipp's] favour is mor pretious to me then lyff, which I am resoulfed to enjoy, or loose, by wittnessing my self, Madame, your La[dyship's] truely obedient servant to the uttermost of my power. ROXBURGHE.

Addressed.—*Thes for the Countes of Solms at Utrick.*
Indorsed.—*The Earle of Roxbrough to his Majesty.*
Receaved, Oct. 18, 1653.

CXL

COLONEL LILBURNE to the LORD GENERAL CROMWELL.[1]

MAY ITT PLEASE YOUR EXCELLENCY,—Intelligence from all parts of this nation speaking one language makes mee beleeve some suddaine action is intended by those desperate people gott together in the Hills. There are daily some straglers steale through the Country to goe to them, and I heare many are come over from Ireland, and some landed with Middleton, and they have resolved to have 12,000 on foote by the 20th

---

[1] Clarke Manuscripts, lxxxvi. 81.

of this month, and in the interim to bee falling downe in
parties to force people to joyne with them, threatning fire
and sword to those that refuse, and to see if they can disturbe
us any where, which I hope they will nott bee able. I have
apprehended the Lord Blantire, Swinton's (?) brother in law,
and some other Lairds and Gentlemen in the West, who were
ready to start if they had nott bin prevented; but doe what
wee can they steale uppe into the Hills in the night, though I
have parties laid att the new bridge on the River Clyde and
other parts to apprehend them; some few wee take, but the
most gett by us; and my intelligence sayes, the Lord Glencairne is their Generall, and that they are uppe in armes in
the Lewes to resist us. The winde being contrarie hath given
them abundance of time to prepare themselves, and our
shippes gott but from Frizleburgh[1] on Sunday last, and can
hardly yett bee at Lewes. I once againe intreate your Lordshippe that those officers that have their charges heere, especially them in the North (for there I feare most danger), may
bee sent away speedily, Col. Morgan fearing a distemper, and
that hee shall nott bee able to attend the service, though att
present hee bee gone to Invernesse. I intreate alsoe that the
powder wee lent to the shippes may bee restor'd to us speedily,
and some monie to pay the forces, as alsoe those supplies for
the traine and garrisons, that when wee have occasion to use
them wee may nott want. I should humbly offer to your
Excellency that a Declaration might bee drawne uppe speedily
against the Lord Glencairne, Lord Seafort, Lord Balcarres,
Lord Kenmore, Sir Arthur Forbes, and others that joyne with
them to proclaime them traitors, or as the Parliament shall
thinke fitt, as alsoe that whoever shall suffer damage in their
estates by resisting those in rebellion and owning the Commonwealth shall have the benefitt of that law that provides
reparation in such cases (heerin the Lord Hopton will bee able
to tell you what I meane, knowing that law to bee still in
force in Scotland), and which is conceiv'd will tend much to
the incouragement of our freindes and discouragement of our
enemies. Though the General Assembly was rooted,[2] yet

---

[1] *i.e.* Fraserburgh.   [2] Routed?

they have their provintiall assemblyes, and whether I should allsoe discharge those I should bee glad of your Lordshipps commaunds, for I doubt the people are not well able to beare any more against their ministers,[1] but to distemper their minds too much unlesse the good newes from our navie proove true, and then they'l be tame enough.[2]—I humbly remaine, your

Dalkeith, 6 *August* 1653.

CXLI

Col. Lilburne to the Lord General Cromwell.[3]

May itt please your Excellencie,—I conceive itt still incumbent uppon mee to give your Lordshippe an account of such intellegence as I have of the motion or action of those wilde people in the Highlands, who would faine bee acting something that might bringe a dissadvantage to our affaires in this nation, which I have us'd all possible meanes to prevent them of bringing to passe, by placing the forces in the best posture I can to receive them, the best intelligence I have being various as to what their designe is. Glencairne, their

---

[1] Manuscript, 'Mistrs.'

[2] From Edinburgh, August 9.—'There hath bin published a Declaration by the Commissioners for visiting the Universities in Scotland, and placing and displacing of ministers, which doth much amaze them, after so long forbearance. The Declaration you have here enclosed. It especially forbids preaching or praying for the king; and yet the day after it had been proclaimed here at the High Cross, Mr. Lowrey preached and prayed for him more earnestly than before; for which he was apprehended when he came down from the pulpit, and committed to the Castle, but on promise of better demeanour in time to come he was released. The rest of the ministers are, since the proclamation, more fierce than ever in praying for the king (as they call him), especially the Remonstrators, who till now have been either silent, or but cold in their petitions for him. Mr. John Starling declared himself in opposition beyond all men's expectation, and paraphrased upon the proclamation very boldly.'—*Mercurius Politicus*, p. 2659. The Declaration, which is dated August 2, is printed in *Mercurius Politicus*, p. 2672; and on p. 2704 of the same newspaper is added, An answer to a paper entituled 'Some Reasons why the Ministers of Christ in Scotland ought not to be troubled for praying for the King.' The Declaration of August 2 is reprinted in the *Spottiswoode Miscellany*, ii. 121. On Robert Lowrie and John Stirling, see *ibid.* p. 119.

[3] Clarke Manuscripts, lxxxvi. 77.

Generall, was lately towards the Westerne Highlands, where some Irish are landed. Report speakes them many, but I cannott heare certainly of a[ny] considerable. The 3d instant they had a Randezvouz in Loughaber, towards which place the Lord of Lorne is gone, and with him Mac-naughton, lately Bayliff of Cantire. The Marq. of Argyll I heare hath declared all his sons adherents traitors, and indeavours to keepe all thinges quiett in his Country. The Earle of Atholl was lately in the Blaire of Atholl, and advis'd by the Gentry of that Country nott to engage with those in the Highlands ; hee hearkned nott to their counsell, but is gone with 20 inconsiderable to Loughaber, threatning to seize the estates of those that refused to joyne with him, and uppon that score is likely to forfeite his owne to the Commonwealth. Glencairne summoned in Bagenoth to bee in a readinesse to joyne with him, which caused a meeting of the Clans the first instant, where they resolv'd nott to engage with him. Kenmoore is lately gon againe to the hills, with 50 in his companie ; divers vagabonds goes up, but some we light of; none considerable stirres from the Lowlands. Huntley stays at home, it's said they will not trust him. Many comissions are issued by Glencairne, and terrable threates of fire and sword to provoake men to rise, but I doe not yet heare they are considerable. About 60 ministers were to meete yesterday at Bigger, neare Cornewath, but I sent to discharge them. Mr. Robt. Duglas was amongst them, and I am told he and those that came from London are more refractory then many others.[1] I have advised the judges to send some of them up to London, which, though they get noe other punishment, will terrifie them most for their disobedience and contempt of the present aucthority.

Dalkeith, 11 *August* 1653.

---

[1] Robert Douglas and James Hamilton, prisoners in the Tower, had been discharged by the Council of State on Feb. 11, 1653, and allowed to return to Scotland on promising to live peaceably. The same liberty had been given to John Smith, Andrew Kerr, Macguire, and David Siddell.—*Cal. S. P. Dom.* 1652-3, pp. 158, 160, 161, 185, 205. See also *Spottiswoode Miscellany*, ii. 111.

CXLII[1]

Col. Lilburne to Col. Reade.[2]

Sir,—I have sent orders for 4 troopes of horse and one troope of dragoones to come uppe to you to Cardros, and that you might understand my direccions the better to them I have sent you the copies of those orders, and shall desire you to meete Capt. Hope att Bonhannon or att Cardros, to advise what may bee best to bee done for suppressing those insurreccions you mention in your letter; and if those people you speake of in the Hills doe vanish, or that you doe finde out a way to disperse them, to send those troopes to these great Houses following, to prevent those parts both from insurreccions as alsoe from straglers, vizte. Cardros, Ballendolla, Downe Castle, Carmichall, the Lord Fuller's House, and Strablaine, or any other Houses that are most fitting for that purpose in those parts, till the storme bee over, which I thinke will nott continue very longe. Glencairne is above Bagenoth and towards Invernesse, and Lorne, Glengary, and divers others are with him. They are about 1200 stronge, but both Atholl people and Bagenoth people doe refuse to joyne with them, and they will never come to any considerable number. I have sent order to the Comptroller to send you 8 barrells of powder, which is as much as wee can well spare att present. You may send an officer hither for monie. I wish you to draw out some more of your owne men, if you see itt convenient, and dispose of those troopes as I have sent to you as you shall see fitting to doe further then these directs, and lett mee heare from you as frequently as you can.—I remayne, Your very loving freind,

R. L.

Dalk., 13 *August* 1653.

---

[1] Clarke Manuscripts, lxxxvi. 84.
[2] Colonel Thomas Reade was governor of Stirling.

CXLIII
Col. Lilburne to the Lord General Cromwell.¹

May itt please your Excellency,—Understanding that the Lord Kenmore, with the Tutour of Macgriggor, were betweene Sterling and Dunbarton endeavouring to raise the country therabouts, threatning fire and sword, I sent a partie of horse and dragoones uppon whose approach, and some other ill newes that came to them, they retreated to the Hills. Another partie of them are gone into the Fraser's country, neare Envernes, to engage all of that name, and if they can keepe in a body they intende I heare towards Winter to fall uppon some of our garrisons. They make the people beleeve strange stories that the Duke of Gloucester and Middleton are to land the 20th instant att Portpatrick with 10000 men, and then they say they are to fall into the Lowlands and joyne with them. I heare Col. Morgan hath dispersed some of those in the North. I intend on Thursday and Friday to goe towards Sterling and S. Johnston's for the better putting the forces there into a posture, in case any attempt should bee made uppon them. I beseech your Excellency that you will not forgett your promise about the powder you borrowed of us, for wee are straightned in the want of itt, I alsoe hope to heare of the other supplies coming speedilie. Notwithstanding the great successe God was pleased to give us att sea, yett the malignants heere strongly affirme and beleeve that wee were beaten. I have drawne Col. Fairfax to S. Johnston's, and Col. Overton's to Sterling, the better to strengthen these places and passes.—I remayne, Your Excellencies most humble servant,

R. L.

Dalk., 16 *August* 1653.

CXLIV
Col. Lilburne to the Lord General Cromwell.²

May, etc.,—My intelligence tells mee now the clouds in the Hills are dispers't uppon the newes of the defeate of the Dutch,

---

¹ Clarke Manuscripts, lxxxvi. 85.   ² *Ibid.* lxxxvi. 86.

which was brought to them by the Lord Oglebye's Brother about the 13th instant, to a place called Bonnywher, neere Ruthven Castle, where they lay in a wood about 1300 stronge and 80 horse. The Lord Lorne and M'Clane (which is the Clan that belongs to Mula Island, of whose men there were soe many slaine att Innerkethen), presently march't homeward; Glencairne and Glengary went towards Loghaber, and the whole number were dispersed, and soe are the Macgriggers and the rest uppon the west of Sterling; and though there were very great reports lately of strange thinges that they would doe, heere is now a very great calme in these parts, and much dejection amongst the Highlanders. I heare nott yett from the Lewis, only that our shippes about ―― dayes agoe went from Orknay, nor can I heare any thinge from those shippes I sent towards Loghaber from Aire. I am inform'd that one Mr. John Eyton, a Scotchman, who was formerly an usher to the late kinge, is now an agent for Charles Stuart and the Hollanders, and lies ―― here about Kingestreete. I cannott but intreate your Excellencies furtherance to the dispatch of that powder and furniture of warre, which hath bin soe longe since writt for, for our supply, and that your Lordshippe will remember your promise unto my Lord, Your Excellencies, etc.

Dalk., 18 *August* 1653.

CXLV

ENGAGEMENT of the GENTLEMEN of RENFREW.[1]

Paisley, 22 *August* 1653.

THE Gentlemen of the sheriffedome of Renfrew convenned, Considering divers prejudices hath arisen, and like more to ensue uppon jealousie that there is some designe of concurring or corresponding with those in the North now in armes, wheruppon as is conceived some of their number have bin apprehended, and others searched for: Therfore for cleering and vindicating the said Sheriffedome of Renfrew of any suspition theranent, and preventing any further trouble or burthen that

---

[1] Clarke Manuscripts, xxv. 117.

may bee imposed uppon the said Sheriffedome in reference
therunto; They doe therfore nominate and elect Sir Lodowick
Houstoune of that ilke, knight, and Sir Adam Blaire of Bigtoune, knight, forthwith to repaire to the right honourable
Col. Robert Lilburne, Commander in Cheif of the forces in
Scotland: And to all others needfull; And[1] to indeavour by
all faire meanes to vindicate and cleare the said Country and
shire of any designe, correspondence, or intercourse, directly or
indirectly, with any in the North in armes, or any purpose of
rising or troubling the peace of the Country: And to doe all
other thinges needfull for the good of the shire: promising to
hold firme and stable whatsoever their Commissioners above
named doe theranent.

         COCHRANE.
         MEATHER POLLOK.
         A. BLAKHALL.
W. BLACKHALL.   F. BRINOCK.
ARCHIBALD STEWART. BISCOPTOUNE.
         CORNELIUS CRAUFURD.
         JOHN MAXWELL.

CXLVI

COLONEL LILBURNE to CAMPBELL of GLENORCHY.[2]

SIR,—Although that relation which I had from your servant
doth nott agree with that information which I have had these
2 or 3 dayes from other parts, which spoke all the Highlanders
to have dispersed themselves and bin going to their severall
homes,[3] yet for your better security and defence in case of any
stirres about you, I desire you will place such strengthes in

---

[1] 'The like was sent from the Sheriffedome of Aire.'
[2] Clarke Manuscripts, lxxxvi. 88.
[3] The sixth report of the Historical Manuscripts Commission, p. 617, contains
the following abstract of a letter from the Marquis of Argyll to Lilburne, which
illustrates the rumour that the Highlanders had dispersed, mentioned above, and
further elucidates Argyll's relations to the English Governor. It is dated Rose-
neath, 30th August 1653:—'The Marquis acknowledges receipt of one from
Col. Lilburne from Dalkeith, dated 24th August; informs him that the Highlanders who came together were divided, and most part gone home, only he hears

your severall Houses which are defensible, as you shall conceive necessarie, and further to secure the peace of the Country as you shall bee able; and when as you have putt your selves into a posture of defence I shall desire to heare from you to know what your demands may bee about some consideration for your paines and charges in securing the peace of that country.—I remayne your very loving freind, R. L.
Dalk. 29 Aug. 1653.
Laird of Glenurquie.

CXLVII

Colonel Lilburne to the Lord-General Cromwell.[1]

May itt, etc.—I have little to acquaint your Lordshippe withall, but as I was going towards Sterling the Lord Cockran and some other Lords and Gentlemen mett mee about Falkirke, with commissions from the shires of Aire and Renfrew to vindicate those shires from any jealousies of joyning with the Highlanders, or disturbing the peace, as your Lordshippe will perceive by the inclosed copie.[2] They desiring to know what I would demand of them, I propounded that they should declare against those men in the Highlands, and in the name of their Country to engage to owne and indeavour to preserve the

---

that Lord Kenmore, McNaughton, and his own son are toward the heads of Monteith, bent on mischief, and threatening to fall upon any one who will not concur with them. What he wants anent the assess his lordship is striving to make good, though all the impediments are cast in his way that disaffected people can, and he fears it will be impossible to get it in money. He acknowledges that it was a great oversight that Colonel Lilburn was not informed before the gentlemen in Kintyre had sent for certain commodities referred to, and while professing his own ignorance of it also, until it was done, gives certain explanations in extenuation of the offence. He concludes by entreating Colonel Lilburn to command him what is his pleasure, and it will be done, for "I trust in the Lord whatsoever the malice of men shall either openly calumniate me in or privately suggest against me, my way shall be found straight, doing no other than what I profess; and that in his strength alone, who is able to sustain his own, and guide them in a way they know not. I want not presently the malice of all who are perversely disposed in this nation, which wants not its own weight of trouble and difficulty. But the wrath of man works not the righteousness of God."'

[1] Clarke Manuscripts, lxxxvi. 91. [2] Number cxliv.

peace of the Commonwealth and the Governement established; which in regard the full number of Commissioners were nott present, especiallie those of Aireshire, they desir'd time to meete mee heere att my returne within a few dayes, and then I suppose I shall bee able to give your Lordshippe a more full account. I can heare noe certainty of our shippes arrivall att the Lewes nor att Loghaber, the windes have bin soe crosse, but I hope they were there 10 dayes agoe. Of late the Higlanders (as I gave your Lordshippe formerly an account) retreated from the Breas of Badenoch towards Loghaber, and dissolu'd, being soe much dissappointed of their expectations every way both from abroad and att home, yett as my intelligence sayes, intend nott altogether to cease, but are resolv'd now to gather uppe as many vagabonds and loose men as had noe fortunes in the world nor any other thing to rely uppon but some desperate businesse, to gett as many of them together as they can, and to try conclusions with them. The fortification at St. Johnston's goes on very well, they have already gott uppe one house that will hold 600 men. I have disposed most of the forces now to the Winter quarters, which I am constrayn'd to lay as thick as I can to prevent suddaine infalls. I humbly intreate, that your Lordshippe will be pleased to befreind us in dispatching some monie downe for the forces, as alsoe those other supplies of ammunition which I formerly moved your Lordshippe in, for wee are drawne to a very great scarcity.—I remayne, Your Lordships, etc.

Dalkeith, 1 September 1653.

I should bee glad to know what is resolu'd concerning those men that have endeavour'd to disturbe the peace in the Highlands, and how I may deale with them in case they submitt, as some of them doe already offer : I conceive itt would doe well to make them exemplary.

CXLVIII

Colonel Lilburne to Sir James MacDonald.[1]

Sir,—I received yours yesterday dated the 12th of August, wherin you express much innocencie concerning any corre-

---

[1] Clarke Manuscripts, lxxxvi. 90.

spondence with any that are about to disturbe the peace, and withall you seeme to give a further engagement of your peaceable resolutions under the present Governement. I am very inclinable to beleeve the reality therof, and am satisfied in those particulars, and shall desire you to be confident that uppon the application to any officer of our's that shall come neere your parts they will nott disturbe you in the least, but give you any protection or assistance as shall bee necessary, and therfore when any of our forces come neere unto your habitations you may acquaint them with Major Generall Deane's protections and with the contents of this lettre, which will bee sufficient to you in all cases of that nature : yet because you desire particular proteccions I have sent them heere inclosed,[1] as alsoe those proteccions you desired for the Captain of Clanrannold, who as yet hath given noe engagement, and therfore this favour is done to him out of respect unto your selfe. I have sent unto the Judges to grant you a suspension according to your desire,[2] which I hope you will receive accordingly.—I remayne,

CXLIX

Lord Newburgh to Charles II.[3]

2 Septr.

Mistres,—Ther never com so much truble, greife, and fear to the harts of al loves yow, as this last danger ye was in, nor so great joy as the certentie it was over, as ye had the prayers

---

[1] 'These are to require you on sight heerof to forbeare to prejudice any of the inhabitants of the Island of North Eust belonging to Sir James Mac-donald of Slate, either by taking away any of their horses, sheepe, or other cattell or goods whatsoever, or by offering any violence to their persons or houses, or the persons of any of their families : they doing nothing prejudiciall to the Commonwealth of England and giving obedience to the present Governement. Given etc.'

[2] 'Gentlemen,—For divers reasons I must entreate you to grant some further time unto Sir James Mac-donald of Slate for making his appearance to give security amongst the rest of the Clans, and that hee may have 2 or 3 monthes att least. I desire you will please to deliver the same to this Bearer, which is all att present from, Your affeccionate servant.

'*Dalkeith,* 2. *September* 1653.'

[3] Clarendon Manuscripts, xlvi. 224.

of many for your recoverie, so it oght to ingage bothe yow and them to thankfulnes to him who hes bein gratiously pleased yet to preserve yow, to be myndful of past mercies is the only way to procur new favors. . Let this be a means to make yow whos lyfe is againe given yow to endevor to lead a new and more holy on. I wil now leave this subject, that louks lyker the discource of a devyne then a lover, and tel yow that my absence from yow and incapacitie to expresse my devotion to your service is my greatest unhappines; for the present I can contribut nothing but my prayers, nor sal I ade more but the telling yow that my zeal and afection is witheout by end and incapable of the least cheng, nothing being able to put a period therto but the end of his lyfe who is your most faitheful and most obedient servant　　　　　　　　De.

Mistrs ye wilbe pleased to louk on the berar of this as my freind and a kynd on too. I must at this tyme give him no moe charecters albeit I could in justice doe it.

Addressed.—*For Mistres Heart thes*
Indorsed.—*Sept. 2d.*

Mr. Whyte to his Majesty. Rec. Dec. 10*th*, 1653.
Lord Newburgh to the King.

CL

CHARLES II. to the EARL of SEAFORTH.[1]

RIGHT TRUSTY, ETC.,—Wee understande as well by the dispatch which Coll. Bampfeilde brought from you in Aprill (which came to our handes within these few dayes, though himselfe be not yett come, nor do wee know what is become of him), as from severall other handes, of the greate affection and courage which you have so seasonably shewed to our service, for which wee do returne you our very hearty thankes, and assure you that wee shall never forgett the good service done to us by your father and your selfe, but shall rewarde you for both, as soone as wee shall be able. We doubte not but you

Sept. 7.

---

[1] Clarendon Manuscripts, xlvi. 225.

will proceede with the same alacrity you have begunn, and dispose all your frends and dependance to that concurrence and unity, which may best advance the good worke in hande, which wee hope God Almighty will prosper, and make you a principle instrument in redeeminge your Country from the slavery and misery it suffers under, by the mischeive, pryde, and cruelty of our English Rebells, who are not greater enimyes to our Royall person then they are to the Nobility and auncient gentry of that our Kingdome, which they resolve to extirpate, if it shall be in ther power. Wee shall not neede to desyre you to use your utmost endeavours and interest to prevent all faction and animosityes amongst your selves, upon any private groundes soever, and to dispose all persons to unity and an intyre submissyon to all derections wee have and shall give, without which nothinge can prosper you take in hande; and as wee have formerly sayd, wee shall no lesse esteeme the affection and service of those who do cheerefully obey, as of them who do commande with the best successe. Be confident wee are takinge all possible care for your assistance and supply, and leave nothinge undone on our parte. Wee hope Lt. Generall Middleton will be shortly with you, and in the meane tyme that by degrees you will receave armes, ammunicion, and good officers. And so wee bidd you heartily farwell.

Earle of Seaforte.

Indorsed.—*The King to the Earle of Seaforte*, 12 *Sept.* 1653.

CLI

Col. Lilburne to the Lord General Cromwell.[1]

May itt please your Excellencie,—Receiving an account from Lieutenant Col. Blount this day, that Col. Cobbett had entred the Lewes about 14 dayes agoe without any resistance, and that the armes of that Island were brought in unto him, I thought itt my dutie to acquaint your Excellencie therewith, itt being the first account that is come to my hand of Col.

---

[1] Clarke Manuscripts, lxxxvi. 95.

Cobbett's arrivall. That day they sail'd from Orknay Major Birde died of a feavour,[1] soe that there will want a Major to Col. Fitche's regiment, which will bee necessary to bee supplied speedily, because there is none but Lieutenant Colonell Blount to take care of the regiment, and hee hath very much businesse lying uppon him. I shall nott presume to offer any for the supply of that place; only I doubt the oldest Captaine is hardly soe fitt a man as might bee thought on, but Col. Fitch himself can better informe your Excellency. The Lord Argyll sent mee intelligence the other day that his sonne and Kenmore were drawne downe towards the west parts of Sterlingshire, and itt seemes itt is true, for Col. Reade this day gave mee an account of about 260 horse and foote that lay within 7 miles of Sterling, tis conceiv'd to have surpriz'd some of those houses wee were constrayn'd to garrison for the present security of the Country that lies neere unto the Hills. A partie of our's going uppe towards them, one of our horses was shott by an ambuscadoe in a wood, but had noe other losse, nor could doe noe further service in that place. I conceive that Argyll having left his sonne to run his owne course, hee is growne into a little desperation, and joynes with Kenmore and any vagabonds that will come to them, and hopes to make a partie to disturbe us in the winter, and to live in the meane time uppon the spoyle uppon the Breas of the Hills, which will bee impossible for us to prevent this winter. Col. Reade is gone with 2 or 3 companies of his owne and 3 troopes of horse, to try if hee can engage them, but I am confident itt will bee in vaine, for they will nott dare to doe any such thinge without great advantage. Glencairne is gone into Mula Island, what his businesse is I cannott learne, some conjecture itt is to make his escape away. Seafort is indeavouring to secure his house att Kintaile, but his owne people desert him very much, and I hope wee shall bee masters of that house before Col. Cobbett returne. I thinke itt some unhappinesse that your Lordshippe hath nott vouchsafed an answer to any of those lettrs formerly sent your Excellency from your Excellencies, etc.

Dalkeith, 3° September 1653.
Lord Generall.

---

[1] Aug. 15, *Mercurius Politicus*, p. 2719.

CLII

Col. Lilburne to the Marquess of Argyll.[1]

My Lord,—I perceive that newes of Kenmore's being in Menteith was true. Concerning those proposicions your Lordshippe makes for my accepting cowes and trees in lieu of the sesse of your shire, I have offer'd 26s. or 28s. for each cowe your Lordshippe or the Country shall send, provided they bee fatt, and 4s. a tree [for trees] that are betweene 20 and 24 foote longe, and about 12 or 14 inches square, to bee deliver'd att a convenient place where our shippes may load them in safety, and some reasonable time to bringe them away in. Butt, my Lord, if these rates bee too much, which I doe a little question my owne judgement in, I hope your Lordshippe will consider those abatements that are given the shire, and afford the more reasonable penniworth, seing I am willing to accept such thinges as the Country does produce for the payment of the sesse.—I remayne your Lordshippes, etc.

Dalkeith, 5° September 1653.

Marq. of Argyll.

CLIII

Col. Lilburne to the Lord Generall Cromwell.[2]

May itt please your Excellency,—In my last I acquainted your Lordshippe with the Lord Kenmore and Lorne's coming neere Sterling with a partie, and that Col. Reade was gone to repell them, but they having the advantage of the Hills, they gave ground presently, Col. Reade pursuing them about a mile and half amongst cragges and strange places, killed but 2 or 3 in the pursuite, was glad to retreate, the night being neere, and noe provisions to bee had for man or horse in that place,

---

[1] Clarke Manuscripts, lxxxvi. 94.
[2] *Ibid.* lxxxvi. 88.

which the Highlanders perceiving, run very fast to the Hills that flank't him as hee retreated, killed 2 of his men, and Major Creedes Trumpett, and 2 horses, and gall'd divers both men and horse besides; but as for Glencairne, hee is in the Isle of Mull, and the rest of the Highlanders are dispers't for the present, nor doe I heare further from the Lewes.—I remayne your Lordshippes most humble servant, R. L.

Dalk., *6 September* 1653.

Lord Generall.

The inclosed was sent to the Lord Cardross.[1]

CLIV

Charles II. to C. M.[2]

Madam,—I have trusted Mrs. Jannett Browne to sollicitt a businesse in which I am much concerned, and I cannot doubte of your readynesse to assiste her in it, which I pray do, and I shall lyve to thanke you, and give you cause to believe that I am heartily, Madam, Your very affectionate constant Frend. C. M.[3]

---

[1] 'My Lord,—I doubt not that your Lordship knows the intentions of this Kingdom; also the posture of affairs, and how they are ordered: therefore your Lordship is hereby required to put out your proportion of horse and foot, your horse to Sir Mungoe Murray, your foot to the Laird of Duchraye, with assurance so long as their bounds be deficient, I must expect quarters of you, but in expectation of your forwardness I remain your humble servant,

2 *Septemb.* 1653. Kenmore.

'I also desire provision, conform to my Quartermaster's note, may be provided this night, so that it may be conveniently brought where I shall be.

'For my Lord Cardrus.

'These are to require the Commissioners of Cardrus to bring in to John Neipers house, within two hours after sight hereof, 30 wedders, 4 and 20 pecks of meal, and 16 stone of cheese, as you will answer upon your highest peril.

'John Inglish.'

Printed in *Mercurius Politicus*, Sept. 8-15, 1653.

[2] Clarendon Manuscripts, xlvii. 238—cliv. and clv. are both written on one sheet.

[3] It is suggested by Mr. Macray that C. M. signifies the Countess of Morton. *Cal. Clarendon Papers*, ii. 455.

CLV

CHARLES II. to the EARL of SOUTHESK.

My Lord,—You cannot but know the straights I am in, and how impossible it will be for me to subsiste or attempte any thinge towards my recovery without the assistance of my frends, and I can not doubte you will be ready to do your parte. I would not aske a summ of mony from you the disbursinge wherof might be very inconvenient to you; and therfore I only desyre you to lend me 300t, which if you deliver to the person who gives you this letter, it will come safely to my handes, and I doubte not I shall lyve to repay it to you or yours; your affection will not suffer you to deny this to, My Lord, Your very affectionate Frende.

For the Earle of Southaisk.

The like to the Earle of Eythy for 300t.
The like to the Earle of Panmure for 500t.

Indorsed.—*The Kinge* 18 *Sept. by Midd.*

CLVI

The EARL of LOUDOUN to CHARLES II.[1]

Reasons why the Lord Chanceller did noe sooner give ane Accompt to the King's Majestie of the state of affairs in Scotland.

That after his Majesties removeall out of Scotland till the defeat at Worcester ther was noe safe passadge, and after that sad defeatt wherin it pleased God to preserve the King, and soe miraculously to give him a way of escape to France, the Enemie was soe powerfull at sea, and was soe carefull and vigilant to catch all passingers, and stopp all intercourses and intelligence, as ther was noe safe passadge to send to his Majestie.

That ther wer such miserable divisions and animosities in

---

[1] Clarendon Manuscripts, xlvi. 246.

Scotland after his Majesties removeall, as did impede and hinder all conjunction of counsells and forces, and did obstruct all acting and vigorous opposing of the Enemie.

That after the defeat at Worcester ther was such a generall despondencie of spirit and faintnes of heart seazed on most of men, as ther was noe hope of doeing any gude for the King or Cuntrie from people in such a distemper.

That dyverse wer insnaired by the Enemies profession of pietie, and their specious pretences and fair promeises of libertie, eas, and advantage to the people, and others by terror and compulsion of armes forced to submitt to them.

That the Lord Chancellor did with all faithfullnes endevor to compose and remove all differences and divisions which wer in Scotland, and to move them to joyn their counsells and forces for defence of the Kingdome, as his wholl deportment in the procedour and manadging of affairs doe clearly testifie, yet such wer the miserable animosities and prejudices that noe intreattie nor means culd prevaill with them to joyn and unit themselfes against the invasion of the comone Enemie.

That after the defeat at Worcester all forces of Scotland disbanded, and all the judicatories and the meittings of the Committee of Estates wer relinquished, and the meitting of the Parliament deserted, notwithstanding the Lord Chanceller did his utmost endevour to preserve those judicatories in force and in the exercise of their power.

That such as hade for some tyme keiped themselfes from the Enemie accepted passes, and returned home, and ther was a universall inclination in the most pairt of men to coutch under the burthen, and undergoe any bondage and servitude for fear of ruine, and out of a desire of selfe preservation. And the Enemie was soe prevalent by sea and land, as ther was noe opposition at home, nor any visible and pro[ba]ble means of delyverance to be expected speedily from abroad.

The information or relation of such a miserable condition and sad posture of affairs being verie unpleasant and comfortles, and such as culd contribute noe thing to the advantage bot rather to the prejudice of his Majesties service and affairs, the Lord Chanceller did conceave it was a tyme to be silent rather then to speak, and be the relater of soe bad newes.

And after assaying all means he culd for defence of the Kingdome and maintaining his Majestie's just authoritie, and that he culd gett noe concurrence therin, he did retire to remote pairts in the Hi[g]hland montains, still suffering great oppression and persecution against his persone, means and estate. All which being rightly considered he trusts will clear his faithfullnes and loyaltie, and will sufficiently plead his excuse, that he did noe sooner give ane accomptte to the King's Majestie of the condition of affairs in Scotland. Bot soe soon as it hath pleased God to put in the hearts of the people a earnest desire and resolution to take hold on any fitt opportunitie to break the yoack of the oppression and bondage of the Enemie, and that ther is some door of hope that the King may gett asistance from abroad, the Chanceller thought it his duetie to give a true accompt to his Majestie of the proceedings and state of affairs in Scotland.

Indorsed.—*Reasons why the Lord chanceller did noe sooner give an Accompt to the King of the affairs of Scotand. Rec. Sep. 19th, 1653.*

CLVII

The EARL of LOUDOUN's NARRATIVE of the UNION of ENGLAND AND SCOTLAND.[1]

A trew narrative of the precedour and artificiall wayes taken by the pretended Parliament of the Commonwealth of England and ther Commissioners for obtaining the consent of Scotland to be incorporated and unyted to ther usurped Commonwealth.

AFTER all the forces of Scotland wer disbanded, and all the meittings of the Committee of Estats and the meitting of Parliament deserted, and all judicatories and exercise of ther power relinquished, the pertended Parliament of the new usurped Commonwealth of England sent their Commissioners to Scotland with a Declaratione toutching the setlement of Scotland, wherin they establishe tolleration to all sorts of

---

[1] Clarendon Manuscripts, xlvi. 248.

religion under the nam of any meaner or way of service and worshipe of God in any Gospell way everie man pleaseth to chuse. And they doe lykways declare as to that concernes the freedome to be established to the people and for the securitie of ther Commonwealth for tyms coming, That Scotland shall and may be incorporated into one Commonwealth with England, wherby the same Government established ther under the free state and Commonwealth of England, as it is now settled without King or House of Lords, may be deryved and communicated unto Scotland with such convenient speed as the same may be made practicable amongst them.

And they doe farther declare that towards satisfaction and reparation of the vast expenss and damnadges that the Commonwealth hes alreadie undergone, by reason of the invasion in anno 1648, by the Scottish armie under the D[uke] of Hammiltoune, etc., and that late invaisione under Charles Stewart, and for lessening the future chairges of the Commonwealth, all the lands, houses, goods, revenewes whatsoever belonging to the said Charles Stewart, King of Scotts or to the Croune and State of Scotland; And all the Estats whatsoever of thos (reall or personall) who did invaid England under Duke Hammiltone in the yeir 1648, or wer advysing, contriving, or promotting therof, or in any way abating, aiding or assisting him in Scotland, or who did with the said Charles Stewart latly invade England, or who wer abating, aiding, or assisting therinto, or since the same hes raised armes, or bein promotors, aiders, or assisters therto in prosecution of the said invaision, or in oppositione of the forces of the Parlament of England remaining ther, shall be confiscated and forfalted to the use and benefitte of the Commonwealth of England (except such who at the Battle of Dumbarr, 3d Sepr. 1650, deserted the said Charles Stewart and not borne armes since against the Parlament, and all such whose merit and service to this Commonwealth shall rander themselfes capable to be taken into a more favourable consideration by the Parlament. The Parlament doe declair that all such persons of the Scotische nation [as] are not comprehended within the former qualificacions bot have keept themselfs free from the guilt of such things as have compelled this warr, and shall now upon discoverie of their own trew interest be disposed [upon] to concurr and promott the ends formerly declared by the Parlament, shall injoy their liberties and estats as others of the free people of the Commonwealth of England; which declaratione doeth containe some other us[e]les and frivolous exceptions which doeth no wayes contribute nor tend to the advantage of any of the Scotish nation, but only to some verie few persons who not being sound and orthodox in ther principles concerning religion, nor Loyall to the King, nor trew to ther native cuntrie, did (contrarie to ther dewtie and former engadgements) joyn with the Enimie; And by which Declaration the wholl estats personall and reall of all trew Scotish men are most unjustly confiscated and forfaulted for the use and benefitt of the Commonwealth of England, without any caus other then for the defence of ther religione, lawes, liberties, King and Cuntrie against a most unlawfull and injust invasione which Scotland was obleged by all obligations, religious, civill and politicall, to defend. And the aforsaid Commissioners from England did mak intimation to the severall shyres in Scotland to meitt and chuse Commissioners, by vertew of and conforme to the authoritie given to them from the Parlament of the Commonwealth of England, and to authorize them with full and ample power to wait upon the Commissioners of the Parlament to treat, agree, and conclud with them; according to which warrant seaven or eight Gentl[e]men or therby did meitt in each shyre, and did nominat and chuse Commissioners to meitt and treat, and some of the Commissioners or deputies who wer chosen haveing only power to hear and report bot not to conclud any thing till first they should mak report and communicatt the desirs of the English Commissioners to ther shyres, thes Commissions wer rejected till the deputies should returne with full and absolut power. But some shyres wold give no such power, and so have still refused to send any Commissioners or deputies to treat and conclud. When the deputies from the shyres come to Dalkeith to wait upon the Englishe Commissioners they did prescryve and sett doun in wryting the answers which they did positively requyer from the aforesaid deputies, viz.: Wee [blank] deputies of the shirifdom of [blank], on the behalf of our selfes and thes represented by us, declaire our free and willing acceptance of and consent unto the tender made by the Parlament of England, that Scotland be incorporated into and made one Commonwealth with England, that therby the sam Government that is established and injoyed without King or House of Lords under the free Statt and Comonwealth of England may be deryved into the people of Scotland, And wee desir that the people of England and Scottland may be represented in one Parlament and Government of Representatives wherin is the suprem government and authoritie of the wholl Iland, And in the mean tyme wee shall live peaceably under and yeild obedience unto the authoritie of the Parlament of the Commonwealth of England exercised in Scotland. By which answer they mak them renunce ther duetie and former obligations to Religione, King, Governement, Lawes, Liberties, and Cuntrie, and to accept of and assent to the tender of the Parlament of the Commonwealth of England, which doeth evict and forfault the wholl estates personall and reall of all men in Scotland, which the adversaries themselfs culd never have expected from rationall men. But the only excuse by them pretended is the fear they had of the enemie, and they affirme they had reasone to apprehend (if they had not speedily complyed and ingratiated themselfs with the English), That thes whom they call remonstrators and dissenters wold have prevented them and complyed with the English, to ther utter ruine, and that they werr necessitated to what they have done for ther own preservation.

And in farther persewance of ther treattie with the Commissioners from England they did (by order of the aforsaid Parlament) chuse and send some of the former deputies to Londone to prosecute the former treatie, the results of whose proceidings in England not being yett reported nor intimated to Scotland are passed over and pretermitted. But it is most clear and apparent by the wholl former progres that Scotland hes no ways accepted of nor given any legall nor valid consent to the tender or declaracione of the pretended Parlament of the Commonwealth of England, nor that Scotland shall be incorporated into and made on Comonwealth with England, for many reasons :—First, Becaus Scotland being under the power and force of the armie of the Parlament of the pretended

Comonwealth of England had no freedome and libertie to meitt, nether wer they desired nor permitted to meitt according to the libertie, lawes, practize and consuetude of Scotland, bot wer requyered to meitt by vertew of and according to the warrant, authoritie, and command of the pretended Parliament of the Comonwealth of England, and to nominate and chuse Commissioners or deputies according to the qualifications, restrictions, limitations, and to the ends prescryved by them, so as ther was noe freedome nor legalitie or laufullness in the meitting nor in the election of Commissioners from the shyres. Next it wold be considered that the establishment of religion and the worshipe of God and promoveing the Gospell is pretended and held furthe as the cheif pairt and end of the Declaratione and Tender of the Parlament of England, which for its worth and excellencie ought indeed to have preference befor and above all worldly and civill interests; And it is agreeable to the word of God, to all eqwitie and reasone, and to the lawes and constitution eclesiastick and civill of the Church and Kingdome of Scotland, that the Church have the pryme and antecedent judgement in all matters of religion; And yett the advyce and consent of the Church of Scotland nor of any representative therof was never sought, nor so much as any notice att all taken of them in the consent sought to the Tender [and] Declaration of the said Parlament and approbatione for establishment therof in Scotland. Thirdly, the consent of the Nobilitie, who are on of the three estates of Scotland, by whom all lawes and statuts of Scottland wer made and maintained, and without whom ther is no trew, full, and adequat representative of Scotland, was never sought, nor notice given to them of any such meitting or consent to be united and incorporated into the Comonwealth of England. By all which and many other reasons it is most evident that ther is no consent from the Kingdome of Scotland nor any trew representative therof who have given or could give consent to such a chainge, nether are these usurpers of the pretended Comonwealth so ignorant as not to know, that the consent of the sex or seaven Gentlmen or heritors from each shire chosen in maner aforsaid, can give noe legall nor valid consent to subvert religione, and to chainge the fundamentall ancient Government Lawes and Liberties of Scotland, without consent of the

Church, the Nobilitie, and Gentrie, and which wer contrarie to their alleadgence, dwetie and Covenant. Bot that all which hath bein done to that end is nothing bot violence, usurpation, and meir forgerie, for accquyring and extorting a show of consent, only to deceave and abuse ignorant peopell, and to delude forrain kingdoms and estates, and to mak them belive that they have obtained the consent and approbatione of Scotland for strengthening ther usurped and unlaufull power, and authoritie; And ther intertaining a show of a treatie att London with som of the aforsaid deputies from som of the shires of Scotland, who wer bot choysen in manier aforsaid, is only to the sam end; and that they may falsly suggest and hold furth to the world that Scotland goes alongst with them in the perverse and crooked wayes they tak for establishing of that power which they have accquyred and doe still maintaine by craft and violence; and yett it is not strainge that a faction who's power and dignitie is from themselfs, and who have destroyed the fundamentall Government of England under which it did florish long in peace and plentie, and can notwithstanding dreame themselfs to be a lawfull Parliament without King or Hous of Lords, and after violent expelling the farr greater pairt of the House of Comons, should lykways fancie and imagine that they have obtained the consent and approbatione of the Kingdome of Scotland for establishment of ther usurped Comonwealth, without consent of the Nobilitie and Gentrie of Scotland, by getting a constrained forced consent from seven or eight Gentlemen or heritors in each shyre.

Indorsed.—*A narrative of the ways the English Rebells have taken for incorporating the two Kingdoms into a Common wealth. Rec. Sep. 19th, 1653.*

CLVIII

A Proposed Declaration of Charles II. drawn up by the Earl of Loudon.[1]

Some grounds of a Declaration to be emitted by the King.

Yow shall show that (when it shall pleas God to enable his

---

[1] Clarendon Manuscripts, xlvi. 252. This proposed Declaration, together with other papers sent by Loudoun, including No. IV., was presented to the king at Paris on September $\frac{7}{16}$.

Majestie to enter into any of his Kingdoms in persueance of his just rights) it will be verie fitt that he emitt a Declaration of his intentions and resolutions, wherin it will be expedient in the begining or introduction therof to give some reasons of his Majesties long silence, and not making any applicatione sooner to his faithfull and loyall subjects in respect of his Majestie's conditione and thers, etc. And that although it hath pleased God, whose counsells are a great deipth, and who is righteous in all his wayes, for the sines of the King and the sines of his fathers house, and for the sines of his people justly to chastize and bring him and them verie low, and that the hearts of the enemie, who judge of love or hatred by that which is befor them, ar hardned and sett upon mischeife becaus they prosper, and that sentence is not speedily execute against thair evell work; yett the King (trusting that the loud cry of the wrongs and oppression of the enemie, and the cryes and prayer of Gods people ar and will be heard by him, who is the righteous judge of all the world, who executs righteousness and judgement for the oppressed, and that he will ryse to plead and mantaine his own caus, and turne back the captivitie of his people) is resolved by the blissing and in the strength of God Almightie to imploy all such assistance and lawfull means as it hath pleased or shall please him to affoord, for reformation and defence of religione according to the Covenant sworne and subscrybed by his Majestie and his subjects, being resolved in the Lord's strength firmly to adhere therto; and for recoverie of his Majesties just and undoubted right and establishment of Monarchicall Government, togither with the lawfull libertie and estates of his subjects, against the unlawfull usurpation and violence of a rebellious faction of Sectaries and Independents, who by craft and creweltie have subverted religion, murthered his Royall Father, changed the ancient fundamentall Government of the Kingdomes (under which they did florish for many generations in peace and plentie) and have destroyed the priviledges of Parlament and libertie of the subject, and have imprisoned and taken the lyf's of many of his Majesties faithfull and Loyall subjects, and confiscated and forfaulted ther estats, and are dayly waisting and consuming the estats and wholl means of the subjects of all his dominions, and enslaveing and enthralling ther persons and consciences to mantaine ther most unlawfull and usurped power by sea and land, and to satisfie ther insatiable ambitione and avarice. And as his Majestie doeth esteim such as have bein firme and constant in ther dwetie to God, to him, and ther countrie, and shall continew therin unto the end to be his most faithfull and Loyall subjects, whom he intends according to ther merits to recompence by such means and ways as he trusts God in his providence will affoord, so that the world may see how desirous his Majestie is to recover his Croun and his Government by peacable means, and how much he tenders the saftie of his people, his Majestie is willing in relation to others who have bein involved in thes late commotions against religion and Government to pas an act of oblivion, excepting only some few persons who have bein chief opposers of the work of Reformatione, and cheif authores of the change of the Government and of the unparaleled murther of his Royall Father, provyded that they who ar to have the benefitt of this act lay doun ther armes, and returne to the obedience of ther laufull Soveraigne betwext and next to com, and shall offer themselfs willingly and hartily to joyne with his Majestie and his forces for the aforsaid ends when they shall be requyred. Bot if any shall be so pertinatious and perverse as to contemne this offer, and persist in ther oppositione and rebellion, they are not to expect any such favour, bot to the end some just difference may be made betwext the cheif authors, contryvers, and obstinat leaders on of thes unnaturall warres, returning so latte to ther dwetie, and thos who never depairted from it, they must expect that towards the publict burthens of the King and Kingdomes and the defraying of the necessarie charges his Majestie may be putt to in the recoverie of his rights, and which in a great pairt occassioned through ther default, ther estates in som proportion shall be lyable in such a reasonable and moderat meassure as the wisdome and discreation of the King and Parlaments of either Kingdome respectively, being called by his Majesties warrant and authoritie and lawfully constituted, or such as shall be authorized by them (who will be as carefull to prevent ther ruine, and not lay on them more then they may tollerably bear as to supplie and defray the just and necessarie publick debts and burthens his Majestie must be att for recoverie of his just rights and establishing the peace of his Kingdomes) shall find to be just and necessarie for that end. And albeit his Majestie knowes he must rancounter many difficulties and dangers in this undertaking, yett the sam being so necessarie a dewtie as that he is in conscience and honour obledged by all bonds religious, politicall, and naturall to prosecutt, he resolves to cast himself and his interest wholly upon God, and mantaine his trewth and laus and his oun just rights against injust usurpers, the enemies of treuth and peace, whose dignitie is from themselfs, and who mantaine sects and heresies and a tirannicall arbitrarie power over the consciences, persons, and estats of his good subjects, and his Majestie as a Cristiane doeth exhort, and as a King doeth reqwyre all his subjects who have trwe zeall to religion, loyaltie to ther King, or naturall affection to ther native Cuntrie, and who have any sparkles of the ancient valour of ther ancestours, and who desir to liberatt themselfs and ther children and posteritie from perpetuall infamie and servitude, to tak hold on such an opportunitie, and concurr with ther wholl hart and strength with his Majestie in so pious and just a caus; and as Cæsar said to a trimbling mariner who was in the shipe with him [in] the tym of a storme, 'Fear not, for thow caries Cæsar and his fortune,' so doeth his Majestie desir all who shall sincerly joyne with him, and inbark themselfs in this so noble ane interpryse, not to fear bot to be of gude couradge, not becaus they carie ther King (whom God hath bein pleased to save out of many dangers) and all his interests alongst with them; bot becaus that God the King of Kings and Lorde of Lords and his honour, who can save with few as weill as with many, is in the shipe with them.

Indorsed.—*Some grounds for a Declaration.*
Rec. Sep. 19th, 1653. Scotch Paper.
Q rejected.

By way of Instructions to the Person whom Ld. Loudon sent with the other Papers.
Indorsed by Lord Loudon.

CLIX

Colonel Bampfield's Advice.[1]

That your Majesty woulde please to dispatch Leut. Coll. M'Cloyde with all possible expedition, whoe I beleive is soe honest and faithfull to your Majesty's service, that he will say all things that may encourage your servants in Scotland.

That if your Majesty shall thinke fit, you may please to write three or four lines with your owne hand to the Chancellour, to the Lord Lorne, and to the Earle of Seaforth, which I beleive they will expect, by reason they knowe your Majesty has done the like to others, and may be discontented if you doe it not to them, and in this exgencye of your affayres, to doe some things extraordnaryly that looke like kindenesse in my humble oppinion may be dispenced with.

That letters may be written by els your Majesty shall thinke fit, to Glengary, to Lochele, to the Tutor of Mack Cloyde, to the Tutor of M'Cleve, the Laird of M'Kinnon, and the Laird of Coll, and that your Majesty will please to write a particular letter to the Gentry of Argylle and Lorne, to followe my Lord Lorne.

That your Majesty will thinke of some way that may obleidge M'Cloyde, whoe is considerable in the interest of his frends, and in his reputation amongst the rest of the Highlanders, and whose reports there will weigh much to the advantage or disadvantage of your Majestyes affayres.

That if your Majesty shall thinke fit, you will please to tell him, that whither the business bee ended suddeynly betwixt the Dutch and English or not, yet you are sure of money both from Prince Rupert and my Lord of Rochester, and that before Winter be ended you will certay[n]ly send them assistance both of armes and ammunition, and peradventure of men, and that some ships which are abroad with your Majesty's Commissions shall have order to plye upon theyr coasts, for the security of the Westerne Isles; all things that can be sayd or done to encourage them not to let your title fall totally, in my

---

[1] Clarendon Manuscripts, xlvi. 254.

humble oppinion ought to bee performed, for if it quite fall, it will infinitely change the constitution of your business in all your Majesty's Dominions.

That your Majesty will send a Commission for the Councell of war, with power to choose theyr precedent, and with all powers by them desired in the instructions, except the putting in and putting out new members at theyr pleasure, which will cause factions if your Majesty doeth not nominate the persons.

That your Majesty will please to make some pretence to detayne Shawe a while, till you may see whither the condition of your affayres abroad may be a little bettered, for I doubpt a great part of his business was to discover the true state of things in foraigne parts, and to advertise the Chancellor thereof, whoe may yet have a back dore to returne at, if he finds either none or but weake hopes of assistance.

If your Majesty will command M'Cloyde and I to present the names of such persons as wee thinke fittest for to be in the Councell of war, wee shall consider of it, and put them downe in writing.

Indorsed.—*Mr. Bampfeild's advises.*
Sept. 1653.[1]

CLX

Col. Bamfield's Advice.[2]

To the Earle of Atholl, from your Majesty's owne hand.
To Collonell Gilbert Stewart, only subscribed by your Majesty.
To the Tutor of Stroan the like.
To the Earle of Cateness from your Majesty's hand.
To the Master of Cateness, only subscribed.
To Sir James Synclare of Murcoll the like.
To the Laird of May the like.
To my Lord Rea and my Lord Duthoss in your Majesty's hand.

---

[1] Bampfield is mentioned in one of Hyde's letters, dated September 12, as not having yet reached Paris, and his arrival is mentioned in one written a week later. The memorial was no doubt presented at once.

[2] Clarendon Manuscripts, xlvi. 256.

[1653] A PROVISIONAL GOVERNMENT 219

The names of the Committee for the Government of affayres in the Kingdome of Scotland, till your Majesty sends a Commander.

The Lord Chancellour.
The Earle of Atholl.
The Earle of Glencarne.
The Earle of Cateness.
The Earle of Seafort.
The Lord Lorne.
The Lord Kenmore.
The Lorde Rea.
The Lord Duthoss.
The Master of Louet.

The Tutor of M'Clene.
Sir James M'Donald.
The Tutor of M'Cloyd.
The Laird of Glengary.
The Laird of Lochele.
The Captain of Clan Ranold.

These, or any seaven of them, with the president, to have full power to confirme what has been done, to authorise for the future.

To the Laird of Mack Farlan.
To the Laird of M'Knab.
To the Tutor of Clangrigar.

A Commission for the Tutor of M'Cloyde for a Regiment of Horse.

A Commission for Leut. Collonell Norman M'Cloyde for a Regiment of foote.

Indorsed :—*Coll. Bampfeild's paper, delivered the Kinge Sept. 9ʳ 1653.*

CLXI

Order concerning the Shire of Dunbarton.[1]

Wheras severall orders have bin issued out for the revaluing of the shire of Dunbarton, and that by reason of some differences amongst the Heritors of that shire, they cannott agree uppon fitt persons to bee chosen with generall satisfaction. I doe therfore againe order, That every individuall parish in the shire of Dunbarton may before the 22th instant chuse itt's proportion of 13 Commissioners, and that the names of all such may bee

---

[1] Clarke Manuscripts, lxxxvi. 94.

return'd unto mee, with the parishes for which they are elected, that out of those 13 I may appoint 7 of that number that may bee a standing Committee, to intend that worke for revaluing the whole shire, together with some officers of the army that shall bee appointed to joyne with those 7 therin: unlesse the shire amongst themselves agree uppon a better expedient for the settling of the valuations: and that if itt doe appeare any of those said number of 7 doe any thinge unjustly in favour of themselves to the prejudice of their neighbours, itt shall bee lawfull for those officers I shall appoint to sitt with them to rectifie the same, and to inflict such penalties uppon the offenders as they shall see fitt. Given under my hand att Dalkeith, the 12th day of September 1653. R. L.

CLXII

A Letter of Intelligence.[1]

Sept. 12, 1653.

The Highlanders purpose is to have a 1000 men together about Michalmas next, which shall bee a standing partie under the command of Glencairne. M'Aldey is to give 200 men, M'Laine 200 men, Seaforde 300, and Glencairnie and Glingary is to make up the rest. They resolve to keepe togeather till they have aid from the late King of Scotts, which they give out will come to them shortly, or however the next Spring.

They report that the English daire not (or at the least cannot) doe them any prejudice, except they fall doune in the Lowlands, which is not intended by them untill they have more strength. It's determined by this partie to prevent the contriey ajacent to the Lowlands for [from?] payeing sess to the English, but to themselves, and they perswade Commanders that the intent of the Parliment by their late summoning all to ingage (or bring ingagement for their peaceable liveing), is to git them togather, and soe distroy them, which they will prevent by men appereing. Lord Lorne and Glingary fell out, and drew each upon the other, but was prevented of fighting by some then present, how [ever] parted great enimies.

---

[1] Clarke Manuscripts, xxv. 126.

CLXIII

Col. Lilburne to the Lord Generall Cromwell.[1]

May itt please your Excellency,—Since my last to your Lordshippe, I have had a more particular account of the proceedinges of Col. Cobbett in reducing the Lewis.

The Lord Seaford had left his bastard brother Governour there. Uppon the approach of our forces he and the inhabitants quitt the fort, where there was 2 greate guns and 4 sling peeces, and towne of Loughsternay, and fled to the Hills, but uppon Proclamation from Col. Cobbett they came to their houses, and divers of them brought in their armes. Major Crispe is left there with 4 companies, and is fortifying Loughsternay, and a little fort in an Island which is almost inviron'd by the sea. The Harbore is very commodious for shipping to ride in with security under the fort. The 27th of August Col. Cobbett sayl'd thence, and by intelligence sent from the Marq. of Argyll the 3d instant, hee entred Mula Island, and tooke in the stronge Castle of Dovart;[2] the 3 shippes sent from Aire, with Captain Hargraves Company, mett him before his going into Mull.

Uppon the appearance of these forces they had a generall alarum throughout the Highlands, and pretended to march to the releife of M'cloud, who they heard was prisoner; they have appointed 1500 to bee in readinesse by the first of October, uppon the repute wherof they hope for credit abroad,

---

[1] Clarke Manuscripts, lxxxvi. 95.

[2] 'From Dalkeith, September 22.—While Col. Cobbet staid in Mula Island, the Marquis of Argile came thither; and by his advice and assistance the heritors of the countrey were brought to engage, that themselves and tenants shall live peaceably, obey the authority of Parliament, and pay sesse as the rest of the shire of Argile doth; and further engage not to act, nor suffer MacCleane the Tutor to act, anything prejudiciall to the affairs of the Commonwealth, nor to the garrison settled in Dowart, nor to pay any rent to the said MacCleane, out still in rebellion, and was at our coming thither in the Isle with Glencarne to raise them to joyne with those that are to meet at Loghaber the first of October, but upon our coming they went to Tyrree Island.'—*Mercurius Politicus*, Sept. 29-Oct. 6.

or att least to prey uppon the Lowlands for the maintenance of those mostroopers and fugitives that are amongst them, and intends to joyne with them. The Lord Lorne and Glengary lately fell out and drew each uppon other, but were prevented from fighting, yet parted great enemies. A shippe being lately come from Norway to Invernesse reports, that many Dutch men from the Indies, France, and Spaine, and other southerne parts, to the number of 100, are in Norway, in great feare of our fleete.

About 14 dayes agoe, betweene 30 and 40 sayle of Dutch were seene by the inhabitants of Orknay, judg'd to bee some Dutch Merchants from severall parts. One of them, of 200 tun, was wreck't uppon those Islands, the greatest parte of her loading being tobacos: seaven of her men were drown'd, and 20 sav'd.

Mr. John Waugh is committed by the Judges to Edinburgh Castle for praying and preaching for Charles Stuart.[1]

Dalkeith, 13° September 1653.

Lord Generall.

CLXIV

WARRANT from COL. LILBURNE.[2]

WHERAS by a former order from Major Generall Deane you were appointed to respite in your hands all the sesse that should bee due from the Laird of Genurque for his lands in Argyll for severall monthes expressed in that order. And wheras, by my late order of the 19th of August last, you were to respite his said sesse in Argyll for the said monthes of November, December, January, February, March, and Aprill last, I doe heerby order That you abate the sesse of the said Glenurque for the said six monthes, as alsoe That you forbeare to exact any sesse from him for six monthes, commencing from

---

[1] Compare the letter from Lilburne to Secretary Thurloe, written the same day, and printed in *Thurloe Papers*, i. 478; see also *Mercurius Politicus*, p. 2750, where it is said that Colonel Cobbett entered the Lewis the 16 of August.

[2] Clarke Manuscripts, lxxxvi. 101.

the first of May last, provided That the said Laird of Glenurque have nott acted, nor shall act, any thinge prejudiciall to the Commonwealth. Given under my hand and seale att Dalkeith, the 14th day of September 1653.   Rt. Lilburne.

To the Collector of the shire of Argyll.

CLXV

General Douglas to Charles II.[1]

May it pleas your Majeste,—I receaved your letter from Major Durahm, written in Paris the 18th of Aprill last, and with thatt submissive deutic I aught, do retorin your Majeste most humble thankis for that honor.[2] For the confidence yow are pleased to repois in me I shall indevour to deserve it be my comportment in thois rancounters thatt my service can be of use to yow, and that I may not delud your expecttation, be pleased to kno that from my infancie I have folloued the service of this Croune, whair I am now satlid, and so deipe in ther inter[i]stis be the trost reposid in me that I cane nather act personaly, nor furnish such advice as it may be is necessary for the advancement of your Majestis affairs. The greatte succes of the English heath much preveled over the spirits of some of the most pouerful heir, who for the publicke interist of traid do necessarle yeald to that pouer which they ar not abil to oppois. Generall Lieutenant Middiltoune did wishe not to com in person for manie reasons, which so particularlie cannot be impairted to your Majestie yeat, I make no questions bot from other handis youe receave frequent advertisements of the temper of this Court. All I cane do for your Majeste is and most be in a privat way, which can not produce any thing material to your service; however I am confident that your goodnes will not reject the harte affections of your subjects abroad, quhairoff a few with my selfe have maide bould to send your Majeste a somme of 5200 rixdollers, to that effect we have writt and sent our securitie to

Sept. ⅔

---

[1] Clarendon Manuscripts, xlvi. 269.
[2] See p. 105.

William Davidson, merchant in Amsterdam, appointing him to advance that small somm upon your Majestis demand. Ther are lykewayes som others of your subjects who live at a remot distance from this, I have alreadie writt to them, and maike no questione bot according to ther abilities that they will followe our example. Whain I have a retorin from them, itt shalbe convayed to yow with all possible speed. The rumor of your Majestes sicknes hath mutch afflicted me, for I doe not onle wisch you perfect health bot everie thing belonging to it in that fulnes as may rander your conditione pourful and glorious, and with an unalterable constance off deutie I doe title my selfe Your Majestes Most humble, ever Loiall, and most reallie affectionat subject, Ro. DOUGLAS.

From Stockholm this 24th off September 1653.

Addressed.—*For his most sacred Ma^te. The King off Great Brittaigne.*

Indorsed.—*Generall Douglasse, 24 Sept.* 1653, *to the Kinge.*

CLXVI

COL. LILBURNE to the LORD GENERAL CROMWELL.[1]

MAY ITT, ETC.,—Having newly received the inclosed relations from Col. Cobbett and the Marquesse of Argyll I thought itt my duty to send them to your Lordshippe to reade, that you may understand the account that is given of the Lewis and other places; the particulars in that paper mencioned [in] Col. Cobbett's lettre are most of them such thinges as doe yett lie before the Councell of State or Committee for the Ordnance, as amunition and other furniture of warre, which I humbly intreate your Lordshippe will consider and further the dispatch, especiallie that powder which I lent uppon your Lordshippes lettre, wherof indeed wee are in very great want, and I cannott handsomely supply the Lewis and other parts as I would for want therof. I humbly minde your Lordshippe of further supplies of monie that your Lordshippe will vouchsafe

---

[1] Clarke Manuscripts, lxxxvi. 97.

a worde or two to the Committee of the Army to give us timely supplies. I have nott further to acquaint your Lordshippe withall but what I lately have given you an account of, only that I heare other 4 ministers are under examination before the Judges. I remayne, Your Excellencies, etc.

Dalk. 15 September 1653.

His Excellency.

CLXVII

Col. LILBURNE to the COUNCIL of STATE.[1]

RIGHT HONORABLE,—Before I received your commands I had intelligence of armes shipp't by Middleton in the Netherlands, and have given orders to those shippes northward to bee watchfull, and shall according to those Instructions now received from you send further directions unto them, as alsoe that man of warre that is heere ; but I cannott omitt to acquaint you with the great disservice our shippes are putt uppon constantlie once in 6 weekes or 2 monthes in going to Newcastle or Hull for provisions, itt many times falls out very unhappily, and to the great neglect of service and losse of divers opportunities. I shall humbly intreat some speedy course bee taken for supply of victualls in this place for all such shippes as shall come for the guard or service of these Coasts, and that your Honours will bee pleased to appoint some monie for victualling of them, or otherwise that a good store of beefe and porke may bee laid in heere for them ; for other things the Country will afford them for monie ; and having all this summer disburs't divers summes for the supply of those shippes that are heere, and being exceedingly straightned for monie to carry on the fortifications and for pay of the forces, I humbly intreate that those summes may bee reimburs't unto us, and that the Treasurers of the Navy may have orders accordingly to discount with us : and shall alsoe humbly intreate that more monie may bee sent for the pay of the forces. I have received an account this day from Col. Cobbett concerning the Lewis, which seemes to bee a

---

[1] Clarke Manuscripts, lxxxvi. 98.

considerable place, and shall observe your commands as to the fortifying therof, humbly offering itt to your considerations that hee that shall bee left there Governour may have some additionall incouragement besides his pay, and that you would bee pleas'd to cause those supplies of ammunicion and other furniture of warre I formerly writt for to bee despatch't hither; for indeed heere is a great want of them, and I cannott supply the Lewis and other places as I would through that deficiencie. I have alsoe an account from the Marq. of Argyll that Col. Cobbett hath possess't Mula Island, which lies in the Mouth of Loughaber about 80 or 100 mile from the Lewis, that I doe nott doubt but one way or other wee shall meete with Middleton's armes if they come over.—I remayne, etc.

Dalk. 15 *September* 1653.
C. of S.

CLXVIII

Col. Lilburne to the Lord General Cromwell.[1]

May itt please your Excellency,—I received your Lordshippes, and have already putt garrisons into the frontiers on the Breas of the Highlands, and shall looke as strictlie to them as possibly I can, but when all is done I doubt they will make incursions and rob us of some of our sesse. I have already sent your Lordshippe an account of the Lewis Island as itt came to my hand, when Col. Cobbett returnes I shall queere further into all those thinges according to your Lordshippes commands, and give your Lordshippe a more ample account; but though itt may bee apprehended (as your Lordshippe sayes) that the Dutch have an eye uppon that place of Lewis, I rather find their conveniencie lies att Shetland, and their constant correspondence going and coming is att that place, as you may a little better perceive by the inclosed. There have bin sometimes 1800 saile in and about Birssie Sound in Shetland, a place where they can goe in att one end and out att the other, that end that lies most commodious for them where they commonlie touch att, being nott above half a mile over, may

---

[1] Clarke Manuscripts, lxxxvi. 105.

easily bee secured with a very small fort, which, if the season of
the yeare would permitt, and that your Lordshippe did approve
of itt, I should give order about itt; and if there were a guard
or a squadron of shippes there undoubtedly itt is the most
commodious place to give check to the Dutch trade of any, for
from thence I am told they can see neere the Coast of Norway,
that a shippe can hardly goe by them either way. Yesterday
a partie of my regiment hath happily apprehended Capt. Hume
(who was now going to his old trade of Mosse trooping) amongst
many others, who I hope may be deterr'd by his being taken;
the Country are full of Glencairne's round about us, but I hope
to scatter the nest of them if I can light but of one man more
that I have sent to apprehend, which is Col. Hume of Ayton's.[1]
I finde they have correspondents in England, and they are yett,
or att least seeme to bee, confident their designes there are
prosperously going on, notwithstanding the late discovery of
those in the west towards Southampton and Poole. Heere is
one of my most able intelligencers does propound the raising of
some voluntcers to serve the Kinge of Spaine, or Archduke
Leopold, or any other forraine prince that is not in enmity
against us, will undertake to draw away the most considerable
of all that rascality that seeme now to disturbe us. Hee offers
good security, and I perceive Marq. Huntley is alsoe driving
att some such businesse, which truly I thinke in my weake
judgement may bee very considerable as to the establishing of
peace heere, but I only lay these before your Excellency to
consider of as you see fitt. Your Lordshippe is pleas'd to tell
mee of a speedy course taken for monie, amunition, etc., but
they are slow in coming, and I assure your Lordshippe wee have
very great want: and for the supply of Lewis I was constrain'd
to send to Lieth and Edinburgh Castle for divers thinges out
of those stores, which Col. Fenwick was unwilling to parte with,
hee having found itt difficult to procure such thinges. I was
gladd to order the Comptroller to . . . (?) him supplies
assoone as they came under the disposall of Your Excellencies, etc.

Dalkeith, 20 September 1653.

---

[1] A commission to John Hume, 4 Oct. 1653, to command a regiment of horse, was intercepted about this time. Thurloe i. 503.

I have given notice to the severall Corporations to forbeare new elections of Magistrates according to the command I received from the Councell of State.

I wonder your Lordshippe hath nott all this while sent downe some good Ministers.[1]

CLXIX

A WARRANT from LORD KENMORE.[2]

Sept. 22, 1653.

HAVING taken uppe armes for defence of Religion, Kinge, and Kingedome, and being now by Gods providence in a condition able by God's blessing to protect you from the violence of the English rebbells, who have most unjustly invaded this Kingedome, and endeavour to subject the people thereof under the power of their usurped and pretended Commonwealth, and haveing directed orders to other parishes soe, these are to discharge all heritors and tenants in the parish of Criff to pay any more sesse to the enimie; and instead heareof you are required to make ready your proportion of monthly maintenance for this present month of September, which shall be three parts of fower of what your sesse extended to, which is three pence for ane groat, and the heriters are heareby required to bring every one his proportion to John Campbell's house att the East End of Lochearne, where there shall be some with orders to receive itt from you, and to give you discharges for what maintenance they receive; you are hereby discharged of what sesse is resting in your hands unpayd to the English, and in this you shall not fayle as you will not incurre prejudice of being esteemed enemies to religion, to king, and kingdome, and quartered on as deficents. KENMORE.

You are to bring for the month of September and October the foresaid maintenance against the day appointed, which day is the first of November 1653 as you will answer.

---

[1] On Sept. 26, 1653, the Council of State ordered that forts should be raised at convenient places on the Shetland isles, and that £4000 should be at once provided for the cost of fortifications there and elsewhere in Scotland.

[2] Clarke Manuscripts, xxv. 131.

CLXX

PROCLAMATION by COL. LILBURNE.[1]

By the Comander in Cheif of the forces in Scotland.

WHEREAS his Excellency by his proclamation of the fifth day of November 1650 heertofore published (remayning still in force) requiring plenary satisfaction for goods, and life for life taken from any of the English Army, of those parishes and places where the fact should bee committed, unlesse they should discover and produce the offender. And whereas the Commissioners appointed for the administracion of justice have lately published their Proclamacion of the fourth of July last for the suppressing vagabounds and masterfull beggars, notwithstanding which Proclamacion many theftes, robberies, and murthers are frequently committed (upon both Englishe and Scotes) by the gathering togeather of many desperate, rebellious, and broken people upon the Breas of the Highlands and in some other partes of the Nacion, for prevencion whereof and for preservacion of the peace for the tyme to come, These are strictly to require all Magistrates and officers, as well civill as military, and all other persons whatsoever to take care that noe suspected person or persons travaile or abide within their bounds or jurisdiccions without calling them to account for the same, and if they shall not give an good account of themselves to cause them to be secured. And if any of the said rebellious persons, or any person suspected belonging to them, or travailing to joyne with them, or coming from them, or any spy or intelligencer of theirs, shall come within any Burgh or parishe, such Burgh or parishe are hereby strictly required to apprehend them and keepe them in safe custody, or cause timely notice to be given to the next adjacent forces of the Englishe forces, whoe are hereby required in like manner to apprehend and secure them. And such person or persons as shalbe soe apprehended and secured notice thereof is to be given in writing to the Judge advocate of the Army and Advocate Generall of the Commonwealth,

---

[1] Clarke Manuscripts, xliii. 36.

whose order for their further disposall by the direccion of my selfe or civill Judges is to be observed. Or if any person or persons shall refuse or neglect his or their duty in the premisses they shalbe judged, deemed, and taken as disaffected to the peace of the Commonwealth, and proceeded against accordingly. And if any shall at any tyme furnishe the before said rebellious persons with monyes, horse, armes and amunitions, victual, or any kind of necessaries or provisions whatsoever, or be any waies aiding, abetting, assisting or countenancing them by advice, councell, or intelligence, connivance or any other correspondencie whatsoever, such person and persons shalbe adjudged, deemed, and taken as enimies to the Commonwealth and proceeded against accordingly. And for the encouragement of all such as shall apprehend any of the aforesaid persons, or shall bring or give tymely notice to the next forces as aforesaid of any partyes falling from the Highlands into the Lowlands, or of any persons hereby intended, or of any person or parishe whoe shall neglect his or their duty in pursuance of this Proclamacion, such person or persons shalbe lookt upon as frinds to the peace of this Nacion, and gratified and rewarded for his or their good service done therein.

Given under my hand and seale at Dalkeith the 27th day of September 1653. ROBT. LILBURNE.

To be proclaymed at the Market Cross in each Burgh according to the usuall manner.

CLXXI

COL. LILBURNE to the LORD GENERAL CROMWELL.[1]

MAY ITT PLEASE YOUR EXCELLENCY,—By the last post I received 2 or 3 lines from Mr. Malin, wherin hee signified your Lordshippes pleasure concerning my having a speciall eye to the security of the Orknay and Lewis Islands, and that all care may bee taken for the further fortifying of them; wherin I have already bin as carefull as I can, and done what can bee expected this season, and more cannott well bee done without a greater supply of monie, and more men to bee sent to those

---

[1] Clarke Manuscripts, lxxxvi. 103.

places then may conveniently bee spared att this time; and if wee should weaken our selves heere more by supplying those places, I conceive itt to bee exceeding hazardous to all our quarters and garrisons; and if more could conveniently bee spared to goe to the Islands, unlesse itt were a considerable partie indeed to each, consisting of att least 700 or 800 men, if the Dutch and Middleton doe agree, and that they come over any thing considerable, as itt may bee expected they will if they undertake such a businesse, then our small force there could nott prevent their landing and fortifying either one harbour or other; however, what your Lordshippe commands, if you please to particularize what you would have done, I shall either bee carefull to putt itt in execution, or give your Lordshippe sufficient reason to the contrarie. Those broken people, vizt., Glencairne, Kenmore, Sir Arthur Forbes, and the rest, doe continue stealing horses, wherby they increase their numbers daily, and lately ventur'd downe in the night time as farre as Falkeland, and tooke Captain Penne, and 4 or 5 more that had the charge of some timber in that parke, prisoners, for the releasement of whome Sir Arthur Forbes demands 80li, which uppon advice is consented to rather then to suffer the destruction of our freinds; in regard some of the towne were accessorie to that businesse I intend to make them responsible. They had another partie of about 300 Highlanders lately fell into Dunbarton Towne in the night, and kill'd 2 souldiers, and tooke 2 prisoners that lay in the Towne out of the garrison, and this day I heare the Lord Glencairne is coming that way ward, and is within one dayes march of that place with 1000 men, as the Governour of Dunbarton informes mee, but this particular I beleeve nott: however, wee doe strengthen our quarters and provide against the worst. I heard this day of the Lord Huntley's proposition concerning transporting of some men to any forraine princes service that is in amitie with us. I humbly intreate your Lordshippes directions how I may expresse my self in this particular, either to him or any other that shall make any such overture; I humbly conceive itt may bee for the advantage of the Commonwealth to helpe forward such offers. I must further importune your Lordshippe for the dispatch of powder and other amunition, etc., for indeed,

my Lord, wee are in want of those supplies that are necessary.
—I remayne, your Excellencies, etc.

Dalkeith, 27° September 1653.

Lord Generall.

CLXXII

Col. Lilburne to the Lord Generall Cromwell.[1]

May itt please your Excellency,—Yesterday I received an expresse from Mr. Malin, wherin hee signifies itt is your Lordshippes pleasure to fortifie the Islands better, and to putt some more force in them; and though I have already given your Lordshippe my thoughts of that businesse, yet having consider'd with Col. Cobbett and some others that understand those Islands, I finde them clearlie of opinion with my selfe, that more men then wee can conveniently spare will nott bee sufficient to secure those places, butt that an enemy may land in one Island or other, doe what they can, though there were 4000 of ours, without there were a squadron of shippes, which would bee more considerable for the safety and defence of those parts then other wayes, and without shippes Middleton or any other may land in 20 places, and wee know nott how to hinder him. But after your Lordshippe hath read my former and this, and after your Lordshippe has well consider'd the premisses, if your Lordshippe shall thinke fitt to command any thinge further to bee done, I shall bee very ready to obey your Lordshippes commands, haveing already given notice to the Governours of those forts in the Islands to strengthen themselves. There being nothing else worthy your Lordshippes trouble, I humbly subscribe my self, your Excellencies, etc.

Dalkeith, 29 September 1653.

Lord Generall.

---

[1] Clarke Manuscripts, lxxxvi. 107.

CLXXIII

Memorial from Lieut. Gen. Middleton to the States General.[1]

Memorial pour les treshauts et trespuissants Seigneurs Messeigneurs les Etats Generaux des Provinces Unies de la part du Monsieur Middleton, Lieutenant Génerall de sa Majesté Britannique au Royaume d'Escosse.

Lequel présente treshumblement à leur treshautz et trespuissantz Seigneuries les considérations suyvantes.

Imprimis. Qu'il est du tout impossible aux pretenduz Parlementaires d'Angleterre pour le présent de maintenir la guerre par terre et par mer ensemble, pourvu qu'elle soit vigoureusement poursuivie contre eux; comme il est tresaisé de veoir par les grandes despenses qu'ils ont fait depuis l'An 1649. Combien que depuis ce temps là ils n'ayent pas eu affaire à maintenir la guerre par terre et par mer ensemble, n'ayants pas esté embarquez en guerre avec ces Provinces icy, qu'apres avoir ruiné la partie Royale par terre en Escosse et Angleterre; car outre les grands imposts et taxes mises sur le peuple, ils ont vendu le Domaine Royal, les meubles, et la plus grande part des joyaux de la Couronne, ils ont delapidé les revenues du Roy et de l'Église, et ont eu des compositions pour les biens confisquez de ceux qui ont constamment adheré au service de sa Majesté, jusques à la somme de dix millions sterling et d'avantage, neantmoins ils se trouvent accablez des grandes debtes, ayants emprunté des sommes des deniers excessives de beaucoup des gens riches et incorporations particuliers des villes, combien que jusques icy ils n'ayent eu à faire à une fois qu'avec un ennemy, et ne payoient alors a leur infanterie par teste que huit sols par jour, et à ceste heure on leur paye douze sols. D'avantage les imposts sur les marchandises tant transportées dehors, qu'emportées dedans les Royaumes d'Escosse et d'Angleterre, leur manquent à present par faute de trafficq par mer. D'ou les treshauts et trespuissants Seigneurs peuvent claire-

---

[1] Clarendon Manuscripts, xlvi. 216.

ment prevoir la ruine évidente de ces Parlementaires, pourveu qu'ils soient vertement attaquez par terre et par mer ensemble.

2. Que les Escossois ont et la volonté et le pouvoir de leur faire la guerre, est assez évident par le mauvais traitement qu'ils ont reçeu d'eux; leur Noblesse estant deshonorée et privée de la liberté de porter des espées; le trafficq osté aux Bourgeois ausquels ne reste pas aucun navire de consequence; la liberté de l'Église opprimée; et les communs foulez en leur personnes, ayants esté ou venduz comme esclaves, mesmes aux Turcs et infidèles, après la bataille de Worcester, ou exposez dans les champs à une mort languissante par la faim et par les injures de l'air. D'avantage le pais montagneux d'Escosse possedè maintenant par les Royaux comprend bien les deux tierces du Roiaume, et est inhabité par des gens guerriers, vaillants, et preferants leur liberté à leur vies, ausquels rien ne manque que des armes et ammunition; desquelles s'ils estoient fourniz, les Anglois seroient ou ruinez par les incursions quotidiennes, ou contraints de s'assembler en un corps d'armée; ce qui rendroit les Escossois aussi maistres de la plus grande partie du Pais Bas; lesquels pourroient ou combattre les ennemis à leur avantage, si l'occasion se presentoit; ou les necessiter à une guerre d'hiver; laquelle il leur est impossible de maintenir, pour l'incommodité du climat et la faute des choses nécessaires à leur armée; les transport desquelles en hiver par terre est impossible, et par mer peut estre empesché par les navires de ce pais icy. Par ainsi la guerre pourra estre aysement transportée d'Escosse en Angleterre, et les Anglois contraints de quiter la mer pour se defendre par terre.

3. Que s'il plaist aux treshauts et trespuissants Seigneurs d'assister avec armes et ammunition les fideles sujets de sa Majesté en Escosse, sa Majesté accordera à leur Seigneuries la permission de faire bastir des forteresses, tant dans la terre ferme d'Escosse vers l'Occident qui est encores à sa Majesté, que dans les Isles, ou par tout il y a quantité des bonnes havres, pour l'asseurance de leur commerce tant des Indes qu'ailleurs, et l'avancement de la pescherie.

4. Quant aux difficultez qui se pourront presenter touchant le contenu dessus, ou touchant la quantité des armes et d'ammunition nécessaire pour faire la diversion de forces Angloises;

le susdit Lieutenant Générall de Sa Majesté en promet un prompt esclaircissement et information plus particulière ; pourveu que leur Seigneuries ayent pour agréable, ou de deputir quelq'un de leur corps, quis çache parler Anglois, pour conferer avec luy ; ou de luy octroyer la permission d'emmener avec luy un interpret.

CLXXIV
A Second Memorial from Lieut.-Gen. Middleton.[1]

Autre Memorial pour les treshauts et trespuissants Messeigneurs les Estats Généraux des Provinces Unies, de la part de Monsieur Middleton L. Générall de sa Majesté Britanique au Royaume d'Escosse.

Lequel présente treshumblement à leur treshauts et trespuissants Seigneuries les considérations suyvantes.

Imprimis. Que l'Escosse peut mettre en campaigne à present 30000 hommes, et n'a des armes que pour environ 6000 de Cavallerie et d'Infanterie ; il est bien vray que les montaguards ont des arcs et flesches, et lances en nombre considerable ; mais ces armes ne sont pas utiles pour opposer à celles desquelles les ennemis se servent, ains seulement pour se defendre, s'ils sont attaquez en leur pais.

2. Que si les treshauts et trespuissant Seigneurs ont pour agreable d'envoyer des armes pour les autres 24000 la diversion des forces Angloises sera tant plus grande et utile à ces Provinces icy : mais pour rendre la diversion aucunement considérable, il faut pour le moins avoir.

Carabins 2000.
Fusées 4000.
Mousquets 2000.
Piques 4000.
de poudre 1200 livres, et bales en proportion convenable, et mesches selon la proportion de 4000 livres de poudre.
Hoiaux et Bêches 2000.
deux Pièces Mortaires avec quelques grenades.

---
[1] Clarendon Manuscripts, xlvi. 217.

Petards 24.

de Pistolets 1000 pairs, avec 1000 selles et autre equipage convenable aux 1000 cavalliers, comme morions et corselets.

de Canon 8 pieces, pour la defense de quelque havre ou forteresse qu'on pourra faire bastir.

3. Que pour asseurance de remboursement des fraiz que leur Seigneuries seront en fournissant les armes et ammunition susdites, sa Majesté leur engagera les revenues des Isles Orcades, qui montent pour le moins tous les ans a 80000 livres, jusques à ce que leur Seigneuries soient payés.

4. D'avantage sa Majesté accordera à leur Seigneuries de faire bastir telles forteresses qu'elles voudront, dans les Isles Orcades, Hetland, et Isles Occidentales d'Escosse, ce qui servira grandement pour asseurer leur trafficq des Indes et vers le Septentrion; La pescherie aussi s'y pourra continuer tant en hiver qu'en esté, et avec beaucoup moins des fraiz et des gens qu'ils n'ont accoustumé d'embarquer pour la pesche, les havres dans ces Iles leur estants tousjours ouverts, ou estants aidez par ceux de ce pais là a saler et dresser leur poissons, ils pourront plus faire avec cent, qu' à ceste heure avec trois cents.

5. Pour oster l'apprehension que leur Seigneuries peuvent avoir d'aucune garnison qui est desja dans les Iles: je respond que dans toutes ces Iles, il n'y a qu'une seule garnison Angloise, à sçavoir en la ville de Kirkwall, et que les autres Iles ne la recognoissent aucunement en payant contribution ou autrement, tellement que les ennemis la semblent plustost estre dans une prison que dans une garnison: et que s'il plaist à leur Seigneuries d'y envoier seulement 1200 pietons et 200 cavaliers, Je m'oblige sur l'hazard de ma vie et honneur, de les mettre en possession de ceste place là, dans 24 heures après nostre arrivée.

6. Quant à la difficulté qu'on pourroit apprehendre à maintenir ces Isles contre les ennemis, je respond aussi que ces Isles là peuvent aysement fournir 1000 hommes pour assister ceux de ce pais icy à les maintenir; et s'il plaist à leur Seigneuries d'y envoier des armes necessaires, les inhabitants des Isles seront obligez de les acheter en payant argent contant, et authorisez par le commandement de sa Majesté de les assister contre tous opposants, et toutes choses estantes mises en ceste posture, il sera impossible aux Anglois de leur nuire en ces Isles, sans

forces extraordinaires et beaucoup plus grandes, tant par terre que par mer, qu'ils ne sçauroient fournir.

7. Si en la prosecution de ce que j'ay cy dessus proposé, les treshauts et trespuissants Seigneurs trouveront la fascherie et incommodité grande ; qu'ils ayent pour agréable d'avancer seulement la somme de 180000 livres, et la mettre entre les mains d'un Commissaire deputé par eux pour la debourser pour l'avancement des desseins proposez : Je m'oblige de faire en sorte que les armes et ammunition susdites seront envoyées en Escosse avec le nombre de Cavallerie et Infanterie cy dessus specifié, et de mettre leur Seigneuries en la possession desdites Isles ; pourveu aussi qu'il leur plaise d'escrire à sa Majestè de Denmarck, de favoriser le transport de ces armes et soldats, et que je puisse avoir la liberté en payant de louer des navires en son païs pour ce sujet.

8. Outre plus ce peu des gens estant envoyé là encouragera grandement les natives et tout le pais d'Escosse de s'eslever contre les ennemis, qui auront (dieu aydant) assez à faire de se tenir sur le defensif ; tant s'en faut qu'ils seront en aucune façon capables de molester ceux qui seront dans ces Isles.

9. Ainsi il est clairement monstré que dans deux annees les treshauts et trespuissants Seigneurs seront remboursez des frais qu'ils seront ; outre le grand avantage que ces Provinces tireront de l'asseurance de leur commerce des Indes et vers le Septentrion, et de la pescherie continuée, et sans vanité Je pourray promettre, par la benediction de dieu sur nos entreprises, devant la feste de Noël suyvant de rendre sa Majesté maistre de tous les havres et ports d'Escosse (ou les navires de ce pais icy seront protegez en toutes asseurance), horsmis la ville de Leith, laquelle seule ils ont fortifié et qu'il est bien mal-aysé d'assieger en hiver.

10. Pour l'accomplissement des conditions cy desus specifiées, Je m'oblige de procurer la ratification d'icelles de sa part de sa Majesté : esperant aussi que les treshauts et trespuissants Seigneurs ayants conferé cet escrit avec le premier, et meurement considéré le contenu de tous les deux, y trouveront l'esclaircissement des difficultez qui se pourront presenter sur le sujet proposé.[1]

---

[1] This is doubtless the memorial from Middleton read in the Assembly of the States of Holland and Friesland on Sept. 12, 1653. See Thurloe i. 446. The

CLXXV

Col. Lilburn to Lord General Cromwell.[1]

May, etc.,—I have nott any thinge considerable to acquaint your Excellency with att this time, only that in regard 3 of our men of warre are disabled by the late storme[2] I have sent them upp to [?] London to refitt themselues, and desire they may bee returned hither with all convenient speede, or some other in their stead, of the usefulnesse of which I have already given your Excellency my poore thoughtes, and shall againe humbly intreate that 4 or 5 (if nott more) good men of warre might be sent to lie about Shetland. Certainly itt would bee very considerable service they might bee able to doe there, besides preventing of Middleton's landing, and without shipping all our fortifications in those islands signifies little or nothing. Col. Riche's regiment being come Col. Berry's troopes are most of them march't for England, as alsoe by virtue of an order from M. G. Lambert (I suppose by your Lordshippes appointment) three troopes of mine are march't towards Westchester, and the other 3 order'd shortly to follow; but as yett I heare of none coming in their stead, though the truth is wee stand in neede of horse, and I doubt if the Enemy increase much more wee must either increase these numbers that are heere by recruiting, or other wise move for some more supplies from England, the troopes being soe very small; which makes mee the rather bold to intreate your Lordshippes allowance of my owne troopes continuance heere for some time

---

states of Holland resolved on 17 Oct. to assist the Scots with the sum of 180,000 gilders, and by order of 24th Nov. he was given leave to transport to Scotland a specified quantity of arms and ammunition, *ib.* pp. 528, 594. The progress of the negotiations was well known to the English Government through its spies (*ib.* pp. 447, 449, 450, 460, 463, 469, 485, 496, 508, 514, 520, 531, 557, 585, 599). For Hyde's comments on the attitude of the Dutch, see *Clarendon State Papers*, iii. 192, 196, 199, 202.

[1] Clarke Manuscripts, lxxxvi. 102.

[2] The storm was on 23 Sept. Cobbet's expedition lost three ships: the *Swan*, a small man-of-war, and the transports, *Martha and Margaret*, and *Speedwell*.

longer, aud if your Lordshippe signifie nothing to the contrarie I shall take this for granted unto, Your Excellencies, etc.

Dalkeith, 3d October
1653.

CLXXVI

COL. LILBURNE to the SCOTTISH JUDGES.[1]

GENTLEMEN,—Haveing heard of the hard condicion the Earl of Marr is in through those greate ingagements that lye upon his estate, and being perswaded he is free as yett from any corrispondence with those in armes against us, and that he is come in to give security for his peaceable living, according to your late proclamacion, and because allsoe of severall reasons tending to the peace of this Commonwelth, and that he may not be put upon any extreeme course for his owne preservacion through the violence of some creditours, I desire you wilbe pleased to grant him suspention in such cases as are depending before you for 3 months, or longer if you see cause for it; his creditours have condecended, which I could not but recomend unto you, and remaine, etc.

Oct. 3. 1653.

Commissioners for Administration of Justice.

CLXXVII

PASS for the MARQUESS of ARGYLL.[2]

WHERAS the right honorable the Marquesse of Argyll is to repaire to the Head Quarters about some affaires of publique concernement, These are to require you on sight heerof to permitt and suffer the said Marquesse of Argyll with his servants, horses, armes, and necessaries to pass from Inverara to Dalkeith, and to passe about his occasions in these parts for the space of six weekes after the date heerof, and to returne

---

[1] Clarke Manuscripts, lxxxvi. 126.   [2] *Ibid.* lxxxvi. 120.

without interruption or molestation. Given under my hand and seale att Dalkeith the 4th day of October 1653.

RT. LILBURNE.

To all officers and souldiers and others whome these may concerne.

CLXXVIII

COL. LILBURNE to the LORD GENERAL CROMWELL.[1]

MAY ITT PLEASE YOUR EXCELLENCY,—Col. Reade and others giving mee intelligence that 5 or 600 are coming towards the Breas of the Hills to joyne with the Lord Lorne and Kenmore, by which addition I am told they will bee about 1000 or 1200 stronge horse and foote. I am doubtfull by reason I heare they Randezvouz neere the Head of Lough Lomond, that they may designe something uppon our new garrisons att Buhannon and Cardrus, or uppon the towne of Sterling or Glasgowe, which itt seemes they threaten, therefor I am drawing some forces that way to prevent any thinge of danger.[2] I am told they have gott that incouragement, either from abroad or some way from the Lowlands, that they are going to putt forth a Declaration to invite their Countrymen to joyne against the common Enemy, and to lay doune the grounds and reasons of these their proceedinges. I must confesse this businesse begins to looke more suspitiously then hitherto ; but yett I cannot see what they can doe this winter, without itt bee by putting some affronts uppon some small garrisons or parties marching to and fro by stealing downe in the night time, which I have made itt my study to prevent, and to lie as stronge and considerable as I can in each quarter. Heere is a very great want of the assistance of those officers that are absent, there being neither

---

[1] Clarke Manuscripts, lxxxvi. 107.

[2] 'From Colonel Lilburn at Linlithgow, October 8.—Hearing that the Highlander Tories were to have a rendezvouz near the head of Lough Lomand not far from Sterling, we are drawing some forces that way to prevent their in-fall, but they take their opportunities in the night time, and steal horses and increase their body daily ; and we perceive the ministers are not altogether ignorant, nor free from correspondence with them. Could we tell how to come at them I should

Colonell nor Major of horse in all Scotland but Major Bridge,[1] and the want of Col. Overton or some body to bee with those forces in the west makes mee humbly to propound itt to your Excellency, that in case Col. Overton doe nott speedily come by reason Col. Cooper is ordered for Aire, that hee may bee forthwith dispatch'd hither with other officers that are too much wanting, and that the amunition and those other supplies may bee dispatch't away. I thought itt my duty to give your Lordshippe these accounts as they come unto, Your Lordshippes most, etc.

Dalkeith, 6th October 1653.

CLXXIX

COL. LILBURNE to the LORD GENERAL CROMWELL.[2]

MAY ITT, ETC.,—By reason of the partie under Kenmore making incursions by the advantage of the boates in Lough Lomond into some parts of Dunbartonshire, and having intelligence that Sir Mungoe Murray and Sir Arthur Forbes were come out of Perthshire to joyne with him, not knowing but they might intend something uppon this place or Country, I came hither to prevent any danger of that kinde;[3] and since my coming have heard that they are march't from this side Lough Lomond to the Head of Lough Longe, and soe towards Argyll's country, pretending as the report is to force those people to rise with them or else to plunder them, nor doe I heare that the Lord Arg[yll] is in any posture to oppose them. I am nott able to understand the mistery of their proceedinges, nor from whence they gett soe much incouragement, but am inform'd many of the Ministers have a great hand with them;

---

hope to give a good accompt of them. Glengary is gone to meet Sir James Macdonald. Kenmore hastens all he can together. The Marquis of Argile stands firm yet, and some that have formerly been out, are now (notwithstanding the present stir) come in, and desire to live peaceably under protection.'—*Mercurius Politicus*, p. 2809, Oct. 13-20, 1654.

[1] Tobias Bridge, Major of Okey's dragoons.
[2] Clarke's Manuscripts, lxxxvi. 109.
[3] From Scotland, October 18.—'The Commander-in-Chief marched from Dalkeith to Linlithgow, where two companies of Lieut.-General Moncke's

though I perceive Mr. Galeaspe of this towne, who was with mee, and these Westerne people, doe much detest the thoughts of their actions or countenancing of them, yet generally the people are true to them, and will nott discover any partie that comes downe till they bee gone without our reach, unlesse itt bee some few that are peaceably inclin'd and suffer under them. They goe on in their trade of stealing horses in severall parts, and pretend themselves to bee stronge, as your Lordshippe will perceive by the inclosed copies, the originall wherof I have under Kenmore's owne hand. I could wish the Scoutmaster-Generall heere with some other officers to looke after their charges, if your Lordshippe see fitt to command them.—I remayne, your Lordshippes, etc.

Glasgowe, 12 *October* 1653.
Lord Generall.

CLXXX

COL. LILBURNE to the LORD GENERAL CROMWELL.[1]

MAY ITT PLEASE, ETC.,—Having on Friday last march't within 160 miles of the Marq. of Argyll's house att Inverara, with Col. Overton's regiment of foote and 150 horse, to see if wee could have done any thinge to have either engag'd or snap't Kenmore or any of his partie; hee was farre before and the way soe impassable for us, especiallie att this season of the yeare, that after I had taken a view of a great house some 10 miles hence, I returned hither, and am going over Clyde into Renfrew and Ayre shires, to see in what temper the people are there. Since my coming back hither I heard from the Lord Argyll, who gives mee an account that his Country men and Clan doe nott answer his expectation in joyning with him to

---

Regiment, and three troops of horse lay that night. We had intelligence that Kenmore went from Busse to the head of Lough Long, the 7th instant, with all his men, to meet Colonel Macnaughton, who came over the Lough with him about six days since with a party of foot. His men run away from him daily, so that what he increases one day he loseth another. He marches with a rundlet of strong waters before him which they call Kenmore's Drum.'—*Mercurius Politicus,* Oct. 20-27.

[1] Clarke Manuscripts, lxxxvi. 109, 6.

oppose Kenmore, who itt seemes is nott yett above 5 or 600 horse and foote; yett the Lord Argyll tells mee hee cannott advise mee to advance further, though hee suffer never soe much by those Tories, who (according to my intelligence yesternight) are neere unto Cantyre, where there are a partie of Lowland men unwilling to receive them, as I am inform'd, and pretends they will oppose them: if they doe nott, they being many of them of the Kirke partie, and most of them officers, both Colonells, Lieut. Colonells and Majors, that were of Gibbee Kerr and Straughan's partie, and perfectlie creatures to Argyll, I shall then more aptly beleeve there is absolute jugling amongst them. I heare they intend when they are growne a little considerable (as they doe promise themselves very much of itt, they being in places wee cannott come att them in) they will for Invernesse, and hope to reduce that place, and then to drive us out of the North, after which they are confident to forme a considerable Army.

I humbly conceive if the Marq. of Huntley and others had incouragement to draw off as many of those men as they can gett, itt would bee a great meanes to weaken and dissappoint them, and a way might bee found out for the doing therof without any hazard or danger to our forces, and after that party were gone men enow might bee found to undertake any service abroad, that they might bee lawfully call'd to, and heerby I thinke a great many of our enemies would bee dispatch't from this Nation, and might very much conduce to the setlement of a lasting peace heere. I hope your Lordshippe will further the dispatch of a guard of shippes for the Northerne parts, which doubtlesse will bee of great advantage. I should humbly intreate alsoe that a shippe or two might been sent to the Westerne Coasts, to assist us about Aire and the Islands where wee have garrisons. I must againe intreate your Lordshippe to dispatch Col. Cooper, for uppon the removall of Col. Alured's men itt will bee very fitting Col. Cooper should bee uppon the place, least our affaires goe slowly on there, though I am confident the Lieutenant Colonell will doe his utmost indeavours whilest hee stayes.—I remayne, your Excellencies, etc.

Dunbarton, 16 *October* 1653.
    Lord Generall.

CLXXXI[1]

Colonel Lilburne to the Marquis of Argyll.[2]

My Lord,—I suppose your Lordship may have heard that divers horses are stolne and other insolencies committed in Ranthrow [?] and Ayreshire [?] of the Lord Glencairne's and Kenmore's partie, or other loose persons who intend to joyne with them, and that divers of them are frequently transported to and fro, neare Lough-Long and other places in your Lordshippes bounds, by some of your people who have boates; the which tending to the disturbance of the publique peace, I conceive itt my duty to desire your Lordshippe to give strict order to your people to forbeare to lett any of their boates bee made use of by any such men, or to lett them att any time to transport any stranger or suspitious person; which if they shall persist to doe I shall bee constrayned to suppresse or seize uppon all boates in any of their possessions who shall soe offend; wherein a word from your Lordshipp may both prevent many inconveniences to these Cuntries, and much trouble to such parties of ours as wilbe commaunded to take inspection hereinto, and may tend much to the preserving of the peace, and shalbe owned amongst many other your good workes and civillities unto my Lord.   R. L.

Dunbarton, 17 October 1653.

CLXXXII[3]

Oct. 21. ### Sir Edward Hyde to Lieut.-Gen. Middleton.[4]

Sir,—This inclosed from his Majesty is written by advice of

---

[1] Clarendon Manuscripts, lxxxvi. 111.   [2] No address is given.
[3] Clarendon Manuscripts, xlvi. 364.
[4] In a letter to Nicholas, Hyde explains the origin of the published intention of the king to go to Scotland himself. 'When you see or hear that anything is resolved, which seems contrary to evident reason, be so kind to those upon the place to imagine that it is either not resolved, or that there are other reasons than appear to you. You very well know that in the condition the king is in, and to comply with the unskilful humours of those who wish well, and the

the Councell, which consideringe how very convenient it may probably be for his Majesty himselfe to goe into Scotlande, and himselfe resolvinge not to be longer doinge nothinge, thinkes that he can never be sufficiently informed of the state of his affayres ther, to know what is counsellable for him to doe, till you be ther and can returne him your advice; and I am perswaded the very fame of your goinge would gett some

turbulent humours of others, many things must be given out to be resolved which in truth are not, and many things may be generally resolved under some notion which must depend upon accidents before they can be executed; and I have said enough heretofore of this argument to you, of the king's positive resolution concerning himself, to persuade you not to be much moved upon general discourses, and you may reasonably conclude, if you know it not, that there is no very positive determination of moment. You apprehend the king's going into Scotland unreasonable, which be confident will never be done with less caution than you wish, and yet it is very necessary that the resolutions should be taken, which are, and therefore taken that they may be spoken of. I will tell you as shortly as I can the state of the business, and then you will find the journey from Chantilly was nothing to the point. You must know most of the letters from Scotland and from the prisoners in London very earnestly press the king to go himself into Scotland, and in the meantime to hasten Middleton hither to prevent and compose the factions there, and all people wish that he were in Scotland; not that they really wish it, but to raise the odium and the envy against those whose counsel they think the king takes too much, and whom they would have believed to be the cause that his Majesty is not active, which is now the word used to lead on all discourses to folly and madness. To comply with the good wishes of the first, the king writes to his friends in London and Scotland, that Middleton shall be shortly there, and then upon advice from him and evidence that the king is counselable, he will be himself with them, if there do not appear somewhat to be done more reasonable for the common work; and this he is contented should be in all places believed, and therefore it is no wonder, it having been so oft said, that Middleton hears it from London or from any other part of the world. To reform if it be possible the other more pernicious humour, the king calls his Council, tells them he takes notice of the general imputations and reproaches, that he is willing to be advised what to do with his own person, that he is so weary of sitting still, he would if they thought fit go into Scotland. This being so unexpected and so concerted by those they thought so much of another opinion, it was alledged that the state of Scotland was not understood at the board (where indeed it had never been opened), and therefore advice could not be given. Hereupon, as it was necessary, Colonel Drummond (whom you will know; and is a very discreet, honest, gallant person) was called according to appointment, and made a relation of all matters there which neither were or ought to be a secret, and then all were of opinion that such a letter should be written to Middleton, and that the king would be ready to follow when fit, and in the meantime go out of France as soon as they will supply him with money.'—*Clarendon State Papers*, iii. 196. Nov. 14, 1653.

good company with you, and you finde by what my Lord Wentworth writes that Denmarke, though it promised nothinge positively, hath a good disposicion to know what could do us good, and people do not use to aske such questions who do not intende to administer some helpe, at least privately, which will doe our businesse. I pray consider well 'of it, and lett me know your minde. Ther is likewise a clause in your letter, to that purpose you mencioned in your last, in which I know you will proceede with that warynesse as is necessary, and expose your selfe as little as may be, to be denyed. Coll. Drummonde will be with you within very few dayes, and shall bringe with him the letter for Collonell Greene and many other dispatches, which I conceave will not be unwellcome to you. By him I shall say much more, that is not so fitt for paper. God preserve you and make you a blessed instrument to restore our deere Master, which I hope you will be.—I am most heartily and faythfully your, etc.

Lt. Generall Middleton.

Indorsed.—*Myne to Lt. Gen. Middleton*, 31 Oct. 1653.

CLXXXIII[1]

INSTRUCTIONS for our Trusty and Wellbeloved COLLONELL WILLIAM DRUMMONDE: imployed by us upon our especiall service into our Kingdome of Scotlande.

Oct. 23.
Nov. 2.

1. As soone as you have communicated with L^{nt} Generall Middleton all those particulers which wee have given you in charge, and ascertained with him as well as is possible the tyme for his owne departure into Scotlande, to the which wee have trusted him by our owne letter, and taken such other derections from him as he will give, you shall proceede in your jorney for that our kingdome that way you judge most safe and expedient; and deliver the severall letters wee have intrusted you with.

---

[1] Clarendon Manuscripts, xlvii. 7.

2. You shall as soone as you can with safety and conveniency repayre to the place wher the Earle of Glengarne is, and assure him in our name that wee are very well satisfyed with what he hath done, and very gladd that he hath taken the commande upon himselfe, accordinge to our Commission, and that wee will not fayle to protecte him to the utmost of our power in the execution therof; and as wee are very well assured that he undertooke that charge only out of his zeale and affection to us, and to prevent those inconveniences and mischieves which might otherwise have insued, so wee are most assured that he will proceede therin with all candour, and use his utmost power and dexterity to unite and dispose all persons to our service; and as heartily receave all who do wish the same end, though they may have hearetofore (before our pleasure was knowne) differed in the way, as severely proceede against those who, upon what pretences soever, are obstinate and refractory to those orders, without an intire obedyence wherunto the service cannot be carryed on.

3. You shall as soone as may be reporte unto the Lord Balcarris, and commende us heartily unto him; and tell him that wee have nothinge to add to what wee have of late written to him, which wee presume is come by severall wayes to his handes, and you shall assure him wee cannot have more confidence in and kindnesse for any man then wee have for him, whose affection to us, or ability to serve us, can never be doubted by us.

4. Since wee know you are so particularly knowne and esteemed by the Earle of Glengarne and the Lord Balcarris, that they will not only give creditt to what you shall say as you are imployed and trusted by us, but as you are a person loved and valewed by them both; and therfore you shall with all freedome expresse to them the trouble and griefe you founde us possessed with upon the newes of the interrupcion of that confidence and kindnesse which hath bene betweene them, the preservation wherof is of so high importance to our service, and indeede to ther owne and ther Countryes service. You shall remember them, that they well know themselves to be the two persons upon whome wee more depended, and in whose affections and usefulnesse to our service wee have a greater

confidence then in any whome wee left behinde us in Scotlande, and not more for ther wisdome and undoubted fayth to us then for ther intire frendshipp to each other, which wee well knew would be able to prævent the devices and designes of others; and therfore they will easily conclude in what perplexity wee must be, whilst wee have an apprehension of any breach or distance betweene them: or indeede whilst other men imagyne that ther is such. Wee cannot but believe that those who endeavour to wyden that breach are farr from the desyringe the good of our service, and wee wish that they will both looke upon them as such. Wee have informed you at large of the grounds of all our proceedings, and you shall use our name to both of them to conjure them as they ever intende to gratify us, that they will returne to ther old confidence in each other, and departe from all misapprehensions, and be irreconciliable to them who oppose that reconciliation, as an infallable marke of disaffection to the publique worke.

5. You shall lett the Lord Balcarris know that the reason why wee did not make any answer in our letter to him, to that parte of his which mencioned his purpose of comminge to us in person, was not that wee have not the same opinion of him, or desyre not his presence neere us, which he knowes wee have formerly expressed to have; but that wee saw by his letter that that resolucion proceeded from discontent, and the difference betweene him and the Earle of Glengarne, and in that case, and whilst the people conclude it proceeded from that grounde, wee neede not say how inconvenient and mischievous his leavinge the Kingdome may prove to be.

6. You shall informe the Earle of Glengarne, and the principle persons ther to whome in your judgement it ought to be communicated, that our longe abode in this Kingdome (how unactive soever wee have appeared to be) hath bene upon good reason. They well know how longe it was since the warr first begunn betweene the Dutch and the Rebells, and what reason wee had to believe that they would before this have thought fitt to have considered our interest, at least to have used it, in the carryinge on the warr. That as wee have left nothinge unattempted within our power to dispose them to such a concurrence, by the best meanes and expedients which occurred

to us, so wee have followed the advice of our wisest frends, both in Englande and Hollande, in stayinge in this Kingdome, till wee might see the conclusion and resolucion the other would take, and in the meane tyme preservinge to our selfe the reputacion of havinge this Crowne our frende, and indeavouringe by its countenance, and by promoting the allyance in treaty betweene France and Hollande, to procure our owne affayres to be consider'd by the other. That the delayes and factions in Hollande have prooved greater then wee could reasonably expecte, yett that wee hope for a conclusion to our advantage. That wee have tryed all other wayes with other Princes to putt our selfe into a posture of beinge active, by gettinge men, armes, and mony, and though our purposse hath not bene yett answerable to our expectacion, wee are not discouraged. That wee are resolved (if wee do not quickly finde some opportunity to make an impressyon upon some other partes of our Kingdome, wherby wee may deverte and devyde the power of the Rebells, and make the worke the more easy to our armes in Scotlande), to transporte our selfe to them, and runn our fortune with them, as soone as they shall give us such an accounte of ther posture and condicion as may make such a resolucion counsellable and fitt to be executed: and concerninge this particular you shall procure advice to be sent to us as soone as may be: and in the sendinge expresses to us, you shall lett them know what wee desyre should be observed.

7. Wee neede not putt you in minde of the recepcion of all such who shall resorte to you out of Englande, that all encouragement may be given to them: of which wee have spoken to you at large.

Indorsed.—*Coll. Drummond's instructions*,[1] 2 *and* 3 *of November* 1653.

---

[1] Drummond was still at Rotterdam on Nov. 21. A letter from him to Glencairne, of that date, was intercepted, and is printed in the *Thurloe Papers*, i. 585.

CXXXIV[1]

INSTRUCTIONS to our Trusty and Wellbeloved COLL. NORMAN MACKCLOUDE: imployed by us to our good subjects now in armes in Scotlande.[2]

Oct. 23.
Nov. 2.
1. You shall repayre with what speede you can into the Province of Hollande to L^{nt} Generall Middleton, whome you shall informe of what you know of the affayres of our Kingdome of Scotlande, and the particular affections of those with whom you are best acquainted ther, and shall lett him know the reasons that you called not on him in your way towards us; and you shall observe such derections as you shall receave from him, ether for your speedy repayre into Scotlande, or for your stay with him, or repayre to any other place for the advancement of our service, accordinge to such orders as he shall give you, which you are to obey as if they were under our owne signe manuall.

2. When you shall come into Scotlande, you shall deliver the severall letters wee have intrusted you with, and you shall lett those from whome you were imployed to us know, that it was the middle of September before you came to us, and the reasons why you stay'd so longe on the way, so that wee had putt our affayres of that Kingdome into that way of conducte they are now under longe before the letters and advices sent to them by you came to our handes.

3. You shall lett them know, that upon the first newes and assurance of many of our good subjects of the Highlands beinge in armes for us, of which wee had a very confused intelligence without knowinge more then the names of very few of the heades of the Clanns who were united in that resolucion, nor what correspondence they had with the rest, Wee graunted our Commissyon to some selecte persons to order and conducte those affayres, and to make choyce of one Commander in chiefe,

---

[1] Clarendon Manuscripts, xlvii. 9.
[2] Altered from 'in our Highlands of Scotlande.'

to whome all the forces raysed and to be raysed should be
obedyent, untill such tyme as L^{nt} Generall Middleton should
arryve ther. And because wee were not sure that all those
persons nominated by us had then thought it seasonable
publiquely to declare ther purposes, or could be present at
those first meetinges in the Highlandes, wee authorized the
persons nominated by us to choose others to be joynt Commissyoners with them, that so ther might still be a competent
number of persons of the best quality and interest present at
all councells, presuminge that they would still restrain themselves to such a fitt number, as both for secrecy and dispatch
might not too much exceede. That havinge formed this modell,
wee foresaw that ther might be still roome for faction and
devisyon to gett in, upon jealosyes or old animosityes, and the
weekely printes from London, which are our constant and most
perticular intelligence gave us still cause to believe, that even
amongst those of whose zeale and affection to us wee made no
questyon ther was not unity enough. Therfore beinge at the
same tyme, and by the same meanes, informed of the Earle of
Glengarnes beinge gone into the Highlandes, whome wee knew
to be a person not only of unquestionable fidelity and affection
to us, but likewise of so universall a reputacion, and of so
particular an interest and esteeme with most of those upon
whose councell and conducte wee depended, that wee doubted
not his creditt with any who wished well to our service. Wee
sent our sayd Commissyon and instructions to him, to be
delivered by him at such a tyme and place as he thought fitt:
with our expresse commande, that if he founde greate diversity
of opinion amongst the Commissyoners, or any faction and
animosity amongst other persons, wherby our service was not
like to be carryed on with that unanimity and consent which
was to be wished, and which indeede could only give reputacion
to what they went aboute, that in such a case he should
produce a Commissyon which wee had sent to himselfe, to take
the sole commande upon him, untill L^{nt} Generall Middleton
should arryve, which in our owne judgement wee then thought
(and so expressed to him) was the best expedient for our service,
well knowinge that he will in all matters of moment be ready

and desirous to take the advice and assistance of those persons who were thought fitt to be our Comissyoners.

4. This beinge the case, you shall lett all those who professe a desyre to advance our service, upon which the recovery of ther Country from the tyranny and slavery and dishonnour it grones under depends, know, that wee shall expecte from them an intyre complyance with the commandes wee have given, and submissyon to the power and authority with which wee have invested the Earle of Glengarne, untill such tyme as L^{nt} Generall Middleton shall come thither, and that wee shall looke upon any refracterynesse in this particular, or upon an absence of the cheerefulnesse and alacrity which is necessary both for the reputacion and successe of our service, as the true and reall cause of any misfortune that can fall out.

5. You shall use your utmost diligence and endeavours to dispose those of your owne family, and all others in whome you have a particular interest, to a cheerefull submissyon and concurrence with those who are intrusted by us, and to lay asyde all old or new grudges and faction, as a thinge the most acceptable to us that is in ther power to doe, and you shall lett them know, that wee shall looke upon any offices of this kinde, which they shall performe, ether in departinge from any pretences they might reasonably make, and the insistinge wheron may be prejudiciall to our service, or in removinge the indisposicion and jealosyes of other men, and disposinge them to that temper which is fitt and necessary, as the greatest service they can doe us, and which wee shall hereafter rewarde no lesse then any greate and signall action which can be performed in the most important occasyon.

6. You shall informe the Earle of Glengarne, and the other principle persons to whome affayres of that nature are proper to be communicated, that as wee are assured that L^{nt}. Generall Middleton used his utmost endeavours in a private and secrett way, accordinge to the Commissyons and Powers wee have supplyed him with to procure men, armes, and ammunicion, for the reliefe of that our Kingdome, so wee are endeavouringe by the Earle of Rochester at the Dyett, and by the Lord Wentworth in Denmarke, and by Coll. Ballentyne in Sweden, and by other persons in other places, to procure supplyes

of that kinde, wherby wee may be able to appeare in person in some action that may be worthy of us.

7. You shall lett them know that upon ther desyre of some supplyes of men, wee have sent private directions into Irelande, to some whome wee trust, that they use all possible endeavours to transporte souldyers from thence into Scotlande, which wee hope will be done by degrees in reasonable proporcion, and if it shall so fall out, wee doubte not but they will finde that recepcion and treatment that is fitt.

8. You shall lett them know that wee have not bene wantinge to make all fitt overtures to the States of the United Provinces, as Lt. Generall Middleton well knowes, but ther slow proceedings in the prosequcion of the warr against the Rebells, and ther continued treatyes with them, makes them delay the givinge any answer to the proposicions and overtures made by us; and that is the reason wee have not bene hitherto able to procure any shippinge to attende that Coast, which wee shall still endeavour all wee can.

CLXXXV

Instructions for Capt. Shaw.[1]

1. And if by Lt. Generall Middleton's order your journy into Scotlande be for some tyme deferred, you shall send the letters as before wee have intrusted you with, by the first opportunity, accordinge to the advice of our Lt. Generall. *Oct. 23. Nov. 2.*

2. You shall, when you come into Scotland, commende us to the Lord Chancellour and Lord Lorne, as in the 2d.—3 as before—4 as before.

5. You shall informe the Lord Chancellour and the Lord Lorne, that as wee are assured that Lt. Generall Middleton, etc., as in the 6.

6. As the 8th.

7. You shall lett them know that wee intende that Lt. Generall shall make hast to them, and that when wee receave an accounte from him, and finde the condicion of Scotlande to be such that it will be counsellable for us to repayre thither in

---

[1] On the same sheet as clxxxiv.

person, we will not fayle to do it, except some other accidents and alteracions make it fitter to make some other attempt upon some other parte of our dominions.

8. You shall lett the Lord Lorne know that though the Rebells bragge much of the greate assistance and benefitt they have receaved by his Father's comunication with them, yett wee are well pleased with the professyons he makes for himselfe and his Brother of ther resolucions heartily to engage in our service, and wee doubte not but the frends and dependants of that family will attende and follow them in that engagement, and to that purpose you shall in our name speake with the principle persons of Argyleshire and Lorne, and of the other dependants of that family, and lett them know, that as wee believe and expect that no example or inducement whatsoever shall be able to corrupte ther affections and duty to us, and leade them into rebellyon against us, or to a complyance with those who are so, so wee are very gladd that the Lord Lorne, beinge the heyre apparent of that family, and his Brother, are so forwarde to leade them into our service, and therfore wee requyre them that they follow him, and in all places submitt to that authority wee have derected to conducte our affayres in that Kingdome, and wee shall take particuler notice of all those who expresse at this tyme greate zeale to observe our commands, in the advancement of our service, by which only they can provyde for ther owne preservation.

Concerning ball for the demi Culuirin you are to confer with L[t.] G[enerall] M[iddleton].

Indorsed.—*Coll. M'Clouds and Cap. Shaw's Instructions*, 2 *November* 1653.

CLXXXVI

The King to the Laird of Macnaughton.[1]

Oct. 23.
Nov. 2.

Trusty,—Wee are informed by the Earle of Glencarne with what notable courage and affection to us you behave your selfe at this tyme of tryall, when our interest and the honour and liberty of your Country is at stake, and therfore wee cannot

---

[1] Clarendon Manuscripts, xlvii. 5.

but expresse our hearty sence of such your good carriage, and returne you our Princely thankes for the same. And as wee hope all honest men who are lovers of us or ther Country will follow your example, and that you will all unite togither in the way wee have derected, and under that authority wee have appointed to conducte you for the prosequcion of so good a worke, so wee do assure you wee shall be ready as soone as wee are able signally to rewarde your service, and to repayre the losses you shall undergoe for our sake. And so wee bidd you farewell.—Given, etc.

Macnauchton.

CLXXXVII
The King to the Tutor of Macleod.

Trusty and well, etc.,—This Bearer, your Brother, will informe you how well wee are pleased with the assurance he hath given us of your forwardnesse in our service, and your resolucion cheerefully to concurr in all those wayes wee have derected for the carryinge on and conductinge that good worke upon which our interest, and the honour and liberty of your Country, and the preservation of the whole nobility and gentry so much depend: and he will tell you our resolucion to rewarde you for so doinge. He hath proposed to us on your behalfe the erectinge a Borough in one of the Islands, which you are willinge to builde, but he findes that wee are without any of those officers who can prepare such formes or passe those actes in the manner that is necessary, therfore wee can only encourage you to proceede in that way of buildinge as is best for your owne advantage, and expecte such a season as may be fitt for us to add any grace and favour to it that shall be fitt and agreable to our purposes of gratifyinge you in all thinges reasonable, wherof you are not to doubte. And so wee bidd you farewell.

Oct. 23.
Nov. 2.

The Tutor of McCloude.

Indorsed.—*To the Laird of M'Naughton and Tuteor of M'Clounde, [sic] by Coll. M'Clounde, 2d of November 1653.*[1]

---

[1] On the back of the sheet containing these two letters are the names of the following persons, to whom probably similar letters were written :—The Lord Viscount Kenmore, the Lai[rd] of Locheille, the Laird of Keilhead. 2 November.—Laird of Coll, Laird of M'Kinnon, Laird of Logh-bay, Laird of Ardgour, younger, Coll. John Hume.

CLXXXVIII

Charles II. to the Tutor of Struan.

Oct. 23.
Nov. 2.

Trusty, etc.,—As wee have heretofore receaved frequent and ample testimonyes of your greate fidelity and loyalty to our blessed Father and to our selfe, and your sufferinges for the same, so the Bearer heareof, Generall Majour William Drummonde, hath given us a full accounte of the continuance and constancy of the same affection and courage in you towards us and our service, for which wee have thought fitt to returne you our Princely thankes and acceptances, and to assure you, that when God shall inable us, wee will rewarde your faythfull services, and repayre your sufferinges. Wee know well wee neede not encourage you to use your utmost power and creditt to assiste those who are intrusted by us to conducte our affayres ther, and who, wee hope, with God's blessinge will be his instruments to redeeme your country from the oppressyon, slavery, and tyranny it now grones under. What wee have done, and intende in person to do towards it, you will understande by this Bearer, who will likewise tell you the good opinion wee have of you: And so wee bidd you farwell. Given, etc.

Tutor of Struan.

Indorsed.—*The Kinge to the Tutor of Struan, 2 November 1653, by Coll. Drummonde.*[1]

CLXXXIX

Col. Lilburne to the Lord Generall Cromwell.[2]

May itt please, etc.,—Since that account I gave your Lordshippe from Dunbarton, and that I found the wayes after Kenmore and his partie unpassable, and those bounds where they were inaccessible without too great hazard to us, I went to

---

[1] A packet of letters from Lord Newburgh to Lord Balcarres and others was intercepted about this time. They are dated Oct. 4, and are printed in the *Thurloe Papers*, i. 501-4. There was also one from the King himself to Balcarres, *ibid.* p. 495.

[2] Clarke Manuscripts, lxxxvi. 112.

Aire, where I found the Forte in very great forwardnesse, and the out workes compleatly built; itt is a most stately thinge, and will bee very stronge, only I conceive itt is a great deale too large, and will putt the state to much charge in maintayning itt, which now cannot bee help't. Since my returne hither my Lord Argyll is come to mee, and gives mee a relation of his proceedinges, and of Kenmore's marching through his Country, which by reason of the Lord Lorne's being with him hee could nott prevent, his people being unwilling to oppose his sonne; and this hee seemes to speake with much sadnesse, especially that Kenmore should make spoyle uppon those Lowland people in Cantire;[1] which itt seemes to their power have oppos'd him, and uppon his approach into that Country drew into a stronge house, where they received his demands, which was, that they would forthwith furnish him with fourscore horse, and deliver uppe all their armes and amunition. But they resolutely refusing, hee desir'd only to come into the house with a guard, and to stay there all night, and to carry away in the morning 6 musketts and 2 or 3 pound of powder, but they refusing all his propositions and demands, hee drove away their cattell and plundred them; and one Ralston, that was formerly Lieutenant Col. to Straughan, following them with a partie of horse, overtooke some of Kenmore's number, wherewithall hee was in hopes to redeeme their cattell agen, and before Ralston and his partie return'd, they had intelligence of Mac-naughton, the ringleader of Kenmore's partie, and tooke him prisoner, whom they say they will keepe till they have order from the Lord Argyll. My Lord hath shew'd mee their letter to that purpose. He seemes to bee very much afflicted with these proceedings, and threatens his sonne very much, and seemes to

---

[1] An account of Kenmore's expedition into Cantire is given by Baillie (*Letters*, vol. iii. p. 250). Speaking of the Lowland gentlemen he says: 'They, on hope of the English assistance from Aire, fortified the castle of Lochheid; but while neither Argyle nor the English appear in their defence, they render the house to Lorne's discretion. Kenmure, thinking the besieged better used by Lorne than they deserved, fell in a discontent, and went from Lorne to Glencairne with many complaints.' See also *Mercurius Politicus*, pp. 2843, 2858, and *Spottiswoode Miscellany*, ii. 137, 138. William Ralston of Ralston, in Ayrshire, had commanded a regiment in the battle between Lambert and Ker at Hamilton in 1650.

wish that there were a good force of ours in the Country, though hee gave us his owne house for our entertainement, but att this season of the yeare noe officers I can advise withall thinke itt practicable to venture into those parts, and the rather because of the want of shipping uppon the West Coasts for the transporting of men thither. I received a lettre from the Counsell of State, wherin they give mee power to dispose of some monies towards the carrying on of fortifications in Shetland, which fort being to bee rais'd out of the ground in that place where a fortress will bee most usefull to the state, there cannott any such thinge bee taken in hand till the Summer season, there being nott any houses to harbour our men in, and those parts are extreame cold, and itt is fear'd would bee the losse of all those men that should bee sent thither; but I shall bee thinking of preparing materialls against the time they can bee made use of. Our wants of monie are very great att this time, being now about 3 monthes in arreare. I humbly intreate your Lordshippes furtherance in dispatching some hither, for the souldiers are glad now to live uppon biskett and cheese, which seemes very unsavoury to them att this time, and I perceive the forces in England are paid uppe almost to a day.— I remayne your Lordshippes, etc.

Dalkeith, 25 October 1653.

CXC

ORDER CONCERNING the SHIRE of ARGYLL.[1]

In consideration of a watch or guard to bee kept by the gentlemen of the shire of Argyll for the keeping the publique peace: I am content to allow them the sesse of the said shire, commencing the first of September last untill the first of January next, provided the said gentlemen doe use their indeavours for opposing the present disturbers of the publique peace, or any others that shall practice the like courses. Given under my hand and seale att Dalkeith, the 27th day of October 1653. [R. L.]

---

[1] Clarke Manuscripts, lxxxvi. 132.

CXCI
Proclamation by Col. Lilburne.[1]

Wheras severall persons of desperate fortunes have rebelliously combined and joyned together in armes to disturbe the peace of this Nation, contrary and against the lawes and acts of Parliament, and have already committed murther and severall outrages, and shelter themselves in the mountaines and inaccessible places in the Highlands, with whome severall persons out of the Lowlands doe daily joyne themselves, and sometimes returne back to their dwellinges for the gayning intelligence and other opportunities to their partie for stealing horses and doing other mischeifs. For the better prevention wherof for the time to come, and to the end a discovery may bee made of all persons who shall soe run to or assist the enemy as aforesaid, I desire you on sight heerof to issue forth warrants to the Provosts, Bayliffes, and other officers in the respective Burghes and Parishes within your quarters, that they doe forthwith send you a list of all such persons who are inform'd to bee gone from their habitations to the enemy, or who they doe suspect to bee gone to them, and that they doe from time to time give you an account of the same, and of their returne, or of any who usually lie from their houses without a knowne lawfull occasion. Of all which they are to returne you a true and exact account as they will answer the contrarie.

To Col. Reade, Col. Daniell, Lt.-Col. Mason, Lt.-Col. Talbott, Col. Cooper, Col. Fitch.

CXCII
Sir Edward Hyde to Lieutenant-General Middleton.[2]

Sir,—I have seene yours to my Lord Newburgh of the 6: and finde it fitt to answer some partes of it my selfe for your satisfaction. It was not imagyned that upon the receipt of the King's letter you would take yourselfe oblieged to be gone the

Nov. 14.

---

[1] Clarke Manuscripts, lxxxvi. 119. [2] *Ibid.* xcvii. 51.

next day, but that you would consider of all thinges necessary to take with you, and goe your selfe as soone as is convenient; and when you have conferred with Coll. Drummonde, and with the good Secretary to whome I have written at large upon that subjecte, and desyred him to communicate it to you, you will finde ther was greate reason for that councell, and that the discourses upon it from severall places hath not procceded from levity or corrupcion in those who are trusted. What is in the nature of it fitt to be a secrett I hope will be kept, and the more easily if other thinges be comunicated which may well enough be knowne. As you will not make more hast then is agreable to the worke you goe aboute, so no question you will finde that your presence in Scotlande, though with lesse supplyes then they exspecte, will prevent much mischieve, which may fall out by the[ir] devissyons, and I hope you will be able to carry more with you then yett appeares. I send you a note (in high Dutch I thinke) which Sir William Bellenden sent me, and I have writt to my Lord Wentworth aboute it; he says if Quarter-Master Generall Swingle[1] be encouraged he will be ready to goe alonge himselfe with you into Scotlande, and sure others may be gotten. This acte of the Dyett will give new life to us: you must thinke what instructions may be fitt to be added to yours, and send me the leaders, and all shall be dispatched. For a Declaracion I shall be gladd to see the notes you promise, but lett me tell you it is the hardest piece of worke I have yett thought of; if the Kinge courtes the kirke as they exspecte, you know what my opinion is; if he setts out a Declaracion and lightly passes by them, they will be exceedingly incenced; so that really I thinke he were better say nothinge, it beinge hard to cutt a feather in that pointe, and in all these extravagancyes I am out. I send you in this, and in my Lord Newburgh's packett, all the letters, orders, and warrants, which you or Coll. Drummond or the other gentlemen do expecte.

---

[1] General George à Schwengolln wrote to Charles II. from Stockholm on September $\frac{18}{28}$, 1653, about the sale of some artillery and ammunition. The King's advisers hoped to persuade him to transfer himself and his war material to Scotland, but his terms were too high.—*Cal. Clarendon Manuscripts*, ii. 252, 331, 337.

The King's letter to Coll. Gunn[1] I have inclosed to him in myne, and send you the copyes of both; if you do not thinke fitt that it goe soe, open myne, and dispose it as you thinke fitt; but I did it that I might excuse the superscripcion as you see, and which I know he will take well, since I my selfe give him the title you derecte, and he and I are old frends, yet it may be it will be necessary for you to tell him that. All is done to Mr. Davison you requyre. Remember me very kindly to Coll. Drummonde, whome I wish with all my hearte in Scotlande with our frends, who I hope will be well satisfyed with what is done. God preserve me, and, Sir, your, etc.

Indorsed.—*Myne to Lt. Ge. Middleton*, 14 *November* 1653.

CXCIII

A LETTER to COL. LILBURNE.[2]

I HAD yester-night notice from Innerary, that the malignant people who are in Argyll came to itt Thursday night, and that Sir Arthur Forbes, and a partie with him, then advanced before the rest, uppon some intention to fall into some place in the Lowlands; themselves give itt out for the Lenox, but that seemes nott soe probable; always marching they are, and they doe affirme they are called to meete Middleton. I may assure you they are nott att all strengthned by leavies from this shire, for this parte Cowall hath nott putt out one man, and the Gentry resolve to suffer the totall ruine of what they have before they doe itt, except one or two: Lorne hath resolved the like. And I heare their champion in Argyll, Auchinbrek, and they have differed, soe they have come to noe good speede there; however I doe nott thinke but there are some sons of Beliall amongst us as in other places, vaine men who may joyne with them, but they will nott be considerable.

---

[1] Colonel William Gunn was in the Imperial service, and had just been made a Baron by the Emperor. 'I am exceedingly gladd,' writes Hyde to Gunn on Nov. 14, 'to heare that in this generall calamity your virtue hath raysed you to so good a condition.' In 1657 he collected 1000 dollars in Germany for Charles II.—*Cal. Clarendon Papers*, ii. 274, 441; iii. 67, 357.

[2] Clarke Manuscripts, xxv. 151.

You may make your owne private use of this, and ever command mee as, your freind to serve.

Carick, November 5, 1653. [Unsigned.]¹

CXCIV
Col. Lilburne to the Lord General Cromwell.²

May itt please your, etc.—I have little to acquaint your Lordshippe withall, but that I heare Kenmore is still in Argill towards Lorne; hee hath nott Ralston prisoner as was reported,³ nor any of that partie in Canteir. Glencairne and Glengary are allsoe busy uppe and downe, and many small parties fall downe into the Lowlands in the night time and stealc horses; indeed the people doe many of them voluntarily give them, and will nott att give us any intelligence of them. Their numbers increase, and they had within these 2 or 3 dayes a Randezvous, and probably will bee able to disturbe the country this Winter, and some of our forces alsoe, though wee have put our selves into the best posture wee can for the safety both of our selves and country. The Westerne Gentlemen have bin with mee this day expressing their willingnesse to preserve the peace, and pretend to abhominate those people under Glencairne and Kenmore. Our amunition is nott yett come, nor any of those shippes for the Northerne Coasts that I heard was intended thither.—I remayne, Your Excellencies, etc.

Dalk. 5° November 1653.
Lord Generall.

CXCV
Col. Lilburne to the Judges.⁴

Right honorable,—Though I suppose the sad conditions of Sir William Dick,⁵ and his sons', Sir Andrew, and Mr. [blank]

---
¹ Evidently from Argyll to Lilburne.
² Clarke Manuscripts, lxxxvi. 115.   ³ *Mercurius Politicus*, p. 2858.
⁴ Clarke Manuscripts, lxxxvi. 124.
⁵ Sir William Dick died in Westminster, the 19th day of December 1655, in great misery and want, and without the benefit of a decent funeral.—*The Lamentable estate and distressed case of Sir William Dick, folio* 1657.

Dicke, are nott unknowne to you, yet being very sensible of the sufferinges of the old gentleman, their father, by reason of his engagements for the publique, and of their being continuallie liable to bee imprisoned for his debts, while hee is att London agitating for some publique satisfaction which may free him and them from further trouble, I doe therfore recommend itt unto you to dispense as much as may bee with the letter of the law, and to grant a suspension unto the said Sir Andrew and Mr. [blank] Dicke from personall execution, soe longe as you may conveniently grant the same.—I remayne, your very affeccionate servant, R. L.

Dalkeith, 9° *November* 1653.

To the Judges.

CXCVI

A Warrant by John Graham.[1]

These are requiring John Wright of Posed, and Walter Lackey of Dasher, as Commissioners for the parish of Kippen, to convene their whole parish of fensible men, and bring them along to the Kirke of Aberfoyle on Munday next. This doe as you will nott bee esteemed as dissafectors to religion, disloyall subjects, unnaturall Countrymen, and under the penalty of apprehending your persons, loosing your estates, sesing uppon your whole goods and geere whatsoever: lett none pretend ignorance herein for by the assistance of God I intend to putt my Commission to execution in despight of all pretence to protect or hinder you. Att Knickmell the 11th of November 1653. Jo. Grahame.

CXCVII

Letter from John Graham.

Lett this bee sufficient to acquaint you to cause [to] bring

---

[1] Clarke Manuscripts, xxv. 154.

alonge to the House of Douhray,¹ for maintenance of those in the service, out of every plough of land one furlitt of meale, one stone of cheese, one sheepe, or one cow for 6 sheepe, on Tuesday night, to eschue further losse. If you faile blame nott

Jo. Grahame.

CXCVIII
Warrant from Sir Mungo Murray.[2]

These are to require the Heritors of the parochnir [?] of Blair, That imediately after sight heerof [you are] to send to my Quarters to Dunkell, six martis, thirty wedders, six bowes oates, six bowes meale : you are likewise to bringe with you all the sesse restand to the English preceding the date heerof, with the last discharges given to the severall Heritors of the said cesse. And this must bee performed against Munday next the 14th of this instant, by 8 of the clock, with certification that who shall faile I will cause exact from them the 3 last monthes sesse by past, or drive their guides for the use of the arms. This is your warrant conforme to the generall order. Given att Dunkeld the 11th of November 1653.

M. Murray,
Quarter-Master Generall.

The Commissioner is required to bee att Dunkell himself the time appointed to give uppe Deficients, this uppon his perill.

M. Murray,
Quarter-Master Generall.

For Henry Anderson, Commissioner of Blaire parish.

CXCIX
Col. Lilburne to the Lord General Cromwell.[3]

Kenmore being returned from Argill, where I am informed he hath not much increased his number, is now active in Dumbar-

---

[1] John Grahame of Duchrie is believed to have been the author of the narrative of Glencairne's Expedition printed in the Appendix to the *Memoirs of John Gwynne.* Edinburgh, 1822. See p. 158 note.
[2] Clarke Manuscripts, xxv. 155.
[3] *Ibid.* lxxxvi. 150.

tonshire and towards Sterling; and from Lough Lomond to
the Brayes of Aberdeene, and soe to Strathspay, there are
parties of horse and foote falls downe every night in one place or
other, and steeles horses, and cannot be prevented. The Cuntry
is soe falce to us, and complyes soe with them, that though at
present there is not soe visible an enimie that speakes much
dainger, yett their dayly accions and growing strength may
(together with what ill spiritt is generally found in the ministers
and people, who doubtles are readie to rise if any visible
strength appeare) give reason to beleive they have some notable
designe in hand, and finde good incouragement one way or
another to proceede; though we doe what we can to prevent
them, soe farre as these forces are able, who peradventure might
doe a some what more if their officers were with them, whereof
there is greate want, and many times I can hardly gett a feild
officer to advise withall.

But if the officers were here, the troopes are soe little I
cannot lay any horse at all in many places, where they are very
needfull by way of prevention, and we have not a troope to
spare to all the south parts of Scotland, where I have some
intelligence they are beginning to be busie, and somewhat
hereof I had from Major Tolhurst lately, that I doubt, as I
told your Excellencie formerly, we must crave some more
assistance ere it be long. In the interim if your Lordshipp please
to send hither a troope or 2 of dragoones, if they can be spared,
they would be of greate use, for I am constrained to lay soe
many horse in petty garrisons for proteccion to the Cuntry
(who indeede deserves it not) that I have but very few to
attend other motions. Th'other night (as your Lordshipp may
partly perceive by one of the inclosed letters) Sir Arthur
Forbes fell downe to Kirkentalloe, and there plundered onely
the poore congregated people,[1] and did noe more harme; and I
thinke the same night a party from Kenmore boated over
Clyde, and tooke Sir Ja. Hamilton, for complying with us as
they pretended, and not a man would give us any timely intelligence. That by many circumstances I gathered there is a
generall complyance and well wishing towards these desperadoes,

---

[1] See *Mercurius Politicus*, Nov. 17-24, p. 2875.

and I doubt those we count godlie in this Nacion are not cleare in their harts as to these accions. One passage remarkeable th'other day at a presbetry of Remonstrators about Hamilton (as I am credibly informed from 2 good men), the question being put whether they ought to accompt us or Kenmore greater enemies, it was resolved they ought to esteeme us greater; that even in all these people there is a secrett antipathy against us, doe what we can to oblige them, unlesse in some few that are convinced, and those but a few. I might tell your Lordshippe alsoe our number of foote, as they are dispers't, are nott very considerable if an enemy appeare in the field, soe that I could wish one regiment of foote more to strengthen us. In case of further danger, I am thinking to stay 3 of Col. Saunders troopes untill your Lordshippe send further orders for them.

Dalk., 12° *November* 1653.

If your Lordshippe desires a particular account of the quarters of the whole forces I shall give itt.

CC

Col. Lilburne to the Council of State.[1]

Right Honorable,—There being many Lords and Gentlemen (that have had good fortunes) in this Nation that are now reduced to great extreamity,[2] and by reason of their creditors pressing hard uppon them for satisfaction of their debts, divers are fledd to the hills and joyned with the tories; and finding that many doe at least pretend to incline to give what satisfaction they are able to their creditors, which theyre creditors sometimes refusing putts some uppon desperate courses, and in these broken times constrains them to lay hold uppon any advantage to save themselves, and therby to run into those courses and joyne with those parties out of meere necessity, to the disturbance of the peace of this Commonwealth; and

---

[1] Clarke Manuscripts, lxxxvi. 116.
[2] On the ruined condition of the Scottish nobility see Baillie, *Letters*, iii. 249, 387: 'Our nobilitie weel near all are wracked.'

being often prest to grant them protections or suspentions for some time, which I cannott doe by any lawfull aucthority (though I often see much reason in what they desire), I am bold to recommend their condition to the Commissioners for the Administration of Justice, who being tied uppe much to the letter of the law leaves them in an unsatisfied condition; and conceiving itt better that some particular men's debts were awhile longer delayed unsatisfied, rather then by their too earnest pressing the peace of the whole Nation should bee disturb'd, as indeed itt seemes to bee much occasion'd by these extreamities uppon men, I humbly offer itt to your consideration to give some direction in these cases, untill such time as the publique may bee in greater safety. Many broken men and those of desperate fortunes running to the Hills daily, and from thence fall downe in parties in the night time into the Lowlands, and steale horses, wherby they grow more considerable every day then other; and the mindes and affections of the generality of the people in this Nation being very much towards them, and against the Commonwelth, and some Ministers publiquely praying for their successe, and generally are uppon great expectations of a chainge some way or other, I thought itt my duty to give you this breefe account, and humbly intreate your speedy directions unto, your most humble servant.

I humbly intreate further directions about the monthly assesse, your former authority to mee being expired the first instant.

Novr. 12°.

Council of State.

CCI

A Letter from Lord Lorne to the Gentlemen of Badenoch.[1]

Loving freinds,—Seing that for the carrying on his Majestie's service, it is thought fit that the whole Highlands in

---

[1] Clarke Manuscripts, xxv. 157.

Scotland send out such proportions of men as are condescended upon for that purpose, these are to require you to send out of the whole lands of Badenoth two hundred sufficient men well armed, and let them be ready against my next advertizement. I referre the particulars to the Bearer, and rest Your loving friend, LORNE.

Finlarig, 14 *November* 1653.

CCII

THE GOVERNOR of RUTHVEN CASTLE to the GENTLEMEN of BADENOCH.[1]

GENTLEMEN,—The next day after I had a meeting with some of you the Guide man of Nide (I suppose directed from the rest) came to mee with that which seemed a very strange overture, howbeitt I beleive itt to be the result of that your convent, viz., to inquire of me whether or not (in case the enimy should approach these partes) yow might have liberty to give them some men and provissions to put them by the Country; to which I have taken this occasion (by the hands of the same Agent) to give you the ensuinge answer, the effect wherof I gave Nede at such time as he made that needless offer) that you may take itt for granted that whosoever shall either directly or indirectly assist those thevish rebells, either with men, money, or provissions, shall be deemed by us as one of them, and shall forfeit whatever he hath both reall and personall; and whereas itt hath beene said that some of our cheife officers have granted such liberty, or (as yow call itt) favour, to other partes of the Country, I must assure yow (as I first tould Nede) that report was and is as false in itt selfe, as itt hath beene weakely seconded by your beleife, neither will those who first spake itt to be able to hould upp their faces when called to account for itt. Gentlemen, you may be confident that if you suffer any thinge by submission to the present power, the state is better able to make yow some kinde of satisfaction, as on the contrary they are to give yow the

---

[1] Clarke Manuscripts, xxv. 155.

reward of your doings in case yow submitt or give assistance to their (and indeed your owne) enimies, then any other now in Scotland who may seeke such things from yow. And that I may reason with yow a litle, what may yow expect from an inconsiderable party (you thought they were more numerouse) of desperate men, of broken fortunes or none att all, who dare not keepe their homes for feare the just lawes of the Country should be executed upon them, but that they should bring yow into the same headlonge and vagabond condition with themselves? Wherreas on the contrary, your selves may in greate parte witnesse the care of this state to setle your peace and indeavour your prosperity, and (if yow will but cast your eye upon things most probable) is not this state more likely to protect and make yow prosperouse then those who not onely seeke to destroy your peace, and devoure that litle morsell which they and others like them have left yow, and which this state indeavours to preserve to yow, but even like vipers gnaw out the bowells of their Mother Country? Againe, is not the State of England imediately about to incorporate and make yow one free Common wealth with themselves, and what greater favour could they cast upon yow? and are yow not very tenderly dealt with your condition considered? what burden doe yow undergoe which England is free from? and (if freindly and civill dealeinge may gaine any thinge upon yow), I am sure their was never any people (under the lash of the sword) more freindly intreated and civilly ussed by those in whose power itt is to exact and sweepe their all from them then yow are; soe indeed I could almost afford to aske yow what was become of your reason while yow assaulted mee with this unreasonable overture. Againe, consider that God hath delivered into our hands the most potent and best apointed armies that Scotland hath beene able to raise, and is itt likely that this handfull of theeves and robers should stand before us? Gentlemen, what I have spoken is out of a desire to your welfare, and I hope you will consider itt accordingly; as alsoe that yow will give mee some testimony of the reality of your intentions towards this state (to whom yow stand ingaged), and soe take of that doubt which by your late offer you have given me occation to harbour, att least by hasteinge in such fieringe and other things as are by yow deficient for the use of this garrison, and the speedy payment of your Assess. To conclude, this is to require yow neither to aide, abett, or any wayes assist the Enimy with men, money, armes, provisions, or ought else, either directly, or indirectly, as yow will answer the contrary with the loss of your estates and hazard of your persons, and such as your carriage is herein you may expect the like from, Gentlemen, your humble servant

[JOHN HILL].[1]

Ruthven Castle, 14*th November* 1653.

CCIII

COL. LILBURNE to the LORD GENERAL CROMWELL.[2]

MAY IT PLEASE YOUR EXCELLENCY,—By my last I gave your Lordshipp an account of the increase of the Enimie, and since that a party of them have infested [so] all the Cuntry betwene this and Glascow and Sterling that noe small party of ours escapes them, the Cuntry is soe active for them, and treacherous to us. Three Captains of Col. Overton's, and some other officers with their wifes, lay on Saturday night at Faulkirke, and about 10 or 11 of the clock in the night were sett upon, and 2 of them taken, viz., Townesend and Scrope, but much feare being upon the party they ventred onely upon that one house,[3] and tooke those

---

[1] This letter is probably the letter to the gentlemen of Badenoch referred to by the Earl of Glencairne in his letter of Dec. 30 to Captain Hill. Hill's answer, and a second letter from him to the gentlemen of Badenoch are also printed in the *Thurloe Papers*, i. 657-659. See also *Military Memoirs of John Gwynne*, p. 231. Hill, who is said to have died in 1697, was a lieutenant-colonel in 1691, and governor of Inverlochy. He was implicated in the Glencoe Massacre. The account of his life in the *Dictionary of National Biography*, xxvi. 396, does not mention his services during the Cromwellian occupation of Scotland. In addition to the authorities there referred to, see *Letters from Roundhead Officers in Scotland*, pp. 134, 140; *Memoirs of Captain Carleton*, p. 41, edition 1741; *Mackay's Memoirs*, pp. 105, 107, 108, 320, 332, 337, 343, 347, 354.

[2] Clarke Manuscripts, lxxxvi. 123.

[3] *Mercurius Politicus*, p. 2889. Captain Dennis and Lieutenant Waller who lay in the house opposite escaped their notice.

prisoners, and since that tooke 2 souldiers (goeing with orders at 11 a clocke in the night towards Glascow) at Killsith, and yesternight they plundered the Lord Warriston neare Edinburgh and the Lord Dundas. Yet hardly any of these people will appear either to give us intelligence, or doe any thing for preserving the peace; though I must confesse, when I talke with them hereof, the Remonstrants espetially seemes much to disgust both Kenmore and all that party, and their proceedings; but undoubtedly even this small appearance of this inconsiderable Enimie (as yet he is) hightens the spiritt of the generality of people here, who have a deadely antipathy against us, though I thinke I may truely say it they have had from the generality of us a very large share of civillityes. Undoubtedly many of the ministers of the Assembly party blowes these coales, which indeede seeme to increase towards a flame, and I wish your Lordshipp would send us a few more horse and dragoones, and if a regiment of foote could be spared they might be very serviceable, and helpe us much to stopp some more gapps; for our quarters are soe longe and large, and the Enimie in soe many places round about us steeleing opportunities, and the hills soe neere, that if they should be able to fall downe any thing considerable, we should be hard put to it to repell them in severall places, being soe farre from one another, and the least accion will call all forces from hence, and leave Edenburgh, and these whole cuntrys wholy distitute. I have sent your Lordshipp a coppie of our quarters, and am goeing to Linlithgoe to stay there with those forces, to be readie to joyne with Glasgow or Sterleing as there shalbe occasion, and am constrained to leave Edenburgh very empty, and this is allsoe occasioned by the many petty garrisons which we cannot be without for saifety to the Cuntrys, which takes up soe many of our forces, and were it not for these garrisons that is some awe [?] and a checke upon the Cuntry, I doubt many would appeare that yet dare not. The Lord Atholl is now joyned with them, and very active in his Country, which is one of the most considerable in the Hylands. Many of these people are necessitated to this desperate course for want of livelyhoods, and being soe much pinched by that justice done upon them in causeing them [to] pay their debts. If they might be allowed to transport themselves to forraigne parts it would be one of the best diversions. I am told that Ralston, and some other of the honestest sort, would ingage against these Tories, and if the Lord Argill would joyne, would undertake to firrett them out of the Hills; but these things to be done without the state and your Excellencies direccions or approbacion, I conceive somewhat above.—Your, etc.

Dalkeith, 15 *November* 1653.
Lord Generall.

CCIV

Col. Lilburne to the Committee for the Army.[1]

Gentlemen,—Having received an order of Parliament that the monthly summe of ten thousand and sixteene pounds and tenn shillinges be charged upon Scotland [to be] issued forth for the pay of the forces and other contingencies heere by warrant and order of the committee for the army, and least any obstruccion should bee to those fortifications in hand, and other necessary services that will nott allow of longe delayes for supplies of monie I make bold to intreate your pleasure and direccions heeranent unto your very humble servant.

Dalkeith, 17 *November* 1653.
Committee for the Army.

CCV

Col. Lilburne to the Lord General Cromwell.[2]

May it please your Excellencie,—Though I am loath to give untrue allarums, yett the visible appearance of that dainger that dayly more and more threatens, will not permitt me to be alltogether silent, if I performe that duty I owe to your

---

[1] Clarke Manuscripts, lxxxvi. 125.
[2] Clarke Manuscripts, lxxxvi. 123. The original is undated.

Excellencie. Though as yett things are much in the clouds, and darkness as yet swallowes up much of that which is breaking forth to light, yet some beames are darting I may say allmost in each corner; for hardly any parte of the Cuntry is free from those nightwalkers, who continew praying upon Gentlemen's horses, and by their secrett wayes conveys them to the hills where they have riders in readines, and beside many younger brothers and desperate persons that privately steale to them, well mounted and fitted for service, nor doe they want the companie of divers, both English and Irish, and that my intelligence speakes them somewhat numerous. But yett all these signifie little in comparison of those secrett contrivements, and incouragements the generallity of this people affords them, and are bringing forth to ripenes, if their darke and wicked designes may take effect, which I doubt not but the Lord will blast; though I assure your Lordshipp (not as from my owne judgment, which is inconsiderable, but the judgement and dayly experience of most officers and freinds I meete with) there is a necessity of some more forces to helpe to stope this currant, unlesse we run too greate a hazard in these southern parts, or by drawing off force from other parts northerly we give those cuntries wholely to the Enimie. I have bene adviseing (for the better preventing this inundacion) to seize the horses in cuntrymen's hands, but findes these people soe ticklish to deale with all at this time (out of that strainge expectacion they have of a chainge), and soe readie to take the wing, that it's feared we shall not onely loose the horses, but drive many to the hills (who seeme to be peaceable) rather then part with them to us, and without we could seize all together, which is impossable, it is doubted we shall doe more hurt then good. I could humbly wish your Lordshipp would thinke of one way or other to helpe with some more force in time before the flame increase any further. Or if the state see it fitt to send downe Col. Lockart, or Swinton, or both, to assist in the ingageing some honest Scotchmen here that would be forward to imbarque with us, and might be had in such a way as the state might not be at any greate charge more then at present. Or if we should in a faire way gaine the horses from the people here, allow some thing towards their prise, and the incouragement of such foote souldiers as might be mounted with firelocks upon them. But its conceived it would be best to ingage some honest Scots, both by reason of the knowledge of the private wayes in the cuntry, their better possabillity of corrispondence with intelligencers, and their language, which would gaine intelligence where we could not, and their habituall hardines to undergoe the duty that this Enimie will put us upon, and further that it may appeare to the world we have a party here.

I understand they are endeavoring to raise men in Galloway, and now there is not any horse that way, nor can we spare any; they are allsoe begining to steale horses and rob in the March and that way, where allsoe we can send noe horse; that if those garrisons at Barwick and Carlile could spare any to send parties to garrison some greate houses, to gaine intelligence, and prevent riseings in those partes, it would be very necessary and usefull; and they might sometimes mount their men and scower the Cuntry of any of the Tories, though they are soe cuning, and the Cuntry so true to them, they wilbe round about on every hand close by, and we shall not know it. But I feare I trespas too much upon your Excellencies patience, and therefor humbly makes bold to subscribe my selfe.

As yet I heare nothing of our amunicion.

CCVI

Col. Lilburne to the Lord General Cromwell.[1]

May it please your Excellencie,—Col. Cobbet being come hither, and his party saifely arrived at Dumberton, haveing in all his voyage not had one man died but Major Bird, which I looke upon as a very great mercie, and thought it my duty to give you an accompt thereof; he being constrainded to march through the Hilands this sad season, and indeede way laide by Kenmoore and the Hylanders, that are in a bodie with him upon any occasion of advantage or plundring, that had not Lo. Argill

---

[1] Clarke Manuscripts, lxxxvi. 124.

and his people bene good guides to him, and assisted him with
any thing they could, the party in all likelyhoode might have
miscarried, that Col. Cobbet acknowledges his saifety was under
God in the Lord Argill's favour to him.[1] I have spoaken with
him about those particulers in Lewes Island your Excellencie
required an accompt of: as to the Cuntry and harbours, etc., he
saith the Cuntry is very hilly and mossie, not very much corne,
yet plenty of cattle and sheepe; there are considerable harbours
where greate shipps may ride, vizt., Lough Sterneway, which is
the best and which we secure, Lough Tarbett, Lough Harres,
these 2 last lyes towards the Hebrides which is southward, and
there is onely 2 or 3 bays to the northward of Lough Sterneway,
wherin there is not very saife rideing yet very convenient places
for landing men; there is not timber in the Cuntry, nor any good
free stone that he could heare of, and very little fresh water,
yet he caus'd sinke a well at Lough Sterneway which proved
very well; he saith that Lewes lyes 30 leagues off the trade roade,
and very seldom or never that any Dutch shipps tooch there,
but constantly at Shetland, by which I conceive that Lewes is
not soe considerable for the Dutch as was supposed, but rather
Shetland is much more considerable, and would be of greater
advantage to us if fortified dureing the warre with Holland.

CCVII.

Col. Lilburne to Major Gen. Lambert.[2]

Honoured Sir,—The Enimie growing strong in the Edge of
the Hills and presseing much uppon us, and the secrett designes
and mallice of the generality of this nation, with the scarsity of
forces both horse and foote to prevent all growing daingers,
many officers being meett have thought it there duty to send
Capt. Spencer to represent the condicion of affaires here above,

---

[1] In consequence of the loss of provisions in the wrecks of Sept. 23, Colonel Cobbet had to return by land: 'To boat over his men to Dunstaffenage, and to march through Argiles country, a dangerous passage in case the rebels, which are now on foot, should interrupt them in their passage, which they are preparing to doe, though I hope he will get through the Highlands before they can be in a readiness.'—*Mercurius Politicus*, Sept. 29-Oct. 6.

[2] Clarke Manuscripts, lxxxvi. 130.

and to move for more forces to assist us. And because the Enimie is soe active in all parts, and now have as we heare sent 100 horse towards Carlile and Galloway, it is humbly desired you would please to order 6 or 8 troopes of horse that are nearest to come up to the borders, untill his Excellencie signifie his further pleasure about our supplyes, and that you will please to acquaint his Excellencie with what you doe or thinke fitting to be done herein.

Dalk. Nov. 21, 1653.

To Major Generall Lambert.[1]

CCVIII

ORDERS ISSUED by the JUDGES.[2]

At Edinburgh, the 23 day of November 1653.

Orders to be Observed hereafter in the Court of Justice, For the more clear Regulating of Processes, And the Commissioners Procedure in their Administration, for the satisfaction and good of the People.

1. THAT the under-Clerks who are appointed to serve in the Outer-House attend at the accustomed place appointed for calling of Causes. And in the first place call Processes, to see *vicissim* before the Judge come to the Outer-House; Wherein if there be no compearance, the Summonds may be decerned. And after the Judge cometh to the Outer-House, the said under-Clerks are to call *vicissim*, First Witnesses, next Parties Oaths, Thirdly Copies of Suspensions and Advocations, Fourthly Acts and Diligences, And then ordinary Summonds. And if any after reading of the Minute-Book desire a Decreet given for non compearance to be rescinded he may be admitted; That all Causes wherein the dispute is closed, and ready to be advised, be given in of consent of the Advocats for both Parties, And

---

[1] On Nov. 23 the Council of State appointed a committee of seven of its members, including Cromwell, to confer with Major-General Lambert, and such other army officers as they should think fit, on the state of affairs in Scotland, and to report accordingly.

[2] From a broadside in William Clarke's collection in Worcester College Library.

that the affixt Roll serve for Intimation, except when any priviledged Cause is to be advised, that the same be intimat at least twenty-four hours before. After the in-giving whereof it shall not be lawfull to either of the Parties to alter or add any thing in the Processe, Neither shall any Bills be heard to be presented by any, either concerning the advising of the Cause or merits thereof, but such as shall be seen by the Adverse Party, to the effect he may answer thereto if he will.

2. That all Copies of Suspensions and Advocations be not called oftener then once. And all Parties are to have four dayes to produce the principalls, with the Verifications, if they any have, or declare they have, and will use none. And if they fail, that the under-Clerks without calling admit Protestation. And wherein there is compearance, that the Charger deliver to the Advocat for the Suspender his Charge, some time before the day assigned to him to produce.

3. That all Calling, either before or after Litiscontestation, shall be either upon Acts or Minutes of Processe, as shall please the Advocat or Party-Caller of the Diet. Only after Litiscontestation the Processe shall remain *in retentis*, and neither the Pursuer nor Defender be Master thereof.

4. That the Dispute close, and be holden concluded at a Duply, and given in to be advised; and if after perusall of the same, that the Commissioners find it necessary to say further in the Cause, They will ordain them to do the same. And in case the Advocats transgresse herein, the Commissioners will take speciall notice of the Advocats for the Defenders their delay, and will censure them according to the nature of the offence.

5. That the Processe put to *Avisandum* as they are to be received, be marked with the day of the Moneth on which they are received and put to *Avisandum*.

6. That in place of the Keeper of the Minute-Book, all Acts, Decreets, Protestations, and Remits, be insent in a Book after the same are past by the under-Clerks in the Outer-house, *per vices*, successively, and the Minute-Book to be read every day after twelve a clock, as formerly; and the same to be subscribed every day by one of the principall Clerks, and nothing to be deleted or inter-lined, except it be marked by one of them. The Clerk Subscriber of the Book staying a competent

time after the reading to delete such Decreets, Protestations, or Remits, as that day are given for not Compearance, where Advocats desire to see, or take a day to produce principall Suspensions, the same with the Verifications being presently produced, or at the least before the morrow at twelve a clock.

7. That of Processes at *Avisandum*, there be made up a Roll by both Clerks, bearing upon the head of every Cause the day of the Moneth whereupon the same was given in to be advised. And if any Processes be ordained to be seen after *Avisandum*, that the same be in the Clerks hands, and neverthelesse keep its place in the Roll, according to the first *Avisandum*; and the Clerks in making the Roll of concluded Causes are not to prefer any Party to another, wherein if they fail they are to pay Five pound sterling *toties quoties*. Without prejudice alwayes to Parties or Advocats to represent Cases of extreme necessity, which the Commissioners reserve to themselves, and will take notice of as they shall see just cause; and have appointed Friday in every week for the Poors Causes, Suspensions, Advocations, Spoyles, Removings, Ejections, Aliementary actions, actions to make arrested goods forth coming; and Saturday for concluded Causes, wherein Parties Oaths and depositions of Witnesses are taken, and will proceed in discussing thereof, as they stand in the order of the Roll.

8. That no Advocat or Party get up a Processe from the Clerk to see, but upon consignation of Ten shillings sterling, to be disposed upon for the use of the Poor; if the Receiver of the said Processe fail to re-produce the same at the precise day or hour prefixed to him by the Clerk; and the keeper up of the Processe is also to be called, and ordained to re-produce the Processe, and further censured at the Commissioners pleasure.

9. That the testimonies and depositions of Witnesses examined in any Causes be sealed by the Judge Examiner, immediatly after reading and subscribing the same, untill the advising of the Cause.

10. That the benefit of seeking out Bills at the Signet, and giving Copies thereof to the Parties, be brought into the Thesaury at Twelve pence the Copy of every Bill that shall be attested by the Keeper. And that no attested Copy from the

Signet be respected but such as shall be also attested by the Thesaurer, bearing the receipt of the Twelve pence thereupon.

11. That upon the first appearance of the Judge in the Outer-house, the Advocats and their Servants forthwith betake themselves in a quiet manner to the respective seats designed for them.

12. That no Advocates Servant, or person priviledged to come in the House, presume to enter or sit in the Seats designed for the Advocates, under the pain of one shilling sterling *toties quoties*.

13. That none of the Advocates come to the Bar or plead but when the Action and Suit wherein they are employed is called; and when the same is for the time ended, that they forthwith return to their Seats.

14. That no Advocate compear, or cause his Name to be marked for any person or persons, unlesse they be employed; and that no Advocate be marked compearing but upon his own or his Servants desire.

15. That all Complaints against Advocates, for keeping and detaining Processes be subscribed by an Advocate, and be called before any other matter in the Outer House, and the Advocate, deteiner of the Processe, is for the first fault to be sharply rebuked by the Judge, and pay five shillings sterling: and for the second fault, ten shillings sterling, and to be further censured at the Judges discretion.

16. That all Advocates, Clerks, and their Servants, and all other Members of the Court, or depending thereupon, forbear Swearing, Cursing, and Banning, Wherein if they fail, they are to pay, every Advocate two shillings sterling; and every other person, one shilling sterling for every fault: And the Maissers, or any others, are to take notice of all persons who shall transgresse, and are to delate none but of their own hearing, and make the same known to the Judge in the Outer-House, who will cause the said persons failing pay the said Mulct, and further censure them as he shall think fit.

17. That hereafter, full Copies of Suspension be given to the Charger, and be subscribed by a Messenger at Arms, or the Party, or by a Notar at his command, and that the Copies be given before the day of Compearance; otherwise the Sus-

pension to be void, and it shall be lawful to the party Charger to proceed, notwithstanding thereof. And this to take effect from the first day of *December* next.

18. That no Judges Servant, Clerk, Clerks Servant, or Maisser, solicite or agent, in or for any Processe or businesse relating to the Court, Wherein if they fail, they are to be condignely punished, at the Judges discretion.

19. That no Petitions be offered but to the Clerks, or such as are appointed by them to attend for receiving thereof in the Outer-House, at the ordinary place of Calling, between seven and eight hours in the morning, and two and three hours in the afternoon. And that if any Party shall complain, and make it appear that their Petitions are refused, being offered, The Clerk is to be fined therefore in five shillings sterling, *toties quoties*, and further censured at the Commissioners pleasure.

20. For escuing of Alterations and Debates, after that the Sentence of the Court is pronounced, and for security to the Parties, It is ordered, That all Interloquitors and Sentences of Court, shall be first written by the Clerk on a paper apart, and being approven by the Court, shall be clearly transcribed upon the Summons, or some material Act, or Writ of the Processe, (which must lie for the Warrant of the Decreet) and then shall be read publickly, before the dissolving of the Court, which shall then presently be subscribed by the President, against which no opposition shall be made in publick, by any Advocate, or other person; But it shall be lawfull to any person grieved, to represent the same by a Petition within fourty eight hours after pronouncing thereof, that it may be rectified as shall appear just; And that at the pronouncing thereof, the same be read by the Clerk of the Paper so approven, *verbatim*, as it stands without any alteration.

21. That all Papers given in by either party, Pursuer or Defender, be subscribed by the Advocate in-giver thereof, in these words: *Seen and answered by*, or *seen and referred to the Court by*; and then to subscribe his Name, that for preventing any Additions to any part of the Processe after they are given in to be advised.

22. That if any Clerk shall write, *Refused*, upon any Bill, without Order of the Court, or some of the Commissioners, nor

add unto any part of the Processe, or blot out, or abstract any part thereof, he shall be, *ipso facto*, turned out of his place, upon due proof made thereof.

CRAIGHALL.   GEO. SMYTH.
E. MOSLEY.   A. PEIRSON.[1]

CCIX

COL. LILBURNE to ANDREW HAY.[2]

SIR,—I understand that you are summon'd to appeare by a writt out of the Chancery att London to appeare there att the suite of one Mr. Dickson, butt as my informer saith you have refus'd to answer that summons. Wherfore att the request of a freind I thought fitt to give you notice, that itt will bee look't uppon as a very high contempt, and that you may doe well to take notice thereof, in time to prevent further inconveniencies, which is only hinted unto you att present by your very loving freind,   R. L.

Linlithgowe, 24 November 1653.

For Andrew Hay the younger, att Hayes Towne, neere Pebles.

CCX

A LETTER of INTELLIGENCE.[3]

Sterling, November 28, 1653.

I suppose I neede nott acquaint you with the Enemies removall from the parts about Loughearne, only they have left 30 or 40 plundering rogues that are sometimes in those parts

---

[1] On 24 Oct. 1653 the Parliament on a report from the Council of State that Mr. March and Mr. Owen late Commissioners for the administration of justice in Scotland had been recalled, appointed Mr. Edward Hopkins and Mr. William Lawrence to fill their places, and added also Mr. Alexander Peirson of Southall in Scotland. Hopkins desired to be excused, and on 28 Oct. Mr. Goodyeare was appointed instead. The powers of the Commissioners were at the same time enlarged.—*Commons Journals,* vii. 338. 341.

[2] Clarke Manuscripts, lxxxvi. 127.   [3] *Ibid.* xxv. 163.

towards Lough Tay, and the Borders of Atholl. My Lord
Atholl had gott some men to appeare for the incouragement of
their late Randezvouz who would goe noe further with him,
but returned to their homes, wheruppon the Governour of
Blaire sent for them, and they have ingaged themselves never
to follow his Lordshippe any more in such courses ; hee thought
itt therfore wisedome nott to deale roughly with them, because
respective dealing would make them disposed to knock of from
such desperate courses. The Gentry of that Country say the
Earle of Atholl shall gange his owne gate for them.

CCXI

Col. Lilburne to the Lord General Cromwell.[1]

Uppon the Enemies Randezvouz and drawing into Menteith neere this Towne, I sent some forces to strengthen Glasgowe, and drew others hither, and intended this night to have done something uppon them, though they had block't uppe and guarded all passes very strongly, but a partie of our's some 7 or 8 miles hence uppe the River giving them an alarum, they fled to the Hills, and I heare are gone towards Broad Albin with the greatest parte of their body, which I conceive comparing intelligence were nott many above 1000. The Lord Atholl, Sir Art. Forbes and Mercer went towards Conny, and from thence fall to their old trade againe, falling downe in the night time to the Lowlands. I understand their great businesse att present is to goe on with their leavies, which businesse they follow very close ; but since my coming hither, having summon'd the Heritors of severall shires to meete to enter into an engagement for their peaceable living (which they were willing to doe in some shires) to enter into bond uppon hazard of life and fortune nott to act anythinge against the Commonwealth of England, I doe gather that there is nott that great designe on foote soe generall as wee suspected when I sent to your Lordshippe from Dalkeith ; which I thought itt my duty to give your Lordshippe an hinte of, that you

---

[1] Clarke Manuscripts, lxxxvi. 127.

might nott bee possest with too great an alarum, and your Lordshippe will perceive something more by the inclosed intelligence, which compar'd with other I conceive much truth therin, that I hope there is nott that eminent danger in soe great a measure as formerly seem'd to threaten. Yett notwithstanding, if my poore advice may be taken, there is noe likelier way to breake the heart of these peoples designes then the sending some more forces hither; for your Lorshippe may bee confident of this, if wee should receive the least foyle, which wee indeavour to prevent by extreame hard duty, there are nott a few ready to joyne with them against us, and this divers ingenuous Gentlemen doe assure mee; and undoubtedly uppon the least advantage of this nature[1] they would increase exceedingly, and probably drive us into our garrisons doe what wee can with these forces. I am inform'd they have an agent now with the Dutch Ambassadors att London, newly gone uppe to assure them of their considerable strength, which they pretend to bee 10000; his name is Col. Drummond, Brother to the Lord Madderdy. I heare alsoe that Balcarres and Sir Ro. Murray are gone for their Kinge. Wee are in straights for amunition, and I heare nott of any arriv'd. I intreate your Lordshippe that some more may bee sent downe hither, and that those thinges I mention'd formerly by Capt. Spencer may bee taken into consideration and sent hither.[2]

Sterling, 30° *November* 1653.

CCXII

ORDER of the JUDGES on the CUSTODY of DEEDS.[3]

Edinburgh, the second day of December 1653.

THE COMMISSIONERS for Administration of Justice to the People in Scotland, taking to consideration the predjudices which have ensued to the People of this Nation, through the

---

[1] 'nre.'

[2] *Mercurius Politicus*, Dec. 9-16, contains a long letter from Sterling, Nov. 26, on the movement of Kenmure, Athole and others, and on the state of feeling in Scotland. It is reprinted in the Spottiswoode *Miscellany*, ii. 142.

[3] Broadside from the collection of William Clarke.

keeping and detaining (by the respective Clerks within the same for their warrand) the principall Bands, Contracts, Dispositions, Assignations, Indentures, Discharges, and other Writs Registred by way of Decreet, or for custody in the Registers, commonly called the Registers or Records for Bonds; And finding it necessary to remove the fears and jealousies of the People, and to make use of all wayes, tending to a more sure preservation of Writs and Evidents of the nature abovementioned: And withall taking notice of the former and present allowed practices observed in the Registration of Hornings, Inhibitions, Relaxations, Seasings, Reversions, etc., Have therefore Enacted and Ordained, and hereby Enact and Ordain, That in all time hereafter, there shall be no necessity for the Clerks of the Courts of Justice, Sheriff, Commissar, or Town Clerks within this Nation, to keep and retain the principall Bonds, Contracts, Dispositions, Assignations, Indentures, Discharges, or other Writs that shall occur in their severall offices, to be Registred by way of Decreet, or for custody, or by way of action, in the Records or Registers, commonly called the Register of Bonds; But in place thereof, the respective Clerks aforesaid are to transcribe the just Doubles of those principal Writs, and after collationing and comparing thereof with the Principall, are to subscribe the said Doubles by way of Extract, according to the custome presently observed: And at the same time to write upon the Principall Bond the subsequent words, and subscribe their names thereto; *At   the   day of   165   The ' Principal Bond, Contract, etc. abovewritten within sheets of Paper, presented by   and registred by me under-subscribing, the Clerk to the Court of Justice, Sheriff, Commissar, or Town Clerk of   ,*
And then deliver the same to the presenter of the Writ; Which Doubles shall be a sufficient warrant to the said respective Clerks for the Register, or for giving forth, or delivering Extracts thereof, according to the present form, one or more as the same shall be desired. And the Commissioners Declare, that the said Extracts shall be as valid and effectuall in all Cases, as the present Extracts of any Bonds or Writs Registred, as aforesaid, according to the Rules presently observed: And Ordain all manner of execution to passe thereupon as fully and

freely in all respects, as upon the present extracts of any Writs of that nature. And the Commissioners Declare That these presents shall be extended to all Bonds, Dispositions, Contracts, or other Writs comprehended under this present Act, which have been Registred before the date hereof, since the eighteenth day of *May* 1652, and are presently in their custody; So that upon the desire of Parties, or their Trustees, the said Clerks are to deliver to them all Principall Writs of the foresaid nature, which have been Registred since the said day, and are presently in their custody; The said respective Clerks writing alwayes upon the Principall, and subscribing his name to what shall be so written by him, according to the form hereby prescribed, which shall be fully sufficient for giving forth one or more Extracts thereof, as the same shall be desired. Like as at the desire of Parties, or their Trustees, and upon the presenting of the Principal Writs aforesaid, and deleting what is written and subscribed thereon by the Clerks, as aforesaid, The same respective Clerks are to give up and deliver before Registration of the said Doubles so retained by them for the Register, or for giving forth Extracts thereof, the said Doubles to the said Parties, or their Trustees. And Ordains these presents to be published at the Mercat Crosse of Edinburgh, and Printed.

CRAIGHALL.   GEO. SMYTH.
ED. MOSLEY.   A. PEIRSON.[1]

CCXIII

ROBERT LILBURNE to LORD GENERAL CROMWELL.[2]

MAY ITT PLEASE, ETC.,—Yester-day I had intelligence from Berwick that some of the Enemy had bin within 4 mile of that place, att a markett where divers Berwick men were, which they tooke prisoners, disarm'd them, tooke their horses, and after-

---

[1] On 9 Sept. 1653 Parliament, on the motion of the Council of State, made an order that such registers in the Town as concerned private persons' rights, securities, and conveyances, etc., should be sent down to Scotland to be disposed of by the Commissioners for the administration of Justice.—*Commons Journals*, vii. 316.

[2] Clarke Manuscripts, lxxxvi. 130.

wards lett the men goe, and amongst the rest 2 souldiers of
the garrison.¹ They are said to bee about 7 score stronge in
those parts of the old stock of Mosse Troopers. There is alsoe
parties out towards Dumfrize and Galloway, by which your
Lordshippe may perceive how hard wee are putt to itt to preserve the peace, that without some speedy supply wee shall nott
bee able to prevent the mischeifs this broken desperate partie
may doe; they are soe subtle and cunning, and the Country soe
true to them wee cannott possibly reach them; they are uppe
and downe in soe many places att once, in such small parties
as ten or twenty, and broken and desperate people rising with
them in every Country. I am sending some troopes southward
to conduct the mony, and in the interim run some hazard neere
the Hills in the absence of these horse, and indeed the horse
doe generally begin to complaine of their hard duty. But I hope
I neede nott say any more of these thinges; your Lordshippe
has already, I doubt nott, taken them into consideration, and
found out some effectuall meanes to assist us, for itt must bee
store of forces that will breake the neck of this designe, which
though nott soe generall, [is] yett I assure you exceeding dangerous, and people almost universally have a kinde of muttering and
expectation of some change. I understand when they have
rang'd these Southerne Countries, and gott what they can (which
they doe commonly in the night), they intend to returne to the
Hills, and there to joyne their forces, and imediately to fall
uppon action, though I know nott well what they can bee able
to doe; I doubt nott but one hundred will bee able to fight
300 of them, though most of them are Worcester men, and such
as have bin formerly our prisoners, and indeed have hardly any
other way of livelihood. I sent Major Tolhurst about 10 dayes
agoe to mount a partie of foote, and he hath sent threescore
towards Galloway to scoure that country, but I doubt they
will nott signifie much, though there be a small partie of horse
with them. I stay Col. Saunders 3 troopes here till I know
your Lordshipp's further pleasure. If liberty were given for
some of the northerne regiments to recruite (if the State be
able to beare itt, which they had better doe then run a greater

---

¹ See *Mercurius Politicus*, Dec. 16-22, p. 3039.

hazard), I am confident in a monthes time there would bee men enow to supply these defects.

Linlithgowe, 3° December.

CCXIV

Col. Lilburne to the Committee for the Army.[1]

Gentlemen,—I had before the receipt of yours of the 28 of the last, or the resolves of Parliament, issued out warrants for the bringing in of the Monthly Assesse of Scotland for the monthes of November and December, in the same manner as was appointed by the Councell of State for the last 6 monthes; which I was necessitated unto in regard of the difficulty of the collecting of the sesse without allowing sufficient time for the same, and could nott (by reason of the present distempers) revoake those orders (which were gone to the furthest parts of Scotland) without much inconveniencie and disadvantage to present affaires; and therfore I intreate you, that you will please nott charge any more then 8500*l* monthly (as formerly) for those 2 monthes; and for the 4 monthes ensuing I conceive it most adviseable, that during the continuance of these distempers heere, the sesse may nott bee augmented, or laid on without those abatements formerly allowed, which was for the most parte distributed to depopulate places, and to Burroughes who (through the decay of trade) will nott be able to pay the one half of what is laid uppon them;[2] as, for example, Argyll and most of the Hyla[nds] pay nothing at all, and Edenb[urgh] hath 200*li* a month abated, and sues for further abatements; and how seasonable itt will bee to heighten the sesse of the shires, and cast all the abatements of the Hyl[ands] and Broughs upon the Lowlands in this juncture of time, when what is already laid on in all places comes in heavily, (especially neare the Hills, the Enemy having soe much infested

---

[1] Clarke Manuscripts, lxxxvi. 132. No address given, but evidently to a committee, and not to the Council of State.

[2] In the margin: "S. Johnston's, Dundee, Glasgowe, and other great Burroughes, pay little or nothing att all, though their sesse in the booke of rates is considerable.

those parts) I humbly offer to consideration, and that you will please to move the Parliament or Councell of State for their further direction therin. As for the disbursements about fortifications and other incident charges, they have for about these 12 monthes past necessarily required betwene four and five thousand pounds monthly (besides maritime expenses, which are greate), which charge is nott likely to bee lessen'd as yet, considering the severall Isles and other places which have bin lately garrison'd, and must unavoidablie bee kept, and more fortificacions raised, while these insurreccions continue. What further particuler satisfaction you shall desire as to these particulars, Mr. Thompson, Auditor Generall, or Mr. George Bilton, Receivour Generall of the Monthly Assese heere, will bee able fully to informe you: and for Commissary Eldreds' accounts, hee is by this time in London ready to answer your desires, and the Auditor Generall will informe you of the state of Commissioner Hulinges accounts and present stores. I perceive by the Treasurers Deputies heere, that they have noe orders for the returne of monies, which is aswell prejudiciall to the Merchant in point of trade as to the souldiery, whose necessities will nott bee answer'd by that summe now coming downe, unlesse the rest of the monie appointed by your selves for the forces heere bee speedily transmitted. I therfore earnestly intreate you will give direccions to the Treasurers that bills may bee charged and accepted att as few dayes sight as may bee: and that I may receive further and speedie direccions about the monthly asses here, both what shalbe required of the Cuntry, and what order I shall observe in the issuing of it forth in poynt of pay or incident charges.[1]

Dalkeith, 6° December 1653.

CCXV

Col. Lilburne to the Lord General Cromwell.[2]

May itt please your Excellency,—I am lately inform'd, Middleton and Massie have already laden 4 shippes with armes

---

[1] On Nov. 12, 1653, Parliament had voted that there should be an assessment of £10,016, 10s. per month levied upon Scotland towards the payment of the forces there, and had directed Lilburne to raise that sum.—*Commons Journals*, vii. 350.   [2] Clarke Manuscripts, cxxxvi. 133.

and ammunition, and are ready to saile. I only hinte itt to your Lordshippe againe, because of dispatching those shippes intended for the guard of these Northerne parts, in regard though I was inform'd some were order'd hither, none of them have yett appeared, nor can I heare any thinge yett of the shippe with amunition, a thinge which wee exceedingly want, and which I dare hardly speake of att this distance. These broken people doe still more and more breake forth, and I have often inform'd your Lordshippe that affaires heere doe very much require some further supplies of forces, and I hope your Lordshippe hath itt under serious consideration, and will nott suffer much longer delayes heerin. I alsoe made bold humbly to minde your Lordshippe how necessary itt will bee to putt forth a Declaration against these mens proceedings, and to give incouragement to those that would appeare against them, together with divers other particulars, wherin I have nott had the happinesse to know your Lordshippes pleasure, but shall waite your further commands, and remaine, your Excellencies, etc.

Dalkeith, 6° December 1653.

Lord Generall.

I am senceable the Court of Justice, throug their strickt proceedeings, and through the scarcity of money here, drive many to desperate courses, and at this time, as [the] Judge Advocate informes, there are 35000 captions out against men. Marquess Huntley being one of that number, sent this day to me for proteccion, which, by reason I have noe order from the Councell of State in (haveing formerly writt about such things) I am not free to doe it, by which meanes he may be driven to the hills among the rest, though hitherto very quiet, yet to prevent such inconveniencies, I ventured for peace sake to send him a passe to come over hither for 2 months.[1]

CCXVI

COL. LILBURNE to the ADMIRALTY COMMISSIONERS.[2]

RIGHT HONORABLE,—Those men of warre that have attended

---

[1] A letter from Edinburgh, dated Dec. 18, says, 'The Marquess of Huntley died last week at his house at Bogy-geith.'—*Mercurius Politicus*, p. 3146.

[2] Clarke Manuscripts, lxxxvi. 134.

this Coast most of them being driven from hence by the stormes, their remaines only Capt. Robinson of the *Plover* frygott, who I am now constrain'd to order as Convoy to that shippe with masts coming from Invernesse, by reason wherof ther is nott any man of warre left to doe any service heere; and having intelligence that 4 shippes are laden in Holland by Middleton and Massie with armes and ammunition bound for the Highlands, I thought itt my duty to give you this account, and to move you once againe that some men of warre may bee speedily dispatch't for the safety of these Coasts and your affaires in this Nation, and that you will please to order Capt. Robinson back againe assoone as his shippe is in a condition. I conceive you cannot butt thinke itt necessary that some shippes of warre were heere as the state of thinges stands, especially considering those shippes coming from Holland to the Enemy, which I leave to your further consideration, and remaine, your most humble servant.

Dalkeith, 8° Dec. [16]53.
Commissioners of the Admiralty.

CCXVII
A LETTER OF INTELLIGENCE.[1]

Dec. 8, 1653.

ALL our Commission'd officers are going now to their severall localities for leavies (which was nott till now determined uppon), both of horse and foote. The Earle of Atholl is to levy a regiment of horse in Perthshire and the whole foot thereof. Kinoule hath the horse of the shire of Angus, and Caithness, Sutherland, Rosse, and Murray, and to be commander in cheif of the foot leavied there. Kenmore is to leavey the horse of the shire of Aberdeene. Col. Blakader of Tulliallen is to levy in a part of the shyre of Fyfe. Sir Mungo Murray left us two nights, being discontented for not getting a localitie on the North side of Forth; he was and is generall Quartermaster, and is again reconcilled, and is to have Sterlingshire for a localitie for secureing the horse there. There was a high

---

[1] Clarke Manuscripts, xxv. 168. Possibly by the author of Letters cvii and cxxxvi.

discontent betwixt M'Naghten and Kenmore. M'Naghten would have left us but that the Generall prevailed uppon him by giving him Commission for the levveying of the horse in ranthrow [?], soe God be thanked wee are all in unitie. Wee are now about a thousand good, wellarmed, resolute foot, and 500 horse; the riders are singularly good; they and the horse are extreamly ill equipaged; saddles and bridles that [are] good are rare here. I have sent you a purse penney. I intreat that there be not a word of the other. This is all. I remaine, Your servant to Death.

CCXVIII

CHARLES II. to the EARL of MURRAY.[1]

CHARLES R.—Right trusty and right welbeloved Cosen, We Dec. 14. greete you well. Since the affeccion of our good subjects in the Highlands is soe notorious now, that the Rebells themselves begin to confesse some apprehension of their power, and the mischeive would be irreparable if after soe gallant an attempt to redeeme their Country from the slavery and dishonour it groanes under, they should for want of concurrence in the whole Nacion be reduced to extremity, and made a prey to the bloody and mercyless English Rebells, who intend an utter extirpacion of the Nobility and antient Gentry of that Kingdome, We have thought fitt in an espetiall manner to recommend soe important a consideracion to you, and to desire you that if upon any private and particular reasons you have hitherto forborne to engage your selfe with those who are now in armes for Us, that you will (as soone as they who are entrusted by Us shall desire you) joyne with them, and use your utmost interest and power to advance Our service by drawing all your freinds and dependants to a conjunction with them. And as We are endeavouring all We can to procure armes, ammunicion, and other supplyes to be sent unto you, by degrees, and in such manner as We finde most convenient, soe We have directed Lieutenant Generall Middleton himselfe

---

[1] Clarendon Manuscripts, xlvii. 136. There are similar letters to Viscount Kingstoun, the Earl of Dalhousie, and Lord Ramsay.

speedily to repayre to you, as soone as he can obteyne such a supply as We hope will not requier much more time. And We doubt not but God Almighty will blesse you in this enterprize, and We shall never forgett the service you shall doe Us, and the alacrity you shall expresse therein. And soe We bid you very heartily farewell.

Given at Paris the 18th day of December 1653. In the fifth yeare of our Reigne.

Addressed.—*To Our right trusty and right Welbeloved Cosen the Earle of Murray.*

CCXIX

A COMMISSION from the EARL of GLENCAIRN.[1]

William, Earle of Glencairne, Lord of Kilmort, Commander in Cheif of all his Majestie's forces within the Kingdome of Scotland.

By virtue of a Commission granted to mee by his Majesty for leavying of forces within the Kingdome of Scotland for opposing of the common enemy, I doe by these presents appoint Col. Alexander Blakiter to leavy out of the shire of Clackmannan one sufficient troope-horse and man well arm'd out of every thousand pound of rent, with certification if they fayle after sight of my order they shall bee esteemed enemies to their Kinge; and the said Col. Alexander Blakiter, or any having his power, is heerby aucthorized to take the persons of the Deficients, and to bring them prisoners to the armie, and to drive all their goods while they doe duty. Given under my hand att Glenervie this 6th of December 1653.

GLENCAIRNE.

CCXX

AN INTERCEPTED LETTER.

Lo[ving] FREIND,—I desire that you will intimate this order to all the Gentlemen in Clackmannanshire, and send mee the just

---

[1] Clarke Manuscripts, xxv. 170. This letter and the next were intercepted, and are printed in *Mercurius Politicus*, p. 3153, where the first is dated 'Glenertie.'

rentall of every man's estate with this Bearer; and if you shall feare any danger by giving you this order, I will answer for itt. Noe more, butt [I] expect your diligence and your answer as you will have your selfe freed from trouble, and rest your loving freind, JOHN BLAKITER.

From Comerie parish the 10th of December 1653.

For his loving freind Wm. Morris, Clarke in Alloway, these.

CCXXI

SIR EDWARD HYDE to LIEUT.-GEN. MIDDLETON.[1]

SIR,—I have seene both your letters of this weeke and the Dec. last to my Lord Newburgh, and trust me I have so greate a desyre that you should be satisfyed in all thinges you propose, that I exceedingly suspecte my owne judgement when I finde it differs from yours; and therfore though I expressed somewhat of my owne opinion the last weeke of the letter you wished the Kinge should write to Mr. Junius of Amsterdam in Latine, yett I was farr from contractinge any positive judgement in it till I had spoken at large to the Kinge of it, who sayes it can be by no meanes fitt for him to do it, for these reasons. He hath beene pressed by many to write letters to some of the Clergy ther, who are sayd to be leadinge men, and who wish well as they pretende to his service, but he hath alwayes declyned it as a thinge that would be quickly knowen, and would then be misunderstoode by the States as an endeavour to worke upon the people without them, which would be a juster pretence then any they have yett had for any disrespecte towards his Majesty: and if it were once published that the Kinge had written to one Minister ther would noe other be his frende without a letter, nor is it (if all other consideracions were away) a very easy matter to write such a letter upon that occasyon, which would not displease as many and as good men as it would satisfy. Therefore the Kinge desyres you would tell this person, that you have particular order from his Majesty to lett him know that he takes notice of his good affection, and

---
[1] Clarke Manuscripts, xlvii. 145.

to desyre him to continue it, and to assure him of rewarde when his Majesty's condicion is improved, and to say all other thinges which you thinke seasonable. You will receave with this all those letters you desyre for Scotlande, and one in the King's owne hand to M[arquis] Huntly, whome his Majesty hopes you will keepe in good humour. I send you the copy of what the Kinge hath sayd to him. In earnest I believe your presence ther will produce notable fruite, and I am confident the advice you shall sende from thence will be followed by the Kinge. Be sure the Kirke be modest, which will be the greatest argument to the Kinge to venture with them, and that he [be] sure they will not use him as they did. His Majesty does not understande what the old Order of the Thistle was, nor how it is to be revived, but all thinges of that nature must be performed with most exacte forme, and any declension from the rule spoyles the businesse, therfore the Kinge would have you informe your selfe punctually of it, and then what you shall advice shall be done. I have no more to say, but that I wish you as much good fortune as I could do if you were my brother, and will serve you as heartily, and God send us a good meetinge, and prosper me as I am very heartily, Sir, your, etc.

Remember my service to Coll. Drummonde, whose safe arryvall in Scotlande I longe to be assured of.

Lt. Gl. Middleton.

Indorsed.—*Myne to Lt. Gen. Middleton.* 19 *Decemb.* 1653.

CCXXII[1]

COLONEL LILBURNE to the COMMISSIONERS at LEITH.

GENTLEMEN,—The Laird of Pluscardies being Cautioner for the Earle of Seafort, and having an Infeoffement uppon his estate for his security, and his owne estate being comprized for the said Earle's debt, wherby hee will bee ruin'd without

---

[1] Clarke Manuscripts, lxxxvi. 135.

releif uppon Seafort's estate, in which respect, and for that the said Laird of Pluscardie, being one of the Cheif of a great Clan, in case hee should bee putt to extreamity, might bee necessitated to fly to the Hills, and with himself and partie joyne with those now in armes, which would bee of greater disadvantage to the Commonwealth then any benefitt that can bee made by the estates; I desire you will forbeare to proceede in the sequestration of soe much of Seafort's estate as concernes Pluscarty, but that the Laird of Pluscarden may have the benefitt of the Enfeoffement theruppon without molestation.

Dalkeith, 10 *December* 1653.

Commissioners att Leith.

CCXXIII

Proposals from Col. Lilburne.[1]

Sir,—I have severall times represented divers thinges of consequence to his Excellencie, wherof I have nott yett received answer, and having yesterday uppon a meeting with divers officers thought itt advisable to offer some thinge which itt's conceived may conduce to the peace of this Nation to the Generall and his Councell, and because that you are well acquainted with thinges of this nature, it is recomended to offer them as you see an opportunitie.

1. That the Sequestrations of this Nation, and forfeitures of estates may bee all taken off, but 5 or 6 grand offendors for examples sake, and that uppon the passing of the Act of Union, an Act of Oblivion may bee passed for what is past, with a free pardon to all that are now in armes if they will bee quiett, and in the same Act good rewards may bee promis'd to any that shall bringe in any of the present rebells dead or alive, especially the Heads and Cheif of them that will not otherwayes submitt.

2. That libertie may bee given to any Scotchman to transport regimentes to Forraine princes in amity with us uppon good security.

---

[1] Clarke Manuscripts, lxxxvi. 136.

3. To hasten doune a supply of forces, both horse and foote, to prevent the present proceedinges of the Enemy in their leavies in divers parts, where without more forces they cannott bee prevented without too great hazard to some of our garrisons and quarters, they being very active att this time in that worke, and have lately dispersed themselves on purpose.

4. That some men of warre may be sent speedily to guard this coast to prevent Middleton's landing, all our men of war being gon hence.

5. That some Instructions may bee thought on by the Councell of State to stay proceedinges in the Courts of Justice, with some more liberty to the Judges to moderate sentences given out by them, and that the rigour and extreamitie of their decreetes may nott bee presentlie executed, but that aucthority may bee given to the Judges to allow considerable time for the payment of any summe adjudged to bee due, and to appoint the crediter to take land in satisfaction for his debt or interest for his monie till the debtor bee able to satisfie itt, or somethinge to this purpose to save men from being driven to extreamitie by Caption, and therby forc't to fly to the Enemy; which itt is conceiv'd is a very great cause of the present troubles.

CCXXIV[1]

Letter to Col. Lilburne.

Sir,—On Saturday last Sir Alexander Murray and I, having accidentally mett heere at Peblis, gott notice that some 20 English horsemen had layne heere all night, wherof I wrote to your Honour imediately, and Sir Alexander was to dispatch it. I have learned the certentie since, and finde it was Collonell Ogan, that same man whoe in the yeare 1648 (when Duke Hamleton lead his armey in against England) came into this Country with some 80 horse, and joyned with him; that same man who commanded the Earle of Ormond's life Guard of foot

---

[1] Clarke Manuscripts, xxv. 169.

when he was routed before Dublin in Ireland, 1649, and he who was all last engagement here with the king in Scotland, and was at Worcester with him; he with these men have come straight the road doun togeather from London without a challenge (as they have given it out here); they seemed to those that saw them to be all men of good quallitie, for they are gallantly mounted, richly clothed, and well armed, had aboundance of gould about them; they gave out to some that spake with them in private, and to whome Ogan revealed himselfe, that he and some others of that number are come soe lately from Paris, as they reckned that Friday night when they were here to have beene the 27 night since they came from thence (to witt from Paris), and the King is expected shortly in the North. All this I thought fit and my duty to acquant your Honour with, and begs your Honour will deale favourably with me in keepeing these from any of my owne Country men's knowledge, at least the writer. I must acquant your Honour that we feare [?] a broken Country, and not soe much from any within our owne countrys, as from strangers who come from below us towards the borders; and here at home too, there is a young man, one Tweedie [?], who last weeke came to some of my Lord Yester's ground, abused some of his tenants (haveing some more with him of these loose sorte of people), set fire to a beane yarde, tooke away a horse; the fire was got quenched, but they caried away the horse, he is a mad, drunken, roareing young man. Honoured ever, if there be any more of that sorte you are to heare it, and we who are thought to interest in your power and Governement are sure to be the first sufferers. I had allmost forgotten to let your Honour know that Ogan caried away Mr. Hares horse, the minister's here. Thus craving pardon for my prolixitie, I am, your Honour's humble servant.[1]

Peblis, 12 *December* 1653.

---

[1] On Wogan's arrival in Scotland, see *Mercurius Politicus*, pp. 3151, 3185; and *Spottiswoode Miscellany*, ii. 151; *Military Memoirs of John Gwynne*, pp. 166, etc. For an account of Colonel Edward Wogan, see Clarke Papers, i. 421, 2, Camden Society, 1891.

CCXXV

Col. Lilburne to the Council of State.[1]

Right Honourable,—Before I received your Commands concerning the landing of some persons in Lancashire from Forraine parts, who [were] intending for this Nation, I had intelligence of Col. Wogan and about 20 Cavaleers being come within 16 mile of this place, that they lay att Durham severall dayes,[2] and labour'd there to seduce divers persons, some wherof came alonge with them. I have sent out parties before I received your commands, and shall againe give notice to our forces to bee watchfull to apprehend any of them they can meete with; but those horse wee have heere being soe few and their quarters soe remote from one another, are uppon extreame hard duty, and very much harassed in ranging the Country for preventing those dangers that threaten daily more and more. I heare nott as yett of those supplies of amunition which you were pleas'd longe agoe to appoint to this place, nor are any men of warre as yett come to guard this Coast, by reason wherof I doubt some armes are landed from Holland, and the rather I beleeve it, because the Enimie are most of them drawne Northward, but in what particular place noe account as yett is come unto your most humble servant.

Dalkeithe, 13 December 1653.[3]
Councell of State.

CCXXVI[4]

Proclamation by Col. Lilburne.

By the Commander in Cheif of the Forces in Scotland.

Forasmuch as itt is apparent, That (notwithstanding my

---

[1] Clarke Manuscripts, lxxxvi. 137.

[2] Two letters of Wogan on his march are printed in Thurloe, i. 607, 623.

[3] On Dec. 13 Lilburne wrote to Lieutenant-Colonel Mayer and Major Tolhurst, informing them of a report 'that certain persons are speedily to land in Lancashire from foreign parts (some of which being of the quality of officers), who intend privately to pass from thence into Scotland.'

[4] Clarke Manuscripts, xliii. 37. See *Mercurius Politicus*, p. 3190.

Proclamation of the 27th of September last), many serviceable horses daylie goe to the Enemy, to the greate disservice of the peace of this Nation, which could not bee with out too much connivance of the owners or possessors; These are therefore strictly to requiere all manner of persons, whoe nowe are or hereafter shall bee possessed of any servicable horses or mares exceedinge the value of Five pounds sterleinge, To bringe in the same with in fortie eight houers next after publication hereof unto the next adjacent Garrison or quarter of our Army; under the penalty not onely of forfeitinge treble the value of such horses and mares as shalle not be brought in; the one moyetie thereof to the use of the state, and the other moyetie to the partie informinge, but alsoe deemed as an open enemy, and dealt with all accordinglie; which horses and mares soe brought in shall neverthelesse be at the owners choice, either to have meette satisfaction for them, as they shall be reasonably worth, or keepe them with in the said Garrisons or quarters of our army. And the respective Sheriffes and theire Deputies within theire Sheriffdomes, are hereby required to cause these presents solemnly to be proclaymed and published, according to the accustomed manner of publishinge proclamations. And afterwards (that none may pretend ignorance) to cause to be distributed to the severall Presbyteries within theire said Sheriffdomes a competent number hereof.   R. LILBURNE.

Given under my hand att Dalkeith, the 14th of December 1653.

CCXXVII

INSTRUCTIONS to OFFICERS for the SEIZURE of HORSES.[1]

1. THAT parties with an order under your hand in writing be sent imediately after publicacion of the proclamacion of the 14th of December instant to all Heritors and others possessed of horses included within the said Proclamacion in the sheire of [blank] to bring them into your [blank] upon a day certaine according to the tenor of the proclamacion.

---

[1] Clarke Manuscripts, lxxxvi. 154.

2. That you appoint two able and indifferent persons to value what each horse is worth, and register the same, takeing care that noe horse be over valued.

3. That for all such persons as shall desire to keepe theire horses in your [blank] that you allow thereof.

4. That for such as are willing to part with theire horses as they shalbe valued, that you give a tickett under your hand of the receipt and value.

5. That if any officer or souldier of our army shall desire to have any horse att the said valued price you cause such horse to be delivered unto him or them, and the moneyes to be paid to the owner, takinge his discharge in writing under his hand.

6. That if any horse shalbe valued above 25t sterling, the owner shall not be compelled to sell him, but have libertie to keepe him within your quarters or garrison.

7. That soe many horses as shall not be valued to 5t sterling, or not judged serviceable, be restored, takeing securitie for the forth comming of those that are serviceable whensoever required if living.

8. That you examine each person who shall bring in any horse, what more he hath, and what horses his neighbours have; to the end those conceal'd may be discovered, and the parties prosecuted according to the said Proclamacion.

9. That all such horses as shall fall into your hands upon reasonable prizes undisposed of to officer or souldiour[1] [you cause] to deliver proportionably to each company in your regiment, as they shalbe valued; that then you chuse out such foote souldiours as may be capable of riding them and preserving of them in good case, and that you charge provisions of oates and straw proportionably for them.

10. If any trooper having a serviceable horse for Dragoones shall be desirous to exchange for a better, it shall be lawfull for him soe to doe, he paying the overplus of what the horse soe exchanged is worth more then his owne, which monye is forthwith to be paid to the Heritor that ought the horse in parte of satisfaccion.   Rt. Lilburne.

---

[1] The position of this clause has been altered.

CCXXVIII

CHARLES II. to the MARQUESS OF HUNTLY.[1]

THAT you may see how farr I am from givinge creditt to all the reportes I heare concerninge you, I do once more assure you I cannot believe you will ever be wantinge to my service when it shall be seasonable for you to appeare in it, and I must tell you Middleton is so much of my minde, that he dependes on no man's assistance more then on yours, and besydes your affection to me, is very confident of your particular frendshipp to him, which, trust me, he deserves. I shall only remember you how much we have all suffered hearetofore by the emulacion and faction amongst our owne frendes, which hath inabled the Rebells to do all this mischieve. I conjure you, as I do all my other frendes, to use your utmost power to prevent all mischieves of that kinde, and then I doubte not but God will blesse us against the common Enimy, and inable me to repayre and rewarde you all for what you have done and suffered for me: and then you will have no cause to be unsatisfyed with, Yours, etc.

Dec. 16/26.

M. Huntly.

Indorsed.—*The King to Marqs. Huntly.*
26 *of December.*

CCXXIX

COL. LILBURNE to the LORD GENERAL CROMWELL.[2]

MAY ITT PLEASE YOUR EXCELLENCY,—I thought itt my duty (uppon that account and report that came hither of the suddaine dissolution of the Parliament) to let your Lordship know that by all the observation I can make I finde nothing but union amongst us heare,[3] and a resolution to stand with your Lordshippe

---

[1] Clarendon Manuscripts, xlvii. 144.

[2] Clarke Manuscripts, lxxxvi. 151.

[3] There was some disappointment in the army in Scotland at the ineffective proceedings of the Little Parliament.—Thurloe, i. 546.

in the management of these weighty affaires that providence hath cast uppon you, and to pray to the Lord to direct and guide you and those that are in Counsell with you; yet I was informed the judges were scrupled whether to act any further or not, which caused me to write to some of them and had this inclosed returne. I have wondred all this while since I first acquainted your Lordshippe with the first increase of the Enemy heere, and my earnest request and humble advice to your Lordshippe for the sending of some supplies hither, that I have had noe answer therunto when the necessity of affaires hath soe much call'd for them, which hath againe and againe bin represented, which I now impute to the late inconsistancie in the Parliament; yet for want wherof doe what wee can affaires doe suffer heere, and the expectations of this untoward people much heightned seing the weaknesse and small number of our forces, though of late [we] have happilie mett with severall parties and putt discouragements uppon them,[1] but I finde they still increase; the greatest body, being about 2000 horse and foote, are gone Northward through the Hills, yett have left divers parties in all these Countries who follow the old trade of stealing horses in the night to ad to their partie, many rogues running in to them daily, yett I heare nott of any English since Col. Wogan came with 20. I heare the Lord Calendar is going in to them, and doubtlesse many more considerable persons waite their opportunitie. I humbly intreate these papers or propositions that I formerly hinted to your Lordshippe may bee taken into consideration, concerning declaring of these people traitors, or some thing of that kinde, and that some forces may be dispatched: yet I hope a happy conclusion with the Dutch will putt an end to these unhappy peoples distempers, and things may come to a settlement againe, though being jealous of my owne weakenes [I] am doubtfull soe great affaires as are here to be managed may suffer for the

---

[1] On Dec. 10 and Dec. 12 Captain Lisle of Colonel Rich's regiment beat up Lord Kinnoul's quarters taking over thirty prisoners and dispersing the regiment. On 12 Dec. Captain Hart defeated Sir Arthur Forbes in a skirmish at Borthwick Brae.—*Mercurius Politicus*, pp. 3142, 3154, 3186; *Gwynne's Memoirs*, 218, 221; *Spottiswoode Miscellany*, ii. 148, 152.

want of one more fitt to wrastle with them then your Excellencies most humble servant. R. L.
Dalkeith, 20th December 1653.
His Excellency.

CCXXX

COL. LILBURNE to the LORD PROTECTOR.[1]

MAY ITT PLEASE, etc.,—This evening brought mee nott only the acceptable newes of your being call'd to soe high a place and trust (wherin I cannott but wish your Lordshippe much joy, and desire the Lord to direct you in the managing these great affaires before you for the glory of his name and the satisfaction of all good people under your Lordshippes protection), but alsoe the good newes of Capt. Harts routing a party of about an 100 horse under Sir Arther Forbes that were gott uppon the borders neere Langham. I cannott yett tell whether Sir Arthur bee kill'd or taken, but Capt. Hart hath both his horse and Major Erwin's, and 63 more, besides 16 prisoners, and 4 kill'd, and did alsoe rescue the High Sheriff of Roxburghshire that was their prisoner; the eagernesse of the souldiery taking horses hindred the taking of some prisoners that were knock't downe, who made their escape, yet their was nott above 28 of the enemy that gott away on horse back. Wee have lately taken severall other prisoners, some of quality, and the prisons beginn now to bee full in divers places; yett notwithstanding they seem to bee so resolute as nott to bee discourag'd att any thing, and goe on very vigorously in their businesse doe what wee can, and the people very much heightned in their expe[cta]tions, and ready to joyne with them uppon all occasions, and very false towards us. I humbly move your Excellency once againe that some forces may bee speeded hither, as alsoe, seing providence hath call'd you to bee Lord Protector of 3 Nations, that your Excellency will proclaime a pardon to all that will submitt, with some penalty uppon those that should remaine obstinate, and good rewards to those that should bringe in the Heads of those in rebellion; wherby your Excellency may more happily bee

[1] Clarke Manuscripts, lxxxvi. 155.

able to protect the people of this Nation, many of whom are now under very great oppression by the Enemy. Their greatest strength is gone Northward through the Hills, and is doubtfull will much increase in these parts. Our shippe with amunition is nott yett come, nor is there any man of warre heere. I humbly move that some may bee sent downe for the guard of the Coasts, and preventing Middleton or any other enemies landing heere; but I hope if a good peace bee with the Dutch these vapours will quickly vanish, though att present wee are putt to great toyle and hard duty. I humbly remayne, Your Excellencies most humble and reall servant.

Dalk. 22 *Dec.* 1653.

CCXXXI

Col. Lilburne to the Lord Protector.[1]

May itt please your Highnesse,—Though I have often troubled your Highnesse with an account of affaires heere, and of the great dangers that have longe threatned this Nation, the manifold difficulties that wee have to wrestle withall with only this handfull of horse that is heere, yett have I nott had the happinesse this longe time to receive the least commands from your Highnesse, or any thinge to give mee hopes of those supplies which I often told your Highnesse was most necessary to bee sent downe hither ; yett must I nott cease (if I discharge my duty) still to importune your Highnesse to consider affaires heere, before they breake out into such a flame as may nott be easily quenched. The people generally having a very great aptnesse to rise against us, by stealing to the Hills in the night time, [the enemy] are growne considerable, and as I told your Highnesse in my last their greatest body are gone Northward. Itt is reported they are att least 400 stronge, and att this time are nott above 16 miles from Aberdene ; and by reason of the severall parties of them that are heere uppe and downe wee cannott safely spare one hundred horse from hence to adde to

---

[1] Clarke Manuscripts, lxxxvi. 137.

those that are there, our hands being full in every place, and wee are nott above 200 horse in Aberdene, nor is there att present in all Scotland above 1200 or 1300 fighting horse, which is a very inconsiderable body being soe dispers't as necessity requires, wee having our quarters neere 300 mile in length, and every man has his taske sufficient.[1] The Enemy being now gone Northward (the Marq. Huntly being newly dead) wee finde divers of that Clan breaking out already, and I heare the Lord Calendar is lurking in some parts of the North to take his opportunity to joyne with them. My Lord, I beseech you lett these thinges bee seriously consider'd, and supply heere a little more soe as may make us capable of securing the southerne parts, and [to] send such a considerable party Northwards as may nott bee only able to secure themselves but kepe the Enemy uppe in the Hills, which doubtlesse will bee the greatest discouragement we can putt uppon them this winter time. Our shippe with amunition is nott yett come but is gott into Holy Island with much difficulty, yett I hope will bee heere very shortly.—I humbly remaine, Your Highnesse, etc.

Dalkeith, 24 *December* 1653.

I understand divers men are transported out of Ireland into the Highlands, which I humbly intreate your Highnesses order to prevent.[2]

CCXXXII

PROCLAMATION against SIR ARTHUR FORBES.[3]

WHERAS Sir Arthur Forbes escaped after the engagement

---

[1] A letter from Dalkeith dated Jan. 4 states that the regiments of horse of Major-General Lambert and Commissary General Whalley, and the foot regiment of Sir William Constable are on their march to Scotland.

[2] In a letter from Lilburne to Lambert dated Dec. 27 he reiterated his appeal for reinforcements. Captain Scrope of Col. Overton's regiment, who had been some weeks a prisoner with the enemy, had just returned, and said that 'by the most probable guess he can make of the enemy's strength in the hills they are able to have 8000 men at a call,' which Lilburne thought an exaggeration. Lilburne thought it might possibly be necessary to abandon some of the garrison, and withdraw troops from the north,' and so 'to give the enemie all beyond Dundee except Inverness,' in order to bring together a sufficiently strong field army.—Clarke Manuscripts, lxxxvi. 149.

[3] Clarke Manuscripts, lxxxvi. 139.

betweene Capt. Hart and him, and lies concealed in some part of the Lowlands, These are to declare, That whosoever shall discover the said Sir Arthur Forbes and bring him unto any of the garrisons of the Commonwealth, or shall give such certaine intelligence wherby hee shall bee apprehended, shall have one Hundred pounds sterling for the same, and whosoever shall harbour or conceale him shall bee proceeded against as publique enemies.¹   RT. LILBURNE.
Dalk., Dec. 27, 1653.

CCXXXIII
FORM of ENGAGEMENT for PRISONERS.²

WHERAS Capt. J. M., now prisoner to the Army, is uppon caution to bee inlarged for some short space of time to manage his civill affaires att Edinburgh, and to render himself prisoner whensoever required: Bee itt therfore ken'd to all men by these presents, That wee ———— as his Cautioners doe heerby binde and oblige us joynetlie and severallie to the keepers of the liberties of the Commonwealth of England in the summe of Five Hundred pounds sterling, That the said Capt. J. M., being sett att libertie, shall att all times uppon reasonable notice to either of us, given or left in writing att either of our usuall habitations, render him self true prisoner, either att Sterling, where hee now is, or elsewhere as to the Commander-in-Cheif shall bee thought fitt. In witnesse whereof wee have heerunto sett our hands this ———— day of December, 1653. Before these witnesses.

CCXXXIV
COL. LILBURNE to ————³

RIGHT HONOURABLE,—These inclosed will tell you something of the number and proceedinges of the Enemy. Besides divers

---

¹ Forbes was wounded, and a party of horse was sent to seize him as he lay ill in a cottage near Glasgow, but he received warning in time to escape.—*Gwynne's Memoirs,* p. 225.
² Clarke Manuscripts, xlvii. 37.
³ *Ibid.* lxxxvi. 152. Probably to Lambert.

other parties that are throughout the Nation, and in each Country very active, wee are hunting them day and night, but the Country are nott our freinds, they lie in the Mosses, and now begin to murther our men as they meete with them in small parties. You may easily judge the straightes wee are in especially in the North, I meane only those att Aberdene, where I tolde you in my former what number of horse wee have or can make in that place. I am labouring to mount some foote, and have required all the Heritors in severall countries [to send in all horses] that are above £5 price. Some yeild obedience, but the generality are too nimble. I have also intelligence of a designe that Seafort is about to transport a considerable partie into the Lewis to force them of that garrison, and hath the conjunction of diverse neighbours, and at this time I have nott a shipp to send there to countenance them or to give them intelligence. I have againe and againe complained of the want of shipping, and I heare but of three yet sent, though there were 7 ordered. If what I have written formerly or now be rightly apprehended you cannot but be sensible both of the streights wee are in, and of the consequences which these things may bring; which I humbly lay before you, as being deeply upon my owne spirit, and that calls for a timely and serious consideration in those that sit at the Helme. Wee have all this Summer bin exceedingly pincht for pay, and at this time the forces are above two months in arreare, and the sesse of this Nation growne very inconsiderable; that what wee can force from the people that are within our reach, there wee gett something, otherwise wee loose all for the present; that I thinke halfe of the sesse of this Nation will not be received by us, nor dare a Collector stay in the Country but where there is a garrison to receive it, and the many hard duties our horse are upon, and want of supplyes, makes us many times wee cannot assist them with forces. The wants of the souldiers this winter season through the shortnesse of their pay makes me full with complaints, though I doe the best I can to play the good husband for them. But I feare I am too tedious, though I presume of a pardon from you unto your most humble servant.

Dalkeith, December 29th, 1653.

I heere that a Commander-in-Cheif is to be sent downe hither, I only wish such a one as may pay these people for their knavery. Mee thinkes Monke's spiritt would doe well amongst them.

CCXXXV

COLONEL LILBURNE to —— [1]

RIGHT HONOURABLE,—Since the receipt of your last I heare of Capt. Orton's arrivall at Invernesse, and have by the same hand intelligence of a designe in Seafort to regaine the Lewis,[2] and that great preparations are making by him and his neighbours for that purpose; and at this time I have not a ship to give them intelligence or countenance them in the least. I heare the *Primerose* and the *Dutchesse* are about Holy Island with our ammunition; though I sent to them to hasten hither, yet I heare not of their arrivall. I heare of a Dutch prize they have, which they say will make a good man of war, having all her furniture and tackle about her. I shall intreat to heare from you about her, as also some more ships for these Coasts, and for the Westerne Coasts betweene the Highlands and Ireland, from whence I heare divers Irish are transported and joyne with these people that are in armes against us.—I remaine, your most humble servant.

Dalkeith, December 29th, 1653.

CCXXXVI.

THE EARL OF GLENCAIRN'S INSTRUCTIONS TO MAJOR STRACHAN.[3]

Note for M. R. S.

1. First, and above all, the warrant under the King's hand declaring Argyle traytor. The ground of the declaracion is to

---

[1] Clarke Manuscripts, lxxxvi. 153. To the Council of State?

[2] On this design see *Mercurius Politicus*, p. 3182; *Spottiswoode Miscellany*, ii. 155; *Gwynne's Memoirs*, p. 223. The letter summarised in *Mercurius Politicus* was probably from Lilburne himself.

[3] Clarendon Manuscripts, xlvii. 189.

be for his being in open hostility against his Majesty's forces at
Dowart, for assisting the English with men, and in his owne
person for joyning with them in the takeing of the Castle
of Dowart, and for causing all the Country people lift up
their hands and swear to obey the Common wealth of England,
and generally for his open opposition to those in armes for his
Majesty's service in the Heighlands. By this all the Heighlanders will be encouraged to engage against him.

2. Some two or three blanck letters of encouragement to
severall heads of Clans, assuringe them that his Majesty will
deliver them from under those bonds and yoakes which Argyle
has purchased over their heads.

3. To represent how Argyle only has hindred all this
summer's service.

4. To desire a Commission from his Majesty for me, that I
may comand as L[ieutenant] Generall of his horse next to
Middleton, seeing I have engaged my fortune and all I have for
his Majesties service.

5. That Midleton's English freinds be made use of for obtein-
ing this against Argyle; and likewise for obviating Balcarres
calumnies against Middleton and me.

That this paper be only showen to Newburgh on whose
kindnes I do most rely.

To shew Newburgh that he obviate any credit to be given to
a paper Balcarres has purchased under the hands of severall
Heighlanders, which most of them has done out of weaknes, and
that no credit be given to any paper of that nature, or any
other at which Glengaries hand shall not be found.

That Glengaries Comission as Gen. Major may be sent.

That a warrand under the King's hand be sent dischargeing
all within Argyle or the Isles to pay in anie of the King's rents,
or few duties, or the Bishop's rents to Argyle, but that a
warrand be sent to me, to appoint some to lift them for his
Majesty's owne use to be sent to him.

To crave his Majesties advice for putting forth a declaracion,
and how prejudiciall it may be abroad if the Covenant shall be
much mentioned.

If John Malcolme have already gotten Glengaries patent, that
Newburgh comand him to deliver it to you, or if he be gon

with it, that Newburgh gett the King's hand to a double of it, that it may also come back by your means to me to be given to him.   GLENCAIRN.

Indorsed.—*Glengairnes instructions to Major Straghan.*[1]

CCXXXVII[2]

CHARLES II. to LORD BALCARRES.

My last to you was upon the occasyon of yours to the Earle of Diserte, concerninge Bampfeild,[3] by which you see my minde concerninge him, and though I have since that tyme receved your letter by Roger, I can add little to what I then sayd. You must believe that I am very unwillinge to deny you any thinge you aske of me with so much passyon, and in which you say many of my frends joyn with you: and therfore you may conclude when I do not gratify you, that I am swayed by such reason as is worthy to prævayle agaynst my inclination. The truth is, I know Bampfeilde to well to trust him, nor is it in my power to give creditt to him; nor is his presumpcion of goinge into that kingdome, under pretence of affection to my service, in any degree excusable, since he knew well enough that I would by no meanes imploy him in it, and I am too well assured, that what paynes soever he seemes to take, he hath ends very differente from yours, and is governed by those who never intende to serve me as they ought to do; in a worde I must conjure you to have nothinge to do with him, nor in the least degree to give him countenance, but to secure your selfe, and your other frends who have trusted him, by causinge my order formerly sent to be executed. Concerninge the makinge of Glengary Earle of Rosse, I do assure you I never made any such promise to him in my life, nor do I remember that ever any such thinge was proposed to me; I have a very good

---

[1] This paper is not dated, but was apparently written about the end of 1653, judging from the reference to Argyle's conduct at Dowart. Mr. Macray calendars it amongst the Clarendon Papers, ii. 290, as dated 1653, and addressed to Major R. Strachan.

[2] Clarendon Manuscripts, xlvii. 221. Undated.

[3] Oct. 2, 1653, intercepted, and to be found printed in the *Thurloe Papers*, i. 495.

opinion of his affection and ability to serve me, which I will not fayle in dew tyme liberally to rewarde, but it is by no meanes seasonable yett to mention such pattents, when ther are nether officers to draw them, nor to passe them; I doubt not but he will rely on me to do that for him which is fitt, and when it will be best for him and me, and when you have examined this busynesse, you shall finde that Bampfeild hath both putt this and the other humour into his heade (of not beinge commanded by Middleton in the Highlands); for as no man can imagyne that one man should have the commande in the Highlands, and another in the Lowlands, so it was one of the instructions that Capt. Smith had, who was sent from Glengary to me, to desyre that Middleton might be speedily sent thither to commande; and I am confident you believe that ther is no man in that kingdome willinge to engage himselfe for me, who will not be content to be commanded by him, and the discource of burninge Glengary house by him is without the least grounde, ther havinge never bene any such thinge; so that all this is the artifice of Bampfeilde, and you must make it your businesse to compose Glengary and all others to submitt to that authority which I appointe to conducte them, or else all ther affections will avayle me nothinge.

By this tyme I hope some armes are landed in the Highlands, and other assistance I doubte not will shortly be with them, and I will not promise you that I will not be ther my selfe: however I must conjure you by all your affection to me (which I can never doubte) not to give creditt to any in whome you know I have no confidence, and to dispose the mindes of all to union, and to submission to the commande of L^{nt} Generall Middleton: and I shall not neede to assure you that I will alwayes be very heartily, Your, etc.

Lord Balcarris.

I would have you by all meanes disswade your Unkle Dumfermiline from comminge to me, you know well how little I was beholdinge to him in Scotlande, and if he shall come hither, his entertainment cannot be such as will be acceptable to him; therfore, I pray, prevent his undertakinge such a journey, for his owne sake as well as myne.

CCXXXVIII

Charles II. to Glengarry.[1]

I have writt severall letters to you, which I hope are come safe to your handes, and another messenger hath brought that to me, which you intended should have come by Bampfeild, he knowinge too well the little creditt he has with me, to come with that letter himselfe. I do not wounder that you have beene misinformed in many particulars, when you have had so much reason to believe him who imposed likewise upon many other honest men who knew him better, but I assure you I never sent him into Scotlande, nor knew of his beinge ther till my Lord Balcarris sent me worde of it, and spake much good of him to me: so that whatever he hath sayd to you as from me hath bene purely of his owne makinge, and he well knowes, and knowes good reason for it, that I can never trust him, but am well assured that he is sent over by those who desyre to sow jealosyes amongst us frendes, and to disturbe that service which he pretends to advance. I suppose if my warrant I sent came safely into Scotlande for his apprehension, that he is secured from doinge any hurte, however you must looke upon him as a person who hath deceaved you, and whome I cannot repose any trust in, and proceede with him accordingly.

I perceave he hath (accordinge to his usuall custome of infusinge jealosyes into those whome he findes trusted in my service) wrought in you some prejudice towards Middleton, whome I had constituted Lt Generall before I heard from you, and a man I well knew would be most acceptable to all those who would really and heartily engage themselves in action, and your selfe by Capt. Smith desyred that he might speedily be sent over, and trust me he deserves very well from you, havinge a very good esteeme of you. He is laboringe effectually to procure armes and ammunicion for you, which I suppose he hath already in some proporcion sent over to you, and I hope he will be shortly ready to transporte himselfe with more con-

---

[1] Clarendon Manuscripts, xlvii. 223. Undated, but assigned by Mr. Macray to 1653.

siderable supplyes. In the meane tyme I neede not requyre
you to keepe all necessary correspondence with him, and to
comply heartily and cheerefully with that authority which I
have appointed to governe till his arryvall; for if ther grow
jealosy and dislike amongst those upon whose affection, fidelity,
and interest I depende, our enimyes will have an easy worke to
perfecte ther conquests; but I doubte not those mischieves will
be prevented by a joynt submissyon to what I derecte, and as
I have told you in my former letters, I shall not hold my selfe
more beholdinge to, nor oblieged to rewarde any man more,
then him who hath by readily obayinge as I directe, given
others an example of the same temper, without vehemently
pursuinge ther own pretences how reasonable soever. If God
blesse me in the recovery of what belonges to me, I shall have
it in my power, and in my will, to rewarde all who have borne
good partes in the worke.

My Lord Balcarris, who is very kinde to you, hath mooved
me in a particular conceminge you, but as I have no officers
aboute me to prepare and perfecte businesse of that nature, so
it would not be seasonable in many respects, but expose me to
many importunytyes of the same kinde, which I should not be
able to satisfy; therfore trust me, who cannot forgett the many
good services you have performed to my father and my selfe,
and which I will when it shall be in my power rewarde in such
a manner as shall please you. I have written such letters, and
sent such commissyons as you advise, and shall make good use
of the information you give conceminge the Islands. Middleton
will send you worde in what forwardnesse all provisyons are,
and it is very possible I may my selfe be with you sooner than
you expecte, and I wish you could by your intelligence in
Irelande draw over as many of the Nacion (who are leavyed and
transported into other Kingdomes) as is possible to your assistance, which would add much to your strength. Be of good
hearte, and continue your zeale and affection to your.

Glengary.

Indorsed.—*The Kinge to Glengary: in answer to what was
brought by Roger.*

APPENDIX

EXTRACTS AND LETTERS SELECTED FROM
NEWSPAPERS PUBLISHED DURING 1651
AND 1652.

I

MERCURIUS SCOTICUS:
Or a True Character of affairs in England, Scotland,
Ireland, and other Forraign Parts.[1]

Printed att Leith.

Collected for Publick Satisfaction: Beginning Tuesday,
July 22, to Wednesday, July 30, 1651.

As it is no less prudence to preserve then purchase; so is there no safety in any purchase without a right management of the same, The free People of England after the Lord of Hosts had in their Nation subdued the Royall party, and brought the Head thereof to Justice: Did become even setled in their Rights and Liberties, yet by a confederacy of our former friends in this Nation, or at least such as have been so pretended, not onely the price of our purchase, but the thing

---

[1] From the newspaper called *Mercurius Scoticus*, published at Leith from July 22 to Dec. 23, 1651. A copy of this rare periodical is in the Library of Worcester College. The extract here printed is the leading article with which the paper opens. There are in all twenty-one numbers of the paper. The English and foreign news it contains is usually copied from the English papers, and some of the Scottish news is extracted and reproduced in the English papers. A news-letter amongst Clarke's papers, dated Jan. 20, 165½, explains the sudden cessation of the paper: 'You must not expect any prints from Leith, for that the Commissioners have since their coming to Dalkeith, given order to suppress *Merc. Scoticus.*'

it self became Questionable, by such who had no interest in or to the same, and to whome was declared, That Peace onely was sought for upon just and safe Grounds, in respect there was otherwise no appearance of it; Those of this Nation having entertained into their Bosome our grand Enemy, under a formall pretence of Religion; the Lord well knowing the sincerity of our hearts, and that our entrance into this Nation was upon no other Score, did accordingly judge in the very first Encounter with them, and since in all our proceedings Lenity and Clemency from His Excellency having been extended far beyond any Merit of theirs. It's very observable how the Lord hath carried on his own work in this Nation by a despised handfull, against whole Armies, whereby the mighty have been led Captive, and the crafty ensnared in the snare he laid for others: The consideration of this, and likewise that as many Forreigne expectants eyes are upon our progress here, so our Army being desirous to be informed of passages in England and other parts, hath invited me to use my endeavour briefly to hint them, which I shall continue weekly if this my first borne in Scotland may receive but the warmth of incouragement.

II

A Letter from Col. Okey to the Lord President of the Council of State.[1]

My Lord,—I make bold to trouble you with a few lines to let your Lordship know, that after it had pleased God to give us Sterling town, I with Col. Berry, and two troops of Horse more, and two of Dragoons, marched to Glascoe and the West Country; being fully informed that some Lords [were] returning from the King with full Commission to raise in those parts 6000 Horse and Foot, and accordingly had their Commissioners sitting at Glasco and Paisly for levying of the said Forces, and having already some hundreds listed about, and drawing what they had together to a Randezvouse, we marched with all possible speed to prevent them.

---

[1] From *Several Proceedings in Parliament*, 21-28 Aug. 1651.

And upon the 11th instant set forward from hence, and marched to Glasco, Paisly, and Irwin, and sent out parties all over the Country round about; and through the goodnesse of God have so scoured the Country that we may now march with 100 horse from this place all over the West and South. We have totally broken all their levyes, and have taken some of their cheife Commissioners prisoners, as the Lord Orbiston and some others, and returned backe to this place with our Horse yesterday the 18th present.

A party of ours also, which I sent to Boghall, brought me 14 ministers prisoners, who were all met together in a Barne by a wood side 6 miles from Glasco, but were released again, being about a work that I hope will prove advantagious to us. It is thus: The General Assembly having silenced many of them, and forced them to preach both in publique and in private, they were there met together to seek the Lord, whether they should obey or disobey the Generall Assemblys order. And they assured us, as in the presence of the Lord, that they were about no other work: and that God had set it upon their hearts, that it was better to obey God then men, and so accounted their Generall Assembly a malignant usurped Authority, and ought not to be obeyed. And therefore they being set at liberty by us, they did on the last Lords day, in Glasco and other parts, preach publickly against that wicked authority. The Lord hath done great things for us in these parts, whereof we have great cause to be glad, and we are confident also he is doing great things for you in England. I should inlarge, but must now abruptly break off, the post staying for my Letters. I forbear to trouble you any further, save to tel you that I am, My Lord, your Lordships very humble Servant,

JOHN OKEY.

Sterling, 19 *Aug.* 1651.

III

EXTRACT from MERCURIUS SCOTICUS.

Wednesday [*Aug.* 20].

A MAN of War belonging to Col. Adkins of Leith called the Convert Friggat, Commanded by that Souldier, Capt. Peter

Escot, with nine Guns and 46 men, brought into that Harbour two Prizes, which the Captain about 15 dayes past had seized on (after some hot dispute) before Stextco in Cathnes, the one was a Dutch Pinke of 120 Tun, wherein was good store of Herrings and other fish, Tallow, Hides and Bief, the other Ship of 160 Tun laden with Haver Meale and Barly, in which were many intercepted Letters of consequence to Lord Jermin, Capt. Titus, and many others in Holland from Arguisle, Cleveland, and many more of that Faction. The dispute lasted near 3 houres. and one vessel there our men had sunck, worth as the enemy confesse 4 or 5000l, laden with Wine, Amunition, etc. The Passengers therein, seeing their Wooden Horse faile, exposed themselves to the mercy of the Waves, leaping overboard into the Sea, hoping to escape by swiming; but very few or none of them escaped. There was of the goods onely preserved Ten Hogsheads of wines, and the Fore-saile; the rest the Sea swallowed up in sight of our men. In the encounter the Captain was wounded, one Mr. Manley slain, who with Mr. Wells the Chirurgion and Lieuet. Bradshaw behaved themselves stoutly; the Enemy being about 500 High Landers with Muskets, Bowes and Arrows; of which number near 100 were slain on the place by the active and expert service of our Gunner M. Spring, and the rest of the Officers and Mariners. Also one great Lord (as the country stiled him) was slain by our Cannon. The Enemy had once five of ours prisoners, but by taking one Lords son they were immediatly exchanged, 12 more also of the Enemy were taken, and since exchanged. Captain Read an eminent Commander of theirs was brought in prisoner, the intercepted Letters most of them relating to him [and] what he should further verbally declare.

IV

A Proclamation against Moss-Troopers.[1]

By the Governour of Edinburgh, Leith, and Barwick.

Whereas divers lewd and wicked Persons, named Mos-

---

[1] From a broadside amongst William Clarke's collections.

Troopers, rove up and down the Country, Rob, spoile and Murther upon the High-way, all they can get power over, which could not be done except the said Persons had Protection, Countenance, and Assistance from the Inhabitants of the Country, who can no way be brought to discountenance these wicked Persons and their proceedings, except the evils committed by them be some way returned upon themselves. These are therefore to Declare and give notice, that wheresoever any Person shall be Robbed, or Murthered, by the foresaid Mos-Troopers, that the Inhabitants of that Parish where the Fact is done shall make satisfaction for what shall be plundered or taken away from the Person so Robbed (except they can bring forth the Robber); and if it shall happen that any Person be Murthered or Slain by the foresaid Persons, the Town or Parish wherein such Murther is committed, unless they apprehend and bring forth the Murtherer or Murtherers, shall pay for every person so slain or Murthered, one hundred pounds sterling, Ten Pounds of which shall be paid to whosoever shall discover the said Murther. And whosoever shall be known willingly to harbour and receive any of the aforesaid Mos-Troopers; or if they force themselves upon them, shall not give timely notice of their being there, to the Officer or Forces of the next Garrison, shall be punished by burning of their Houses, or some other severe punishment. And whereas there hath been and are still endeavours to raise new Leavies and Forces in severall Shires of this Countrey, I do hereby Declare, that whosoever shall excite or stir up the people to rise and take up Arms, shall have his, or their whole Estate sequestered, and he or they (if they can be apprehended) sent out of the Land. And such Inhabitants which shall upon the perswasion of any person or persons whatsoever rise or take up Arms to lengthen out the War, shall be taken for, and proceeded against as Enemies.

Given under my Hand and Seale at Leith, August 27, 1651.

This to be Proclaimed and Published.

G. FENWICK.

Printed at Leith, by Evan Tyler, *Anno Dom.* 1651.

V

A Letter from Colonel Alured.[1]

Honoured Sir,—It hath pleased the Lord to give a great mercy to us in the delivery up of a great many of the Leaders and chiefe of the Scotch forces into our hands. I (being commanded forth with a party of Horse and Dragoones) marched on a darke rainey night in rough and tedious way to a Towne neere the High-lands called Ellit, where wee had intelligence that most of the Scots Commanders lay; which we found to bee true, and have taken there these prisoners in this enclosed List nominated. Not above 2 of the most considerable men of the Committee of State are left, besides those who are here.[2] The rest of the Enemy were quartered at two little Townes within a mile, but my party, who were about 800, were so dispersed in getting such rich prizes, that I could not possible goe any further, but having such considerable prisoners thought it most convenient to march away with them; the Enemy were about 4000 who are all dispersed. Some of our party have gotten 500, 300, 200, 100li. a piece, and none of them but very well rewarded for their service. I desire the Lord to give us hearts to be thankfull to him for this and all other his mercies towards us; thus with my service to you, this is all at present from, Sir, your obliged Friend and Servant,

Math Alured.

From my Tent at the Leagure before Dundee
29 Aug. 1651.

VI

Letters from Major Scot and his Party at Drumlanerick of the 3 instant.[3]

Saturday last in our march toward Dunfreis with our Party of Horse, and Captain Battely with 60 Dragoons from Boghall,

---

[1] *Several Proceedings in Parliament,* Sept. 4-11, 1651.
[2] On the night of Wednesday, Aug. 27.—*Mercurius Scoticus.*
[3] From *Mercurius Scoticus,* Sept. 2-9, 1651.

we took severall of the Enemies Scouts prisoners: and understanding that 300 Foot, and some Horse Quartered in Dunfreis, we marcht thither, and about a mile short in the morning spied some of their Scouts; Major Scots Lieut. with a Party being sent out by the Major, made after them, they fled; in the interim the Major with his Party advanc'd towards the Town; upon a hill near it appeared a Party of 30 Horse, which upon Captain Waller with his Parties approach, fled, and he pursued; hereupon the Major marcht a Party into the Town, which was forsaken by the Bailiffs, Officers, and other Inhabitants, 300 of Col. Calheads Regiment being marcht forth the day before to Quarter, as we were informed, and that the last nights march was through all their Quarters, unknown to us before. There we took about 20 of the Enemy, and that night returned to Drumlanerick, where we had before left 30 Dragoons to secure a House appointed for Quarters. On Munday morning hearing of divers Rendezvouzes of the Enemy at severall places, many miles distant from each other, we heard of a party about 5 miles off at Maxilton, to which the Countrey were all coming in; we marcht towards them, and within two miles riding discovered their Scout. Hereupon the Majors Lieut. with a Party of forty Horse was sent before, who coming on a suddain upon their Body, which lay hid behinde the turning of a hill, made a stand till all his Party was come up. The Enemy advanced upon him, which he seeing, resolutely charged them. The Enemy also charged desperately, but our Body fast approaching towards him, the Enemy fled, and were pursued 7 miles; about 15 of them were slain, many wounded, and divers of them taken prisoners, a List whereof is inclosed, as also of those of quality that escaped. Their Body consisted of about 250. 100 Foot of the Lord Johnstons were on this side Dunfreis on their march towards them, which (it is hoped) are likewise disperst; also the Countrey were coming in apace, and 40 of Calheads Foot were within half a mile when these Horse were routed, and appointed to make good a Bridge near adjoyning against us, which had they done we could not have come at them. These Foot we also pursued: some were slain, and the rest took woods and Bogs, flinging away their Armes. In this service 10 or 12 of our men were wounded; its feared three or four of them will not live, Here hath been a generall Command to the whole Countrey to rise, upon the approach of any of our Forces. But wee have declared wee shall protect those that live quietly at their homes from any violence, but give no quarter to any Countrey-Man taken in Armes.

A List of Prisoners taken at Dunfreis.

John Maxwell, Senior,
John Maxwell, Junior, } Gent.
Robert Maxwell,
John Johnston of Dunfreis.
Robert Maxwell of Corndellar.
Francis Evans of Dunfreis.
John Dalrumple of Waterside. William Suthinton.
John Vaugh of Leistenston. John Earn of Aunan.
John Murren of Holywood. William Hood.

Taken at the Engagement.

Col. Kilhead of Douglas.
Lieu. Col. Joh. Hamilton.
Capt. John Douglas.
Capt. John Reame.
„ William Ferguson.
} Officers.
Quarter-Master Charters.
Sir John Dalzell, Knight.
Geo. Douglas, L. Johnstons, Secr.
George Gardner.
William Thomson.
Robert Cuninghame.
George Kauheir.
George Hamilton.
Hugh Kennedie.
John Gilkrist.
Alexander Wallace.
Adam Samson.
James Riddall.
Thomas Andrewes.
One more was exchanged.

Eminent Persons [at] this Engagement that escaped.

Earle of Galloway.
Lord Johnston, Son and Heir to Lord Harris.
The Sheriff.
Captain Ferguson of Crackdorough.
Col. Massell.
Col. Emson.

VII

PROCLAMATION against INTERCOURSE with the GARRISON of the BASS.[1]

By the Governour of Edinburgh, Leith, and Berwick.

WHEREAS I am informed That divers persons, both on the

---

[1] *Mercurius Scoticus*, Sept. 23-30, 1650.

South and North side of the Firth, do aswel receive the Boats of the Bass coming from thence, and supply them with necessaries, and also send in Boats with Provisions to the same: These are therefore to give notice to all persons whatsoever, That who ever from henceforth shall hold any correspondencie with any in the Bass, or entertain any Company from thence, or afford them any provision, or hold any other correspondencie with them whatsoever, shall forfeit all their goods, and be tryed at a Court Martiall for their lives, as Correspondents with the Enemy.

Given under my hand and seal at Leith, Sept. 6, 1651.

G. FENWICK.

This to be proclaimed in the severall Towns on both sides of the Firth, by beat of Drum.

VIII

MR. WILLIAM CLARKE to the SPEAKER of the PARLIAMENT.[1]

For the Honourable WILLIAM LENTHAL, Esq., Speaker to the Right Honourable the Parliament of England.

RIGHT HONOURABLE,—Since the taking of Dundee, there came hither a trumpeter from Aberdeen for a list of the prisoners lately taken at Ellit; but the birds were caged and gone (though not flown), so that thereupon the enemy, fearing they should fall into the same condition, quitted Aberdeen.

Two Souldiers of Col. Berries Regiment were sent back for murdering a Countryman. There have some considerable persons dyed at Leith (where the spotted feavour is something rife), and amongst the rest Col. Hubbard, one of your Commissioners, and Sir John Brown, who was prisoner there.

It hath pleased God to visit Lieutenant Generall Monk with a very desperate sickness since the taking of this town, but now wee hope hee is in a very good way of recovery. He is a very precious instrument, and the most properly fitted for management of affairs here. His temper every way fits him for this imployment, and none could order the Scots so hand-

---

[1] *Several Proceedings in Parliament*, Sept. 18-25, 1651.

somely as himself, he carries things with such a grace and rigid gentlenesse.

On Monday last we had Letters of the routing of the Scots Army about Worcester, which was made knowne to the Country by the shouts and vollies of the souldiers at the line, about eight of the clock at night, and the shot of the Canon both from the Town and ships. The Gentlemen of Fife have sent in Commissioners to the Lieutenant Generall, by whom they have represented some things in order to their submission to the Government of the Commonwealth of England, and now their Army hath had such ill successe in England, it is probable others will follow. The Inhabitants of this Town have petitioned the Lieutenant General for protection for the use of their Trade, etc. The horse which went hence on Tuesday last towards Aberdeen, under Col. Overton and Col. Okey, were gallantly entertained by the magistrates of that place, who provided a banquet for them; and since that they are marched above twenty miles beyond Aberdeen Northwards.— Sir, I am your most humble servant,   WILLIAM CLERK.

Saturday, Dundee, the 11 of Septemb. 1651.

IX

A Proclamation by Major-General Monk.[1]

WHEREAS I am informed, That divers Sutlers and others have gotten possession of the Shops, Cellars, and Ware houses of divers Inhabitants of this Town, and refuse to quit them upon the desire of the Inhabitants, whereby they are deprived of the exercise of their severall Trades and Professions: I do hereby require all Sutlers, Souldiers, and others belonging to the Army, that they do remove their Wine, Beer, and other Goods and Commodities from the Shops or Ware houses belonging to the Inhabitants, within 24 hours after publication hereof, and not to stay in them after that time, without giving satisfaction to the owners, as they will answer the contrary at their perils, any Order or particular Warrant from my self to the contrary hereof notwithstanding.

Given under my hand at Dundee, the 15 day of September 1651.   GEORGE MONKE.

---

[1] From *Mercurius Scoticus*, Sept. 16-23, 1651.

X

A Proclamation against Plundering by Major-General Monk.[1]

Whereas I am informed, That divers Souldiers do still continue to plunder and take away the goods of the Inhabitants and Indwellers in this Town, notwithstanding my former Proclamations to the contrary: These are therefore strictly to charge and require all Officers and Souldiers under my command, That they do forbear to seize or take away any of the Goods belonging to the Inhabitants; but to permit them to enjoy their Estates free from plundering, and to pass about their severall Trades or Imployments, as formerly. Neither are they to presume to affright or disturb the People in their cutting down, or fetching in their Corn; Neither take away any Beives, Sheep, Butter, Cheese, Hens, or other Goods or Provisions from the said Inhabitants, or force them to serve with their Persons and Horses, Carts, or otherwise, upon any pretence whatsoever, without Order.

And I do hereby further require all Officers and Souldiers whatsoever, to permit the People of the Countrey hereabouts to receive in their Corn, as also to repair to this Town with their Horses, Cattell, Provisions, and Commodities, to supply the Markets, as heretofore, without disturbance or molestation. And whosoever shall notwithstanding willfully transgresse herein, shall be forthwith proceeded against at a Court Martial, and receive the sharpest censure and severest punishments which are provided in the Lawes and Articles of Warre.

Given under my hand at Dundee the 15 day of September 1651.   George Monke.

XI

Mr. William Clarke to the Speaker.[2]

To the Right Honourable Wil. Lenthall, Esq., Speaker of the Parliament of England.

Mr. Speaker,—The last march of Col. Okey with his own

---

[1] *Mercurius Scoticus*, Sept. 19, 1651.
[2] *Several Proceedings in Parliament*, Oct. 2-9, 1651.

Regiment and some other horse to Aberdeen, produced little more effect then a meere survey of those parts, and the punishing of some Offenders, who had done injury to the Country, viz., a Scotchman, and a Trooper of Col. Grosvenors Regiment, who extorted mony from the Country, under the notion of being Augustines men, but being apprehended by the Country, were both handsomly whipped at the Market place at Aberdeen, which exemplary justice gave much satisfaction to the Inhabitants.

A Scotch man of War, which fled into Aberdeen for succor, being required to be yeelded up by our ships, those of Aberdeen sent word, they would neither protect them, nor deliver them up; but if they pleased they might come and take her. Whereupon some of our men were sent to seize the Vessell, which they did, but the men fled out of her. She had six peece of Ordnance, store of Wares, and other good commodities. We have intelligence that Marquesse Huntley is marched with his Forces, being about 600 horse, and 1000 Foot, towards Lough Tay in the High-lands, most of his men are much harassed, and but raw Souldiers. The Lord Belcarris upon the comming of our horse towards Aberdeen went toward Longhead where the present Committee sits; he hath about 250 Horse. A Randesvouze is intended on the third of Octob. next, when the whole Country is to come in, under pain of Rebellion, and to be proceeded against as publique Enemies.

The Marquesse of Arguile is expected to be at that Randesvouze with 4000 Foote, which he will hardly get together (though he indeavour it) having some few days agoe not above 300 men. However it were good the Forces intended were speeded hither. Marquesse Huntley hath vowed to plunder and fire Aberdeen, which they are affraid of, so that its probable they must now be beholding to us for protection.

The greatest part of our Horse are quartered about Montrosse, Fairfar, Brachin, and the parts between this and Aberdeen, in order to observe the enemies motion.

In regard none of the Scots Army who were defeated neare Worcester are come into those parts, they will not be perswaded here but that their King hath a great Army. They say when Hamilton was routed in Lancashire they had notice

of it by several partics that got away. Nay we hear, that on Friday last, at Glasco and Dunbarton they made Bonefires for the good successe of their Forces in England; so apt they are to beleeve lying vanities. In our march we had a view of Dum Otyr Castle, which is the strongest place we have yet been befor in Scotland (being seated upon an inaccessible Rock); the Royal Crowne of Scotland is said to be in it. The Lieu. Gen. intends to make some attempt speedily upon it.— Sir, I am your most humble Servant, W. CLERK.
Dundee, 25 *Septem.* 1651.

XII

EXTRACT from MERCURIUS SCOTICUS, Tuesday (Sept. 30).

THIS day the Protesting Ministers of Scotland, and those that adhered to it, met at Edinburgh, and (as is supposed) intend to enter upon no Publick Businesse till the next Week, and to spend the remainder of this Week in Supplication and Fasting to the Lord, every man in particular laying out his own guiltiness, in relation as wel to the Publick as his own private interest (Mr. James Durhame being the first man), that they may be able to read his will in all his dispensations towards this Land; and the next Week to proceed upon business of the Assembly (as is supposed) and other Publick business, in order to the deportment of the People in the midst of these troublous times. The Lord will prosper their proceedings if from a right ground, and that they intend the promoting onely his glory, and cementing the wide breaches of his People in this Land.

Present at this Meeting.

Above 62 Ministers already, and the rest dayly coming in: Mr. John Levingston, Minister of Barketh, is appointed Moderator.

This day also Capt. Hughes, Capt. Knowles, Capt. Newman, Capt. Miller, Capt. Langley, and the rest of the Captains of Leith Garrison, appointed as a Committee for determining differences, and releasing Prisoners, whose wants, wounds, or sickness required present redress, upon Engagements, met at Edinburgh; where after full examination of wounded and sick prisoners in the Tolbooth, taken in severall Fights, they thought fit upon due consideration of their miserable conditions, to enlarge these who are mentioned in the List following. Surely these wondrous Acts of Christian Love and Mercy must needs win upon a People, were they far more stupid then these are reported to be.

XIII

A Proclamation against Enforced Oaths by Major-General Monk.[1]

Whereas I am informed that divers persons within this Nation have of late gone about to ensnare men's consciences, by inforsing Oathes and Covenants upon them: these are therefore to let all know, that what person soever shall tender any Oath or Covenant, unto any person or persons whatsoever; or whoever shall take or enter any Oath or Covenant without Order from the Commonwealth of England, both the tenderer and the taker shal be holden as enemies to the Commonwealth aforesaid, as he will answer the contrary at his perill. Given under my Hand this 6 of Octob. 1651. George Monke.

To the Provost of Aberdeen.

XIV

The Submission of the Gentlemen of Fife.[2]

Wednesday (Oct. 8).

The chief Gentlemen of the Shire of Fife, and towns adjoyning, having experience of the Noblenesse and sweet carriage of Col. Syler, Governour of Bruntiland, and clearly out of a desire to serve him and the publick in what they may, were pleased to send this ensuing letter, directed to the Honorable Col. Syler, Governour of Bruntiland. By this Copy of the Letter you may perceive the willingnesse of all ingenious men under the English power to comply with the English interest.

---

[1] *Several Proceedings in Parliament*, Oct. 16-23, 1651.

[2] From *Mercurius Scoticus*, Oct. 8, 1651, also to be found in *Several Proceedings in Parliament*, Oct. 16-23, 1651.

Honoured Sir,—The under-subscribing within the severall Parishes of their Locality, taking notice of the singular care and discretion by you expressed in all your Deportments, both in relation to the Government of the Souldiery, in preventing abuses that might arise from thence, as in the regular distribution of the Assessments; wherein also is observable your Christian compassion, in pittying the sad distresses of these Parts, both by former and present Cautions, and your inclinations to past remedies. The sense whereof, as it should, so hath it provoked this present addresse, for expressing our thankfulnesse therefore, and earnest intreaty for a further improvement of the same; as also for evidencing our willingnesse and desirousnesse to entertain and setle with you a further measure of correspondence, as may induce a righteous agreement towards a happy and setled Peace, whereof (we hope) our present peaceable residing at home, and readinesse to answer your Assessments, notwithstanding our impoverishments, may be unto you probable evidences. Sir, if any other thing be requisite from us for the present, for testifying our desire to Peace, and aversnesse for the continuance of so unhappy a War, We shall humbly desire to be informed by you thereanent, and of the circumstances of a right Addresse, as how, when, and to whom; wherein if hitherto we have failed, it shall not proceed from any Malignity or evill affection in us, but mens ignorance. We conceive, as the protection from the violence of War relateth to the Chief Commanders and Governours of the place, so Matters belonging to Peace, and transactions thereabouts, hath their proper power and judges, with whom we are not as yet acquainted; and Cooper Presbyteries [commission], at least a great many thereof, by one Master John Hay, to treat for the regulating and moderating the Assessments, to which our consent being required, was refused for severall very reasonable considerations; which we shall beg leave to trouble you with, for your better information, that, if being satisfied therewith your self, you may be pleased to interpose your sense thereanent, for preventing such mistakes as may arise from bad suggestions. Thereupon we hope, Sir, ye will not think it necessary for us to joyn with them upon the Accompts of Assessments, being one distinct

Locality, having closed with your self thereabout, long before their appearing in any such businesse, and which this course could onely but unsetle us, and unequally prejudice us. Neither did we understand, nor were we anything satisfied with that latitude of power forced in in his commission,[1] Freedom, and Peace of our Shire, as being too vast a burden and trust for one single Gentleman to bear, especially having so litle share thereof himself for the present (if the Lawes of our Church and Estate have any respect with you, wherof we dare not yet doubt), neither proper for us to transmit, as being a part of the publicke Inheritance and interest of the Kingdome. Sir, we desire not, far lesse delight we to reflect upon any mans person; but if we must be put to it, to abate indirect means for our Peace, contrary to our judgements and Consciences, we hope and expect ye will not onely allow of these Reasons, and justifie us therein your self, but also interpone your advice with the Honourable Lieut. Generall, Governour of Leith, and remanents Commanders, and in our names give them assurance, that as we are also affectionate to a happy Peace and righteous agreement, as any within this Nation, so shall we be ready to evidence the same by all our future deportments, and on all occasions and seasons which shall call for a testimony from us thereupon, who are Your very humble servants,

     Ch. Arnet. J. Halkett.
     J. Alexander. J. Kytoun of Inderarie.[2]
     H. Wadlaw. J. Malcolme.
     Robert Sped. A. Moncreif.
     Alex. Spittel. W. Orrock.
     Mr. Will. Ged. R. Carliff.
     Robert Logan.

From Auchterdurham, Oct. 6, 1651.

XV.

A News Letter from Leith.[3]

Sir,—These are to informe you of the state of things in

---

[1] The newspaper reads 'condition.' In the next sentence some words are evidently omitted.

[2] 'Slygtoun' is the name given in *Several Proceedings in Parliament.*

[3] *Several Proceedings in Parliament*, Oct. 16-23, 1651.

these parts. Col. Okey with three Regiments of Horse, and five Troops of Dragoons quartered in the County of Angus, and some parts of the shire of Mernes; that is to say, we quartered as followeth: Col. Alureds Regiment in Monrosse, with three Troops of Dragoons; Col. Grosveners at Brechin, and severall places thereabouts; and Col. Okeys owne Regiment at Farfar, and two troops of Dragoons. And by reason it lay farre from the Foot, and neare unto the High-lands where the enemy were, we were not only forced to lye thick (which was a great burthen and charge to the Country), but faine to be upon very great duty, every man having his Horse sadled all night, besides those that were upon the Guard; which was very cheerfully done by the Souldiery, though it was very much wasting both to horse and man. The Gentlemen of the Country, understanding that we intended to quarter there all the Winter (which would very much exhaust them, and drive the Country into a desperate condition, by reason that there would be little left before the Spring either for man or beast), thereupon they drew up severall Petitions to the Lieut. Generall and the rest of the Colonells that quartered there, and did promise, that upon our remove they would not only come in themselves, but also endeavour to bring in those that were enemies unto us. Whereupon Col. Okey, Col. Grosvenour, and Col. Alured went over to L. Gen. Monke, and after a serious debate it was thought fit to march away with two Regiments of Horse, and five troops of Dragoons. So the day before we marched, Col. Okey summoned in the Gentry of the Country to meet at Brechin, five miles from Monrosse, and there met him a very considerable company of Lords and Gentlemen, insomuch that not any one house in the Towne would hold them, so they went into the Church, by reason of the numbers; there met them Col. Okey and Col. Allured. It is too long to insist upon the discourse, I shall only give you the heads of the particulars. So, when they were met together, Col. Okey told them this: that it was not unknown to most of them why we were commanded into these parts, which was to suppresse their severall insurrections, which were daily amongst them, and that the burthen they complained of, they might thank themselves for it (which they did acknowledge was just upon them), and that so long as they continued in that kind of way we could not remove our Forces conveniently from them ; but concerning their Petition, the Lieu. Gen. with the rest of the Colonels had taken it into their serious consideration, and had considered of the burthen that had lain heavy upon them, and that they and all the world might see that we did not delight in oppressing any, further then necessity drives us unto, we were to let them know, that upon their promise to live quietly at home, we would remove two Regiments of Horse and the five Troops of Dragoons; which they tooke as a most acceptable thing, and did ingage, as in the presence of the Lord, not to engage any more against the Common wealth of England. So Col. Okey said, 'Now, Gentlemen, as we have declared what we intend to doe, and what Force we intend to leave, and what we intend to take away, we must also tell you plainly, and what you will assuredly find, that if upon our marching off, it shal give any incouragement to you that are lately come home, and has our protection, or shall incourage any of them that are yet in Arms and not come in, we shall by the assistance of God return with treble the forces we take from you, and if ruine come upon you, thank your selves ; ' and they all as one man (if they did any such thing) desired that the Lord might be as a swift witnesse against them. So next day we marched towards Sterling; and one Cornet Car, a Cornet in Col. Okeys Regiment, being at Dundee with eleven more about businesse, and comming toward the Regiment, met with some Mosse Troopers, by whom they were engaged, who promised seven of them faire quarter, but after it was given them, killed them upon cold blood, so that the Cornet with foure more onely escaped their hands, hee having with that small party charged them twice through and through ; we are endeavouring to find out those who were actors in it. And now, Sir, whatsoever our friends in England may think, that the things that are done here are but small, were they but here as we are, and see how populous they are, and what forces they might have raised against us, had not God struck a feare and terrour among them, and mightily appeared for us, wee could not expect to have seen that which we have seen. The Lord give us and you humble hearts to walke humbly before him, and in some measure answerable for his great goodnesse to you in England, and us in Scotland.

Leith, Octob. 11, 1651.

XVI

THE MARQUESS of ARGYLE to MAJOR-GEN. MONK.[1]

The Marquesse of Arguiles Letter.

SIR,—I know the truth of Solomon's saying (that in the multitude of words there wants not sinne), therefore in that I will not transgresse; but as I beleeve all Christians in every businesse do propose a good end (or at least ought to do), so should they resolve upon just and righteous wayes to attain it. (I judge no man), yet I desire to know from you, as one having cheife trust in this Kingdome; if it were not fit that some men who have deserved Trust in both Kingdomes may not (meet to good purpose) in some convenient place, as a meanes to stop the shedding of more Christian blood? which hath a loud cry in the Lords eares against the unjust authors or contrivers of it. I shall say no more untill I hear from you, but that I am, Sir, Your most humble Servant,   ARGUILE.

The 15 *of Octob.* 1651.
For Lieu.-Gen. Monk, these.

XVII

EXTRACTS from 'MERCURIUS SCOTICUS.'

Thursday [*Oct.* 16].

THIS day at a Court Martiall at Leith it was Ordered that Andrew Bennet, Master of a Boat belonging to the Ferry neer Ely (for that it appeared he was commanded in, and forced to submit to some of the Enemy in the Boat belonging to Bass Island), shall have his Boat and Goods restored; but for his carrying of Souldiers without a Pass, shall forfeit twenty shillings sterling, to be paid to Captain Roleston, to be by him distributed amongst his Souldiers that took them.

---

[1] From *Several Proceedings in Parliament*, Oct. 30-Nov. 6; also printed in *Mercurius Scoticus*, Oct. 21-28 p. 108. See No. xviii.

It was also Ordered That no Souldier of the Regiment of Col. Geo. Fenwick, Governour of Edinburgh, Leith, and Barwick, shall presume to be married to any Woman of or in Scotland, without consent of the Governour, Deputy-Governour, or Major of the same Regiment, in that case first had and obtained in writing, upon pain of being casheered the Regiment; and the Minister that shall marry them to answer it at a Court Martiall.

[*Wednesday, Oct. 22.*]

This day also a Summons issued from the Honourable the Deputy-Governour of Leith, for surrender of Bass Island, thus:—

SIR,—I Desire you upon sight hereof, to deliver into the possession of Captain Roleston, The Bass Island, with all the Forts, Fortifications, Ordnance, Arms, Ammunition, Provisions, Magazens, and Stores therein, for the use of the Parliament of England, to avoid the effusion of bloud, or destruction, which may otherwise happen. This if you shall think fit to embrace, you will render your self sensible of your own good, and you (with the Forces with you) shall receive such Conditions as shall be fit for you to accept, and me to grant: I am, Your servant, TIMO. WILKS.

Leith, Octob. 22, 1651.
To the Chief Commander of Bass Island, these.

Thursday [*Oct. 23*].

A Party of Horse that were Ordered forth with Commissioner Desbrough for apprehending the Wife and Brothers of the Governour of the Bass Island (for relieving him with all Necessaries), brought the said Parties prisoners to Leith Garrison, whence they are to be shipt away by the first conveniencie, except the Governour of the Island shall upon notice thereof seek reasonable terms, and apply himself timely for their remedy.

[*Saturday, Oct. 25.*]

This day also, the Lady, and two Brothers of the Governour of the Bass Island, were by Order of the Deputy Governor sent aboard the Admirall, to be disposed of there till further Order. Likewise their Father and they are to be sent to London, and their Estates sequestred, unlesse the Bass shall be suddenly rendred. In Order to which the Lady hath wrote a Letter to her Husband, with pregnant Arguments (as all Places in these parts have found favour by rendition, and shee being great with Childe, together with other miseries which else may befall him and them) importuning him to yeeld it; the return is not yet come; but without doubt he (if considerate and ingenious) will not stand out.

XVIII

Mr. William Clarke to the Speaker.[1]

For the Right Honourable William Lenthal, Esq., Speaker of the Parliament of England.

Mr. Clerks Letter.

Sir,—On the Lords day last, there came a Trumpeter from the Marquesse of Arguile, with the inclosed Letter to the Lieu. Gen., to which the Lieu. Gen. returned answer, that he could admit of no such Treaty (as was desired) without order from the Parliament of England. At the time of the date of the Letter the Marquesse was at his house in Anderraran, about 16 miles from Dunbarton, in the Highlands. We understand he cannot get either Burgesse or Country man to joyn with him, which makes himselfe tender a complyance. Marquesse Huntley and the Lord Belcarris range up and down the Country, and only leavy mony to buy Horses, which they keep in their hands, but we hear not of any Horses bought. Old John Leshley, late Governor of Brunt-Island, whom some call Wooden Sword, others Omnipotent John, lyes close in Murrayland, where he hath the allowance of 16s. per diem as reformado Maj. Gen. There is a considerable person among the Highlanders come in to the Lieut. Gen., by whom we expect good service. The last week Captain Cresset took a Spy at Arbroath, who came from the Lord Forbs at Innernesse.

---

[1] *Several Proceedings in Parliament*, Oct. 30-Nov. 6. 1651.

The Governor of Dunbarton Castle, since the removall of our Horse from those parts, oppresses the Country much for Contribution, and sends out his Foot for 12 miles together to fetch in Horses and goods, which he keepes till they pay mony. The cheife Commander under him in the Castle is one Col. Sterling; there is also Lieu. Gen. Craford, and about 100 men. The meeting of the Ministers at Edenburgh is dissolved; there were about 66 of them in all. After they had made a kind of confession, the substance whereof you have in the inclosed, they dissolved, and sent some to Glasco, where its said they intend a Provinciall meeting in a judiciall way, and will emit some Declaration or warning. They are much troubled they cannot have that power in civill things, *in ordine ad spiritualia*, which they were wont to have in this Nation, under which pretence they got in all civill power whatsoever. The 4 Companies and a halfe of Col. Cobbets Regiment which landed last week at Brunt Island came to Dundee on Munday last, but were sent back to quarter at St. Andrewes till the rest came up. Sir, I have no more at present, but remaine Your most humble Servant, WILL. CLERKE.

Dundee, 23 Octob. 1651.

XIX

A PROCLAMATION by LIEUT.-GEN. MONK.[1]

Munday, [*Nov.* 3].

Came a Proclamation issued from Lieut. Gen. Monke thus:

ALL Persons whatsover, which inhabite within this Garrison, are strictly required to deliver in to the Capt. of the Watch an exact List of the Names of all such Strangers who lodge in their Houses, and if any of the said Inhabitants shall neglect the same, they shall for every such offence forfeit 20 shillings, and five shillings to the Discoverer.

Given under my hand the 27 of Octob. 1651.

To be published by beat of Drum. GEORGE MONKE.

---

[1] *Mercurius Scoticus*, Nov. 3, 1651. The garrison referred to is Dundee.

XX

A Letter from Lieut.-Gen. Monk.[1]

From Lieut. Generall Monk at Dundee, October 31.

There's no news of the young Lad's being here in Scotland; it is confidently reported by the Scotch people that he is either in Holland or France, which I verily think he is. Some of the peoples hearts are much heightened in hopes, though I know no reason they have for it, unlesse it be for their own ruine in case he should attempt again; but I believe he is more wise then so. Argyle hath summoned a Parliament; for what end 'tis not yet known; the people generally are desirous of a settlement, and in order to which have drawn up some petitions in readinesse to be presented to the Commissioners which are to come down, who I wish they were. There landed here the 28 of this instant two hundred recruits of the foure hundred which were sent out of Colonell Barksteads regiment. I intend shortly to place a garrison at Aberdeen, and to send Coll. Overton thither. I intend when more horse are come out of England to place a garrison about Innernesse. The lamenesse in my knees doth yet continue, but I hope it will shortly be away.

XXI

Extract from 'Mercurius Scoticus.'

Tuesday [*Oct.* 28].

By Letters from Dundee, 26 Oct. 1651, thus:—The Highlanders under Marquesse Huntley and Lord Balcarras, now beginning to despair of any prosperous successe or action upon the English (having habituated themselves to the evill custome of Plundering and Robbery), are now betaking themselves to the High-wayes to play the Tories and Robbers; acting their designes (for want of practice) even upon their own Countreymen; insomuch that indeed none can pass through the North or High-lands with safety, as appears in some of their late carriages, one in falling upon some Houshold stuff, Plate, and

---

[1] *Mercurius Politicus*, Nov. 6-13, 1651.

Goods belonging to the Lord Calendar, with his son, Sir Alex. Livingstoun, and some other Gentlemen, who were conducting it through the High-lands, to carry beyond Murray; and the Goods thus seized on by these desperate High-landers were all taken away, the Gentlemen stripped, and the said Sir Alexander hurt. The Marquesse may do well to make his own peace in time, lest his partaking with such Robbers render him in short time unpardonable.

XXII

Some Heads of what hath been concluded touching an Agreement of a Treaty to be between the Marquesse of Arguile and the Commissioners from Lieutenant General Monke.[1]

1. THAT a meeting be condiscended to of admitting the Marquesse of Argyle to treat with such Officers as shal be appointed for that purpose.

2. That the said Marquesse of Argyle be admitted to come with a passe to St. Johnstones.

3. That he be permitted to come with his Servants, and his and their Horses and Armes (his Servants not exceeding the number of 30) to protect him in the way to St. Johnstones from the violence of his enemies in Scotland. That so his person may passe in safety to St. Johnstones, there to treat with the Officers appointed for that purpose.

4. That Lieutenant-Colonell Brayne and Major Pierson bee appointed to Treate with the said Marquesse of Argyle at St. Johnstones.

5. That the said Treaty of the Marquesse of Argyle with the aforesaid Colonell Brayne and Major Pierson be in order to the comming in of the said Marquesse of Argyle, to submit to the Authority of the Parliament of England.

6. That the day whereon the said Marquesse of Argyle is to meet with the said Commissioners be on Wednesday the 19 of this instant Novemb. 1651.

7. That the said Marquesse of Argyle doe take speciall care to prevent the pretended Parliament by him called to sit at Kickillum, which hee is to use his uttermost endeavours to prevent.

---

[1] *Several Proceedings in Parliament*, Nov. 13-20.

8. That the said Marquesse of Argyle doe not meet with any persons at Kickillum, that were intended to have met in any Assembly there, to sit with them in his owne person.

XXIII

EXTRACT from 'MERCURIUS SCOTICUS.'

From Dundee, Novemb. 14.

SINCE the last we understand that the Marquess of Huntly is come to live privatly at his house of Canygeles upon the Pass sent him. I forgot to acquaint you in the last that one Proposall in his Letter for his coming in was: that the Lieut. Gen. would put him in possession of such Lands as were kept from him by the Marquesse of Argyle; so much are they at ods, notwithstanding they are neer kinsmen. There is come in with Huntly others of quality. The Earle of Calendar is come to his house in Dagettee in Fife. You have had of late an accompt of our condition here by severall hands, and a serious Advice to the States of England to free the poor Commoners, and to make as litle use as can be either of the Great Men or Clergy. The counsell was good, and therefore I shall give another stroke to the fastning of it; as to the keeping out not only the Clergy, but also the Kirk Party here, for having any hand in government. We have had many visible and reall services of late performed by some Gentlemen, whom they call Malignants, who (I believe) most free to serve the English Interest; at which the Clergy are much inraged, and have exceedingly railed against us and them in their Pulpits, against them as Malignants and us as Invaders, and (as they have told some of us) favourers of them. They (like the Dog in the Manger) will neither eat themselves, nor let the Horse eat, so inraged are they that any should tender any service to the Commonwealth before them, and so loath are they to part with their power and preheminence. It were good some of them were removed, or (at least) that a stipend were allowed to some able Preachers from England to preach at Edinburgh, Glasgow, S. Johnston, Dundee, and Aberdeen, and one or more considerable Townes in this Nation; which might convince the People to draw them off from the leaven of their Pharisaical and rigid Presbyterian Teachers, who (even as others of their tribe) are in severall parties fighting for a Bone, which neither of them are like to have.

Col. Fitches Regiment came to this Town yesterday, and are this day to march towards Aberdeen, and so for Innernesse. Col. Augustine was lately at Innernesse with two Troops of Horse, and having the first time exacted Money from the Town they rose upon him. The next time he came they killed and wounded divers of his Troop, whereupon he threatens to burn the Town; but now our Foot are come up our next work will be to garrison that Town, for which purpose Col. Fitches Regiment will be appointed.

I should have acquainted you before, that one reason of Marquesse Huntlies coming in, was; for that having a Meeting the last week at Torrie, 16 miles from Aberdeen, with the Generall of those parts, desiring them to quarter his Forces, that they might be ready to rise with them upon any Action; but they denied, and resolved to come in to the protection of the Commander in chief of those English Forces as shall come in to those parts. The Laird Forbes, the late Provost of Innernesse, is lately come in. The Counties hereabout have chosen Commissioners to meet at Edinburgh the 21 instant.

XXIV

Articles agreed on with the Marquess of Huntley.[1]

The Capitulation in Scotland.

1. I do agree, that the Lord Marquesse of Huntley, with the rest adhering to this capitulation, shal be protected in their persons and estates.

2. That none of their houses shall be Garrisoned, or infested with any of our Souldiers, except upon unavoydable necessity, and that no Officer or Gentleman belonging to the said Marquesse, or adhering to his Lordship herein, shal be denyed to

---

[1] *Several Proceedings in Parliament*, Dec. 11-18, 1651.

travell with offensive or defensive arms in order to their personal protection and safety.

3. I doe ingage to see all conditions made good to the Lord Marquesse, and all other Lords and Gentlemen in this capitulation, which have of late been granted to the Earle of Athol, or any other Nobleman or Gentleman in the like condition, or shall hereafter be granted to any others.

4. I shall give my owne, or indeavour to procure passes from any of our party, with safe-conduct to such Gentlemen or others as desire to go beyond Seas in pursuance of their particular occasions or personal imployments.

5. For the confirmation of the premises, I do expect the disbanding of all forces under his Lordship or their respective command within six dayes. Given under my hand at old Aberden, Novemb. 21, 1651. R. OVERTON.

According to the above-mentioned capitulation, and for the full and finall effectuating thereof, I do hereby ingage, with the rest of the Noblemen and Gentlemen of that party, within six days to disband and reduce all the forces, both Horse and foot, under any of our commands. Witnesse our hands and seales, 21 Novemb. 1651.

XXV

EXTRACTS from 'MERCURIUS SCOTICUS.'

Tuesday.—From Dundee, 17 instant.

SIR,—Since my last the Lord Balcarras hath come in to the protection of the Lieutenant Generall. We have nothing from Aberdeen; but the safe coming of the two Regiments of Foot under Col. Overton thither. In the way about Bourny, within 12 miles of Aberdeen, they left some proportion of Ammunition behinde, for want of horse; but the Town engaged either to send it the next day, else to pay 150 pounds sterling; and carrying it towards Aberdeen the next day, a Party of Augustines horse, about 80, and 60 foot from Dun Ottir, were coming to surprize it; of which Col. Overton, having notice from the Countrey, sent a Party of 50 horse, who conveyed it safe away. Col. Fitches Regiment marched on Saturday last from Dundee, and quartered on Sunday at Forfar, they are to march for Innernesse. Major Generall Sterling is come in to the protection of the Parliament, so that now there is now no considerable Person in Scotland, but hath submitted to the Commonwealth of England. Divers of the Scots Ministers wives, whose husbands were taken at Ellit, are gone up for London in the Coach which brought down the Lady Traquair, and the Ministers here are making a Collection or Contribution to their Brethren of the black Robe who are now prisoners in England. Charity to a declining Party is acceptable.

Wednesday.—From Sterlingshire.

The Committee of the Church (not that appointed by the late pretended Generall Assembly at Dundee, but that which was now chosen out of the former Generall Assembly, and appointed to meet by this last Meeting at Edinburgh the last moneth) did meet here the 12 of this instant, and is not as yet dissolved, though not so frequently conveened as was expected. Yet these Ministers of Linlithgow Presbytery, who refused to come to the Synodicall Meeting of Lowthian, are as frequent to this present Meeting as they were slow to that. The said Ministers also have refused to give obedience to the said Synods Acts, especially in that of giving a willing Contribution to bear the charges of Master Robert Lighton, Minister of Newbottle, whom they have appointed to go to London, to mediat for the relief of their Ministers who were taken at Ellit, and now are prisoners at London, whose Wives went thither the last week in Coach (forsooth); and the reason of their refusall to contribute is, that they say, if they had been following their Calling then they should not have been prisoners there now, so that (it seemes) that the Lord hath called them to be where he would have them, because they were not where they should be. There were some of Edinburgh also about the collecting of the Reek penny for their relief, which was so much upon the pound of the House-Rents and Dues of every House that kindles fire there; but finding so much feeblenesse therein by the aversnes of many, some alledging the ruine of their Houses, others their being exhausted by Quartering of Souldiers the last year, other some Parishes refusing to pay, alledging that they cannot be obliged so to do, their Ministers not being prisoners, they were forced to wave that exaction till they think upon some other course; but we hear that in lieu thereof, they have some Charity allowed them by those who affect them at London, as the common Souldiers and prisoners have there from the Royall and Malignant Party.

We hear also of the most part of all the Shires of the North, who have had the Gentlemen there at Meetings, in order to choose Commissioners from their respective Shires, fully instructed and authorized with power and commission to wait upon the Commissioners which are to come from the Parliament of the Common-Wealth of England, to tender their loyalty, to receive their Orders, and to testifie their willingnes and obedience to them: the president whereof was warrant enough for the Shire of Linlithgow and this Shire, who did meet this last Week for that effect. But all such who have met have disowned the Noble Parliament (justly so called, because it is composed most of Noblemen), who did meet at Lochtay the 12 of this instant. Which Meeting, together with that of the said Commissioners of the Church, did begin both in one day, presaging to have the same like effects and results, they having both the like authority and appointed day of meeting, and both their Prime Heads at London prisoners. So that there can be litle life of action expected from the Body which is so far distant from its Head, except what must flow from the Conjunction of the Two Nations in One, which is like to prove a greater mercy to this Nation then ever it expected, and which Providence would force them to participate of, and they as yet not convinced till they finde the sweetnes thereof.

Thursday.—*From the Highlands thus*:

Mackrage, Mac Lenings, Mac Downings, and Mac Comrings (wilde Highlanders) are up in Arms; and they, or some of their men, seized on the Lord Calendars son, stript and wounded him. Argyle and the Chancellor, Lord Lowdon, are in consultation upon their submission to the Commonwealth of England, and a way for yeelding obedience thereto. Thus the Lord is pleased to bring about his Work, in conquering the hearts of those that have had the thoughts of the greatest Policy. The fore-mentioned Highlanders are not above 500 or 600 at the most, but they are a pestiferous burden wheresoever they come, sparing not either Friend or Foe; they make it a common trade to plunder all they come neer. The Countrey groans by such Heathenish usage. It's said those few men Argyle had daily run away, so that few or none are left.

XXVI

A Proclamation concerning the Price of Hay.[1]

This day another Proclamation issued in these words.
By the Deputy-Governour of Leith.

Whereas the price of Hay is ordered by the Maj.-Generals to be reduced to 2s. 6d. the hundred: It is ordered, that at all times from hence forth, during the continuance of Hay at that price, no Stabler, Inn holder, or Change keeper in this Garrison, shall presume to demand or receive any more then eight pence of any person whatsoever, for a Horse Hay and Stable room, day and night.

Leith, 1 *Decemb.* 1651.

This to be proclaimed by beat of Drum.   T. Wilks.

XXVII

Extract from Newsletter of Dec. 2, 1651, from Edinburgh.[2]

This day the Honourable Lieut.-Col. Wilks, Deputy-Governour of Leith, being informed of the severall abuses of the respective Boatmen and Ferrymen of Bruntiland and Leith, in extorting double the price of the Passage accustomed, to the very great abuse of the English and Scottish People: It is therefore ordered to be published by beat of drum, that no Boatman or Ferryman whatsoever, for the passing of any passenger from Bruntiland to Leith, or thence to Bruntiland, should demand any more then twelve pence sterling for each

---

[1] *Several Proceedings in Parliament*, Dec. 4-11, 1651.   [2] *Ibid.*

horse and man, and foure pence sterling for each single passenger, and no more, upon pain of forfeiting five shillings sterling for every default.

XXVIII

Extract from 'Mercurius Scoticus.'

Tuesday (Dec. 16).

There came this day [a letter] from a good and certain hand, of one who much bewailes the languishing disease of a dying Presbytery, and who is ready to mourn over it's dead Corps, seeing nothing but division and heart-burnings, in so far that Assembly is opposite to Assembly, Commission to Commission, Synod to Synod, Presbytery to Presbytery, yea Minister to Minister, and the fear of Independencie, makes them grow into Apostacie, [and] fall from the rigidnesse of their Presbytery to the cruelty of Episcopacy. And to confirme you in the same, we shall need to go no farther then the neighbouring Presbytery of Linlithgow, where the one half is divided from the other equally, the left-handed Party striving to over-ballance the more moderate Party, by consent of their corrupt Synod, which hath most illegally given way for the reponing of some Ministers (who were formerly deposed for Malignancie, and whose names were found registred in the Records of the quondam Bishop of S. Andrews, consenting to the Service-Book and Prelacie if not Popery, viz., Mr. Edward Wright, Minister of Falkirk); and the good successe they had thereof hath encouraged them to do the like with a Brother of the same stamp, viz., Mr. Andrew Keir, Minister of Caridden, where Mr. Baugh (I should say Waugh) came to the said Church in order to his businesse, with a Congregation of People suitable to his own minde, he inviting onely such to hear him preach; but the late placed Minister there could endure his unwillingnesse no farther, then by cutting the Bell string to hinder it from ringing; yet the said Mr. Baugh (*alias* Waugh) did as zealously play the Beadle, in tying the Bell-string to ring it, as devoutly he did the part of the Minister, in preaching to his Proselized Congregation, so that the Minister of the Place was forced to protest against his proceedings indeed. So that it cannot but end as it began with fears of a dying Presbytery, the Synodians are so deadly as Presbyters, turning Prelaticall though our Prelaticall Ministers elswhere are become Presbyteriall. Yet how can a Ship steer right without a Pilot, which brings to mind the Verses made by a Scottish Presbyterian, upon our taking prisoners the Committee and Commissioners at Ellet in Perth.

> Our Guard'ans of this Kingdome have quite mar'd
> Their Guardianship, wanting Scout, Watch, and Guard
> How can that Ship but dash on ev'ry shelf,
> Whose napping Pilot cannot guide himself?
> Blame not that soure Committee at Dumbar,
> They hors'd like men, but these all Captives are.
> As for the Church Commissions, they were late
> The constant Tutors both of War and State,
> Where was their vigilance? nay, where was all
> The Consort of these Watchmen, great and small?
> I wish the League were buried now or sunk,
> For all these Priests dare not to stir one Munk.

XXIX

A Proclamation concerning Bread.[1]

Edenburgh, 29 Decemb. 1651

A Proclamation by the Deputy-Governour of Leith, 17 Decemb. 1651.

Ordered

That from henceforth no Forreign Baker, not inhabiting in Leith, shall from and after the 19 instant, presume to bring into and vend any manner of bread whatsoever within this Garison, which shall not upon the due search and triall of two or more honest men of this Garison appointed for that purpose, be found sound, sufficient, wholesome, and due weight, according to the price of corn and Book of Rates, upon pain of having their Bread seized on for the use of the poor of this Garison.

---

[1] *Several Proceedings in Parliament,* Jan. 1-8, 165½.

And further, that all Bakers of this Town or elsewhere, set their own marks upon their respective loaves, and that they sell their bread in the usuall Market place at the Bridge end, on their several market-dayes, which shal be on Fridayes and Tues-dayes, and not to run from house to house ; And that no loaf be made but half-penny and two penny, and so higher, according to Assize.

And further, it is Ordered, that the Bakers of this Town have the like liberty to vend and sell bread in Edenburgh, or other places adjacent, on their Market-dayes, as they have here at Leith.

Lastly, that the Order be observed in this Garison, upon the like penalty of forfeiting their bread to the poor.

T. WILKS.

To be Proclaimed by beat of Drum, and affixed upon the most publick places of this Garison, and places adjacent.

XXX

A Proclamation concerning Lighting and Cleaning the Streets.[1]

THE Court Martiall at Edinburgh (out of an earnest desire of the good of the place, and to reforme the usuall disorders there, past these severall Results, as Orders to be proclaimed by beat of Drum in Edinburgh), Whereof at present you shall receive only the brief heads as they came to hand, viz. :

1. That all and every the Inhabitants in and about Edinburgh (in regard of many disorders and losses, that are often unjustly charged upon the private Souldiers, to the great dishonour of the Army), doe from hence-forth hang forth Lanthorns with Candles at their Windows or Doors, from the sixt hour at night to the ninth houre, which practice hath been long (among other good and wholsome Orders) observed in Leith Garrison.

2. That the Provost of Edinburgh (to whom the businesse is recommended) be desired to give present order, that the

---

[1] *Several Proceedings in Parliament*, Jan. 1-8, 165½.

Streets, Closes, and Wynds in Edinburgh be cleansed within fourteen dayes, and so continued from time to time.

3. That no person or persons whatsoever, in and about Edinburgh, doe presume to throw forth any filth or water from their Windowes, upon paine of paying immediately foure shillings sterling, viz., two shillings to the Discoverer, and two shillings to the poore of the same Town.

XXXI

A SUMMONS given by the PRESBYTERY of ABERDEEN to SIR ALEXANDER IRVING of Drum.[1]

I, WILLIAM COOK, officer of the Presbytery of Aberdeen, chief in that part, in name of the Moderator, Mr. John Row, and Presbytery of Aberdeen, doe charge you, Sir Alexander Irving of Drum, elder, to appear personally before the Presbytery of Aberdeen, in the ordinary place in the sessions of Aberdeen, upon the 30 day of this instant December 1651, in the hour of cause ordinary before noon, there to answer to all that is already in dependance before the said Presbytery in relation to you, as you well know, as also to answer for your Opinion and frequent railing on, cursing, and reproaching of the Covenants and blessed work of Reformation: for affirming that no Sectary (the most blasphemous not excepted) is so much to be abhorred as a Presbyterian: That Protestants live by an implicit Faith: That if you were not a Papist already you thought you should turn a Papist shortly: for saying in a publique convention, if Monarchy be gone, let the Devill take Presbytery, and the Covenant, it came from hell, let it go back to it again.

Also, I warn and charge [you], dame Magdalen Scrimgeour, Lady Drum elder, to appear day and place foresaid, to answer for your apostacy from the true Protestant Reformed Religion to Popery, or to purge your self thereof by oath in abjuring all the points of Popery as they are particularly set down in the Negative confession: Also to answer for your scandalous and frequent conversing with excommunicants within the bounds of the Presbytery of Aberdeen. And both Laird and Lady fore-

---

[1] The summons and numbers xxxii. to xxxv. are all printed in *Several Proceedings in Parliament*, Jan. 22-29, 165½.

said to answer for your resetting of Papists frequently and ordinarily within your house, and haunting of their companies.

Also, I warne and charge James Irving, son to the Laird of Drum, to appear day and place foresaid, to answer for your apostacy from the late Protestant Reformed Religion to avowed Popery.

Also, I warne and charge Anne, Olspet, and Jane Irving, daughters to the Laird of Drum, to appear day and place foresaid, to answer for your apostacy from the true Protestant Reformed Religion to Popery, or to purge out the scandall thereof by oath and profession, as the Presbytery shall order.

Also, I warn and charge the Laird of Drum his servants to appear day and place foresaid, to answer for your apostacy from the true Protestant Reformed Religion, or anything depending in proces against any of you, especially John Makewen, or to purge out the scandal by oath abjuring Popery in all the particular heads thereof, or as the Presbytery shal enjoyn. And this I do before witnesses. WILLIAM COOK.

XXXII

The Appeal of Sir Alexander Irving of Drum, from the Presbytery of Aberdeen.

WHEREAS I, Sir Alexander Irving of Drum, am cited to appear before the Presbytery of Aberdeen, in the sessions house thereof upon the 30 of December 1651, and there to answer for all that were in dependence before the said Presbytery in relation to me, and for my alleagit opinion and frequent railing on, cursing, and reproaching of the Covenants and work of Reformation, against Presbyterian Government, and that Protestants live by an implicit Faith, and for the alleagit saying in a publique convention, if Monarchy bee gone, let the Devill take Presbytery, and the Covenant it came from hell, let it go back to it again, and also for the alleagit resetting of Papists within my house, and haunting of their companies, as in the said Summons or Libell at more length is contained.

And I being most unjustly cited for the causes foresaid, and ye the Moderator and Presbytery of Aberdeen being my accusers and Judges, are most suspected to be Judges against me in the said particulars. And therefore I do appeal from your wisdoms Moderator and Presbytery of Aberdeen, to Col. Overton, Commander in Chief within the said Presbytery, to the effect he may hear you and me, and discern in the premise as he shall think fit. And that because yee, the Presbytery of Aberdeen, being my challengers and Judges, are most suspect to be suffered to proceed against me; and because the Lieut.-Gen., by his Order of date at Dundee, 6 Octob. 1651, directed to all Ministers and other Kirk Officers, requiring them that they impose no oaths or covenants upon any person whatsoever, without order from the State of England; and likewise the said Lieut.-Gen., by his other Warrant of the date at Dundee 2 Decemb. instant, requires and commands all civill magistrates not to seize upon, meddle with, or any ways molest the persons or estates of any excommunicate persons, or any ways to discharge any other persons whatsoever to desist from dealing or trading with the said excommunicate persons, without order from the Commonwealth of England or their commissioners, as they will answer the contrary at their perils. And so in respect of the said Warrant, you, Moderator and brethren of the Presbytery of Aberdeen, can no ways proceed in the said matter against me; and therefore I do summon you to appear before the said Col. Overton, commander in chief within the said Presbytery of Aberdeen, at the dwelling-house of Sir Patrick Leisly in the Gaistraw of Aberdeen, at 3 hours afternoon, this 30 of Decemb. 1651, to hear and see the said Col. Overton cognosce in the premise, and you censured for your slander raised against me, my wife, children, and family. Wherefore if ye proceed any farther against me, ye will be reputed according to the said Orders as enemies to the Commonwealth of England; and therefore I professe that I be free of any compearance before you, or of any censure you can or may impose against me for the alleaged facts and speeches contained in your Libell, and for the reasons and causes foresaid, and others to be alledged by me for my own defence before the said Col. Overton, commander in chiefe as is said.

ALEXANDER IRVING.

XXXIII
The Summons of Mr. Row, Moderator of Aberdeen, to Sir Alexander Irving.

I, Mr. John Row, Moderator of the Presbytery of Aberdeen, and in their name, and at their command to our Lieutenants, etc., these are, etc.: Passe, and in the name of the foresaid Presbytery warne, etc., and charge Sir Alexander Irving of Drum, elder, to appear before the said Presbytery in their ordinary seat within the Session house of Aberdeen, on the 13 day of this instant Janu. 1652, at the ordinary house before noon, then and there to answer for what was in his former summons to Decemb. 30, 1651. And as for as much as the Lord in his word hath distinguished the Ecclesiasticall government from the civill, and that appeals from any of Christs courts, Ecclesiastick Judicatories transacting Ecclesiastick affairs, to any civill Magistrates or Judicatories, is Erastianisme; and the acknowledging of Papatus politicus is very contrary to our Covenant, and liberties of this Kirk therin mentioned, [and] doth by the Acts of General Assemblies demerit, summar excommunication (as that at St. Andrews, April 24, 1582, Mr. Andrea Meluils, Moderator); to answer for his giving in an appeal to the Presbytery of Aberdeen upon the 30 of Decemb. 1651 in a very inorderly way (even before calling on the Lord's name by the Moderator, and so before they were a constitute Judicatory), being in a great rage and passion, and in his coming in and going out calling the Presbytery Tyrannical, and their Tyranny intolerable. Wheras the Presbyteries amity to convince, joyned with pains taken on the house of Drum in conferences from time to time, hath not been small. For calling the Presbytery (a Judicatory set over him in the Lord, and labouring by all means of Gods appointment to reclaime him) his accusers, his party; and upon that account appealed to Col. Overton, summoning the said Presbytery to appear at 3 afternoon before the said Colonel to answer, and hear him cognosc and discern, and to be censured by him (from whom we are hopeful and confident he had no such Warrant to cite the Presbytery, neither will the foresaid Colonel own or countenance so foul a businesse), with certification in case the Presbytry do proceed, they will be holden as enemies to the Commonwealth of England, alledging orders from Dundee for that effect, discharging all Oaths to be taken; that religious swearing and taking of an oath with the covenants and conditions contained in the sacred Scriptures of God, is a part of the Lords worship commanded, 'Thou shalt swear by my name,' professing the great Lord God to be Omniscient, Omnipotent; and just for his protesting that he may be free of compearance or censure for anything in their libelled Summon; and all the rest which at more length is contained in his foresaid appeal, declinatory, and protestation, to answer for so unparalleld a disorder, a breach of Covenant, a transgression of so deep a dye, that for anything we know, this Kirk did never hear of the like, nor Scotland of such to hear, and he himself (except he repent) deserveth to be censured and sentenced with the highest censures of the Kirk, for these and other things charged upon him in former summons; the which to do we commit to you, as ye will be answerable.

Given at Aberdeen, 2 Jan. 1652.

XXXIV

A Letter of Sir Alexander Irving to Lieut. Gen. Monke.

Honoured Sir,—Seeing such hath been your pious enclination towards those that are highly oppressed in their consciences, by issuing Orders for their relief, I cannot but next to God, who inspired that in your heart, acknowledge my thankfulnesse to you, with such cordiall acceptance as a low and depressed mind can afford. Yet notwithstanding such is the animocity of our church judicature in their parts that nothing will satisfie them unlesse I make shipwrack of that which ought to be most precious to me (my conscience) by a further pressure of oaths, as if the guilt of such sins has not provoked God to continue his chastisements towards this wretched Land. They have again stormed me with a scandalous summons to appear before their Presbytery. The truth is, I altogether decline their Judicature, as not being established by the Commonwealth of England; for I conceive one that lives under their shelter cannot in equity, without forfeiting their protection to the said State, acknowledge any court not warranted by them. Their main businesse against me is popery, but Col. Overton wil be my witnesse, that if Mr. Cant and the rest of the Ministers would give me a private conference before him, I would clearly purge my self of that in any way that he or they can imagine; which the Presbytery absolutely declined with such violence, as if their authority were by an immediate vocation from heaven, wherefore I finding that there was more rancour and spleen intended to me then the glory of God, I was forced to make use of a lawful means, to appeall from those who may justly be supposed to be both judge and party. Wherefore let it be my earnest desire to your honour, that seeing I have been and still am tender towards the interest of the State of England, by giving punctual obedience towards your commands, that you will be pleased to protect me now from the fury of a superstitious clergy. By doing of this you shall not only discover your candid inclinations to freedom, but in a high measure ingage me to continue, Noble Sir, Your reall friend and servant,   ALEXANDER IRVIN.

Aberdeen, 2 Jan. 1652.

XXXV

A LETTER from SIR ALEXANDER IRVIN to Mr. Row, Moderator of the Assembly at Aberdeen.

SIR,—There came one Paper of yours this day to my hand, insinuating no lesse than a Summons from a kind of Court, which the acknowledging of might possibly bring me in a *premunire* against the interest of the Commonwealth of England, which by the Providence of God is now our Soveraign Lords and Masters; wherefore I desire to be pardoned, if I altogether decline any such businesse of a Presbyterian Judicatory, till such time as I have a Law from my Supreme Powers to command me to it; and then you shall see none shall be more ready to give you all dutifull obedience then I shall be, as becommeth a Peacable Member of the Commonwealth.

As for your Papatus Politicus that is mentioned in your Pasquill, I wish you to take notice that I disclaim both Ecclesiasticke and Politick Popery, which I am jealous ye go about to insnare me in, by pressing infallible beliefe to an humane institution. But I trust God wil not only protect me from thos, but al other works of darknesse of the same kind; and be not offended if I tell you it were much more Ministerial and Christian like to preach those consolations, which the Lord hath dispensed in his word, to such as are lying under the burden of his deserved wrath, as it is visible we in this Nation are, and not to spend your spirits in things indifferent, such as I take your Hierarchical hedge to be, whose luxurant nature will obfuscate and prove destructive rather to the plants of Gods Vineyard then protect it from the wild Boare of Antichristianity; and if ye be not wretchedly infatuated to your own fantasies, ye might have both seen, and see daily sad experiences of the same, but I pray God from my heart to unmask your mistaken zeal from so furious and violent proceedings, and observe the commands of Jesus Christ, to preach to all Nations, and not give way to the frail passions of ambition by indeavouring an unwarrantable obedience to each of your capatious whimsies.

Yet notwithstanding of all, to let the world see I do not shun to clear my selfe from the slander urged by you against me, I am content the third time to invite you before Col. Overton, and there it shall appear who is in the wrong; and be you pleased to appoint the time, and I shall be ready to attend, though in point of civility you might have don it formerly, at my first and second Judicatory. Thus much I have written to you in particular, not any way to prejudice my appeal, for you must know I do and will stand to it, till either Maj. Gen. Lambert, or Lieutenant Gen. Monke, or Colonell Overton, or any of their Substitutes, command the contrary, which when they do, I shall be ready to doe all that is incumbent for a Christian and peaceable man. In the mean time let me not be troubled with more such papers, that are but undigested rapsodies of confused nonsense; in so doing you shal encourage me to be Your Friend, ALEX. IRVIN.

Drum, 7 *January* 1652.

XXXVI

From Aberdeen, January 10.[1]

You have here enclosed a short touch of the present temper of the Kirkmen. The old Malignants have all laid by their Bucklers, but the Kirkmen are still stiffe, and speak little for Peace or truth from the Pulpits; but are secretly insinuating themselves one way, and in the interim persecuting another; the inclosed will tell you they intend no abatement of Prelatical power, but are infallibly faithful, that their Canonical customes both in power and opinion will be kept up, and that their stooles of hyppocritical repentance shal stil stand to chastize the incontinent; the judicatories must also be made good upon specious pretences of punishing impieties, when it is rather to ventilate the Presbyterian spleene upon such as cannot succumbe, nor stoop to their superintendencies. I might here make many instances of notable and abominable memory; take one for all: the Lord of Drum was lately called to account by the Kirk for not striking Saile to the uncontroulable tide of their authority; being summond to appear before Mr. Cant and other compurgators, he hung forth a Flag of defiance, and instead of presenting himself before the Sea of their Soveraignty, he summond his summoners to come before Col. Overton, withal requiring them to cognose that he was under the Parliament of Great Britaines protection, and therefore could not (with due reservation of his duty) acknowlege any judicatory in Kirk or State, which had not the impress of that power upon it; yet if as private Christians they requested him by abjuration to purge himselfe of Popery for theirs and the worlds satisfaction, in that sence he would do it; this is not their work so much as the keeping up the Kirks power, whereunto they look upon Lieut. Gen. Monk, and Col. Overton as great Antagonists. And indeed they are in a little dread of them, but Provost Jeffery (Mr. Cants son in Law, who helpt to fetch home the King, and at Dunbar fought himselfe into a cut finger, for which and former services a Pension is his Plaister) is not only become our convert, but is now at Eden-

---

[1] *Mercurius Politicus*, Jan. 22-29, 1652.

burgh insinuating himselfe and acting for the Kirks interest, and his own, with the Noble Major General, who is sufficiently fortified against all such insinuators. I therefore hope he cannot with all his cunning procure M. Cant a Patent for Presbytry; indeed it was more proper for him to do penance in a Pickadilloon, a Pillory, or to have his buttond Cassack and Bucky Ruffe sent to Rome for Reliques of the Kirk of Scotlands conformity to the Canons and Constitutions of that Scarlet Whore which sits upon seven hils. But I hope these superstitious deceivings are drawing toward a dissolution; the day is dawning; away then with those deeds of darkness, and men-pleasing practices or opinions. Policy and Piety are two pieces of Architecture rarely resting under one Ruff; it was therefore said of Saul, that he no sooner ceast to seem religious, but he became an hypocritical Politician; fools and mad folk how will their craft and cunning befool them which cannot defend them? In the interim one of our best Antidotes against their under-minings is to give a civill respect to all, but National trust to none who are of Twillyones Tribe; I am sure the most honest I meet with amongst them are of this mind. Honest Kirkmen thus cookt may become good servants, who were otherways ill masters and managers of State matters; for they are impostumated spirits, soon pufft up by pride and opinion of great imployments; that which makes them sensible (viz. self-sufficiency) does as soon besot them; wee know desire of being wise made them fools; when Ministers meddle with Civil matters, or put themselves upon imployments improper for their professions, like so many foolish Phaetons they set the world on fire, but I hope we are powerfully protected against all their plots and projects; they may therefore omit the Courting of our Commissioners, let them alone to model them into a more religious Government then either their own pride or policy will permit. But I leave them as fit fewel for Reformations fire to feed upon, and when by this Alchimy their Sin and dross is taken off, the pure and perfect gold, if they have any in them, will appear precious, and become useful to after Ages in those times of richer Reformation for the service of the sanctuary.

A Copy of the Missive sent by M. John Rowe, Moderator of the Presbytery of Aberdeen, to Sir Alexander Irvine of Drum.

HONOURABLE AND WORSHIPFUL SIR,—The Romans say, 'Nox dabit consilium'; and we say, 'Sleep and advise.' I was sorry that yesterday you would not follow so much of your worthy friends advise, as to surcease from giving a present answer to the Presbytery in so weighty a matter, and so nearly concerning yourself. Now, Sir, yet again I desire in cold blood a more moderate Answer; for I shall be loth and sorry to report what was said yesterday; And if you desire, I shall come to your Worships chamber, if you will by this bearer put me in hope of an Answer more satisfactory to the Presbytery, more conducing for your own welfare every way, as I humbly conceive. I expect a present return, and rest, etc.

Answer to the said Missive.

SIR,—I know the mercies of the wicked are cruel. I know by experience what has been your carriage in former times. I have as great reason (yea more) to decline your tyrannical Presbyterian Judicatory as ye have to protest against the proceedings of your National Assembly. To eschew hearing, I am content that Colonel Overton be Judge betwixt you and me, but I shall never be judged (with my own consent) with such partial Judges, and such cruel enemies as ye are. I rest, Your servant, *Sic subscribitur,* IRVING.[1]

---

[1] The 'Protestation' of Sir Alexander Irvine against the sentence of the Presbytery of Aberdeen for his excommunication is printed in the *Miscellany* of the Spalding Club, vol. iii. pp. 205-207, from a copy in the Charter-room at Drum. It is not dated, but as the excommunication was to be pronounced on Feb. 1, 1652, according to the books of the Kirk-Session of Aberdeen, quoted in the preface to the Spalding Club volume (p. xviii), the protest probably took place about the end of January. His letter to the Presbytery, dated Jan. 20, 1652, is printed in Whitelocke's *Memorials* (ed. 1853, iii. 398).

XXXVII

A Proclamation by the Deputy-Governor of Leith.[1]

Whereas the Butchers of this garrison doe frequently forestal the Markets by buying up and ingrossing all the meate brought in by the Country, I doe hereby Order and Declare, that if any Butcher of this garrison shall presume to buy any dead victuall of any person whatsoever at any time hereafter, and not such as such butcher kills himself, he shall forfeit the price of all such meat, the one moyety to the use of the Garrison, and the other to the party discovering such offenders.   TIM. WILKES.

Leith, 24 Feb. 1652.

This to be proclaimed by beat of Drum in and about Leith Garrison, and affixed in the Market place.

XXXVIII

A Letter from Inverness.[2]

Sir,—Since my last there hath been some course thought on for the setling of a constant Post to convey Letters from these parts to Leith, from whence they may be sent for England by the Post as formerly, so that as oft as these parts affords any thing worth your taking cognizance of, I shall be carefull to write to you. The Major-General at his being here viewed a peece of ground, and gave order for erecting a large Sconce with five Bulwarks to hold about 2000 horse and foot; the wall is to bee of free stone, and will bee of great strength when finished, and very usefull and serviceable to the Commonwealth of England in securing for their use these parts;

---

[1] *Several Proceedings in Parliament,* March 4-11, 1652.
[2] *Ibid.* June 24-July 1, 1652.

the ground it is to be built on is by an Arme of the Sea, and the river Nesse, over which there is a Bridge to be made, and neare it there may ride ships of very great burthen, and in good harbourage. On Munday next they intend to begin with digging the grafts which are to partake of the water of Nesse.

This day a Pinnace of above forty Tun was lanched, which by the industry and exceeding paines of Captaine Pestle, Captaine of the *Satisfaction,* and some of his seamen, with almost all the officers and souldiers of Col. Fitches Regiment, was drawne six miles and upward over land, to the admiration of all that were spectators, it being a worke thought almost impossible. Considering the bulke of the vessel, and the ill way she was drawne over, I beleeve the like was never before undertaken; the men broke three cables seven inches about with hawling of her, yet it was incredible to see with what chearfulnesse she was carried away, though with great labour; there is appointed divers Souldiers and Seamen to bee put in her, and foure peeces of ordnance, and to saile up and downe a standing water called Lough Nesse, which hath a property never to freeze, and is foure and twenty miles long, and in some places is two miles, and in others three miles broad, and lyeth betwixt the Highlands, so that she will doe excellent service by preventing the Highlanders to make their passage that way, which is frequented by them; the West end of the Lough is neare unto the Irish Sea, it wanting not above six mile of ground to be cut to make the Shires north of it an intire Island of itself.[1]

XXXIX

A Letter from Glasgow.[2]

Sir,—This fair and beautifull City of Glascow (the flower of Scotland) is a fourth part consumed and burnt down, and

---

[1] This letter is said, in a prefatory note, to be dated 'Innernesse, June 14.'
[2] *Several Proceedings in Parliament,* 24 June-1 July 1652.

much of it besides spoyled with a sad and lamentable fire that hapned here.

The fire began on Thursday last, and burnt with that violence in this dry season, that notwithstanding the help of Col. Overtons Regiment, which at that time quartered there, besides the Townesmen, yet it increased so fast, that it could not be quenched in 48 hours, though great paines and care was used therein.

Some men, both Souldiers and others, have lost their lives in using their indevours to quench the fire. Many poor families that before lived well are now by this fire utterly undone, and brought to great extreamity. It would pitty the heart of any man almost to behold so sad a spectacle.

And yesterday when we went to view it, it drew tears from my eyes, and not mine alone, but many. The object is a sad one. The reports are many and much various concerning the manner of its rise: some say it was occasioned by the firing of a Musket, some by carelesseness in a Scotch house, and some say other waies. We have given the Major-General an account of it.

Much Meal and Corn, besides Merchandise, hath been spoyled by this fire, and Goods and other things to a great value.

The great Draught here hath burnt up the most part of the Summers corne in the fields, so that the condition of the people is sad. We are preparing for our Argile expedition, and if we be not hindred for want of provisions coming seasonably to Ayre, we shall (it is hoped) be some of us over some time this week.

Glascow, 20 June 1652.

XL

A Letter from Major-General Deane.[1]

Sir,—We are marched up into the middle of this craggy country, where we have great difficulty to live in a body

---

[1] *Several Proceedings in Parliament*, 15-22 July 1652.

together for want of provisions both for horse and men. It is a dismall place where we scarce see a man or beast for 40 miles together. The L. Argyle parted with me three daies agoe to his own Country to receive the Forces under Col. Overton, etc.—Your affectionate and humble servant,

R. D.

From the Vale of Baggonoye, 6 July 1652.

XLI

A Letter from the Highlands.[1]

We have had a gallant march, the extremities of heat and cold, wind and weather, by day or night not offending us. Here rarest objects are still visible.

Thursday last (having quartered the night before at Gillogaer), at Noon we past the Earl of Athols bounds, and entered Huntley's, (the Earls lands being better than his here) and quartered that night 12 miles further, being at Barracree, and on Wednesday last wee marched 12 miles further to Sheverton Moor, where we quartered, and yesterday came hither; and all this march from the Blayre, we caused our peeces to be drawne through very unknowne, indented, and ill byassed peeces of ground, beside 400 Baggage horse led by the Country people laden with Bisket and Cheese, and guarded by Capt. Kellies Troop of Dragoons, of Col. Morgans Regiment. Some of the Baggage men muttered much, saying, *That none of their Fore Fathers ever went these ways,* but last night having delivered them money and provisions, we sent them away. We shall, I suppose, stay here two or three daies to Randesvouze, and then march either back Westward or some other way.

Last night on the other side of the Lough some of the Highlanders fired 4 or 5 peeces at some of our men fishing on this side, but they no sooner shot but ran away. We pay here for grasse, and guarde our Horse from the corne.

This day the Maj.-Generall, with Col. Hackers Regiment, some Dragoons and Foot, went to view Inner Loughe near the

---

[1] *Several Proceedings in Parliament,* 22-29 July 1652.

sea, six miles from hence, where that ancient Castle seemes ruined by Times continued waste. It lies near the sea, where we expected the ship intended for us with provisions, but not come. One came, as I heare, with a letter from the cheifest Clan of the Country, who assures, that if he may be accepted, hee will bring in a thousand Highlanders that are fled with all their cattell. A party of Horse and Foot is left there, and tomorrow or Monday we shall remove our quarters.

Tent at Lough Loughe, July 10, 1652.

XLII

MR. WILLIAM CLARKE to the SPEAKER.[1]

MR. SPEAKER,—The Major-Gen. was 4 or 5 daies since in the vale of Baggon, where having setled Garisons in the Bray of Marr and Ruthen, being Captaine Powels Company of Licut. Generall Munks late Regiment, he went to Loquaber.

There is a Garison also sent from St. Johnstones to the Blaire of Athol. There are about 600 Highlanders up in Armes something beyond them, under the command of Allom Mac Dewie; but it is most probable rather to make conditions then to oppose. The Lord Glencatre and others of the cheife of the Clans are come in to the Maj. Gen., and Markets setled in some places, for the bringing in of provision to our souldiers, where there never was any Market before; the people generally speak Irish, go only with plads about their middle, both men and women. There are scarce any houses of stone, but only earth and Turfes.

The party under Colonell Overton, which landed at Tarbut in Cantire, were met by the Marquesse of Argyles Steward by his appointment with a complement, but we heare not what they have done since.

Yesterday ther were ten great Iron guns boated over from hence to Insceith Island, which lyes three leagues off this Garrison, and much about that distance from Bruntiland, where 40 Souldiers of this Garrison are placed, and a strong

---

[1] *Several Proceedings in Parliament,* 15-22 July 1652.

house which was there repairing, and some platformes making for guns to defend the places from being made use of by any of the enemies ships for fresh water, which it hath formerly been.—Sir, I am, your Honours most humble Servant,
WILLIAM CLERKE.

Leith, 13 *July* 1652.

For the Right Honourable Wil. Lenthall, Esq., Speaker to the Right Honorable the Parliament of England.

XLIII

A LETTER from the HIGHLANDS.[1]

SIR,—Our Forces here, blessed be God (after their long march), are in good health. The Marquesse of Argyle doth entertaine Col. Overton, Col. Read, and Col. Blackmore in much state; and makes many pretences of love and affection, but who knows not that it is but constrained? The Marquesse is no stranger in the art of Politicks; but we shal make use of him accordingly.

He hath so sent out commands to the Countries under his Dominions, that the Inhabitants doe somewhat civilly intreat our Souldiers where they come. This is a mountainous and an odde Country in some places, yet in other places rich and good in the vallies. But the people very simple and ignorant in the things of God, and some of them live even as bruitish as heathens.

Lieut.-Col. Cotterell is gone with three ships of Souldiers to the North west Isles of Scotland, where lye many Islands great and small, neer one another, some inhabited and some not. He hath orders to Garison such places as shall be thought fit there. Some of them have places for harbour for ships, which may be of use to us for both the safety and also for better supply of Ireland.

---

[1] *Several Proceedings in Parliament,* 22-29 July 1652.

Some of the Highlanders have heard our preaching with great attention and groanings, and seeming affection to it.

Turbet, 18 *July* 1652.

XLIV

A Letter from the Highlands.[1]

Sir,—Having setled some Garisons in Cantyre, we divided our forces and sent Col. Read, with the major part to Innerary, and yesterday was sevennight begun our march, with above 700 horse, dragoons and foot, from Tarbet towards Dunstaffenage, in hope to have found our ships which garison there; and after four hard dayes march, wee got thither, viewed that and another within a mile or two of that, called Dun-olley, finding them very strong, but no provisions being come, although wee stayed there two nights, we were forced to act the King of Frances part, to face about, and by a neerer cut got hither last night, and found yours of the first instant.

Cap. Thompson went from Leith round about Orkney, to come into Dunbarton Firth, with three horse Boats, who was set upon by two Irish Frigots, and after five houres dispute gave them so much as they bore a loofe. And he went into Carrickfergus Harbour to mend his Vessell and rigging, both which had received almost 200 shot, yet lost not one man outright, but had many wounded.

This he signified with his owne hand, in a Letter to Major Generall Deane, but he speakes nothing of Captaine Drew, nor Lieutenant Col. Cotterell; but Colonell Allured from Ayre writes to us, that he heares for certaine they are both in Ireland. He saw the fight, but could not come forth to assist his friends.

Wee are ready to catch anything that gives us hopes they are safe, much of this Summers service, under God, lying upon their well-being.

And if we doe heare they arrive at their designed Port, we shall take another ramble, and scramble againe; but over such

---

[1] *Several Proceedings in Parliament,* 29 July-5 August 1652. The letter is headed 'from Scotland, July 19.'

Mountaines and Mosses, such Places and passes, such Lakes and Loughs did never poor people wander; yet with such cheerfulness, we do any thing to promote the publick Service, Argyle beyond measure assisting us in person, presence, men, friends, provisions, or any thing else.

Clan Carren, a cheife Clan, with many others, where Major-Generall Deane went, are in opposition to him, and have entered into a league to oppose us, and fall upon all that will not enjoyn with them, which frights the people of these parts exceedingly.

XLV

A Letter from Inverary.[1]

Sir,—Major Generall [Deane] is still here, and we are turning every stone, stroking every man, and seriously endeavouring a right understanding with these people, if it may be to a compliance with us, or at least to no hostility against us; yet we have some cause for jealousie that they will run into Rebellion, or at least be at liberty to take in any interest as advantage, if any opportunity shall offer itself when we are withdrawne with our Field Forces; but God having carried us through our duty in relation to a peaceable and amicable deportment, we shall have our witnesse in us against all calumniations upon their future follies manifested. A few days will put our treaties and conferences to a period, and by reason of the season force us into the Low-lands, leaving happily Argyle behinde us upon a prudentiall consideration. Our ships, men and provisions are all gotten safe hither, and disposed according to order, so that no crosse providence hath attended us in all our expedition. I heare that Glen-gary with his confederates are 4000 strong, watching in several small parties to hurt us, and to ruine those of the Country men that have complied with us, which hath forced us to trust some of them with their Arms, upon engagements taken and subscribed.

Innerary, 18 *August* 1652.

---

[1] *Several Proceedings in Parliament,* 26 Aug.-Sept. 2, 1652.

XLVI

A Letter from Paisley.[1]

Sir,—Having setled our Garisons in the High-lands and concluded amicably with Argyle, the 21 instant wee marched from Innerary 5 miles, where wee incamped neer Arkinlesse for a day, in which time the Major Gen. being formerly gone on board of Cap. Sherwins Frigot, the wind falling fair, he set sail for Ayre; and on Monday morning wee began our march again, and are now, blessed be God, lately arrived at this place; though the treacherous Highlanders, who carried fair to us while we continued in their Country, upon our departure gathered betwixt 1000 and 1500 of them together to an impregnable Passe, called Glen Crow, and where onely we could but file over, they in the interim standing secure upon advantageous and inaccessible Rocks, and undoubtedly fully resolved when they came thither to act according to their opportunity; yet God, who restrains the fury of the most savage beasts, doth also muzzle the mouthes and stop the outrages of bloody-minded men. They pretended the reason of their drawing thither was to know whether or no the E. of Argyle were our prisoner, the contrary whereunto we are confident they were not ignorant of.

In fine, we advanced one by one over the Passe, they stood every way prepared to take their advantage upon us, yet had not the power or the spirit to do it. In all which time wee drew up our men under their noses, untill our Rear-guard was got over, and then we advanced a mile further, and encamped that night, and heard no more of them before we came to Dunbarton, but there too much. For the Major Gen. who went by Sea from Innerary to Ayre, came to us by Boat, and wee heard by him of the surprizall of our Garisons of Lough, Kincarn, and Turbet: I wish Dunstafnage and Dunolle be safe.

I doubt whether wee will or no these things are in order to War with these base and beggerly wild beasts, which we would

---

[1] *Several Proceedings in Parliament*, Sept. 2-9, 1652.

willingly have avoyded for many weighty reasons, especially their poverty and unaccessiblenesse of every passe and place, where each hill, whereof the Country totally consists, is no lesse [than] an invincible Garrison. I doubt the treachery of the Highlanders herein hath been as much designed by the Clergy as by their own Clans; God will in his good time reward their works and wayes.

Peasly, 29 *August* 1652.

XLVII

Mr. William Clarke to the Speaker.[1]

For the right Honourable William Lenthall, Esq.; Speaker of the Parliament of England at Westminster.

Mr. Speaker,—On Wednesday last the 20 instant, the English Commissioners for administration of Justice sat upon criminall matters at Edenburgh.

The first day was spent in reading their Commission from the Commissioners at Dalkeith, calling the Sheriffs of the severall Counties on this side the Frith, viz. Berwicke, Selkirke, Peebles, Linlithgow, Haddington, Mid-Lothian, and Rowborough.

Those Sheriffes that appeared not were fined 200†. Scots each. Afterwards the Gentlemen of the severall Counties who were to do their service, were called, and such as appeared not were fined 100†. Scotch; and then severall Delinquents were called and set down for Tryall. Since that, these three daies have been spent in the Tryall and fining of severall persons for Adulteries, Incests, and Fornications, for which there were above 60 persons brought before the Judges in a day; and it is observable, that such is the malice of those people that most of them were accused for facts done divers years since, and the chiefe proofe against them were their owne confessions before the Kirk, who are in this worse then the Romish

---

[1] *Several Proceedings in Parliament*, Oct. 28-Nov. 4, 1652.

Religion, who doe not make so ill an use of their auricular confession. Some of the facts were committed 5, some 6, 10, 16, 18, and 21 years since.

There was one Ephraim Bennet, a Gunner in Leith, indicted, convicted, and condemned for coyning of sixpences, shillings, and halfe crownes; also two Englishmen, Wilkinson and Newcome, condemned for robbing three men, and killing one Scotchman near Haddington in March last.

But that which is most observable is, that some were brought before them for Witches, two whereof had been brought before the Kirk about the time of the Armies coming into Scotland, and having confessed it, were turned over to the civill Magistrate. The Court demanding how they came to bee proved Witches, they declared, that they were forced to doe it by the exceeding torture they were put to, which was, by tying their thumbs behind them, and then hanging them up by them; two Highlanders whipped them, after which they set lighted candles to the soles of their feet, and between their toes, then they burnt them by putting lighted candles into their mouthes, and then burning them in the head. There were six of them accused in all, 4 whereof died of the torture.

The judges are resolved to inquire into the businesse, and have appointed the Sheriffes, Ministers, and Tormentors to be found out, and to have an account of the ground of the cruelty. The judges inquired of the neighbours concerning these women, who report them to be of a very honest and civill conversation.

Another woman that was suspected (according to their thoughts) to be a Witch, was kept 20 dayes and nights with bread and water, being stript naked and laid upon a cold stone, with only an hair-cloth over her. Others had hair-shirts dipt in vinegar put on them to fetch off their skin. It is probable there will shortly be more of this kind of Amboyna usage, but here is enough for reasonable men to comment upon.

On Wednesday night last the Marquesse of Argyle came to Edenburgh. He had so far perfected the worke in the Highlands, that our prisoners are released out of Carversa Castle (where about 60 of them were kept) 20 miles from Innerary, where they had near perished had they not been allowed some of their own Bisket and Cheese. The Marquesse of Argyle used them very civilly at their coming by his house, allowing them good quarters, some monies to bear their charges, and giving them passes through his Country.

I heare there is a Petition drawne up and subscribed by many of the Inhabitants of Leith, to the Parliament, for making them a Corporation, distinct from Edenburgh; which request is so just and equitable that I hope it will bee granted, that Town having been under the greatest slavery that ever I knew; one should be subject to the other no more then Westminster to London, and besides there is a farre greater distance between them.

The denying of this request would very much loose the Parliaments interest in Scotland, by discouraging the English, who have seated themselves there, which will loose the most considerable Garison in Scotland.—Your Honours most humble servant, WIL. CLERK.

Edenburgh, 23 Octob. 1652.

XLVIII

A Letter from Edinburgh.[1]

Sir,—All things at present are in a strange kind of hush; of a sudden all is quiet at present. It is not long since the Presbytery railed in a scurvy unworthy manner against England and the Government thereof.

What core is at the root, which may be feared is sufficiently hard, I know not; but there is such a suddain change, that now the Kirkists, that have so inveighed against us, begin to be a little tamer, and at present to hardly vent out their spleen against the authority of the Parliament of England. This news I suppose will be as strange to you, as unexpected to us, and indeed may seem a miracle; but God who over-ruleth all hearts, and all things, and turneth them which way soever he pleaseth, can rebuke any enemy, or change any heart at his pleasure.

---

[1] *Several Proceedings in Parliament*, Nov. 25-Dec. 2, 1652.

I doe not say their hearts are changed, but I am sure their tongues are much allayed, and their fury abated as to what they do do, or perhaps dare do. Their Royall influence is almost breathlesse, and its recovery so hopelesse, that some of them begin to deliberate. The Gathered Churches in Scotland go on so successfully, that many who derided them, begin to admire them, and love them; and there seems to be an expectation of the glory of the Lords Temple, to be more illustrious in the ruines of the earthly Monarchs, then any of the worldly Crownes and Scepters will ever nurse up in their protections.

Edenburgh, 20 *Novemb.* 1652.

INDEX

ABERBROTHWICK, abbey of, 17.
Aberdeen, xviii, 14-17, 117, 305, 307, 323, 324, 326, 337, 340, 341.
—— presbytery, cites Irvine of Drum, 348; Irvine's appeal against the summons, xxxvii, 349; letter from Irvine of Drum asking the protection of Monk, 352; Irvine's letter to the moderator, 353; the moderator's summons, 354; letter to Irvine from the moderator; Irvine's reply, 357 and *n*.
Aberfoyle, li.
Advocates, regulations concerning, 278, 279.
Aire. *See* Ayr.
Alexander, J., 330.
—— sir Sigismund, 5.
Allen, captain, 142.
Alpine, bailiff of Dumbarton, 39.
Alured, colonel Matthew, xxxii, 1, 7, 15, 21, 63, 86, 114, 115, 179, 188, 243, 331, 364; captures the committee of estates, xviii, 320.
Alyth (Elliot), capture of the committee of estates at, xviii, xli, 8, 9, 14, 193, 320, 323, 342, 346.
Anderraran, 335.
Anderson, Henry, commissioner of the parish of Blair, 264.
Andrew, Robert, 175.
Andrewes, Thomas, 322.
Anstruther, 16 *n*.
Ardchattane, 169.
Ardgour. *See* Maclean.
Ardkinglas (Orkinlesse), 366.
Ardrosse. *See* Cardross.
Argyll, countess of, 2.
—— marquis of, xx-xxiii, xlvi, xlviii, 19 and *n*, 20, 23, 26 *n*, 27, 29, 42, 57 *n*, 79 *n*, 80, 88, 134, 139, 160, 164, 193, 197 *n*, 203, 221 and *n*, 224, 226, 241 and *n*, 242, 243, 254, 257, 272, 274, 275, 308, 309, 326, 333, 335, 343, 361, 363, 365, 366, 368, 369; endeavours to treat with the commissioners of parliament, 34, 37, 40; letter to, from the commissioners, 40, 42; articles of agreement between Argyll and the commonwealth, xxii, 48, 50 *n*, 55, 57; letters from general Deane to, 59; from Lilburne, 85 and *n*, 161, 204, 244; letters from, to Lilburne, 165, 168, 261-262 and *n*; letter of warning to lord Lorne, 166; obtains a pass to visit Lilburne, 239; letter from, to Monk, 333; summons a meeting of parliament, 337; heads of agreement between Argyll and Monk, 338.
Arnet, Charles, 330.
Arrol. *See* Errol.
Ashfield, colonel Richard, 1, 3, 6, 12, 29, 115.
Assessment of Scotland, xxx-xxxi, 170, 174-180, 287-288 and *n*.
Athole, earl of, xlvi, 6, 19, 23, 150, 193, 218, 219, 271, 282, 283 *n*, 290, 341; letter to, from Glengarry, 141 and *n*; letter from, to Charles II., 183-184 and *n*.
Atkins (Adkins), colonel Jonathan, 150, 151, 317.
Auchinbreck. *See* Campbell, sir D.
Auchterderran (Auchterdurham), 330.
Augustine, col., 8 and *n*, 11, 28, 341.
Ayr (Aire), xxxii, 118, 196 *n*, 198, 257.
Aytoun (Kytoun), J., of Inchdarnie, 330 and *n*.

BADENOCH (Bagenoth), 95, 193, 194, 200, 267, 268.
Badger, captain, 5.
Balcarres (Belcarris), lord, xix, xliii, xlvi, 10, 16, 20, 21 and *n*, 23, 104, 106, 130, 133, 138, 144 *n*, 147, 150, 160, 164, 184 *n*, 191, 247, 248, 256 *n*, 283, 309, 312, 313, 326, 335, 337, 341; letters to, from Charles II., 97, 107 and *n*, 310; letter from, to Lilburne, 146.
Balfour, lord, of Burghley, 21, 26.
Ballendolla, 194.

Ballentyne, colonel, 252.
Bampfield, colonel Joseph, xliii-xliv, 91, 94, 101 n, 104, 106, 107 and n, 128, 130-134, 138, 183, 201, 310 and n, 311, 312; his advice to the king, 217-219.
Bargenny, lord, 9.
Barkestead, colonel John, 21, 136 n, 337.
Barracree, 361.
Bass island, the, 117, 333; proclamation against intercourse with the garrison of, 322; surrender of, 334.
Battely, captain, 320.
Baynes, cornet, 129 n.
—— captain Adam, 129 n.
Beggars, proclamation concerning, 155.
Belcarres. See Balcarres.
Beligarney, Forfarshire, 7.
Bellenden or Ballenden, sir William, 130, 260.
Bennet, Andrew, 333.
—— Ephraim, trial of, for coining, 368.
—— captain James, 13 n.
—— Alexander, 177.
Berry, colonel James, 2, 6, 15 and n, 115, 160, 173, 238, 316, 323.
Berwick (Barwick), 274, 285.
Bigger, 193.
Bilton, George, 16, 113, 114, 119, 149, 288.
Bird, major, 175, 186, 187, 203, 274.
Birssie Sound. See Bressay.
Biscoptoune, 197.
Blackford, 6.
Blackhall (Blakhall), A., 197.
—— W., 197.
Blackmore, colonel, 363.
Blackwell, captain John, 96, 113.
—— John, 113.
Blair, engagement of the gentlemen of, 145.
—— in Athol, 118, 362.
Blaire, sir Adam, of Bigtoune, 197.
Blakader (Blakiter), colonel, of Tulliallen, 290.
—— colonel Alexander receives a commission to levy men in Clackmannanshire, 292.
—— John, 293.
Blantire, laird, 5, 191.
Blount or Blunt, lieutenant-colonel Robert, 83, 89 n, 148, 153, 175, 202-203; letter to, from the earl of Seaforth, 151; letter to, from Lilburne, 153 n.
Boghall, 317, 320.
Bohauty, 186 n.

Bohemia, queen of, 98.
Bonnywher, 196.
Borthwick Brae, li, 302 n.
Bourne, major Nehemiah, commander of the 'Speaker,' 6, 8.
Bourtie, Aberdeenshire, 341.
Boyde, James, royalist agent in Ireland, 87.
Bradshaw, lieutenant, 318.
Brandenburgh, marquis of, 52.
Brassie, captain, 140 n, 148, 157.
Brayne, lieutenant-colonel William, 19, 173, 338.
Bread, proclamation concerning, 346.
Breadalbane (Broad Albin), 282.
Brechin (Brachin), 326, 331.
Bressay Sound, xlix, 226.
Bridge, major Tobias, 241 and n.
Brief Relation. . . . of the Affairs of Scotland by the earl of Loudoun, 21 and n.
Brinock, F., 197.
Brodick (Bradick) castle, xix, 38, 118.
Brodie, lord, 185.
Broughty castle, evacuation of, 10.
Broune, Mr., chaplain, 53.
—— Jannett, 205.
—— sir John, 14, 23, 323.
—— Thomas, 9.
Browne, a gipsy, 29.
Buhannon, 240.
Burntisland (Brunt Island), 5, 34, 116, 344.
Butler, major William, 13.
—— ensign Francis, 13 n.

CADDELL, captain John, 13 n.
Caithness (Cateness), earle of, 218, 219.
—— the master of, 218.
Calderwood, Thomas, 35.
Calender, earle of, 26, 27, 302, 305, 338, 339.
Calhead. See Douglas, sir William.
Cameron, sir Ewan, of Lochiel, 57, 60, 67, 143, 217, 219, 255 n.
—— John, of Locheil, receives a commission from Charles II., 65, 66.
Campbell of Glenorchy, xlviii, 222; letter to, from Lilburne, 197.
—— of Moy, 218.
—— Archibald, 40, 42.
—— Colin, of Strachur, 169.
—— sir Dugald, of Auchinbreck, xlviii, 56 n, 165, 169, 261.
—— Doughall, of Logge, 168.
—— Henry, provost of Dumbarton, 39.
—— James, 165, 168.
—— John, 228.
Cannemashe. See Lamlash.

INDEX 373

Cant, Andrew, xxxix, 109, 353, 355.
Cantire, Kenmore's raid into, 257 and *n*, 262.
Canygeles, residence of the marquis of Huntly, 339.
Car. *See* Ker.
Cardross, 194, 240.
—— lord, 20, 26, 27; letter to, from lord Kenmore, 205 *n*.
Carliff, R., 330.
Carlile, 274, 276.
Carmichall, 294.
Carrick, 49.
Carversa castle, 368.
Caryll, Mr., xxxix.
Castle, captain, of North Leeth, 13.
Castle Sinclair, 83 *n*.
Causes of the Lord's wrath against Scotland, 109 *n*.
Caustell, captain, 13 *n*.
Chantilly, 245 *n*.
Charles II. sends commissions to MacDonald of Sleat, Glengarry, etc., 65; his instructions to the commissioners, 67; grants warrant for Bampfield's apprehension, 94; Loudoun's proposed *Declaration* of, 213 and *n*; Bampfield's advice to, 217-219; his intention of coming to Scotland, 244 and *n*; his instructions to colonel Drummond, 246; to colonel Norman Macleod, 250, and to captain Shaw, 253; reported to be in France or Holland, 337.
—— letter from, to the gentlemen of Scotland, 46.
—— —— to the moderator of the general assembly, 47.
—— —— to the duke of Courland, 78.
—— —— to captain Smith, 94.
—— —— to the Highland chiefs, 101.
—— —— to Glencairn, 102.
—— —— to the earl of Seaforth, 201.
—— —— to C. M., 205.
—— —— to the earl of Southesk, 206.
—— —— to Macnaughton, 254.
—— —— to the tutor of Macleod, 255 and *n*.
—— —— to the tutor of Struan, 256 and *n*.
—— —— to the earl of Murray, 291 and *n*.
—— —— to the marquis of Huntly, 301.
—— —— to Glengarry, 312 and *n*.
—— letters from, to Middleton, 50, 60, 109.
—— —— to Balcarres, 97, 107 and *n*, 310.
—— letter to, from Loudoun, 110, 206.

Charles II., letter to, from Lorne, 120 and *n*.
—— —— from Seaforth, 127.
—— —— from sir Robert Moray, 130.
—— —— from the earl of Athole, 183-184 and *n*.
—— —— from the earl of Roxburgh, 189.
—— —— from lord Newburgh, 200.
—— —— from general Douglas, 223.
Charters, quarter-master, 322.
Cheisley, sir John, 33, 109.
Clan Carren, 365.
Clan Leon. *See* Maclean.
Clanranold, captain of, 200, 219.
Clarke, William, lii-liv, letters from, to Lenthall, 18-20, 33, 323, 325, 335, 362, 367.
Cleare, captain, 175.
Cobbett, major John, xxxii.
—— colonel Ralph, xlviii, xlix, 29, 35, 115, 160, 175, 189, 202, 203, 225, 232, 274, 275 and *n*., 336; letter to, from Lilburne, 186 and *n*; in possession of the island of Lewis, 221 and *n*, 222 *n*, 224; proposed as governor of the island of Lewis, 225-226; in possession of Mull, 226; loses three of his ships in a storm, 238 *n*.
Cochrane, lord, 197, 198.
Cockburn (Crickbourne), John, of Ormiston, 9.
Cockburne, James, 177.
Cockram, colonel, 5.
Coll, laird of. *See* Maclean.
Colvill, major, 13 *n*.
Commissioners, appointment of, by Charles II., 67.
Commissioners for the administration of justice in Scotland, xxviii-xxx, 43, 367.
Commissions from Charles II. to Highland chiefs, 65 and *n*.
Committee for Irish and Scottish affairs, 136 *n*.
—— of estates, xx, *Brief Relation of the proceedings of*, 21-28; capture of, at Alyth, xviii, 8, 9, 14, 23, 320, 323.
Compton, captain, 7, 15.
Confiscated revenues, warrant for the levying of, 181.
Conhead, Thomas, 177.
Coningham. *See* Cunningham.
Conny, 282.
Constable, sir William, 305 *n*.
Cook, William, 348.
Cooper, colonel Thomas, 20, 29, 34, 36, 115, 148, 154, 157, 175, 186, 187, 241, 243, 259; letter to, from Lilburne, 83 and *n*.

Cotterell, lieut.-col., 160, 163 and *n*, 363, 364.
Courland, duke of, letter to, from Charles II., xlv, 78.
Court of justice reforms, 276, 283-285 and *n*.
Courts-martial, 15 and *n*, 16 *n*, 333.
Cowall, 261.
Craighall. *See* Hope, sir John.
Craill, 16 *n*.
Crane, Henry, 9.
Crawford (Craford), an agent of Charles II., 160.
—— earl of, 9, 23.
—— lady, 11.
—— lieut.-general, 336.
—— Cornelius, 197.
Creith. *See* Keith.
Cresset, captain, 335.
Crispe, major Peter, 221.
Crocket, Daniell, 9.
Cromwell, Oliver, letter to, from col. Overton, 36; letters to, from Lilburne, 72, 79 and *n*, 80, 84, 86, 87, 95, 135, 147, 148, 153, 156, 160, 190, 192, 195, 198, 202, 204, 221, 224, 226, 230, 232, 238, 240 and *n*, 241 and *n*, 242, 256, 262, 264, 270, 272, 274, 282, 285, 288, 301 and *n*, 303, 304.
Cunningham or Coningham, captain James, 3, 13 *n*.
—— John, 39.
—— Robert, 322.
—— colonel William, governor of Stirling castle, 3, 4; taken prisoner, 12, 13 *n*.

DALHOUSIE, earl of, 291 *n*.
Dalrumple, John, of Waterside, 322.
Dalzell, sir John, 322.
Daniell, colonel William, 115, 142 and *n*, 175, 259.
Davidson, William, Scotch merchant in Holland, 93, 105, 224, 261.
Dawson, alderman, 112.
Deane, captain, 96.
—— major-general Richard, xix, xx, xxiii, xxxi, 30-32, 40, 42, 44, 45 and *n*, 48, 49, 55, 57, 72 *n*, 73, 75, 76, 112, 115, 169, 200, 222, 360, 364, 365; letter from, to captain Mutlow, 58; letter from, to Argyll, 59; instructions to his successors, 62 and *n*, 64.
Declaration of the Parliament of England, xxiv.
Declaration . . . shewing the grounds for the Dissolution of Parliament, 129 and *n*.

Declaration of the union, 41 and *n*.
Deeds, judges' order on the custody of, 283-285 and *n*.
Denmark, king of, 109, 123, 125.
Dennis, captain, 270 *n*.
Dick, sir Andrew, 262, 263.
—— David, 47 *n*, 163.
—— sir William, 262 and *n*, 263.
Disbrowe, Samuel, xxxi, 16, 44, 45, 74, 334.
Diserte. *See* Dysart.
Dixon, Andrew, 19.
Donne, James, 177.
Dorney, major Henry, 13.
Douglas, George, 322.
—— captain John, 322.
—— lieut.-general Robert, xlv, 105; letter to, from Charles II. 61 and *n*; letter from, to Charles II. in reply, 223.
—— rev. Robert, 9, 160, 163, 193 and *n*.
—— sir William, of Kelhead, 255 *n*, 321, 322.
Downe castle, 194.
Downing, George, scoutmaster-general, ix, 35 and *n* 84.
Drew, captain, 187, 364; letter to, from Lilburne, 188.
Drumlanerick, 320, 321.
Drummond, colonel William, xliv, 185, 245 *n*, 246, 249 *n*, 256, 260, 261, 283, 294.
Duart castle, xlix, 187, 221, 309.
Duchraye. *See* Graham, John.
Duer (Duell), David, 9.
Duffus (Duthoss), lord, 218, 219.
Dull, 145.
Dumbarton (Dumbartane), 24, 25, 37, 39 and *n*, 231, 274; revaluation of the shire of, 219.
—— castle, xix, 18, 116, 118, 336.
—— fryth, 64.
Dumfries, 286, 320; skirmish at, 321; list of prisoners taken at, 322.
Dunbar, battle of, 209.
Dunblane, 6.
Dundas, lord, 271.
—— captain Lawrence, 175.
—— Wm., 177.
Dundee, xvii, xviii and *n*, xx; 6, 7 and *n*, 20, 35, 116, 117, 287 *n*, 336 and *n*, 341; siege of, 11-14; list of killed and prisoners, 13 and *n*; proclamations by Monk at, 324, 325.
Dunfermline, earl of, 139, 311.
Dunkell, 24, 25, 118.
Dunnottar (Dum Otyr) castle, xix, xli, 118, 137 and *n*, 327.

INDEX 375

Dunolly (Donlye), xxiii, 53, 56, 57, 118, 145, 187, 364, 366.
Dunstaffnage castle, xxiii, 53, 56, 57, 118, 187-189, 275 n, 364, 366.
Durahm, major, 223.
Durhame, James, 327.
Durant, Mr., 43.
Dutch ships at Shetland, 226, 275.
Duthoss, lord. *See* Duffus.
Dysart (Diserte), earle of, 106, 107, 139, 310.

EADGER, JOHN, 179.
Earn, John, of Annan, 322.
Edinburgh, 116, 271; election of magistrates, 35 and n; order regulating the quartering of soldiers in, 162; proclamation concerning lighting and cleaning the streets of, 347; letter from, 369.
Edwards, E., captain of the 'Fortune,' 140 and n.
Eileandonan (Ellendonald) castle, xlix, 186.
Eldred, commissary, 288.
Elliot. *See* Alyth.
Ellis, James, an Edinburgh bailie, 35.
Ely, captain, 12.
Empson, captain Thomas, 31, 322.
Errol (Arrol), earl of, 6.
Erskin, president, 105.
—— sir Charles, governor of Dumbarton castle, 18.
Erwin. *See* Irvine.
Escot, captain Peter, 317-318.
Ethie (Eythy), earle of, 206.
Evandale castle, 17 n.
Evans, Francis, 322.
Expenses of the English army in Scotland, 111.
Eythy. *See* Ethie.
Eyton, John, Royalist agent, 196.

FAIRFAX, colonel Charles, 112, 114, 115, 177, 195.
'Falcon' frigate, 73, 97, 150.
Falkirk (Faulkirke), 270.
Farmer, captain, 83 and n.
Fenwick, colonel George, governor of Edinburgh and Leith, xxiii, 5, 15, 16 n, 32, 44, 227, 334; his proclamations against mosstroopers, 318; and against intercourse with the garrison of the Bass, 322.
Ferguson (Forgisson), captain, killed at Dundee, 13 and n.
—— of Crackdorough, 322.
—— captain William, 322.
—— quart. William, 13 n.
Ferry, sir Thomas, 13 n.

Fife, submission of the gentlemen of, 328.
Finleyrig, 26 n.
Fisher, major Fitzpaine, proposes to write a history of the transactions of the English army in Scotland, 75 and n.
Fitch, colonel Thomas, xix, 28, 72, 82, 114, 115, 148, 154, 157, 175, 203, 259, 340, 341, 359.
Fleming, James, 9.
Flemyng, Matthew, 179.
Forbes, general major, 105.
—— laird, provost of Inverness, 340.
—— lord, 335.
—— sir Arthur, xlvi, li, 23, 146, 150, 165, 191, 231, 241, 261, 265, 282, 302 n, 303; letter to, from A. B., 144 and n; letter from, to colonel Lilburne, 147; proclamation against, 305.
—— William, of Skellater, 144; letter to, from Glencairn, 143.
Forfar (Fairfar), 326, 331, 342.
Forfeited estates, xxxi-xxxii, xxxv, 181.
Forgisson. *See* Ferguson.
Fortifications of the English army in Scotland, xxxii, xlix, 152 and n, 228 n, 250 n; 17, 28, 36.
Fotheringham, sir Alex. of Pawney, 9.
Fowlis, sir James, of Collinton, taken prisoner at Alyth, 9.
Fraser of Foyar, 65, 66, 68.
Fraserburgh (Frizleburgh), 191.
Fuller, lord, 194.

GALEASPE. *See* Gillespie.
Galloway, 276, 286.
—— earl of, 322.
Gardner, George, 322.
Gauden, Mr., 112.
Ged, William, 330.
General Assembly, meeting of, 161, 162; dissolved by Lilburne, xxxviii, xlix, 163 and n; provincial meetings of, xxxviii; 191-192; its authority called in question, 317.
Giffen. *See* Govan.
Gilkrist, John, 322.
Gillespie (Galeaspe), Mr., 242.
Gillogaer, 361.
Glasgow, 5, 240, 282, 287 n., 316, 317; letter on the burning of, xxxii, 359.
—— synod of, 19.
Glencairn, earl of, xliii, xlvi, 19, 87, 91, 92, 97, 102, 104, 107 n, 138, 144 n, 150, 157, 184, 186 n, 191, 193, 194, 196, 203, 205, 219,

220, 221 *n*, 231, *passim*, instructions to, 99; letter to, from Charles II., 102; letter from, to Skellitor, 143; letter from, to Middleton, 157; commission from, for levying men in Clackmannan, 292 and *n*; his instructions to major Strachan, 308-310 and *n*.
Glencairne's Expedition, authorship of, 264 *n*.
Glenervie, 292 and *n*.
Glencoe (Glen Crow), pass of, 366.
Glengarry. *See* MacDonald.
Glenorchy. *See* Campbell.
Glenurquhy, 165 and *n*.
Gloucester, duke of, 195.
Glover, Mr., 177.
Gluckstat, 123, 124, 126 and *n*.
Goldsmyth, captain, 38.
Goodyeare, Mr., 281 *n*.
Gordon, Alexander, of Blaire, 145.
Gough (Goff), lieutenant-colonel William, 13, 136 *n*, 160.
Govan (Giffen), captain William, 31, 179.
Graham, John, of Deuchrie 205 *n*, 263, 264 and *n*.
Gray, lord, 7.
—— Andrew, 9.
Greene, captain John, 179, 246.
Grosvenour, colonel Edward, 1, 2, 3, 6, 10, 326, 331.
Gunn, colonel William, 261 and *n*.
Guthrie, James, 109.
Gypsies in the Highlands, 29.

HACKER, colonel Francis, 1, 361.
Halkett, colonel, 33.
—— J., 330.
—— R., 109.
Hamilton, duke of, 74, 209, 296.
—— George, 322.
—— James, 193 *n*.
—— captain James, 13 *n*.
—— rev. James, 9.
—— sir James, taken prisoner by Kenmore, 265.
—— lieutenant-colonel John, 322.
—— Thomas, 175.
—— manor, xxxii.
Hane, Joachim, engineer in Monk's army, 2, 11, 28, 154, 157, 161.
Hargrave, captain John, 221.
Harrison, Ralph, 136 *n*.
—— major-general Thomas, report of his death, 7.
Hart, captain, li, 12, 302 *n*, 303, 306.
Hause, a gypsy, 29.
Hawks at Dunnottar castle, 137.

Hay, proclamation concerning the price of, at Leith, 344.
—— Andrew, letter to, from Lilburne, 281.
—— colonel James, 14.
—— John, 175, 329.
Heart, Mrs., 201.
Helsmore, 10.
Hendson, Mr., 5.
Hepburn, Thomas, 9.
Hill, John, governor of Ruthven castle, letter from, to the gentlemen of Badenoch, xxv, 268-270 and *n*.
Hobart (Hubbard), colonel John, 5, 323.
Holy island, 305, 308.
Home (Hoome), earl of, 26, 27.
Hood, William, 322.
Hope, sir John, of Craighall, 30, 43, 281, 285.
—— captain Robert, 83 *n*, 163, 194.
Hopkins, Edward, 281 *n*.
Hopton, lord, 30, 191.
Houstoune, sir Lodowick, 197.
Howstoun, Mr., collector of the cess, 179.
Hublethorne, captain, 179.
Hughes, captain, 327.
Hulinge, commissioner, 288.
Humby, lord, 9.
Hume, captain John, collector of the cess, 177.
—— —— mosstrooper, 8 *n*; capture of, 227.
—— colonel John, 227 and *n*, 255 *n*.
Huntly, the marquis of, xix, 6, 14, 16, 17, 20, 21 and *n*, 31, 93, 160, 193, 227, 231, 243, 289 and *n*, 294, 326, 335, 337, 339, 340; letter to, from Charles II., 301; articles of agreement with, 340; death of, 305.
Hyde, sir Edward, xli; letters from, to Middleton, 89, 98, 103, 106, 182, 244 and *n*, 259-260 and *n*, 293.

INCHGARVIE (Insgarvey), 116.
Inchkeith (Ins-ceith), 117, 362.
Independency in Scotland, xxxix, xl, 31, 53, 339.
Inglis or Inglish, John, 106, 205 *n*.
Ingoldsby (Ingloseby), colonel Richard, xxiv, 74 and *n*, 136 *n*.
Instructions for . . . Collonell Drummond, 246.
Instructions to . . . Collonell Norman Mackcloude, 250.
Instructions for Captain Shaw, 253 and *n*.
Inverary (Innerary), xx, 49, 364, 366; letter from, 365.
Inverlochy (Inner Loughe) castle, 361.

INDEX 377

Inverness, xix, xxxii, li, 28, 64, 82, 83 *n*, 103, 117, 132, 243, 337, 340, 342; letter from, 358 and *n*.
Irvine (Irwin), 317.
—— major, 303.
—— sir Alexander, of Drum, xxxvii; cited to appear before the presbytery of Aberdeen, 348; his appeal from the presbytery, 349; summoned by the moderator, 351; letter from, to Monk, 352; letter from the moderator to, and answer, 357 and *n*.
—— Anne, 349.
—— captain Gerard, 150, 165.
—— James, son of the laird of Drum, summoned to answer for his apostasy, 349.
—— Jane, 349.
—— Olspet, 349.

JEFFRIES, provost of Aberdeen, 15, 31, 355.
Jermin, lord, 318.
Johnson, A., 109.
—— lieutenant Thomas, 13 *n*.
Johnston, lord, 321, 322.
—— John, 322.
Johnstone, sir Archibald, lord Warriston, 33, 271.
Jones, Philip, 136 *n*.
Jossie, John, an Edinburgh bailie, 35.
Junius, Mr., of Amsterdam, 293.

KAUHEIR. *See* Kinnear.
Keir. *See* Ker.
Keith (Creith), lord, taken prisoner at Alyth, 9.
Kelhead. *See* Douglas, sir William.
Kellie, captain, 361.
Kenmore, lord, xlvi, xlviii, li, 186 *n*, 191, 193, 195, 198 *n*, 203, 204, 219, 228, 231, 240-244, 255 *n*, 256, 271, 274, 283 *n*, 290, 291; letter from, to lord Cardross, 205 *n*; Kenmore's drum, 242 *n*; raids Argyll's country, 257 and *n*, 262, and Dumbartonshire, 264; takes sir James. Hamilton prisoner, 265.
Kennedie, Hugh, 322.
—— John, provost of Aire, 26 *n*.
Ker (Car), cornet, 332.
—— Andrew, minister of Carriden, 9, 193 *n*, 345.
—— Gibbee, 243.
—— Robert, 175.
—— Thomas, of Mersington, 77.
Kickillum [? Kirk of Killin], 19, 338, 339.
Kilhead. *See* Douglas, sir William.
Killin, xlvi, 24, 26 *n*, 144 *n*, 186 *n*.

Killsith, 271.
Kincarn, 366.
Kineale, xxxii.
Kingstoun, viscount, 291 *n*.
Kinnear (Kauheir), George, 322.
Kinoule, earl of, li, 290, 302 *n*.
Kinsmart, Alexander, 5.
Kintail, 186.
Kirkby, captain, 17.
Kirkcudbright (Kirkowbry), 19.
Kirkentilloch (Kirkentalloc), 265.
Kirkmichill, 145.
Kirkwall, xlix, 236.
Knapdale, 188.
Knowles, captain William, 327.
Kytoun. *See* Aytoun.

LACKEY, WALTER, of Dasher, 263.
Lambert, major-general John, xxiii, xxxii, 30-33 and *n*, 123 *n*, 238, 305 *n*, 306 *n*, 354; letters to, from Lilburne, 134, 275, 276 *n*.
Lamlash (Cannemashe), 38.
Langley, captain Timothy, 327.
Law, Mungo, 9.
Lawder, John, treasurer of Edinburgh, 35.
Lawrence, John, 9.
—— William, 281 *n*.
Learmonth, sir James, of Balcolinie, 172, 173.
Ledgard, alderman, 112.
Lee, lord, 9.
Leighton (Lighton), Robert, minister of Newbattle, 342.
Leith, garrison of, 116; Lilburne's letter to commissioners of, 294; spotted fever at, 323; officers in the garrison, 327; newsletter from, 330; court martial at, 333; petition of, for becoming a corporation separate from Edinburgh, 369.
Leman, William, 113.
Lenthall, William, liv, letters from Clarke to, 18-20, 33, 323, 325, 335, 362, 367; letters to, from the Scottish commissioners, 32, 74; letter to, from Lilburne, 120.
Leslie (Leshley, Leisly), sir Patrick, 350. Letter concerning affairs in the Highlands, 220, 361, 363, 364.
Leven, earl of, 6, 14; taken prisoner at Alyth, xviii, 8 and *n*.
Levingston. *See* Livingston.
Lewis, island of, xlix, 140 *n*, 148, 149, 153, 157, 160, 187-189, 191, 202, 225, 227, 230, 232, 275, 307, 308 and *n*; occupied by colonel Cobbett, 221, 222 *n*.
Liddington, estate of, xxxii.

Lighton. *See* Leighton.
Lilburne, lieutenant-colonel John, 161 *n*.
—— colonel Robert, commander-in-chief of the English army in Scotland, xx, xxiv, xxxii, xxxiii, xlviii-lii, 20, 30, 31, 45, 62-64, 71, 115; address to, from the remonstrants, 108 and *n*; warrant from, to commissioners, 159; issues order regulating the quartering of soldiers in Edinburgh, 162; issues proclamations anent the conduct of the English soldiers in Scotland, 139 and *n*, 141, 154; letter of instruction to colonel Cobbett, 186 and *n*; grants letter of protection to MacDonald of Sleat, 199; orders the re-valuation of Dumbartonshire, 220; abates the cess of Glenorchy, 222; letter on the Dutch trade with Shetland, 226; issues proclamation dealing with masterful beggars, etc., 229; letter to the Scottish judges regarding the earl of Mar, 239; grants a pass to Argyll, 239; issues an order concerning Argyllshire, 258; and a proclamation concerning persons in correspondence with the enemy, 259; letter from, on the sad state of sir William Dick, 262 and *n*; his suggestions for a policy, 295; letter to, concerning colonel Wogan, 296; arranges for the procuring of horses, 298-299, proclamation against sir Arthur Forbes, 305-306 and *n*; letters from, on the scarcity of supplies, 306, 308.
—— letters from, to Cromwell, 72, 79 and *n*, 80, 84, 86, 87 and *n*, 95, 135-136 and *n*, 142, 147, 148, 153 and *n*, 156, 160, 164, 190, 192, 195, 198, 202, 204, 221, 222 *n*, 224, 226, 231, 232, 238, 240 and *n*, 241 and *n*, 256, 262, 265, 270, 272, 274, 282, 285, 288, 301, 303, 304.
—— letters from, to the council of state, 73, 225, 266 and *n*, 298; to the commander of the army in Scotland, 74; to the English judges in Scotland regarding Ker of Mersington, 77; to colonel Okey, 81 and *n*; to Rowe, 81, 96; to colonel Cooper, 83 and *n*; to the marquis of Argyll, 85 and *n*, 161, 204, 244; to colonel Alured, 86; to Lenthall, 120; to Lambert, 134, 275; to Rushworth, 151 and *n*; to Thurloe, 152 and *n*; to Pluscarty, 153; to colonel Blount, 153 *n*; to captain Drew, 188; to colonel Reade, 194 and *n*; to

Campbell of Glenorchy, 197; to the committee of the army, 272; to Andrew Hay, 281, 287 and *n*; to the admiralty commissioners, 289; to the commissioners at Leith, 294.
—— letters to, from lord Balcarres, 146; from sir Arthur Forbes, 147; from the marquis of Argyll, 165, 168, 197 *n*, 261-262 and *n*.
Linlithgow, 116, 117, 345.
—— earl of, 19.
Lisle, captain Edmund, li, 302 *n*.
'Little Parliament,' the, lii, 301 and *n*.
Livingston, sir Alexander, 338, 343.
—— John, 327.
—— William, 9.
Loch, garrison of, 366.
Lochaber (Loquhaber), xlvi, 150, 157, 160, 189, 193, 196, 199, 221 *n*, 362.
Lochearn (Loughearne), 281.
Loch Harres, 275.
Lochhead, 59, 257 *n*.
Lochiel. *See* Cameron.
Loch Lomond, 240, 241, 265.
Loch Long, 241, 244.
Loch Nesse, 359.
Loch Stornoway (Loughsternay), 221, 275.
Loch Tarbett, 275.
Loch Tay, 282, 326; meeting of the 'noble parliament' at, 343.
Lockhart, colonel, 43, 273.
Lockyer, sir James, 9.
—— Nicholas, xxxix.
Logan, Robert, 330.
Logh-bay. *See* Maclean of Lochbuy.
Logyerate, 145.
Lorne, lord, xliv, xlvi-xlviii, 38 *n*, 49, 50, 133, 134, 139, 144 *n*, 165, 168, 193, 194, 196, 198 *n*, 203, 204, 217, 219, 220, 222, 240, 253, 254, 257 and *n*, 261; letter from, to lord Wilmot, 120; letter from, to Charles II., 120 and *n*; letter to, from the marquis of Argyll, 166; letter from, to the gentlemen of Badenoch, 267.
Loudoun, earl of, chancellor of Scotland, xx, xxv, 19-23, 133, 144 *n*, 150, 213 and *n*, 217-219, 253, 343; his *Brief Relation of the Affairs of Scotland*, 21 and *n*; letters from, to Charles II., 110, 206; letter from, to Rochester, 121; his narrative of the union of England and Scotland, 208.
Lovat (Louet), master of, 218.
Lowrey, Robert, 192 *n*.
Lumsdaine, Robert, governor of Dundee, 7 *n*, 13.

INDEX 379

Mabbot, Gilbert, 151 n.
M'Aldey (Macheldee), 85, 220.
Mac Clende, 85 and n.
M'Cloyde. *See* M'Leod.
MacComrings, 343.
MacDewie, Allom, 362.
MacDonald of Keppoch, 65, 66, 67.
—— Angus of Glengarry, xliii-xlv, xlviii, 53 n, 65-67, 79 and n, 80, 82, 84, 85, 87, 88, 95, 107, 133, 137, 138, 139, 143, 194, 196, 217, 219, 220, 222, 241 n, 262, 309-311, 365; letter from, to the earl of Atholl, 141 and n; letter to, from Charles II., 312 and n.
—— Donald, of Glengarry, letter from, to Athole, 141.
—— Donald Gorme, 65, 66, 68.
—— sir James, of Sleat, xlvi, 65; 67, 166, 169, 188, 219, 241 n; letter from, to colonel Fitch, 82; letter to, from R. B., 88; obtains letter of protection from Lilburne, 199-200 and n.
MacDownings, 343.
MacEwen (Makewen), John, 349.
MacFarlan, laird of, 219.
Macgrigar, the tutor of, 195, 219.
Macguire, Mr., 193 n.
Mackdowell, sir William, 98.
Mackenzie of Pluscarden, xlix, 138, 140 n, 148, 294, 295; letter to, from Lilburne, 153.
—— sir John, of Tarbet, xlix, 140 n, 153 and n, 160.
Mackhume, Thomas, 179.
M'Kinnon, laird of, 217, 255 n.
Mackrage. *See* Macraes.
M'Lean (M'Clane), clan of, 57, 60, 196.
—— tutor of, 85 and n, 217, 219-221 and n.
—— of Ardgour, 255 n.
—— of Coll, 217, 255.
—— of Lochbuy, 255 n.
MacLenings, 343.
Macleod (M'Cloyde, Mackcloude), colonel Norman, xliv, 217 - 219, 221, 250; his instructions from the king, 250.
—— the tutor of, 217, 219; letter to, from the king, 255.
M'Nab (M'Knab), laird of, 219.
—— clan, rout of the, 142 and n.
MacNachtane of MacNachtane, 165, 169, 193, 198 n, 242 n, 291; letter to, from Charles II., 254; taken prisoner, 257.
Mackpherson, Mr., 165.
Macraes (Mackrage), clan of the, 343.

Malcolme, John, 309, 330.
Malignants, 339, 343, 345, 355.
Malin, William, 230, 232.
Manethes, John, 9.
Manley, Mr., 318.
Mar, earl of, 239.
Marischal, earl, taken prisoner at Alyth, xviii, 9.
Marjoribankis, John, Edinburgh bailie, 35.
Marriage regulations of English soldiers, xxxii, 334.
Marriot, captain, 14.
Marsh or March, John, 43-45, 156, 281 n.
Mason, lieutenant - colonel, 81, 112, 113, 259, 322.
Massell, colonel, 322.
Massie, major-general Edward, 288, 290.
Maxilton, 321.
Maxwell, John, 197, 322.
—— junior, 322.
—— Robert, 322.
—— —— of Corndellar, 322.
May. *See* Moy.
Mayers, lieutenant-colonel, 154, 298 n.
Meare, sheriff, 145.
Melville, Andrea, 351.
—— Ephraim, 109.
—— sir George, 13 and n.
—— lieutenant-colonel Henry, taken prisoner at Dundee, 13.
Memorandum on the Rising in Scotland, 137.
Menteith, 282.
Mercer, an adherent of Charles II., 282.
Mercurius Scoticus, liv, 315 and n.
Middleton, John, lieutenant - general, xlii-xlv, 46, 50, 53 n, 61, 65 n, 66-68, 70, 78, 89, 94, 97, 99, 101, 102, 107, 125 *passim*; letter from, to the count of Oldenburg, 54 and n; letters to, from Charles II., 60, 109; letters to, from sir Edward Hyde, 89, 98, 103, 106, 182, 244 and n, 293; letter to, from the count of Waldeck, 123 and n; memorial to, from Waldeck, 124-126 and n; letter to, from Glencairn, 157; his *Memorial to the States - General*, 233; his *Second Memorial*, 235-237 and n.
Military discipline of the English in Scotland, xxxiii-xxxiv, 2, 15, 16, 139 and n, 141, 154, 325, 326.
Mill, John, 35.
Miller, captain John, 327.
Milnes, colonel Andrew, 9.
Mitchell, lieutenant-colonel William, 112, 113.
Moncreif, J., 330.

Monk, lieutenant-general George, xvii, xxiii, xxxii, 114, 115, 331; besieges Stirling, 1; in Dunblane; Perth, 6; summons St. Andrews to deliver up war material, 7; takes Dundee, 12 and *n*; illness of, xliv, 14, 323; letter to the council of state anent ships taken at Dundee, 17; receives overtures from Argyll, xx, 19 and *n*; leaves Scotland, 33 and *n*; proclamations of, against plundering, etc., 324, 325; proclamation of, against enforced oaths, 328; letter to, from Argyll, 333; proclamation of, concerning strangers in Dundee, 336; letter from, on affairs in Scotland, 337; heads of agreement between Argyll and Monk, 338; letter to, from Irvine of Drum, 352.
Monroe, major-general sir George, 87, 95.
—— Robert, of Foulis, 175.
Montrose (Monrosse), xviii, 14, 15, 326, 331.
Moray, earl of, letter to, from Charles II., 291 and *n*.
More, lord, 20.
Morgan, colonel Thomas, xix, 14, 15, 63, 64, 79, 87, 175, 191, 195, 361.
Morris, William, Alloa, 293.
Morton, countess of, 205 *n*.
—— earl of, 36.
Moseley, Edward, 43-45, 156, 281, 285.
Mosstroopers, xix, 1, 8 *n*, 28, 286, 332; proclamation against, 318.
Moy (May), laird of. *See* Campbell.
Mull, island of, xlix, 187, 203, 205, 221 and *n*, 226.
Mullin, parish of, 145.
Murray, earl of. *See* Moray.
—— sir Alexander, 296.
—— sir Mungoe, 186 *n*, 205 *n*, 241, 264, 290.
—— sir Robert, xlvi, 150, 283; letter from, to Charles II., 130.
Murren, John, of Holywood, 322.
Mutlow, captain, governor of Dunstaffnage castle, 53, 58, 187.

NAPIER (NEIPER), JOHN, 205 *n*.
Nearne, Alexander, 9.
—— Robert, of Stratford, 9.
Ness, the, 359.
Nevay, John, 109.
Newburgh, lord, lv *n*, 61, 70, 89, 90, 98, 103, 104, 256 *n*, 259, 260, 293, 309, 310; letter from, to Charles II., xlvi, 200.
Newcome, trial of, for robbery and murder, 368.

Newman, captain William, 327.
News-letter from Dundee, 28, 30.
News-letter from Leith, 34, 41 and *n*, 43 and *n*, 53.
News-letter from Scotland, 32, 38 and *n*.
Newton, lord, killed at the siege of Dundee, 13 and *n*.
Nicholas, sir Edward, secretary to Charles II., xli, 51, 61, 93, 98, 105-107, 159 *n*, 183, 244 *n*.
Nide, the gudeman of, 268.
'Noble Parliament' meeting of the, at Loch Tay, 343.
Norwich, earl of, 126 *n*.

OGAN. *See* Wogan.
Ogleby, lord, taken prisoner at Alyth, 9.
—— captain George, 13 *n*.
—— James, 9.
Okey, colonel John, xvii, xxxii, 1, 2, 5, 6, 10, 11, 14, 15, 63, 81, 86, 115, 324, 325, 331; letter from, to the council of state, 316.
Oldenburg, count of, letter to, from Middleton, xlv, 54.
Olive, William, 187.
Orange, princess of, xlv.
Orbiston, lord, 317.
Order of the Thistle, 294.
Orkinlesse. *See* Ardkinglas.
Orkney islands, xlix, 34 and *n*, 36, 117, 230, 232, 236.
Ormond, earl of, 296.
Orrock, W., 330.
Orton, captain, 308.
Osbaston, laird, 5.
Overton, colonel Robert, xxxii, xxxix, 6, 7, 14, 17, 20, 21 and *n*, 62, 63, 64, 74 *n*, 80, 86, 114, 146, 147, 195, 241, 270, 324, 337, 341, *passim*. letter from, to Cromwell, 36.
Owen, Andrew, 43-45, 156.
Oxenbridge, Mr., xxxix.

PAISLEY, xvii, 5, 316, 317; letter from, 366.
Panmure, earle of, 206.
Parliament of Scotland, xx-xxi, 19, 20, 338.
Pattullo (Pittilton), George, taken prisoner at Alyth, 9.
Peirson, Alex., of Southall, 281 and *n*, 285.
—— major John, 19, 338.
Penne, captain, 231.
Perth, xvii, 5, 6, 8, 15, 19, 22, 116, 118, 195, 199, 287 *n*, 338, 362.
Pestle, captain, of the 'Satisfaction,' 359.
Pinchbancke, colonel, 2.

INDEX

Pittenweem (Pettenwemb), 16 *n*, 176.
Pittilloh's *Hammer of Persecution*, xl.
Pittilton. *See* Pattullo.
Pluckedy or Pluscarden. *See* Mackenzie of Pluscarden.
Pollok, Meather, 197.
Pounall, major Henry, 38, 179.
Powel, captain William, 362.
Pride, col. Thomas, xxxii, 74 *n*.
Prisoners, list of, taken at Alyth, 9; and at Dumfries, 322.
Proclamation of the union of Scotland and England, xxiv-xxv, 41; for annulling kingly power, etc., 35 and *n*; against plundering by the English soldiers, 154, 324, 325; against beggars, 155; concerning persons in correspondence with the enemy, 259; against sir Arthur Forbes, 305; against mosstroopers, 318; prohibiting intercourse with the garrison of the Bass, 322; against enforced oaths, 328; anent strangers in Dundee, 336; concerning the price of hay in Leith, 344, and the bread in Leith, 346; on lighting and cleaning the streets of Edinburgh, 347; and on the butchers of Leith, 358.

RALSTON, WILLIAM, of Ralston, 257 and *n*., 262, 272.
Ramsay, lord, 291 *n*.
—— Hugh, 9.
—— John, 9.
Rattray, John, 9.
Rea, lord, 218, 219.
Read, captain, 318.
Reade, colonel Thomas, governor of Stirling, li, 1, 5, 63, 115, 177, 179, 203, 204, 240, 259, 363, 364; letter to, from Lilburne, 194 and *n*.
Reek penny, collection of the, 342.
Regimental expenses of the English army in Scotland, 113-119.
Remonstrants, xxxviii-xxxix; address of, to colonel Lilburne, 108 and *n*; Lilburne's letter on, 126.
Renfrew (Ranthrow), 244, 291; vindication of, from sympathising with the rebels, 196, 198.
Retorfort. *See* Rutherford.
Riche, colonel Nathaniel, 238, 302 *n*.
Riddall, James, 322.
Robertson, Alex., 145.
—— —— of Auchleeks, 145.
—— —— of Calbroore, 145.
—— —— Donald, of Kincragie, 145.
—— James, of Castrainervack, 145.
—— captain James, 13 *n*.
—— captain John, 13 *n*.

Robertson, Patrick, of Blarefetly, 145.
—— Paul, 145.
—— Robert, of Faskallie, 145.
Robinson, captain, of the 'Plover,' 290.
—— major, 12.
Robson, captain, 34.
Robyns, captain John, 29.
Rochester, earl of, xlv, 104, 105, 217, 252; letter to, from Loudoun, 121.
Roger, Malcolm, xliii, 91, 93, 98, 104, 106, 130, 138.
Roleston, captain, 333.
Rookesby, major, xxxii.
Rosneath, 25.
Rosse, lord, 5.
Rothesaie, 25, 26.
Rowe, John, moderator of Aberdeen presbytery, 348; his summons to Irvine of Drum, 351; letter from Irvine to, 353; letter from, to Irvine of Drum; answer to letter, 357 and *n*.
—— William, 81, 84, 87, 135; letter to, from Lilburne, 96.
Roxburgh, earl of, letter from, to Charles II., xlvi, 189.
Rucheid, James, dean of guild, Edinburgh, 35.
Rupert, prince, 217.
Rushworth, John, letter to, from Lilburne, 151 and *n*.
Rutherford, sergeant-major, 130.
—— Samuel, 33, 109.
Ruthven in Badinoth, 117.
Rymer, Ralph, receivour-general of York, 112.

ST. ANDREWS, xviii, 6-8, 10, 19, 336.
St. John, Oliver, xxiii, xxvii, 32, 40, 42.
St. Johnstone's. *See* Perth.
St. Magnus (St. Maans), cathedral kirk of, taken possession of by colonel Overton, 36.
Salmon, lieut.-col. Edward, 136 *n*.
Saltonstall, Richard, xxxi, 44, 74.
Salway, Richard, xxiii, 32, 40, 42.
Samson, Adam, 322.
Sandilands, Andrew, 73 and *n*.
Saunders, colonel Thomas, 72, 115, 266, 286.
Sawry, lieutenant-colonel Roger, 186.
Schwengolln (Swingle), general George à, 260 and *n*.
Scott, major, account of his skirmish at Dumfries, 320
Scrimgeour (Serengeor), dame Magdalen, lady Drum, 348.
Scrope, captain Robert, 270, 305 *n*.
Seaforth, earl of, xlvi, xlix, 138, 144, 148, 149, 153, 157, 160, 164, 186,

191, 203, 217, 219, 220, 221, 294, 295, 307, 308 and *n*; letter from, to Charles II., 127; summons the 'Fortune' to surrender, 140 and *n*; letter to, from Charles II., 201.
Seaforth, the tutor of. *See* Mackenzie of Pluscarden.
Serengeor. *See* Scrimgeour.
Sergeant, captain, 29.
Sharpe (Sheipe), James, taken prisoner at Alyth, 9.
Shaun, lieutenant Thomas, 13 *n*.
Shaw, captain, xliv, 218; his 'Instructions,' 253.
Sherwin, captain, 366.
Shetland, xlix, 188, 236; Dutch shipping at, 226, 275; fortifications in, 228 *n*, 258.
Sheverton Moor, 361.
Siddell, David, 193.
Sidserfe (Sedforth), Archibald, 9.
Sinclair (Synclare), sir James, of Murcoll, 218.
Skellitor. *See* Forbes.
Skelton, captain, 29.
Smith, or Smyth, Mr., 43.
—— captain, xliii, 65 *n*, 90-93, 98, 101, 106, 107, 311, 312; letter to, from Charles II., 94.
—— colonel, 136 *n*.
—— George, 2, 44, 45, 156, 281, 285.
—— John, 9, 193.
Smythesby, Mr., 81, 82, 84.
Solms, countess of, letter to, from the earl of Roxburgh, 190.
Southesk, earl of, letter to, from Charles II., 206.
Sped, Robert, 330.
Spencer, captain, 275, 283.
Spittel, Alexander, 330.
Spotted fever at Leith, 323.
Spring, a gunner, 318.
Spynee, lady, 11.
—— lord, 11.
Starling, John, 192 *n*.
States-General, Middleton's negotiations with the, 233, 235, 337 *n*.
Staxigoe (Stextco), Caithness, 318.
Steelhand, the mosstrooper, 28.
Sterling, major-general Robert, 26 *n*, 336, 342.
—— James, collector of the cess, 177.
Stewart. *See* Stuart.
Stirling, xvii, 1-3, 22, 23, 116, 118, 195, 203, 240, 316.
Stornoway, xlix, 221, 275.
Strachan, colonel R., xliii, 13 *n*, 91-93, 98, 102 *n*, 104, 106; Glencairn's instructions to, 308-310 and *n*.

Strachur (Straquhurre). *See* Campbell, Colin.
Strathblane (Strablaine), 194.
Strathfillan, 23.
Strathglass (Straglasse), 79.
Strathspay, 265.
Struan, the tutor of, 218; letter to, from Charles II., 256.
Stuart, Alexander, in Duart, 145.
—— —— of Durghilbey, 145.
—— Archibald, 197.
—— Donald, in Behespick, 145.
—— George, of Castrainervack, 145.
—— colonel Gilbert, 218.
—— James, 145.
—— sir James, 33.
—— John, 145.
—— —— of Glasse, 145.
—— —— of Duart, 145.
—— —— in Ballitine, 145.
—— Patrick, of Tultaft, 145.
—— William, of Archinthall, 145.
Sutherland, earl of, 175.
—— captain John, 13 *n*.
—— lieutenant John, 13 *n*.
Suthinton, William, 322.
Swingle. *See* Schwengolln.
Swinton, John, of Swinton, 30, 43, 273.
Syler, colonel Edmund, xxxi, 17, 44, 45, 74, 152, 160; letter to, from the gentlemen of Fife, 328.
Sympson, Robert, 177.

TAILOR, captain, of the 'Lawrell,' 111.
Talbott, lieut.-colonel Thomas, 160, 179, 259.
Tantallon castle, 117.
Tarbet (Tarbut), 59, 362, 364, 366.
—— laird of. *See* Mackenzie.
Thomson, captain, has a skirmish with Irish frigates, 364.
—— captain James, governor of Dumbarton castle, 39.
—— John, auditor-general of the cess, xxxi, 160, 173, 181, 288.
—— William, 35, 151 *n*.
Thurloe, John, secretary, 222 *n*; letter to, from Lilburne, 152.
Tichborne, Robert, xxiii, 32, 40, 42.
Titus, captain, 318.
Todd, Archibald, provost of Edinburgh, 35 and *n*.
Tolhurst, major, 265, 286, 298 *n*.
Torphichen (Torphesen), lord, 21.
Torrie, Aberdeenshire, 340.
Torture employed in cases of suspected witchcraft, 368.
Townesend, captain, 270.
Traill, Robert, 109.
Traquair, lady, 342.

INDEX

Tulabarding, earl of, 6.
Turner, colonel sir James, xlv, 54.
Tweedie, 297.
Twisleton, colonel Philip, 115.
Tyler, Evan, printer in Leith, 45.
Tyree, 221.

UNION of England and Scotland, xxi, xxiii-xxviii; declaration of the union, xxv, 41; Loudoun's narrative of the union, 208.
Universities of Scotland, commissioners for regulating the, xxxviii, 44.
Upton, John, 136 n.
Urquhart's *Discovery of a most Exquisite Jewel*, xxvi, xxxvii.

VALUATION of Scotland, xxx, 170; an order concerning the, 172.
Vandruske (Vanrosse), major-general, xlii, 5.
Vane, sir Henry, xxiii, 32.
Venables, colonel Robert, 87.

WADLAW, H., 330.
Waldeck, count of, letter from, to Middleton, xlv, 123 and n; his *Memorial* to Middleton, 124-126 and n.
Wallace, Alexander, 322.
Waller, or Walley. *See* Whalley.
Warrant for levying the assessment of Scotland, 180; for levying confiscated revenues, 181.
Warre, George, his accounts of expenses of the English army in Scotland, 111.
Warriston, lord. *See* Johnstone, sir Archibald.
Waugh (Vaugh), John, minister of Borrowstounness, 222, 345.
—— —— of Leistenston, 322.

Weare, major, 179.
Weaver, John, xxxii
Weddall, captain, 59, 85.
Wedderburn (Wetherburne), sir Alexander, 175.
Weeme, 145.
Wells, a, chirurgeon, 318.
Wemys (Weems), D., 109.
—— earl of, 19, 20.
Wentworth, lord, xlv, 106, 109, 123, 124, 182, 183, 246, 252, 260.
Westchester, 238.
Whalley, or Walley, colonel Edward, xxxii, 8 n, 270 n, 305 n, 321.
—— Henry, advocate-general, 41, 156, 160; letter from, to Downing, 35.
White, Mr., 112.
Wilkinson, trial of, for robbery and murder, 368.
Wilks, lieutenant-colonel Timothy, deputy-governor of Leith, 21, 160; demands the surrender of the Bass, 334; issues proclamation anent the price of hay; regulates Burntisland ferry charges, 344; issues proclamations concerning bread, 346, and butchers, 358.
Wilmot, lord, letter to, from lord Lorne, 120.
Witchcraft trials in Edinburgh, 368.
Wogan (Ogen), colonel Edward, 296, 297 and n, 298 and n, 302.
Wood, captain Andrew, 9.
—— James, minister of St. Andrews, 53.
Worcester, battle of, xviii, xxiii, 14, 17 and n, 25, 28, 234, 324, 326.
Wright, Mr., 3.
—— Edward, minister of Falkirk, 345.
—— John, of Posed, 263.
Writers to the signet and the commonwealth, xxviii.

Printed by T. and A. CONSTABLE, Printers to Her Majesty
at the Edinburgh University Press

REPORT OF THE EIGHTH ANNUAL MEETING OF THE SCOTTISH HISTORY SOCIETY

THE EIGHTH ANNUAL MEETING OF THE SOCIETY was held on Tuesday, October 30, 1894, at Dowell's Rooms, George Street, Edinburgh—Professor Masson in the chair.

The SECRETARY read the Report of the Council, as follows:—

THE SOCIETY during the past year has sustained twenty-one losses by deaths or resignations. The vacancies have been filled up, and there still remain thirty-nine candidates waiting for admission.

The Council particularly desire to express their regret at the death of Professor Veitch, who had been for many years a corresponding member of the Council; and at the more recent and unexpected death of Mr. John Russell, assistant editor of *Chambers' Journal*, and author of the excellent family history, *The Haigs of Bemersyde*. Mr. Russell had been an active member of the Council, and was for some time engaged in preparing for publication by the Society the *Ormonde Letters; or the Jacobite Rising of* 1719. This work, which has been long expected by members, will be carried through without fail in the course of next year by Mr. W. K. Dickson, advocate.

Only one of the promised publications of the current year has as yet been issued, viz., Mr. S. R. Gardiner's *Letters and Papers Illustrating the Relations between Charles II. and Scotland in 1650.* Mr. C. H. Firth's volume of *Papers on the Military Occupation of Scotland during the Commonwealth and Protectorate,* 1651-1660, is however in progress, and the first sheets are passing through the press. It may be expected early in next year, and will be followed by the second volume of the *Registers of the General Assembly,* half of which is already in type.

The *Lyon in Mourning,* Bishop Forbes' memorials of 1745, which will occupy two volumes of print, has been transcribed, and is in the hands of the editor, Mr. Henry Paton. Professor Masson will also shortly be at work upon the *De Unione Regnorum* of Sir Thomas Craig, the text of which will be printed in both Latin and English.

It will be remembered that at the last General Meeting the Council reported that enquiries were being made regarding documents in Holland relating to the Scots Brigade and the Scottish churches in that country. These enquiries had a satisfactory result, and in the spring of the year it was thought advisable to send your Secretary to the Hague and to Rotterdam in order to make arrangements on the spot for the selection and transcription of the requisite materials. Instructions were thereupon given to Dr. J. Mendels, an historical scholar of repute at the Hague, to examine and extract from the Resolutions of the States General, the Resolutions of the Council of State, and other collections in the public archives, all documents bearing on the organisation and history of the Brigade from the earliest period. The transcripts already sent to us by Dr. Mendels carry the sources of this history from about 1570 to 1680, and are more than sufficient to make a volume. A second volume will probably be formed by the remaining papers at the Hague. Meanwhile Mr. Leliveld, at Rotterdam, under the supervision of the Rev. J. Irvin Brown, of the Scots Church, has forwarded complete transcripts of the four folio MS. volumes preserved in the Stadhuis of that city, and containing the registers of births, deaths, and marriages within the Brigade, and other statistics compiled by the chaplains of the several regiments from 1708 to 1782. These may form a volume apart. If only on account of their genealogical value these registers should certainly be made accessible to students in Scotland. The Dutch papers will in all cases be accompanied with an English translation, and the whole will be edited by Mr. James Ferguson, advocate. The Council has resolved that the cost of all the researches undertaken at the Hague, amounting to £78, 2s. 6d. up to this date, should be taken from the reserved fund of £300, which was set apart for such special cases.

The selection and editing of the papers relating to the Scottish churches in Holland have been for the present postponed. But Mr. Irvin Brown, who is specially qualified for the work, has kindly offered his aid when the opportunity should arise.

So much for the progress made with works which have already been brought before the notice of the Society. But since the last General Meeting the Council have had the good fortune to be offered some fresh materials well worthy of publication—

1. Mr. Siddons Murray has generously placed at our disposal four volumes of journals and papers written by Prince Charles's secretary, John Murray of Broughton. The first volume deals exclusively with the preparations for the rising, made at home and abroad, prior to the Prince's landing in Scotland. There are certain gaps in the narrative of the campaign, but there is a very full account of the events which immediately followed upon Culloden; and the part played by Murray himself gives to the whole of his narrative a peculiar interest. It is, more-

over, remarkably well written. Mr. Fitzroy Bell, advocate, will be the editor.

2. We are indebted to Mr. A. C. Lamb, F.S.A. Scot., and a member of this Society, for permission to publish the note-book or diary of Bailie David Wedderburne, merchant, of Dundee, 1587-1630, from the original autograph in Mr. Lamb's possession. The early date of this diary and the nature of its contents—illustrating the development of commerce, the currency, exports and imports, and the methods of trade at the time—make this a very acceptable addition to our series of such private journals. It will be edited without delay by Mr. A. H. Millar, who has given a description of it in the *Scottish Review* for October 1893.

3. Mr. David Douglas has also kindly lent to the Society for publication a transcript of a diary of John Lauder, Lord Fountainhall, which gives an account of his travels as a young man in France in 1665 and 1666, before he was admitted advocate. It is full of keen and intelligent observations on foreign manners and customs from a Scottish point of view, and will make a volume of entertaining reading. Mr. Donald Crawford, M.P., has undertaken to edit it.

4. The Council have also accepted the offer of Mr. William Mackay, of Inverness, to edit a series of extracts which he has made from the presbytery records of Inverness and Dingwall from 1638 to 1688. These records have a distinct character of their own, and preserve notices of many curious superstitious survivals or obsolete usages not met with elsewhere.

According to rule, Bishop Dowden, Sheriff Mackay, and Mr. James Ferguson retire from the Council. It is proposed that Bishop Dowden and Mr. Ferguson be re-elected, and that Professor Sir Thomas Grainger Stewart, M.D., be nominated in the place of Sheriff Mackay.

The accompanying extract of the Hon. Treasurer's Accounts

shows that the income for 1893-4 has been £510, 16s. 11d., and the expenditure £671, 14s. 9d., an excess of expenditure over income of £160, 17s. 10d. There is a balance due by the bank as at 24th October 1894 of £175, 6s. 8d. In terms of the Resolutions of Council of 26th March and 29th May, there has been paid out of the Reserve Fund the sum of £78, 2s. 6d., leaving the amount of that fund now £221, 17s. 6d.

On the motion of the Chairman, seconded by Sir Thomas Clark, the report was adopted; and a vote of thanks was passed to the Chairman, Office-bearers, and Council.

ABSTRACT OF THE HON. TREASURER'S ACCOUNTS

For Year to 24th October 1894.

I. CHARGE.

Balance from last year,	£333	1	6
14 Subscriptions in arrear for 1892-93,	14	14	0
400 Subscriptions for 1893-94, at £1, 1s., £420 0 0			
Less 6 for 1893-94, paid in advance, 6 6 0			
	413	14	0
44 Libraries at £1, 1s.,	46	4	0
Copies of previous issues sold to New Members,	26	15	6
Interest on Deposit Receipts,	9	9	5
Sum of Charge,	£843	18	5

II. DISCHARGE.

I. *Incidental Expenses—*

Printing Cards and Circulars,	£6	12	9			
„ Annual Report, Rules, List of Members,	14	8	6			
Stationery (15s. 6d.), Cheque Book (2s.), Tin Boxes (37s. 6d.),	2	15	0			
Making-up and delivering copies,	39	4	8			
Postages of Secretary and Treasurer,	5	8	2			
Clerical Work,	4	12	9			
Charges on Cheques,	0	3	6			
Hire of Room for Meeting, 1893,	0	5	0			
				£73	10	4

II. *Erskine's Diary—*

Composition, Presswork, and Paper,	£57	0	0			
Proofs and Corrections,	13	18	0			
Carry forward,	£70	18	0	£73	10	4

Brought forward,	£70 18 0	£73 10 4
Reproducing, Printing of Collotypes,	3 19 6	
Binding,	19 5 0	
Transcribing,	10 0 0	
	£104 2 6	
Less paid to account, October 1893,	47 0 0	
		57 2 6

III. *Miscellany, Vol. I.*—

Composition, Presswork, and Paper,	£164 4 0	
Proofs and Corrections,	49 16 6	
Reproducing, Printing of Collotypes,	13 15 0	
Binding,	18 9 0	
Printing Special Copies for Editors,	6 2 6	
Binding ,, ,,	8 18 6	
Indexing,	5 13 0	
	£266 18 6	
Less paid to account, October 1893	94 16 0	
		172 2 6

IV. *Foulis's Diary*—

Composition, Presswork, and Paper,	£125 14 0	
Proofs and Corrections,	29 2 0	
Binding,	19 9 0	
Transcripts,	10 0 0	
Indexing,	5 14 0	
	£189 19 0	
Less paid to account, October 1893,	9 19 0	
		180 0 0
Carry forward,		£482 15 4

Brought forward,	£482 15 4

V. *Charles II. in 1650*—

Composition, Presswork, and Paper,	£47 6 0	
Proofs and Corrections,	17 14 0	
Binding,	18 12 6	
Transcripts,	4 1 8	
Indexing,	2 13 0	
		90 7 2

VI. *Records of the General Assembly, Vol. II.*—

Transcribing, ... 25 0 0

VII. *The Lyon in Mourning*—

Transcribing, ... 53 2 6

VIII. *Catholic Documents*—

Transcribing, ... 0 9 9

IX. *Registers of the Scottish Brigade in Rotterdam*—

Transcribing, ... 20 0 0

£671 14 9

X. *Balance to next Account*—

Sum due by Bank of Scotland on 24th October 1894,	£175 6 8	
Less 3 Subscriptions, 1894-95, paid in advance,	3 3 0	
		172 3 8

Sum of Discharge, . £843 18 5

Reserve Fund.

As at 24th October 1893,			£300	0 0
Paid in terms of the Resolutions of Council of 26th March and 29th May 1894—				
1. Dr. Mendels, Researches and Transcripts at the Hague relating to the Scottish Brigade,	£60	0 0		
2. Mr. Law, expenses of visit to the Hague and Rotterdam,	18	2 6		
			78	2 6
			£221	17 6
On Deposit Receipt, 23rd October 1894,			£221	17 6

EDINBURGH, 30*th November* 1894.—The auditors, having examined the Accounts of the Treasurer of the Scottish History Society for the year to 24th October 1894, and having compared them with the vouchers, find the said accounts to be correct, closing with a balance in bank on general accounts of £175, 6s. 8d., and in bank on deposit receipt in respect of reserve fund of £221, 17s. 6d. The subscriptions paid in advance amount to three guineas.

RALPH RICHARDSON, *Auditor.*
TRAQUAIR DICKSON, *Auditor.*

Scottish History Society.

THE EXECUTIVE.

President.
The Earl of Rosebery, K.G., K.T., LL.D.

Chairman of Council.
David Masson, LL.D., Historiographer Royal for Scotland.

Council.
J. Ferguson, Advocate.
Right Rev. John Dowden, D.D., Bishop of Edinburgh.
Professor Sir Thomas Grainger Stewart, M.D.
J. N. Macphail, Advocate.
Rev. A. W. Cornelius Hallen.
Sir Arthur Mitchell, K.C.B., M.D., LL.D.
Rev. Geo. W. Sprott, D.D.
J. Balfour Paul, Lyon King of Arms.
A. H. Millar.
J. R. Findlay.
P. Hume Brown, M.A.
G. Gregory Smith, M.A.

Corresponding Members of the Council.
C. H. Firth, Oxford; Samuel Rawson Gardiner, LL.D.; Rev. W. D. Macray, Oxford; Rev. Professor A. F. Mitchell, D.D., St. Andrews.

Hon. Treasurer.
J. T. Clark, Keeper of the Advocates' Library.

Hon. Secretary.
T. G. Law, Librarian, Signet Library.

RULES

1. THE object of the Society is the discovery and printing, under selected editorship, of unpublished documents illustrative of the civil, religious, and social history of Scotland. The Society will also undertake, in exceptional cases, to issue translations of printed works of a similar nature, which have not hitherto been accessible in English.

2. The number of Members of the Society shall be limited to 400.

3. The affairs of the Society shall be managed by a Council, consisting of a Chairman, Treasurer, Secretary, and twelve elected Members, five to make a quorum. Three of the twelve elected Members shall retire annually by ballot, but they shall be eligible for re-election.

4. The Annual Subscription to the Society shall be One Guinea. The publications of the Society shall not be delivered to any Member whose Subscription is in arrear, and no Member shall be permitted to receive more than one copy of the Society's publications.

5. The Society will undertake the issue of its own publications, *i.e.* without the intervention of a publisher or any other paid agent.

6. The Society will issue yearly two octavo volumes of about 320 pages each.

7. An Annual General Meeting of the Society shall be held on the last Tuesday in October.

8. Two stated Meetings of the Council shall be held each year, one on the last Tuesday of May, the other on the Tuesday preceding the day upon which the Annual General Meeting shall be held. The Secretary, on the request of three Members of the Council, shall call a special meeting of the Council.

9. Editors shall receive 20 copies of each volume they edit for the Society.

10. The owners of Manuscripts published by the Society will also be presented with a certain number of copies.

11. The Annual Balance-Sheet, Rules, and List of Members shall be printed.

12. No alteration shall be made in these Rules except at a General Meeting of the Society. A fortnight's notice of any alteration to be proposed shall be given to the Members of the Council.

PUBLICATIONS

OF THE

SCOTTISH HISTORY SOCIETY

For the year 1886-1887.

1. BISHOP POCOCKE'S TOURS IN SCOTLAND, 1747-1760. Edited by D. W. KEMP. (Oct. 1887.)

2. DIARY OF AND GENERAL EXPENDITURE BOOK OF WILLIAM CUNNINGHAM OF CRAIGENDS, 1673-1680. Edited by the Rev. JAMES DODDS, D.D. (Oct. 1887.)

For the year 1887-1888.

3. PANURGI PHILO-CABALLI SCOTI GRAMEIDOS LIBRI SEX.—THE GRAMEID: an heroic poem descriptive of the Campaign of Viscount Dundee in 1689, by JAMES PHILIP of Almerieclose. Translated and Edited by the Rev. A. D. MURDOCH.
(Oct. 1888.)

4. THE REGISTER OF THE KIRK-SESSION OF ST. ANDREWS. Part I. 1559-1582. Edited by D. HAY FLEMING. (Feb. 1889.)

For the year 1888-1889.

5. DIARY OF THE REV. JOHN MILL, Minister of Dunrossness, Sandwick, and Cunningsburgh, in Shetland, 1740-1803. Edited by GILBERT GOUDIE, F.S.A. Scot. (June 1889.)

6. NARRATIVE OF MR. JAMES NIMMO, A COVENANTER, 1654-1709. Edited by W. G. SCOTT-MONCRIEFF, Advocate. (June 1889.)

7. THE REGISTER OF THE KIRK-SESSION OF ST. ANDREWS. Part II. 1583-1600. Edited by D. HAY FLEMING. (Aug. 1890.)

PUBLICATIONS

For the year 1889-1890.

8. A LIST OF PERSONS CONCERNED IN THE REBELLION (1745). With a Preface by the EARL OF ROSEBERY and Annotations by the Rev. WALTER MACLEOD. (Sept. 1890.)

   Presented to the Society by the Earl of Rosebery.

9. GLAMIS PAPERS: The 'BOOK OF RECORD,' a Diary written by PATRICK, FIRST EARL OF STRATHMORE, and other documents relating to Glamis Castle (1684-89). Edited by A. H. MILLAR, F.S.A. Scot. (Sept. 1890.)

10. JOHN MAJOR'S HISTORY OF GREATER BRITAIN (1521). Translated and Edited by ARCHIBALD CONSTABLE, with a Life of the author by ÆNEAS J. G. MACKAY, Advocate. (Feb. 1892.)

For the year 1890-1891.

11. THE RECORDS OF THE COMMISSIONS OF THE GENERAL ASSEMBLIES, 1646-47. Edited by the Rev. Professor MITCHELL, D.D., and the Rev. JAMES CHRISTIE, D.D., with an Introduction by the former. (May 1892.)

12. COURT-BOOK OF THE BARONY OF URIE, 1604-1747. Edited by the Rev. D. G. BARRON, from a MS. in possession of Mr. R. BARCLAY of Dorking. (Oct. 1892.)

For the year 1891-1892.

13. MEMOIRS OF THE LIFE OF SIR JOHN CLERK OF PENICUIK, Baronet, Baron of the Exchequer, Commissioner of the Union, etc. Extracted by himself from his own Journals, 1676-1755. Edited from the original MS. in Penicuik House by JOHN M. GRAY, F.S.A. Scot. (Dec. 1892.)

14. DIARY OF COL. THE HON. JOHN ERSKINE OF CARNOCK, 1683-1687. From a MS. in possession of HENRY DAVID ERSKINE, Esq., of Cardross. Edited by the Rev. WALTER MACLEOD. (Dec. 1893.)

PUBLICATIONS

For the year 1892-1893.

15. MISCELLANY OF THE SCOTTISH HISTORY SOCIETY, First Volume—
    THE LIBRARY OF JAMES VI., 1573-83.
    DOCUMENTS ILLUSTRATING CATHOLIC POLICY, 1596-98.
    LETTERS OF SIR THOMAS HOPE, 1627-46.
    CIVIL WAR PAPERS, 1645-50.
    LAUDERDALE CORRESPONDENCE, 1660-77.
    TURNBULL'S DIARY, 1657-1704.
    MASTERTON PAPERS, 1660-1719.
    ACCOMPT OF EXPENSES IN EDINBURGH, 1715.
    REBELLION PAPERS, 1715 and 1745. (Dec. 1893.)

16. ACCOUNT BOOK OF SIR JOHN FOULIS OF RAVELSTON (1671-1707). Edited by the Rev. A. W. CORNELIUS HALLEN.
    (June 1894.)

For the year 1893-1894.

17. LETTERS AND PAPERS ILLUSTRATING THE RELATIONS BETWEEN CHARLES II. AND SCOTLAND IN 1650. Edited, with Notes and Introduction, by SAMUEL RAWSON GARDINER, LL.D., etc.
    (July 1894.)

18. SCOTLAND AND THE COMMONWEALTH. LETTERS AND PAPERS RELATING TO THE MILITARY GOVERNMENT OF SCOTLAND, Aug. 1651—Dec. 1653. Edited, with Introduction and Notes, by C. H. FIRTH, M.A. (Oct. 1895.)

For the year 1894-1895.

19. THE JACOBITE RISING OF 1719. Letter Book of James, Second Duke of Ormonde, Nov. 4, 1718—Sept. 27, 1719. Edited by W. K. DICKSON, Advocate. (*In progress.*)

20, 21. THE LYON IN MOURNING, OR A COLLECTION OF SPEECHES, LETTERS, JOURNALS, ETC., RELATIVE TO THE AFFAIRS OF PRINCE CHARLES EDWARD STUART, by the Rev. ROBERT FORBES, A.M., Bishop of Ross and Caithness. 1746-1775. Edited from his Manuscript by HENRY PATON, M.A. Vols. I. and II.
    (Oct. 1895.)

PUBLICATIONS

In preparation.

THE LYON IN MOURNING. Vol. III.

EXTRACTS FROM THE PRESBYTERY RECORDS OF INVERNESS AND DINGWALL FROM 1638 TO 1688. Edited by WILLIAM MACKAY.

RECORDS OF THE COMMISSIONS OF THE GENERAL ASSEMBLIES (*continued*) for the years 1648-49, 1649-50, 1651-52. Edited by the Rev. Professor MITCHELL, D.D., and Rev. JAMES CHRISTIE, D.D.

JOURNAL OF A FOREIGN TOUR IN 1665 AND 1666 BY JOHN LAUDER, LORD FOUNTAINHALL. Edited by DONALD CRAWFORD, Sheriff of Aberdeenshire.

JOURNALS AND PAPERS OF JOHN MURRAY OF BROUGHTON, PRINCE CHARLES' SECRETARY. Edited by R. FITZROY BELL, Advocate.

SIR THOMAS CRAIG'S DE UNIONE REGNORUM BRITANNIÆ. Edited, with an English Translation, from the unpublished MS. in the Advocates' Library, by DAVID MASSON, Historiographer Royal.

NOTE-BOOK OR DIARY OF BAILIE DAVID WEDDERBURNE, MERCHANT OF DUNDEE, 1587-1630. Edited by A. H. MILLAR.

A TRANSLATION OF THE STATUTA ECCLESIÆ SCOTICANÆ, 1225-1556, by DAVID PATRICK, LL.D.

DOCUMENTS IN THE ARCHIVES OF THE HAGUE AND ROTTERDAM CONCERNING THE SCOTS BRIGADE IN HOLLAND. Edited by J. FERGUSON, Advocate.

THE DIARY OF ANDREW HAY OF STONE, NEAR BIGGAR, AFTERWARDS OF CRAIGNETHAN CASTLE, 1659-60. Edited by A. G. REID from a manuscript in his possession.

A SELECTION OF THE FORFEITED ESTATES PAPERS PRESERVED IN H.M. GENERAL REGISTER HOUSE AND ELSEWHERE. Edited by A. H. MILLAR.

A TRANSLATION OF THE HISTORIA ABBATUM DE KYNLOS OF FERRERIUS. By ARCHIBALD CONSTABLE.

DOCUMENTS RELATING TO THE AFFAIRS OF THE ROMAN CATHOLIC PARTY IN SCOTLAND, from the year of the Armada to the Union of the Crowns. Edited by THOMAS GRAVES LAW.

www.ingramcontent.com/pod-product-compliance
Lightning Source LLC
Chambersburg PA
CBHW032009300426
44117CB00008B/951